DATE			

Awakening at Midlife

AWAKENING AT MIDLIFE

Realizing Your Potential for Growth and Change

Kathleen A. Brehony

Riverhead Books
New York
1996

Permissions appear on page 373.

The names and specific identifying characteristics of individuals described in this book have been altered to protect their privacy.

RIVERHEAD BOOKS
a division of G. P. Putnam's Sons
Publishers Since 1838
200 Madison Avenue
New York, NY 10016

Published simultaneously in Canada

Library of Congress Cataloging-in-Publication Data

Brehony, Kathleen A.
Awakening at midlife / Kathleen A. Brehony.
p. cm.
Includes bibliographical references.
ISBN 1-57322-024-8 (alk. paper)
1. Middle-age—Psychological aspects. 2. Middle aged persons—Psychology. 3. Aging—Psychological aspects. 4. Midlife crisis.
I. Title.
BF724.6B74 1996 95-50991 CIP
155.6'6—dc20

Printed in the United States of America
10 9 8 7 6 5 4 3 2 1
This book is printed on acid-free paper. ♾

Book design by Laura Hammond Hough

THIS BOOK IS LOVINGLY DEDICATED TO

My father, Jim, who shows me everything there is to know
about courage and celebrating the sacred in every living being,
and
My mother, Mary, who loved me unconditionally
and taught me to always say a “Hail Mary”
at the sound of an ambulance.

Contents

CHAPTER 1: Introduction: The Challenge of Midlife 1

CHAPTER 2: Growing Up and the Search for Wholeness 17

CHAPTER 3: The Emergence of the Unconscious 43

CHAPTER 4: Losses and Confronting Death 83

CHAPTER 5: Entering the Chrysalis 113

INTRODUCTION TO SECTION TWO: Strategies for Growth in Midlife 149

CHAPTER 6: Building Containers, Healing Relationships, and Finding Our Neighbors 153

CHAPTER 7: Dreams and Dreamwork: The Royal Road 199

CHAPTER 8: Creativity: Breathing Life into the Process 241

CHAPTER 9: The Life of the Spirit: Prayer, Meditation, and Being 267

CHAPTER 10: Living in the Body 287

CHAPTER 11: Understanding and Helping 315

CHAPTER 12: Concluding Thoughts 327

NOTES 337

ACKNOWLEDGMENTS 369

Awakening at Midlife

CHAPTER 1

Introduction: The Challenge of Midlife

Midway upon the journey of my life
I found myself in a dark wood,
where the right way was lost.
DANTE ALIGHIERI,
THE DIVINE COMEDY, C. 1313

THE AMERICAN POPULATION is becoming middle-aged. There are now 81 million baby boomers (those born between 1945 and 1965) in this country. In 1992 nearly 3 million Americans turned fifty. We are aging, like it or not, and many people will be experiencing the midlife passage. The profound changes that accompany this developmental transition will affect us deeply both individually and collectively.

In spite of the great number of people entering or entrenched in midlife, very little attention has been paid to it, compared with other major areas of the life cycle. A great deal has been written about the developmental stages of childhood, for example, and thanks to Dr. Spock and others, it is possible for new parents to read about and understand the changes expected in their infant and toddler on an almost week-by-week basis. Adolescence, too, has been the subject of a great deal of research and writing. But the cultural assumption is that once we hit the age of twenty-one and become adults there are no more real changes left to come. We are grown-up—finished and complete. Gail Sheehy, the author of *Passages,* one of the first popular books about adult development, writes, "Studies of child development have plotted every nuance of growth and given us comforting labels such as the Terrible Twos and the Noisy Nines. Adolescence has been so carefully deciphered, most of the fun of being impossible has been taken out of it. But after meticulously documenting our periods of personality development up to the age of 18 or 20—nothing. Beyond the age of 21, apart from medical people who are interested only in our gradual physical decay, we are left to fend for ourselves on the way downstream to senescence, at which point we are picked up again by gerontologists."[1]

This cultural belief, that there are few changes expected in adulthood, is a dangerous one. It allows us to deny that we will have to make adjustments throughout our life and that these changes will often occur at times when we think we are stable and secure. In fact, many of us prefer to think of the confusion associated with midlife as something that happens to other people or to characters in movies, not to us. We're not going to have an affair or fall in love with someone new. We're not going to fall apart at this late stage of the game. We're going to be perfectly content in our career until we retire. We know who we are and what we want for the rest of our lives.

If we do admit to any trouble, we tend to oversimplify problems; hence the stereotyped notion that midlife for men is only about affairs with younger women or that for women it always involves the loss of the mothering role (e.g., the "empty nest" syndrome). But at midlife the underlying, often unconscious psychological issues that are straining to emerge, the search for wholeness that occurs at this time, and the frequent confrontation of one's own and others' mortality are not so simple, nor are they restricted by gender, class, education, or any other demographic variable. The midlife transition is a deeply *human* experience. Some of us may drift into it unconsciously, barely noticing the effects, while others of us will feel as if we've been knocked over the head with a two-by-four. But all of us will be confronted by the profound and inevitable developmental realities of this time of life.

The opening lines of Dante's *The Divine Comedy,* "Midway upon the journey of my life I found myself in a dark wood, where the right way was lost," summarize the feelings of many people at midlife. Americans today are healthier and live longer than any previous generation. Many of us believe the advertising slogan "You're not getting older, you're getting better," and one has only to look at women and men in their forties, fifties, and beyond—still fit, beautiful, and vibrant—to know that there is truth in this idea. But in spite of our increased life span and enhanced physical fitness, to many people midlife still feels like being lost in the woods.

Most people experience some physical, relational, professional, or psychological changes during their middle years, often in the form of an unhappy marriage, affairs, or divorce; anxiety that may have no clear source; depression; dissatisfaction with career or job; disillusionment; or despair. Some will experience these symptoms at a very intense level, as a true midlife crisis; others may avoid a full-blown crisis but nonetheless will notice a subtle shifting of attitudes, feelings, or behaviors. Many people simply refer to an emptiness that is both deep and inexplicable.

Questions of personal identity often arise at this time. Values and goals that have never been questioned are now subject to internal debate. Spiritual questions, often long ignored, rise to the surface of consciousness. At midlife we begin, perhaps for the first time, to contemplate death. As a result, for many the time of midlife transition is fraught with fear and doubt.

Like so many others, I was very much in denial about the changes of midlife. Even though I had worked as a therapist for many years and had read a great deal about change, development, and human psychology, I was as unprepared as anyone I've ever known for the dramatic transformation that I experienced. My fortieth birthday found me surrounded by good friends of many years, black "over the hill" balloons, and lots of food and music. Forty, like thirty-nine or thirty, seemed like just another great time with my friends. Being children of the sixties, we laughed about how we used to say, "Never trust anyone over thirty"—here I was passing that benchmark by a decade. But I had been having vague and indescribable feelings for at least a year. I was not clinically depressed, but I hadn't felt like myself for a long time either. Several weeks before my birthday I had noticed an odd sensation in my chest. It wasn't pain, just a funny feeling. I went to the doctor and had an EKG, which revealed no problems at all. "You'll probably live to be a hundred," the doctor had said.

Within a month after my fortieth birthday party my life had changed dramatically. I fell in love with someone new and left a long-term relationship with a very good person whom I also loved. I was in a tremendous crisis about my conflicting feelings. I lost a job that was emotionally and professionally unsatisfying to me but provided a good income. The loss of my salary intensified a precarious financial situation that had resulted from a major business reversal, and I found myself economically devastated yet with a hefty mortgage on a house I had recently purchased. Having been accustomed to a great deal of ease and success in my life, I felt like a complete failure. The ground was slipping out from under me and I felt cut loose in space. I couldn't get to sleep at night and when I finally drifted off I would wake every hour or so with a vague sense of dread and fear. Food seemed to stick in my throat. Sometimes when I looked in a mirror I could barely recognize the reflection as my own. I knew I was seeing myself, but it just didn't seem like me. I was empty, hopeless, anxious, and without any sense of direction. The worst part was that I felt totally crazy and very alone.

I remember sitting in a restaurant in Nags Head, North Carolina, where I was living at the time. From what it felt like on the inside, I know that on the outside I must have looked glazed, like a deer in the headlights of a car. A woman I barely knew came over to me. She shook my shoulder, got right in my face and said "Hey, hey. Did you just find out that life ain't fair? Hmmm?" All I could do was nod. I had lived to be forty years old. I was the child of an upper-middle-class family, blessed with good health, a good education, and endless possibilities. Now I was confronting age-old questions: "Where am I going with the rest of my life?" "Who am I?" I vaguely remembered asking these questions as a teenager but had forgotten the answers, if I ever knew them. After that I forgot to ask the questions.

I was certain I was having a nervous breakdown. My family and friends were convinced as well. I had a vivid dream during this time. I was sitting in the back seat of a car and someone else was driving us along a winding road high in the mountains. The road was so high that I could see clouds below us. Through the clouds I could see the rooftops of a little village: I remember the unusual shapes and the spire of a church. I watched as the tire ran over loose gravel and the car lost control. We were pitched over the edge. I woke up suddenly and I could neither breathe nor move for what seemed like several terrifying minutes.

I tried to talk with supportive, loving friends, but no one seemed to understand my state of mind. Being newly in love was a great comfort but my confusion, guilt, and feelings of being split in two were threatening this relationship. My new lover was concerned and fearful that I was losing my mind. I kept thinking about the dream I had, and wrote down what I could remember of it. The dream felt important, though I didn't understand why. I was feeling so crazy, so unlike myself, that I began to work with a therapist and read anything I could find to help me understand what was happening to me.

For the first time I spent a great deal of time really looking at my life.

I had grown up in an extremely extroverted family and like most people had always been focused on the outer world: creating a loving relationship, completing my education, building a career and developing a professional reputation, establishing and nurturing a system of good friends, buying a house, and saving for the future. It seemed like I had everything. But I found myself at age forty in emotional chaos and spiritually bankrupt.

After a great deal of reflection and reading I now understand what this experience was and is for me. I began to acknowledge that first dream as an initiation into places within myself that I had never known before. I now know that, like most people of my culture and generation, I had become separated from my real Self, the deepest, most authentic parts of me. I didn't have a clue as to who I really was short of the roles and expectations that I had so vigorously embraced. I understood, even then and in some intuitive way, that I was on a journey that could only be undertaken alone. This passage has taken the better part of six years and I know that there is still much to learn and experience on this road back to myself.

. . .

My experience will not be your experience. Each one of us is unique and no two people will experience midlife in exactly the same way. In fact, there has never been a generation that has had so many differences among its members. At midlife some of us are grandparents while others are having their first child. Many people are immersed in a longtime career or profession while others have made major changes and are starting out on entirely new ventures. At midlife some of us notice the subtle and not so subtle effects of aging on our bodies, while others are in the best form of their lives, running marathons and entering other athletic competitions. These differences within the same generation of people hold true, as well, for the form in which we will traverse the midlife passage. Some of us may, in fact, experience a true crisis at midlife. Others may simply notice subtle changes in the way we feel about our life, how we relate to other people—especially our spouse/partner—or how fulfilling or unfulfilling our work is to us. But none will remain untouched.

Some will begin the midlife passage as a result of a trauma or loss of some kind, as in the case of Susan. Susan was called by a local hospital late one night and told that her lover had been seriously injured in an automobile accident. She raced to the hospital but it was too late: her lover had died in the ambulance. Susan went through a long period of grieving. Too long, many of her friends said. They felt she needed to get back into life. About two years later, Susan gave up her profitable career as a business executive, sold her home, and moved to a small town in Colorado, where she writes fiction for children.

For others the midlife transition is initiated for no apparent reason by dramatic and unexpected behavior. Jack was a high-powered investment banker whom everyone described as a workaholic. He rarely had time for his three children or his wife of twenty-seven years because of the demands of his career. He increasingly turned to alcohol to reduce his stress and exhaustion. One night when he failed to return from work his wife called the police. Later that night they located his car at the airport. His wife and family were hysterical and assumed that something terrible had happened to him. Several weeks later he was located off the coast of Mexico working on a tourist ferry.

Colleen had been married at sixteen and had her first child the next year. Her marriage was comfortable, but had become stale and unexciting. She thought of herself exclusively as a wife and mother. Her work outside the home had always been limited to low-paying retail jobs due to the frequent moves her husband's career in the military required. In the past, she had considered going back to school so that she could find more interesting, challenging work, but they never stayed in one place long enough for her to complete any classes. Her older children were in college and living away from home. One child, a sixteen-year-old son, still lived with the family. One day Colleen's husband received a phone call from the police. Colleen had been arrested for possession of cocaine. She had been "partying" with co-workers, people in their early twenties, when the police raided the place. Her oldest son was a year or two older than her new friends.

Unlike the serious crises of Jack, Colleen, and Susan, many other people will encounter the midlife transition in less dramatic ways. Perhaps their stories are less dramatic, but their pain can be just as intense. The experiences of Judy and Leon illustrate more typical responses to the midlife transition.

Judy was preparing to retire from the successful business she had started in her twenties. She had turned fifty and decided she had worked hard for a long time and had more than enough money to be financially comfortable for the rest of her life. She had arranged to leave the day-to-day management of her business to others. "I should be ecstatic," she said. Instead she was having trouble sleeping at night, and spoke of a vague sense of anxiety, depression, and a total lack of enthusiasm for the activities that she had previously loved. She continued to function outwardly but spent many hours feeling tearful and confused. Only her closest friends knew that anything had changed for her.

For many years, Leon had enjoyed a successful career as an attorney. By the time he was thirty he had been made a junior partner in the law practice founded by his grandfather. By age thirty-seven he was a full partner and earning a fantastic income. He had a beautiful home with tennis courts and a pool, a good marriage, healthy children who were in their late teens and getting ready to go away to college. In spite of his wonderful life Leon was not happy. "I'm not actively unhappy," he would say, "but something is missing." He said he felt "empty" and could only point toward the center of his body when asked how or where his life felt empty. He became increasingly dissatisfied with his career. Often, he would sleep through the alarm clock and race to work with his heart pounding. He had frightening dreams of dark-skinned people, of lush jungles, of drums and primitive-sounding instruments. He couldn't understand what was happening to his well-ordered life.

Conflict between opposing choices in careers or relationships is the focal point of the midlife transition for many people. Donald's situation is familiar to many—it has almost become a stereotype of the midlife crisis. Donald found himself attracted to a much younger woman in his office and began an affair with her. He felt guilty and frightened by these feelings. After all, he told himself, he still loved his wife of eighteen years. She was a wonderful, loving person and they had much in common. They had built a life together, raised a family, and enjoyed a comfortable and secure lifestyle. With two young sons at home, Donald couldn't imagine breaking up his marriage for this younger woman. Yet he could not stop thinking about her, said he was "obsessed" by her, and couldn't seem to end the relationship. He began to have panic attacks every time he left his house. Donald also experienced frequent bouts of a deep depression. His family physician prescribed Prozac and told him to stop working so hard.

While each of the people described above is undergoing vastly different life experiences, they have one thing in common. They are all individuals in their late thirties, forties, and early fifties and are in transitions associated with midlife. This passage of midlife may take the form of the major crises of Jack, Colleen, and Susan; the dull pain that Leon and Judy are experiencing; or the conflict that Donald feels. You may be tempted to discount the reality of the midlife experience by saying that the lives of these people are not like yours: Leon has an anxiety problem, Judy is depressed, Jack is self-absorbed, Colleen is chemically dependent, Susan is grieving, Donald is a philanderer, and Kathleen, well, she just went crazy. But as we begin to understand the powerful psychological underpinnings of the midlife transition it will become clear that all of the examples given are different responses to the same very real underlying developmental processes.

What we call the midlife transition is actually a spiritual and psychological process, not a chronological one, and it is quite possible that the dramatic symptoms and changes that we associate with midlife can occur at any point in the life span. Some people may experience these changes in their teens or twenties; others may not experience them until their sixties, seventies, or beyond. Generally when they occur other than at midlife, it is because a life crisis (usually a major loss or trauma) forces these psychological and spiritual processes into action. For most of us, though, powerful unconscious forces reach a critical mass at midlife. The vast majority of people will experience these changes and symptoms between the ages of thirty-five and fifty.

What is happening at midlife that creates such upheaval in our lives? First of all, there is a realization, whether conscious or unconscious, that we have lived roughly half our life. We may hear Peggy Lee singing in the background "Is That All There Is?" For some the tune plays quietly; for others it is backed by a full orchestra. But regardless of the intensity, inner psychological forces are pressing us to grow and change. For perhaps the first time at a deeply spiritual and psychological level we know that life is half over. Anthony Stevens, in a brilliant and informative book about the psychology of Carl Jung, writes: "The knowledge that one day we must surely die is one of the most disagreeable discoveries of childhood, but there are a number of ego-defence mechanisms at our disposal to take the sting out of this dreadful truth, and for the first forty years or so we live comforted by the thought that old age is far off and death too remote to bear worrying about. Then suddenly, the realization dawns that it is not such a long way off after all—in fact, it is rushing up towards one like the ground towards a complacent parachutist."[2]

Mary Ann was one of these "complacent parachutists." An active business leader, she lived life in the fast lane. She spent long evenings entertaining business clients and then, after only a few hours sleep, would rush to work for early meetings at the office. She knew that she smoked too much, frequently drank too much alcohol, and was oblivious to healthy diet and exercise behaviors. At age forty-seven she had a serious heart attack. "My doctor told me I was lucky. There is a lot of heart disease in my family and I wasn't helping with my lifestyle. She said that this was a warning signal. It suddenly dawned on me that I wasn't invincible, and I became aware that the things I did in my twenties would have to change if I was to live through my forties. I understand that now. I know that I'll die someday but I want the rest of my life to be healthier and happier than the first half." Today Mary Ann is in her mid-fifties. She quit smoking, drinks alcohol only very occasionally and then only one glass of wine, and walks with her dogs every day on the beach. She greatly curtailed her business activities and has decided that "life is too short" not to spend some part of each day doing things that she enjoys.

Thomas is another example of how we can be unconscious about the important things in our lives. His wake-up call involved not himself but someone he loved deeply. Thomas was a successful real estate broker with his own company and fit the description of a workaholic. He was a good father to his three children when he was home. The problem was that he was rarely there. His children were all good students. Both sons were musically talented and played in various bands and concert groups. His daughter was an excellent athlete who went to the state finals in field hockey and basketball. In spite of his desire to be a good dad, Thomas had never been to any of his daughter's athletic contests or any of his sons' recitals. "I was very busy trying to earn a good income that would allow the kids to go to good colleges." In fact, Thomas could probably have taken some time off in the afternoons to spend with his children for their special events. His income was far more than he needed to provide them with an excellent college education.

Thomas's life and the life of his family changed quite suddenly when one of his sons developed physical problems and was diagnosed with leukemia. "I was shaken to the core," Thomas said. He began to have nightmares of monsters that slithered out of dark shadows and snatched his children away from him. "I prayed to God that if He would only let my son recover I would never miss spending time with my children or my wife again. I would reorganize my priorities in some important ways." Thomas, who could never find time to spend with his children during happy occasions, took off three afternoons a week to accompany his son for blood transfusions at their local hospital. Fortunately his son recovered. And so did

Thomas. "It hit me in the gut that you can't take things for granted. Life evolves. It moves forward and not always according to the plans you have made."

This awareness of death at midlife includes, but is not restricted to, our own inevitable death or the death of someone we love. Sometimes the awareness is of the death or loss of an important aspect of the Self: the loss of youth, the loss of physical abilities, the loss of dreams and ideals. At the center of the crisis is the loss of who we were supposed to be.

We were born whole and have an innate need for this wholeness. But in order to become socialized, to become acceptable members of our culture, we quickly split off parts of our true selves. Our culture, our gender, and our families determine what characteristics are acceptable and unacceptable. We repress the unacceptable aspects of our humanity and push them into our personal unconscious, a place that Jung refers to as the "shadow." But in order to be whole we must embrace those long-forgotten parts of ourselves. At midlife, given our heightened awareness of life's limits, there are powerful pressures to remember who we are.

Leon's experience, mentioned earlier in this chapter, is a good example of the potent psychological and spiritual powers pushing us toward wholeness, toward who we were meant to be. Leon was a very successful attorney in his family law practice. The problems that emerged for him in midlife—anxiety attacks, nightmares, and feelings of emptiness—could be traced to ways in which he gave up his own dreams in the service of becoming what his family wanted for him. "When I think of it now, I realize that I went to law school right after college without even thinking about it. It wasn't even a question whether or not I would go on to become a lawyer. The only question I even remember asking was which law schools will I apply to." It is important to point out that Leon's family was not demanding nor did they insist that he become a lawyer. By the time he was in college he had internalized their preferences and ideas for his future, so it wasn't even necessary for anyone to convince him. He convinced himself. "Now I understand that, in my heart of hearts, I always thought law was too intellectual and restrictive. What I really like to do is travel, meet different people, and see new things. I also like the feeling of helping people. Maybe I should have been a stewardess!" Leon's midlife crisis reached down to the deepest parts of him. His desire to travel or to help people wasn't being given any opportunity for expression in his present life. His symptoms, in all their ferocity, were trying to help him see this. Leon and his wife made certain that their children had the financial resources to complete their college educations, sold their house, and moved to a South American country. There they teach English as a second language at a small village school. Their income has decreased to one three-hundredth of what they earned before. But Leon's symptoms are gone, and he says, "I'm far too busy and happy to spend time feeling empty."

At midlife we realize that if we are ever going to become who we are in the deepest recesses of our being, we have got to begin now. In order to grow, however, we have to let go of many things that have come to define who we are. The ego has a great deal of difficulty letting go of anything; and so we often defend ourselves against losing this sense of who we are with great intensity. We often refuse to give up our view of ourselves and the world, in spite of the fact that many of the values, ideas, and self-definitions that sustained us during the first half of life will become obsolete and often antagonistic to the realities of the rest of our life. James Hollis, a Jungian analyst and writer, likens this stage of the midlife transition to the movement of tectonic plates, the large geological formations of the earth's surface, crashing against each other.[3] The ego and all the values of our youth are in deadly combat with the wisdom of the Self, the deep place inside each of us that understands and knows the realities and the losses yet to come during the rest of our life.

The frightening and painful symptoms of midlife are necessary for the growth of the individual; they are developmental, inherently built into the structure of the personality and the Self, and can no more be sidestepped than can the separation anxiety of a two-year-old or the questions of identity experienced by the adolescent. The deepest inner strivings of the soul press for expression even if that expression threatens our well-structured world and sense of identity. At the most basic level, we must let go of who we are in order to become who we are supposed to be. We will see, in later chapters, why this is the case and why midlife is so different from other transitional points in life. Most important, the midlife passage is an entranceway into the deepest layers of one's soul. The growth and transformation that can occur at this transition is nothing short of remarkable.

Like Leon, many people in midlife speak of an inner conflict that is unconscious until brought to light through a serious psychological or physical symptom. Robert taught economics and management at a university for eleven years. In 1979 he was named dean of the business school. Well respected and highly regarded, he had reached a very successful point in the life of an academician. But in 1985 Robert was rushed to the emergency room with heart palpitations. The diagnosis was a major anxiety attack. "My doctor said the poet within me got in a fight with my other life," Robert said. He resigned as dean and resumed regular teaching duties, but several years later he left the university on an unpaid leave, supporting himself and his family with his retirement fund. Two weeks later he had completed the manuscript of a novel that had been "cooking inside [his] head." In his mid-fifties Robert James Waller, former professor and dean, is the best-selling author of *The Bridges of Madison County*.[4]

Robert Waller was fortunate to have a physician who understood what can happen when the poet inside is in a fight with one's other life. This is unusual. Many physicians and therapists would have looked only at the symptom—the anxiety attacks—and prescribed medication or, far less likely, psychotherapy to develop ways of managing the anxiety. But if it is true, as it apparently was in Waller's case, that there is an internal conflict between parts of the psyche, then medication, indeed anything short of a full awareness of the conflict, will provide only minimal relief from the symptoms. Covering up or minimizing these symptoms keeps us from understanding what is happening in the deepest parts of ourselves.

The illustration of Jack's life presented earlier is an excellent example of how our attitudes toward serious symptoms can abort the process of change. After the police located Jack on the Mexican ferry, he was transported back to a psychiatric hospital in his hometown. He was given medication to control his depression and spent significant time working on his alcoholism. In spite of all the opportunities to learn from this experience Jack continues to abuse alcohol and hasn't changed a single thing about his workaholism or his relationships to others. He continues to believe that he just had a "breakdown" that was unrelated to the way he is living his life. Most people who know Jack are just waiting for the next "breakdown." His wake-up call went unheeded.

Many of my clients look at me as if I'm crazy when I suggest that the symptoms of the midlife experience should be welcomed, that they are a blessing. "What are you talking about?" they'll say. "I feel horrible. I'm depressed and anxious all the time. My marriage is falling apart. I hate my job but I need the income to pay the mortgage. What do you mean welcome the symptoms!" I'll ask them about the last time they felt that they had grown, had changed in important areas of their lives. Most can't remember. The truth is that change is born of conflict, pain, and suffering. Jung was correct when he wrote that "there can be no growth of consciousness without pain."[5]

Most people don't head home from work on a Friday night, walk in the front door, and say, "Honey, you know what I'm going to do this weekend? I'm going to grow." More likely we come home from work exhausted at the end of a long week and say, "Oh rats, *The X-Files* is a rerun." On Saturdays we mow the lawn, do the laundry, make a deposit at the bank, take the children to soccer games, play racquetball, wash the car, sit on a beach, relax on the golf course. On Saturday nights we may take in a movie with some friends, go out to dinner, enjoy country line dancing, or rent a video. On Sundays some people may go to church and then to the in-laws for a late lunch; others make a second pot of coffee and unwind with the Sunday paper. In the afternoon we watch a ball game on television, take a walk, or finish the crossword. Before we know it it's seven o'clock and time for *60 Minutes*. By the time we've finished the dinner dishes, put the kids to bed, read the rest of the newspaper, checked over our schedule for the coming week, called some family or friends, we're ready for sleep. Most people end the day on Sunday dreading Monday, and on Monday morning start the week over again.

Most of us leave no time for introspection, reflection, or any kind of contemplation of the meaning or lack of meaning in our lives, about who we really are apart from the roles we play in life, about God, about death. And yet we are here to grow and to become the person we have always been destined to be. The symptoms of midlife are a wake-up call. If they were not so severe, so disruptive, we could easily dismiss them and continue on unconsciously through the rest of our lives. But our psyches will not have that. The deepest, most authentic part of the soul is crying to be heard and so symptoms of anxiety, depression, relationship problems, dissatisfaction with career or work, or feelings of emptiness collide into our daily lives.

Carl Jung experienced a profound midlife crisis that dramatically influenced his thinking and ideas. His work presents us with a great deal of wisdom regarding the midlife transition and the "second half of life." At the age of thirty-eight, Jung entered a period of great turmoil that he termed an "experiment with the unconscious." At the time, he was very successful professionally: He was president of the International Psychoanalytic Association, held a lectureship in psychoanalysis at the University of Zurich, and maintained a productive private practice. Perhaps most important, he was the heir apparent to the psychoanalytic movement under Sigmund Freud.

Jung had been realizing that many of his views of human psychology departed from the teachings of Freud. But to disagree was to put at risk his professional success. He had, as Joseph Campbell has written of the midlife crisis, climbed to the top of the ladder only to realize it was against the wrong wall. Jung writes, "It was during Advent of the year 1913—December 12th, to be exact—that I resolved on the decisive step. I was sitting at my desk once more, thinking over my fears. Then I let myself drop. Suddenly it was as though the ground literally gave way beneath my feet, and I plunged down into the dark depths. I could not fend off a feeling of panic."[6] Jung's midlife crisis affected every area of his life and work. "I was living in a constant state of tension; often I felt as if gigantic blocks of stone were tumbling down upon me. One thunderstorm followed another."[7] But it would be narrow and shortsighted to think that Jung's crisis was only about his career and profession. Jung began to understand that his devotion to career had, in fact, demanded a one-sided approach to reality and a "channeling of energy in one, highly specific direction, and this, over the years, can result in a serious 'diminution of personality' with much Self-potential falling into the unconscious."[8]

Without a map to guide the way or any outer authority to help him understand what was happening to him, Jung began to look inward. It was this inward-looking, this attempt to understand how often we go unconsciously through our lives, and the wonders that reveal themselves through this introspection that make Jung's work so important to all of us confronting the challenges of midlife. The ways in which we lived our youth are simply not up to the task of meeting the realities of our middle and older years. Jung writes: "Wholly unprepared, we embark upon the second half of life . . . we take the step into the afternoon of life; worse still we take this step with the false assumption that our truths and ideals will serve as before. But we cannot live the afternoon of life according to the program of life's morning—for what was great in the morning will be little at evening, and what in the morning was true will at evening have become a lie."[9]

Midlife is a crisis of the spirit, a gut-level awareness that life in its second half will be different from its first half. But in crisis and change lies the potential for growth. In the midst of a full-blown crisis it can be helpful to remember that the word *crisis* itself is derived from the Greek *krinein,* which means "discrimination," "decision," or "turning point." The Chinese symbol for the word is made up of two separate characters; one stands for the word "danger," the other for the word "opportunity." Both of these symbolize the true nature of disruptive psychological and spiritual change, for midlife is a time of both danger and opportunity, a true turning point.

Sheldon Kopp, a psychotherapist and prolific writer, talks about life's transitional periods as a "loss of innocence" and offers a biological metaphor for the natural and necessary vulnerability that occurs at these times. Most insects, he writes, must go through a period of shedding their shell, a molting. This is necessary in order for the insect to grow. During this time, just after molting, the insect is vulnerable to predators because it lacks the armor of the old shell and has not yet formed the new one. Kopp goes on to reflect that without the analogous losses in humans, there would be no opportunity for awareness or growth.[10]

"What!" you might say, as a friend of mind did. "My life is falling apart and you're talking about bugs!" But the metaphor holds well with the feelings described in the midlife transition. Suddenly, it seems, all of the old values and illusions that held one's life together are coming apart. In our youth we thought we were invincible, immortal. Now in the middle part of our life we know that this is not so. Although Robert James Waller became a best-selling author in the middle part of his life and others have made major changes as they entered life's afternoon, there are some dreams that we will have to relinquish. The opportunities to become a professional athlete are gone. We are most likely never going to be a rock 'n' roll star (unless we already are one). We are going to have to say good-bye to many people we love through death. We ourselves will have to experience the ultimate loss of the ego and the life we have built through our own death. These are the underpinnings, the quiet thoughts, the crashing sounds that herald the midlife transition. All of these realizations of loss are necessary before we can begin to understand what we stand to gain through this passage to the second half of life.

The symptoms of midlife are only part of the story. Because in spite of all its suffering and pain, the midlife transition is an initiation and a necessary part of a journey toward growth and self-realization. When understanding and consciousness evolve from the midlife journey we can emerge truly transformed. This passage can lead to a far greater appreciation and expression of our individuality, an enrichment of our spiritual and compassionate selves, and a greater connection to all of life. On the other hand, the failure to experience the true psychological transformation of the midlife passage can leave us stuck in a half-crazy place. Materialistic values, power, and arrogance may predominate as a defense against the realities of human life and experience. This is dangerous both for the individual and for our world.

The growth of consciousness and increased awareness that can come from each of our experiences of midlife have never been more important than they are right now. The enormous number of people who are engaged in this critical transformative time of life is staggering. Eighty-one million American men and women are now or will be struggling with the powerful psychological changes of midlife. The world is being run by individuals in the midlife stage of development. We are governed by a president and vice president in their mid-forties. The vast majority of the members of Congress are in this age group, as are most parents and leaders and decision makers in business, education, medicine, religion, science, environmental policy, the arts, and the media. How each of us individually and collectively emerges from the journey of midlife will have profound and far-reaching effects on the future of our society and our planet.

I hope that this book can be helpful as you experience the challenges of midlife. My purpose in writing it is not to pretend that it is possible to quickly and easily navigate through the difficulties of the midlife experience. The process of change is never quick or easy. Nor is this book intended to oversimplify the midlife transition or suggest that if you will only do such and such you will be just fine. Rather, I offer suggestions for strategies that can help you grow from the experiences of midlife and add to your awareness that this transition, in all its difficult moments, is the portal to a richer, more meaningful, more contented second half of your life. And while you are on an individual journey that is yours and yours alone, there is encouragement in knowing that others have gone before you. There is comfort in understanding what may be going on below the surface and how those forces may be manifesting themselves in your life. And there is empowerment in the realization that you are on the threshold of becoming the person you were born to be, a more authentic, deeply living, real human being.

CHAPTER 2

Growing Up and the Search for Wholeness

We shall not cease from exploration
And the end of all our exploring
Will be to arrive where we started
And know the place for the first time.
T. S. ELIOT, *FOUR QUARTETS,*
LITTLE GIDDING, 1942

MICHELANGELO WAS ASKED how he created such magnificent sculptures from a slab of cold marble: "How did you create such beauty, such divinity that is the *Pietà?* How did you carve such magnificence into David?" Michelangelo reportedly replied, "I didn't do anything. God put them in the marble, they were already there. I only had to carve away the parts that kept you from seeing them."

We are, like David and the *Pietà,* already inside of ourselves. We are born whole with everything psychologically and spiritually intact. At the very beginning, we are one with our mothers and one with the universe. There is no consciousness or ego, all is in the unconscious. It is only as we develop a conscious sense of "I" that we begin to experience separation from everything that we were once a part of. As they grow and develop, infants begin to see themselves as separate from other people and objects in their environment. Around the time of the infant's second birthday, language begins to reflect this shifting awareness as the child begins to speak of him- or herself in the first person, as "I" or "me." At this stage children are learning, as M. Esther Harding has suggested, to differentiate the "i" from the "not i."[1]

They are experiencing the birth of the ego and the beginnings of consciousness.

As we develop this sense of individuality, we begin to move in a direction that further separates us from the sense of "oneness" with everything and everyone else and our relationship with the Divine. As we move through life we acquire a growing identification with the ego, a thicker coating of persona and an increasing distance from our true natures. "I" becomes a heightening sense of who we are supposed to be in order to adapt to our external environment. In fact, we become more and more like each other as we conform to social prescriptions, gender demands, family designs, and religious caveats. Before long we begin to believe that we are just this personality that we show to the world. There is nothing unique, nothing that says "I am me." But inner forces are brewing and bubbling over as we hit the middle part of life. If we are ever to discover who we really are, we had best begin. Midlife is a time when, like Michelangelo, we can start in earnest the painstaking process of sculpting away the parts that keep us from seeing what is really inside.

Abraham Maslow describes the process of growth and self-awareness as "self-actualization"—becoming everything that one is capable of becoming.[2] Carl Jung calls this path, this journey to our unique Self, the process of *individuation* (from the Latin *individuus,* for "undivided," "not fragmented," or "whole"). Individuation, to Jung, is "the process by which individual beings are formed and differentiated; in particular, it is the development of the psychological individual as being distinct from the general, collective psychology."[3] In fact, to Jung the process of individuation was not limited only to human beings. He believed it to be an expression of a teleological process by which *every* thing becomes what it was destined to become from the start.

This process of "coming home to the Self," fulfilling one's destiny by following one's unique path of development, is not just a personality theory developed by twentieth-century psychologists, such as Maslow, Jung, Carl Rogers, Fritz Perls, and Alfred Adler, but an idea that has resonated in all cultures throughout the history of the human race. It is a philosophy of growth and development of the personality that can be found throughout Western philosophy since the time of Aristotle, and appears in the work of Schopenhauer, Aquinas, Leibniz, Spinoza, and Locke, among others. The ancient world is filled with images, myths, fairy tales, poetry, and prayers that outline this spiraling pathway to the Self. The Navajo called the journey "the Pollen Path," the Sioux named it "the Good Red Road," and the Chinese simply say "Tao." All of these belief systems touch the dimension of divine mystery. *The common theme among these diverse traditions is that life is a journey, and the goal is the discovery of one's true nature, a transformation of one's view of the world, an enhanced wisdom, and an authentic, loving connection to all of life and to some larger universal power.*

The characteristics of the fully actualized human being, the individuated person, demonstrate both psychological maturity and spiritual enlightenment. Abraham Maslow detailed common features of this goal for personality development:[4]

1. Realistic orientation
2. Acceptance of self, others, and the natural world
3. Spontaneity
4. Task orientation, rather than self-preoccupation
5. Sense of privacy
6. Independence
7. Vivid appreciativeness
8. Spirituality that is not necessarily religious in a formal sense
9. Sense of identity with mankind
10. Feelings of intimacy with a few loved ones
11. Democratic values
12. Recognition of the difference between means and ends
13. Humor that is philosophical rather than hostile
14. Creativeness
15. Nonconformism

Maslow's ideas about the self-actualized personality describe a psychologically mature individual who is self-knowing, is able to experience meaningful, intimate relationships with others, has a deep understanding of the human experience, and is capable of great joy and a sense of connectedness to the powers of the universe.

Like Maslow, Jung believed that the purpose of life was the unfolding of the unique, individual inner core or "Self" that is inherent in every person. The natural movement toward the Self, individuation, is both a principle and a process that underlies all psychic activity. Everything that lives matures. The oak tree is already imagined within the acorn. The bloom is present, if not yet visible, within the seed. To Jung, so it was with human beings. We have within us who we are supposed to be. But this way of individuation, according to Jung, is not just a natural process which simply "happens." It is not a passive process. Rather it needs to be experienced *consciously*. That is, with awareness. In fact, it is this idea that individuation is a conscious process that makes it so important. We move toward wholeness as we begin to really know ourselves. This knowledge depends upon a vital relationship, a dialogue, a dialectic, between the ego and the unconscious. To Jung, the aim is not to be perfect but rather to be whole. Wholeness by definition includes an awareness of all aspects of our personality, including those characteristics that we would rather not claim. Jung observed, "The aim is not to overcome one's personal psychology, to become perfect, but to become familiar with it. Thus individuation involves an increasing awareness of one's unique psychological reality, including personal strengths and limitations, and at the same time a deeper appreciation of humanity in general."[5]

No one ever really fully individuates, becomes completely whole or fully enlightened. Instead the value of this process lies in what happens along the way; what we learn about ourselves, about the experience of being human, about our relationship to ourselves, all of life, and the cosmos. It is the journey itself that is the destination. This concept, that the process itself is the important thing, is an alien idea in our outcome-oriented society. We are far more comfortable with the idea of reaching a destination than actively, consciously contemplating the journey. But it is the path itself that needs to be the focus of our attention. Jung wrote, "The goal is important only as an idea; the essential thing is the opus which leads to the goal: that is the goal of a lifetime."[6] In other words, when we are on the path, we are at the goal.

And we are being propelled down this path by our own inner strivings to become who we were always supposed to be. And that process leads naturally to an openness of spirit, a deep inner wisdom, and enlightenment. At this place it is possible to love ourselves and others unconditionally. But the path is never even or easy. It requires courage and faith in the process to leave the collective mentality, to depart from what is safe and familiar. This idea of departure from what is secure to face the unknown and embark on adventures that allow for a transformation of the Self is described in stories and myths from all cultures and throughout all periods of history. Joseph Campbell has more than anyone brought this transformation to our attention in the "Hero's Journey."

On the Path of the Hero

In the popular book and PBS series, *The Power of Myth,* Bill Moyers asks Joseph Campbell, "Why are there so many stories of the hero in mythology?" "Because," Campbell answers, "that's what's worth writing about. . . . The usual hero adventure begins with someone from whom something has been taken, or who feels there's something lacking in the normal experiences available or permitted to the members of his society. This person then takes off on a series of adventures beyond the ordinary, either to recover what has been lost or to discover some life-giving elixir. It's usually a cycle, a going and a returning."[7]

Campbell's prolific work on hero myths from multiple cultures and from all periods of history has revealed the same consistent story in each of them. This "monomyth," this Hero's Journey, Campbell says, is a "magnification of the formula represented in rites of passage."[8] Each journey begins with a call to adventure, followed by a separation, an initiation, and a return. Campbell calls this the "nuclear unit of the monomyth," and describes it as follows: "A hero ventures forth from the world of common day into a region of supernatural wonder; fabulous forces are there encountered and a decisive victory is won; the hero comes back from this mysterious adventure with the power to bestow boons on his fellow man."[9]

This "rite of passage" is consistent as we look at myths and stories that are both foreign and familiar to us: Prometheus stealing fire from the gods; Psyche fulfilling the tasks required to be reunited with her lover, Amor; Inanna's descent and emergence from the depths of the underworld; Jason battling the dragon to claim the Golden Fleece; Luke Skywalker in *Star Wars,* becoming a man and finally emerging from the shadow of his father.[10] My favorite myth that makes this process clear is a story written for children and familiar to most of us—the Hero's Adventure of Dorothy in *The Wonderful Wizard of Oz*.

At the beginning of the story, Dorothy is lamenting the boring life she lives on the Kansas farm of her Auntie Em and Uncle Henry. She yearns for wider horizons and more interesting people and surroundings. She is given the *call to adventure* with the sudden development of a tornado. Unable to reach the family storm shelter with the others, she, her little dog, Toto, and her house are sucked into the spiraling wind of the tornado and dropped down in a land that is both magical and frightening. *Separated* from all that is familiar, safe, and reassuring, Dorothy first appeals to the strangers that she meets to help her find a way to get home again. Inadvertently, her house has landed on the Wicked Witch of the East and she is treated as a hero by the local residents of Munchkinland. They would like to help her out. In most myths, as in life, there is help along the way. Glinda, the good witch, arrives and points her in the right direction. "Follow the Yellow Brick Road," she tells Dorothy. At the end of this road lies Emerald City and an all-powerful, all-good Wizard who will help Dorothy return to Kansas.

As she travels, Dorothy makes new friends who are also looking for important things in their lives. She meets the Scarecrow, who agrees to accompany her and ask the Wizard for a brain. She meets a Tin Woodsman who wants a heart, and a most Cowardly Lion who wishes only for courage. These characters are looking for things that are important to all of us: brains (wisdom), heart, courage, and home.

Although they are terrorized by the Wicked Witch of the West (Dorothy's house had dropped on her sister, after all), our heroes finally arrive for an audience with the Wonderful Wizard of Oz. They are told that they must complete one task before their wishes will be granted. They must return with the broomstick of the Wicked Witch of the West. Since the broomstick is extremely valuable to her and is always in her possession, they must do away with her in order to retrieve it.

Dorothy and her friends are frightened at the thought of confronting the Wicked Witch, because she is both powerful and evil. They reluctantly begin their *adventure,* since it appears that this is the only way that they will get what they need from the Wizard. In the process they learn to care deeply for each other. Most important, the Scarecrow makes many wise decisions, the Tin Woodsman acts out of loyalty and heart, and the Lion responds with courage and bravery in spite of his fears.

After melting the Wicked Witch and retrieving her broomstick they *return* to Emerald City, where the Wizard helps them to understand that each of them already has what they were seeking. "For the Scarecrow, it was not a problem of lacking brains, but of avoiding the experiences that would yield knowledge. Now that he would risk being wrong, he could sometimes act wisely. So too with the Tin Woodsman: it was not heart he lacked, but rather a willingness to bear unhappiness. And, of course, the Cowardly Lion needed, not courage, but the confidence to know that he could face danger even when he was terribly afraid."[11]

Dorothy learns that she always had the power to go back to Kansas, through the Ruby Slippers that she found on her feet after arriving in this strange new land. All she ever had to do was click her heels together three times and say, "There's no place like home."

Like all true hero's myths, this story reflects the call to adventure, the separation, the adventure, and the return. As in all classic myths, Dorothy returns changed forever by her experience. She now understands that there really is no place like home and that everything she ever really wanted was there all along.

This initiation, this rite of passage undertaken by Dorothy and all other "heroes," is a familiar process for many people who have felt the sting of the call to adventure when they least expected it.

At thirty-eight, J.T. was successful in business and had built his own company from the ground up. He was a true workaholic, often spending fifteen hours a day grinding out more money and profit. J.T. was born into a large family in which all the children had a close relationship to their mother. Their father left the family when J.T. was just twelve years old, and that was the last time J.T. saw him; his father had no contact with him or any of the rest of the family, and was irresponsible in sending financial support. The lessons of his childhood were very painful, but J.T. worked hard to better himself and his situation in life. He held two part-time jobs and attended an urban university where, in spite of the great demands on his time, he graduated with honors. Over the years, he devoted more and more of his life to work and to maintaining a strong position of leadership in the community and a high profile in a business group for African-American entrepreneurs. But something had to be sacrificed in order to devote all this energy to his work and community, and he rarely had time to spend with his wife or children. Since his mother's death several years earlier, he had become increasingly distant from his brothers and sisters, in spite of the fact that the rest of the family remained very close. His siblings always invited him to family gatherings and reunions, though he rarely had time to attend them.

Two days after his thirty-ninth birthday, J.T. had a routine physical which revealed that he had cancer. The cancer had already spread to his lymph system and his physician told him that his prognosis was poor. J.T. was terrified and confused. "Why me?" he asked. Everything was going so well. He had devoted his life to becoming everything that his father was not: a responsible, hardworking citizen. He had always tried to be fair, honest, and to give something back to his community. He and his wife were drawing up plans for their dream house, and his oldest son was leaving for college the following year. J.T.'s reaction is not uncommon: He didn't deserve this. He was learning that one of the realities of life is that it is *not* always fair. James Hollis notes: "One of the most powerful shocks of the Middle Passage is the collapse of our tacit contract with the universe—the assumption that if we act correctly, if we are of good heart and good intentions, things will work out. We assume a reciprocity with the universe. If we do our part, the universe will comply."[12]

During the next six months, J.T. dramatically cut back on his work schedule. He had no choice: the chemotherapy made him sick and weak. He gave over most of his day-to-day responsibilities for his business to one of his most loyal and experienced managers. In spite of the fact that he had become so remote from his brothers and sisters, they rallied to his support. One sister in particular spent hours and hours with him. She remembered how much he had loved tangerines as a child and ordered some for him. There in the cold, gray winter afternoons in their northeastern city, his sister would peel the tangerines and gently squeeze the juice to his lips. His brother helped J.T.'s wife and children with household jobs, picked up groceries, and drove him to his twice-weekly chemotherapy and radiation appointments. J.T.'s youngest brother, whom he had always considered a ne'er-do-well because he had never completed his schooling or been successful in holding down a job, took J.T.'s son to college night at the high school. J.T.'s wife, whom he loved but had grown distant from, greatly reduced her volunteer activities and spent many afternoons cuddled up next to him, something they had both loved to do very early in their relationship.

In spite of all the loving attention given him, J.T.'s condition continued to worsen. The doctors determined that his only chance to live was a bone marrow transplant, a highly dangerous procedure which would require months of isolation in a special unit in the hospital. They gave him less than a fifty-fifty chance of survival with the transplant and zero chance without it.

Between life and death in the ICU, J.T. began to pray. He was completely separated now from all the ways he had previously defined himself: strong, independent, competent, successful. Now he couldn't even use the bathroom. Because the medical procedure had weakened his immune system, he could only have occasional visitors and, even then, only one at a time and for just a few minutes. One afternoon, a figure entered the room wearing green hospital scrubs. The mask covered most of the face but J.T.

recognized his father. His father sat and held his hand, never saying a word. "At that moment, I knew that something inside me could heal," J.T. said.

Over the months J.T.'s physical condition improved, and the doctors released him. At the moment, his cancer is in remission. But he had a kind of cancer that often recurs and J.T. is fully aware that he is not yet out of the woods. He may never be.

J.T. has changed. No longer a workaholic, he works a normal eight-hour day, going over plans and strategies with his management staff. He has spent time fishing with his daughter and younger brother. He recently drove his son to four different colleges to really get a feel for them. They took their time, often stopping at different places along the way to see sites of interest, something that he would have put off in the past. J.T. and his wife have started a support program for cancer patients and their families. He has invited his father back into his life and they are spending time getting to know each other. J.T. has experienced a *transformation.* He has deeper, more loving relationships with his own family and his family of origin. He has followed the path of the hero: he was called to adventure, separated from what was familiar and safe; he battled the dragons and demons and, finally, returned home transformed, changed in fundamental ways. One thing is for sure: J.T. will not live out the rest of his life as he lived the first thirty-nine years. He has regained a greater sense of balance in his life, an awareness of what is really important to him. He has opened up his heart to the love that others have for him. He has allowed for a far deeper expression of love toward those he holds dear and to other human beings.

J.T.'s call to the Hero's Journey was a loud and savage one. He could hardly have missed the bell that rang for him. It is important to point out that J.T.'s experience could happen to anyone and at any age. We are more likely to experience serious illness as we grow older, but at any time in life we can be confronted with a life-threatening illness or other crisis that threatens our sense of how the world is "supposed" to be.

Kate had no particular wake-up call that she can remember. "I only know that I was walking my dog on the beach one night when the stars were particularly clear and close. I sat down and just looked up there and felt the presence of questions that I don't think I had ever asked before." Kate, at age forty-six and on a familiar beach at night, began to ask, "What am I doing here? What will happen to me after I die? Who made all this?" Kate began her spiritual quest in the process of her mundane daily life. She was, after all, simply walking her dog, something she had done several times a day for years. Her call to adventure was subtle and easy to ignore. She did not choose to ignore it.

"I felt myself change that night. I began to write some of my thoughts down as soon as I got back to the house. I noticed that I was changing in the days and weeks that followed." Always an extremely social and people-oriented person, Kate observed that she seemed to want to spend more time alone or with a few close friends. She wasn't becoming antisocial, she just knew that she would have to make time to ask herself more of these questions. She described most of her relationships up to this point as "superficial." She began to make room for quality time with people she cared about. Her "separation" came not with the physical isolation that marked J.T.'s but simply with a changing sense of her own identity. Her dragons were not a life-threatening illness but a quiet and unfocused, yet demanding, search for greater meaning in her life. Instead of ignoring this subtle call, she began to introspect and look carefully in a new, more honest way. "I began to really think about the things that I have always believed to be the most important. My career, my house, my possessions, were overly important to me—all these attachments to things. But my values are changing now. I'm not quite as ambitious. I'm taking more time for myself and my close friends. I'm not as guarded with them as I've been in the past. I guess I just figured out that I better find some other ways of letting people know that I love them and how important they are in my life."

Kate's heroic journey, while not as dramatic as some others, demonstrates how subtly these psychological and spiritual changes may occur at midlife. Kate is reflecting, maybe for the first time, on her life and who she is. She doesn't always like what she learns about herself, but that hasn't stopped her from looking. Schopenhauer compared life to a piece of embroidery: during the first half we look at the right side, while during the second half we see the wrong side—which, he points out, is not as beautiful but is more instructive, since we can see the way in which the threads have been worked together.[13]

Many people will ignore or avoid the call to adventure. In spite of the remarkable rewards, we fear letting go of safety and the world we have known. Marion Woodman, a Jungian analyst and writer, tells an engaging story about the temptation to avoid the journey. She speaks of a particular session with her analyst in which she spent most of the hour finding ways of avoiding the issues that were right there in front of her face. "I was in quite a terrible state. I felt like I was being taken where I didn't want to go, which I was, and I was doing my best to try to control it." Her analyst barely said anything throughout the session. As she was leaving and he was showing her out the door, he said, "You know, Mrs. Woodman, you are going to walk down the road. You can either go like a pig being drawn to the slaughter—squealing all the way—or you can walk with as much grace and consciousness as you can muster." Marion Woodman allows as how most of us go squealing all the way.[14]

We resist our path, our destiny, because of fear. And the fear and trembling that we may experience as we are given the call to leave behind our safety cannot be overemphasized. It is, for most of us, a terrifying experience: we are desperate to know that things will work out, yet all we can see is the abyss. The journey requires letting go of the fundamentals of who we have been and what we have believed about ourselves and about life itself. We want assurance that we will not be annihilated along the way.

Mary Oliver's poem "The Journey" captures for me the darkness of those feelings:

One day you finally knew
what you had to do, and began,
though the voices around you
kept shouting
their bad advice—
though the whole house
began to tremble
and you felt the old tug
at your ankles.
"Mend my life!"
each voice cried.
But you didn't stop.
You knew what you had to do,
though the wind pried
with its stiff fingers
at the very foundations—
though their melancholy
was terrible.
It was already late
enough, and a wild night,
and the road full of fallen

branches and stones.
But little by little,
as you left their voices behind,
the stars began to burn
through the sheets of clouds,
and there was a new voice,
which you slowly
recognized as your own,
that kept you company
as you strode deeper and deeper
into the world,
determined to do
the only thing you could do—
determined to save
the only life you could save.[15]

This poem speaks to the real emotion of the initiation of this journey to the Self. The images are of houses trembling, wind prying with stiff fingers, terrible melancholy, a wild night with a road full of fallen branches and stones. Saint John of the Cross called this place the "dark night of the soul," Kierkegaard called it "despair."[16] The Greeks referred to *nekyia,* or a symbolic death. This is the frightening terrain of the journey. It can scare the life out of you. During the initiation to my midlife journey I wished I had a map.

Jung's Landscape

Carl Jung, as described in the introduction, experienced his own great "confrontation with the unconscious" in the middle part of his life. More than any other thinker and writer, he lays out a landscape that can help us to understand our own responses to the psychological and spiritual realities that confront all of us at midlife.

You will have your own story to live and to tell. There is no map, but to have a general understanding of the territory of your journey is to have a helpful and powerful tool.

The meaning of Jung's work and life cannot be explained or grasped easily. Jung himself always claimed that his psychology wasn't worth anything if it couldn't be understood by a Swiss farmer.[17] This is a little hard to accept when faced with his writing and the depth of concepts that he presents in his *Collected Works,* when your eyes glaze over and you find yourself wondering how it is that your intellectual dyslexia has gone undiagnosed for so long. Jung was an inspired thinker and prolific writer but his theories and ideas have a natural movement and flow that is not linear or easily organized. Jung thought of himself as a scientist, a physician, and he attempted to bring empirical methodologies to support his theories. In spite of this, many of his ideas do not easily lend themselves to the kind of scrutiny that we have come to expect from science. His work has sometimes been criticized for being too "mystical" in its approach to human psychology, and yet that is precisely part of his appeal for many people. In fact, I suspect, many of these critics have lost sight of the fact that the word *psychology* itself comes from the Greek *psyche,* which means "soul." Psychology then, in essence, can be seen as the science of the soul.

In addition to offering practical ways of looking at the human personality, relationships, and interventions for psychological problems through psychotherapy and analysis, Jung was open-minded to larger transpersonal, transcendent ideas. There is a sense, in his work, that the individual can come to experience him- or herself as part of a divine cosmic plan.

Just as our physical bodies are composed of various parts, so too, according to Jung, is our psyche. Jung's analytical psychology invites us to experience and understand all that is deep within us. The goal of his psychology is to make conscious that which has been unconscious. He wrote, "As far as we can discern, the sole purpose of human existence is to kindle a light in the darkness of mere being."[18]

Jung uses the word "psyche" to refer to the totality of all psychological processes. "The psyche embraces all thought, feeling, and behavior, both conscious and unconscious. It functions as a guide which regulates and adapts the individual to his social and physical environment."[19] The psyche holds within it a self-regulating ability and desire to balance conscious and unconscious material. Just as most living systems seek homeostasis or equilibrium, the psyche will attempt to *compensate* our waking consciousness and unconsciousness. This balancing may become evident in dream material, for example. The following schematic[20] provides a visual reference for Jung's description of the "anatomy" or "psychic organs" of the psyche. This system is not static. Quite the contrary, there is dynamic interplay, harmony and conflict, flow and stagnation, tension and integration of opposites. To Jung, the psyche is a living, dynamic reality and this schematic is simply a metaphor for explaining the relationships between its different components.

My intent here is not to present a thorough description of Jung's theories of psychology. In fact, the discussion that follows is a very succinct and cursory overview of only a few of the main tenets of his theories and enough, I hope, to help you have a foundation for understanding much of what is contained in this book. Jung wrote extensively, and those who are interested can read the numerous volumes of his *Collected Works* or the many other books that provide excellent summaries, analyses, and reviews of his work.[21] The following illustration describes some of the major concepts of Jung's ideas.

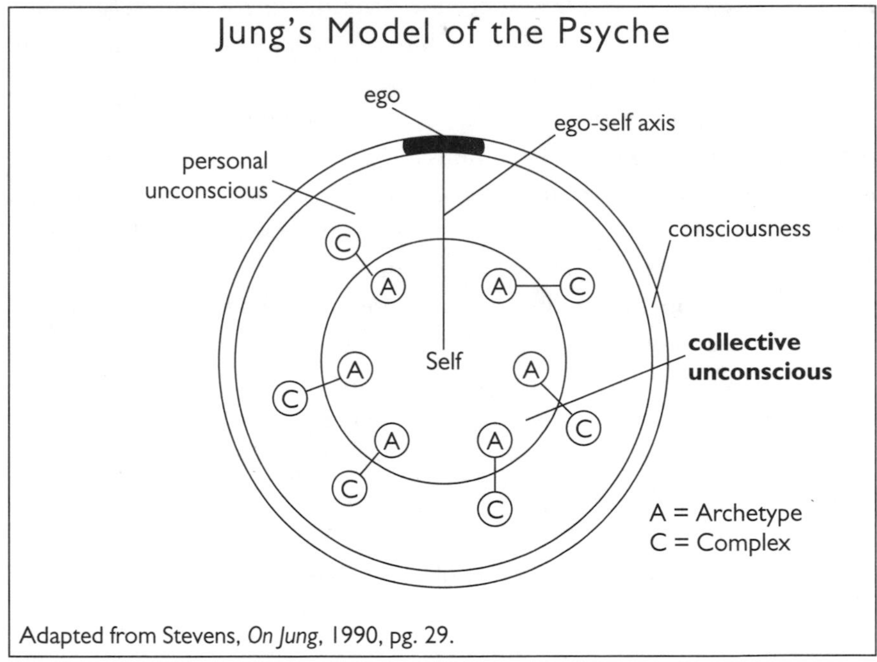

Adapted from Stevens, *On Jung*, 1990, pg. 29.

Jung proposed three levels of consciousness within the structure of the psyche: consciousness, the personal unconscious, and the collective unconscious.

CONSCIOUSNESS

The word *consciousness* comes from the Latin *conscius,* meaning "knowing with others, participating in knowledge, or aware of." *Consciousness includes all the things that we are aware of and know.* But it is more than this, for animals act purposively and skillfully through their instincts and *know* many things about their environment and the world around them. Consciousness, from the perspective of human psychology, also includes an understanding of "knowing that we know." Consciousness implies a *self-awareness* and a sense of the meaning of that awareness. There are many definitions for consciousness and there is an ongoing debate about its nature and evolution.[22] But the understanding that I most appreciate is related in a story of the Buddha. Jack Kornfield retells it in a wonderful little book called *Teachings of the Buddha:*[23]

> It is said that soon after his enlightenment the Buddha passed a man on the road who was struck by the Buddha's extraordinary radiance and peaceful presence. The man stopped and asked, "My friend, what are you? Are you a celestial being or a god?"
>
> "No," said the Buddha.
>
> "Well, then are you some kind of magician or wizard?" Again the Buddha answered, "No."
>
> "Are you a man?"
>
> "No."
>
> "Well, my friend, then what are you?"
>
> The Buddha replied, "I am awake."

Our consciousness expands based upon our experience and our willingness to become aware of ourselves and our world. To "become conscious" is to become aware of something that had previously been unknown. The goal of the process of individuation is to become increasingly conscious, self-aware, and, like the Buddha, awake. As we awaken, as we move toward a wholeness of being, we experience an increasingly authentic and more complete view of ourselves—both our positive and negative aspects.

Consciousness often emerges in a flash of blinding insight. If you have ever experienced a sudden realization—"I suddenly realized that . . ."—then you have felt the real-life version of the cartoon character drawn with a light bulb over its head shouting "Eureka!"[24] Jung observed that "consciousness does not create itself—it wells up from unknown depths. In childhood it awakens gradually, and all through life it wakes each morning out of the depths of sleep from an unconscious condition. It is like a child that is born daily out of the primordial womb of the unconscious . . . It is not only influenced by the unconscious but continually emerges out of it in the form of numberless spontaneous ideas and sudden flashes of thought."[25]

A good metaphor for this sudden flash of insight or consciousness can be found in poster shops and bookstores in shopping malls throughout the world. You have probably seen computer-generated pictures, called stereograms, which have become quite popular. Their colorful, wild, wallpaper-like repetitive graphics contain an underlying three-dimensional picture. Some people discern the image almost immediately. I have observed that children have an easier time seeing the embedded images, perhaps because they are less locked into habitual ways of seeing the world, while others can stare at the images for hours and, with great frustration, throw up their hands in disbelief that there is anything more there than meets their eyes.

Like seeing an image in a stereogram, consciousness emerges when we allow ourselves to look beyond the limits of our normal perceptions. Once you have seen the hidden image, it is easy to see it again. What we know becomes part of the experience of our conscious ego. Once having seen, we cannot unsee. Once having known, we cannot unknow. What we have become conscious of becomes an integrated aspect of our personal reality.

Coming to consciousness is not an either/or, all-or-none phenomenon. We do not on one given day come to full consciousness, though pieces of awareness often arrive with stunning suddenness. Rather, it is a dynamic process, one of growth, change, and evolution, which follows, according to some, a spiraling path. Jung referred to the process as *circumambulating,* or circling around. His choice of this tongue twister comes from the root of the word, which means "walking around," and it has strong ritual meaning as well. As Jean Shinoda Bolen[26] points out, when Buddhist and Hindu pilgrims circumambulate the holy Mount Kailas, they walk completely around the base of the mountain as a spiritual offering. Coming to consciousness and individuation itself takes a spiral path as we indirectly and gradually gain awareness about our inner life. Jung wrote, "The way to the goal seems chaotic and interminable at first, and only gradually do the signs increase that it is leading anywhere. The way is not straight but appears to go round in circles. More accurate knowledge has proved it to go in spirals . . ."[27]

EGO

Jung used the word "ego" to describe the organizing function of the conscious mind, what gives us our sense of identity, continuity, and personality. Composed of conscious perceptions, memories, thoughts, and feelings, the ego is the "gatekeeper to consciousness," poised at the threshold between the inner and outer worlds. It is the part of ourselves that allows us to say "I" or "me," and through it we are able to see ourselves as separate beings, differentiated from other people and the rest of the world. The ego actually represents a very small part of the overall psyche, but many of us conclude that what we know about ourselves through the ego is all there is. Most of us, unprepared as we are to look within ourselves, generally think that we are who we think we are. That is, we believe that we know everything there is to know about ourselves. We mistake our *ego* for everything that we are or can be. In other words, the ego often thinks of itself as the center of the psyche. After all, what else is there?

This belief, that the ego is the center of our personality, is like that of primitive people thinking that the sun revolves around the earth instead of the other way around. Though science and observation proved them wrong, many people refused to give up their long-held assumption. The dogmatism that allows people to hold viewpoints that are completely false in the face of incontrovertible fact is among the worst aspects of human nature and all too common; it wasn't that long ago, after all, that Galileo was forced by the Inquisition to recant his "heresy" that the earth revolved around the sun. As Galileo rose from his knees in front of the Inquisitors, he was heard to whisper, *"E pur si muove"*—"And still it moves."

The idea that the ego represents all that we are can lead to a dangerous sense of *inflation:* I am all that there is, I am the most important entity in the universe. Nevertheless, the major task of the first half of life involves the development of the ego and the progressive separation between the ego and the deeper parts of the psyche. In other words, it is necessary to the development of a human being to perceive oneself as a distinct, independent being. Although this is a natural course of development, this sense of separateness can cause us to feel *alienated* from others and from some vital connections with the universe.

PERSONAL UNCONSCIOUS AND COMPLEXES

Jung described the personal unconscious and its contents thus: "Everything of which I know, but of which I am not at the moment thinking; everything of which I was once conscious but have now forgotten; everything perceived by my senses, but not noted by my conscious mind; everything which, involuntarily, and without paying attention to it, I feel, think, remember, want, and do; all the future things which are taking shape in me and will sometime come to consciousness; all this is the content of the unconscious."[28]

As Jung points out, personal experiences that are not recognized by the ego are stored in the *personal unconscious*. The events, experiences, feelings, and thoughts that we choose not to keep in consciousness do not necessarily disappear from the psyche. Though nothing that has ever been experienced ceases to exist in some form of memory, some of these experiences are relegated to the unconscious simply because they are irrelevant or unimportant to our lives. Other experiences, however, remain unconscious because they are or were traumatic. As the words to the song "The Way We Were" express, "What's too painful to remember, we simply choose to forget." The personal unconscious often reveals itself in slips of the tongue and strong emotional reactions (both positive and negative) to other people. It most often expresses its contents in the production of dreams, art, poetry, and other spontaneous symbols.

The functional units that are part of the personal unconscious are called *complexes*. This is a Jungian idea that has found its way into our popular language, as in "power complex," "inferiority complex," "mother complex." Complexes are groups of unconscious contents that cluster or constellate together. A complex then is a group of associated "feeling-toned ideas" bound together by a shared emotional charge. Complexes are unconscious, highly emotional, and feel autonomous. That is, complexes feel as if they are not "me." In fact, the more unconscious a complex is, the more autonomous or separate it feels. In spite of being unconscious, or more likely because of it, complexes act like split-off, partial, independent, and separate personalities. They dramatically affect our choices, behavior, and relationships. Most important, Jung saw complexes as vital parts of everyone's psychological makeup, normal aspects of a healthy personality. We all have complexes of various sorts, and as we grow and develop, many of these become conscious to us. But some complexes will remain deeply unconscious, and the less conscious the complex, the greater its degree of autonomy and the more we will project its contents onto others. That is to say, we will see in other people what we refuse to see in ourselves.

Jung's ideas of the ego and the personal unconscious, including the notion of complexes, were not considered to be controversial. Freud first introduced the "Oedipus complex," and he and others had been writing and talking about these ideas since the 1860s. Jung entered into the arena of greater controversy when he wrote about the third area of consciousness.

COLLECTIVE UNCONSCIOUS AND ARCHETYPES

The *collective unconscious* (which he later called the *objective psyche*) to Jung was the layer of the psyche which contains inherited elements that are unconscious but distinct from the personal unconscious. The functional units of the collective unconscious he named *archetypes,* meaning "first" or "original," a "prototype." Jung originally referred to archetypes as "primordial images," and he saw them as similar to the ethological view of innate releasing mechanisms that were observed in animals by behavioral biologists. Jung wrote that archetypes are "not meant to denote an inherited idea, but rather an inherited mode of functioning, corresponding to the inborn way in which the chick emerges from the egg, the bird builds its nest, a certain kind of wasp stings the motor ganglion of the caterpillar and eels find their way to the Bermudas. In other words, it is a pattern of behavior."[29] Jung has often been misunderstood to have claimed that the collective unconscious (and its contents, the archetypes) was the inheritance of *acquired* characteristics that had been learned by an individual ancestor of a species and then passed on to its progeny by some genetic mechanism. But this is not what he meant. Instead, he was arguing that human beings, all animals in fact, are born with responses to "typical" situations. Jung did not believe that human beings were born like blank slates, tabulae rasae; rather, they were prepared for the experiences of a human life in the same fashion that birds were innately ready to build nests or female sea turtles were set to return to the site of their hatching to lay their own eggs. Like these animals, human beings are born with a kind of "blueprint" for life. For example, a human infant has a natural fear of falling, and "visual cliff" experiments show that this fear is present even in very young infants who have not had any experience with falls. It is obvious that this inborn fear of falling holds tremendous survival value for our human species since we would perish without this innate knowledge. Some of these typical situations relative to the human condition and represented by archetypes include the predisposition to experience the concepts of mother, father, child, God, the Great Mother, the wise old man, birth, death, rebirth, separation from parents, courting rituals, marriage, and so on. Jung's ideas about the collective unconscious and the archetypes brought the work of psychodynamic psychologists into the realm of the biological sciences. Scholarly disciplines such as structural anthropology, psycholinguistics, and sociobiology all include concepts similar to Jung's description of the archetypes. The idea of archetypes did not originate with Jung. Jung acknowledged that his ideas were described by philosophers as early as Plato.

To Jung, archetypes were universal. Regardless of one's personal experiences or the culture in which one grows up, everyone inherits the same archetypal forms, which are then rounded out and developed into a definitive psychological image by actual experience. Complexes are the ways in which the archetypes specifically express themselves in the personal psyche.[30] While there are as many archetypes as there are "typical" human situations, at midlife it is critical to have an awareness of four of these in particular: the Self, the persona, the shadow, and the anima/animus.

Details of the persona, shadow, and anima/animus and their relation to midlife will be discussed in detail in the following chapter. For now, let us turn our attention to Jung's notion of the Self. It is with his ideas on the Self, the collective unconscious, and the archetypes that Jung makes the leap from the psychological to the spiritual. And a spiritual, transcendent awareness of ourselves is a critical aspect to understanding and navigating the midlife transition.

The Self—the Soul

According to Jung, the *Self* is the center of the psyche. It is the "central archetype in the collective unconscious, much as the sun is the center of the solar system. The Self is the archetype of order, organization, and unification; it draws to itself and harmonizes all the archetypes and their manifestations in complexes and consciousness. It unites the personality, giving it a sense of 'oneness' and firmness."[31] The Self is the archetype of wholeness and the regulating center of the psyche. It is the aspect of the psyche that is responsible for fulfilling the blueprint for life.

All is Self at birth: the latent ego is in complete correspondence with the Self. Over time, however, the ego begins to separate from the Self. As we grow up and in the course of normal, healthy development, the ego becomes increasingly differentiated from the Self. This is as it should be, for the tasks of the first half of life require the establishment of a firm identity and the development of a strong ego, a clear sense of "I." Establishing a sense of personal identity, developing a career, marrying or entering into a significant relationship, giving birth and raising children, contributing to the society, and becoming independent of one's family of origin all depend on the establishment of an ego-identity and a clear sense of "I." At midlife, the psychological challenges change. *In the absence of some traumatic event that initiates the beginnings of individuation in a younger person, this process is a task reserved for the second half of life.*

The goal of the Self is psychological wholeness and completeness. But the Self is more than a construct of a personality theory. To Jung, the Self incorporates soul, mystery, God-image within, the ultimately unknowable essence. Western logic is poorly equipped to understand that which is *numinous* or awe-inspiring and appears to lie beyond the grasp of rationalism, and Jung's notion of the Self lies within that realm. In his autobiography he described the power of the archetypal Self in experiencing both one's unique personality and one's connection to all that is: "In such awareness we experience ourselves concurrently as limited and eternal, as both the one and the other. In knowing ourselves to be unique in our personal combination—that is, ultimately limited—we possess also the capacity for becoming conscious of the infinite."[32] But it is the language of art, poetry, imagination, myth, and religion that comes closest to describing the power and mystery of the Self. The poet Rilke understood the transcendent, soul-like energy of the Self as it merges with the Divine: "I am circling around God, around the ancient tower/and I have been circling for a thousand years/and I still don't know if I am a falcon, or a storm/or a great song."[33]

One reason that our logical thought has such a difficult time with the idea of transcendence (such as embodied in Self or soul) is our assumption that mind/consciousness is located at a certain place in space and time. In Western thinking the location of mind is in the brain.[34] In this limited view, we are bound to one brain, in one lifetime, and worse, we are doomed because if mind/Self/soul is located there, then it dies with the brain and the body.

How then does one form a basis for the belief that there is some spiritual aspect of human beings that can transcend death and be in eternal relationship with God, Christ, the Divine, Jah, the Great Spirit, the Cosmic Mother, Tao, or whatever one chooses to call this force? Why do millions of people from Mahayana Buddhists to Taoists to Fundamentalist Christians hold such beliefs?

Jung wrote that "there are indications that at least a part of the psyche is not subject to the laws of space and time. . . . [T]he psyche at times functions outside of the spatio-temporal law of causality."[35] This statement requires a belief in the nonlocal nature of mind. Jung here maintains that our very essence, our beingness, is not restricted to our body and our brain. Rather, some nontemporal, nonspatial aspect of ourselves exists beyond the limitations of the world as we perceive it through our five senses. This is the realm that Jung enters with his ideas of the Self and human consciousness.

This transcendent aspect of human consciousness and the spectrum of consciousness that exists, while not embraced by rationalistic Western thought, finds itself quite at home in Eastern philosophy, where more value is placed upon expanding consciousness and merging with the infinite. This spectrum of consciousness is what Jung is talking about when he describes the collective unconscious, the archetypes, and the central role of the Self. "Day after day," he wrote, "we live far from the bounds of our consciousness. . . . Without our knowledge, the life of the unconscious is also going on within us . . . communicating things to us . . . synchronistic phenomena, premonitions and dreams that come true."[36] Jung's idea of the Self is closer to Eastern schools of thought and the mystic Christians than to the usual concerns of contemporary psychology. At the level of the collective unconscious, a person perceives the unity and interrelationship of all things. Every thing, every person, animal, plant, from the smallest atomic particle to the largest galaxy are all part of the One.

The Self is the connecting bridge to this unity, according to Jung. As Jean Shinoda Bolen writes that "just as stars cannot be seen in midday, yet are there nonetheless, in our Western minds the conditions are not right for 'seeing' a pattern of underlying oneness."[37] But thinkers from all ages have been convinced of this "oneness" of all things and the underlying unity that is around us:

- The more God is in all things, the more He is outside them. The more He is within, the more without.

From Meister Eckhart, medieval Christian mystic[38]

- Do not ask whether the Principle is in this or that; it is in all beings. It is on this account that we apply to it the epithets of supreme, universal, total . . . It has ordained that all things should be limited, but is Itself unlimited, infinite . . . It is in all things, but is not identical with beings, for it is neither differentiated nor limited.

From Book of Chuang Tzu *(Taoist tradition, turn of the fourth and third centuries* B.C.)[39]

- Jesus said, "I am the light that is over all things. I am all:
From me all has come forth, and to me all has reached.
Split a piece of wood; I am there. Lift up the stone,
and you will find me there."

From the Gospel of Thomas (the Coptic texts)[40]

- The Buddha pure and like space, Without shape or form pervades all.

From the Kegon Sutra[41]

- I live, yet not I, but Christ liveth in me.

From the Holy Bible, *Saint Paul (Galatians 2:20)*[42]

- When you contemplate the Creator, realize that his encampment extends beyond, infinitely beyond, and so, too, in front of you and behind you, east and west, north and south, above and below, infinitely everywhere. Be aware that God fashioned everything and is within everything. There is nothing else.

From the Kabbalah (Jewish mystic tradition)[43]

- In the one, there is the all.
In the all, there is the one.
If you know this,
You will never worry about being incomplete.

From Believing in Mind, *Seng Ts'an (third century* B.C.)*—Zen*[44]

- He who dwells in the seed, and within the seed, whom the seed does not know, whose body the seed is, and who pulls (rules) the seed within, he is the Self, the puller (ruler) within, the immortal; unseen, but seeing; unheard, but hearing; unperceived, but perceiving; unknown, but knowing. There is no other seer but he, there is no other hearer but he, there is no other perceiver but he, there is no other knower but he. This is thy Self, the ruler within, the immortal. Everything else is of evil.

From the Brihadaranyaka Upanishad[45]

- Mitaukuye Oyasin ("We are all related.")

From Dakota/Lakota Sioux tradition[46]

- Everything that rises, must converge.

From Teilhard de Chardin[47]

Jung was well aware that his concept of the Self reflected the sense of oneness with all things and that this idea necessarily evoked the idea of the Divine. And it is this powerful, underlying mystery that he engages when he speaks of the Self. He wrote, "Does this mean that the Mind is 'nothing but' our mind? Or that our mind is the Mind? Assuredly it is the latter . . . there is no hubris in this; on the contrary, it is a perfectly accepted truth (in the East), whereas with us (in the West) it would amount to saying 'I am God.' "[48] Jung is clear. He is not saying "I am God." He is, however, making a strong case, as has been so fundamental to Eastern thought, that we are one with God and that God is in all of us. We are all intimately and ultimately connected.

At first blush, it appears that there are fundamental contradictions in this process of coming to greater consciousness and individuation. First, the more conscious and individuated we become, the more we are able to understand ourselves as separate and unique individuals. On the other hand, the notion of the Self speaks to the idea of being one with the universe. Again, we must depart from black/white, either/or thinking. We are both at once. It is through the individuation process that we recover the original wholeness from which we emerged. But now we have an opportunity to recover a sense of oneness that is no longer unconscious. Instead, it is perceived directly and consciously.

Throughout our lives, our initial inflation ("I am everything") has been in a constant conflict with alienation ("I am separate from everything"). The conscious discovery of the Self allows for a new experience, a dialectic between ego and Self which replaces what Jungian analyst Edward Edinger calls the "pendulum swing between inflation and alienation."[49] We can begin to realize that we are unique in all the world, that no one else has ever been exactly who we are. At the same time, we are a grain of sand on the beach. We will all experience the fundamentals of the great human drama. We are all part of the same mystery. Like a teaspoon of water taken from the greatest ocean, we are ultimately made of the same stuff as all the rest of the cosmos and destined to return to it.

At midlife when we speak of the Self pushing for expression, it is critical to realize the depth of mystery that is the power behind the symptoms and the confusion so often experienced. At midlife the power of the emerging Self is an awesome force that we reckon with, a confrontation nothing less than an encounter with the Absolute. At midlife we question our relationship to God and the sacred and ponder the meaning of our existence. For some, these questions are asked consciously. For others, they are unconscious and expressed through physical, psychological, and spiritual symptoms. Most of us live disconnected from parts of ourselves, from others, and from a relationship with anything larger than ourselves. At the core of the midlife transition lies our search for spiritual meaning. Jung said that he had never seen a patient past the age of thirty-five whose problem was not "that of finding a religious outlook on life."[50]

Knowing the Self requires looking deeply inside and making that which is unconscious conscious. But this process requires letting go of many beliefs that appear to have served us well. It is necessary to look honestly inside and understand ourselves in new ways. This includes knowing our own dark, shadow side. Consciousness depends upon knowing what has been unknown. Within the darkness lies the rest of our humanity, wisdom, compassion, an understanding of the meaning of our life, and our connection to spirit. Jesus said, "If you bring forth what is within you, what you have will save you. If you do not bring forth what is within you, what you do not bring forth will kill you."[51]

Many people will attempt to defer or delay this terrifying journey of transformation through addictions that will blunt the pain of the passage. Others will find all manner of avoidance behaviors and devote themselves to constant "doing" so as never to leave even a brief, unguarded moment when the questions that prompt the initiation might appear. Some people will look for simple solutions to the pain they are experiencing. Often they will seek an instant sense of spirituality (I call it "Spirituality Lite") to deal with the demands of life's second half and the inevitability of death. Jung wrote that "far too many people are misled into snatching at such 'magical' ideas and applying them externally, like an ointment. People will do anything, no matter how absurd, in order to avoid facing their own souls."[52]

But face our own souls we must. The task of midlife, for each of us, is to illuminate that which has been unconscious and to bring light to the darkness. Midlife is the time during which the unconscious emerges with great power and energy.

CHAPTER 3

The Emergence of the Unconscious

But when the self speaks to the self, who is speaking?—
the entombed soul, the spirit driven in, in, in
to the central catacomb; the self that took
the veil and left the world—a coward perhaps,
yet somehow beautiful, as it flits with its lantern
restlessly up and down the dark corridors.
VIRGINIA WOOLF, "AN UNWRITTEN NOVEL,"
MONDAY OR TUESDAY, 1921

WE LIVE IN A WORLD in which the vast majority of our energy is devoted to making things happen. We strive to achieve goals, to build and produce. It is hard for us to accept what we cannot find concrete evidence for, and as if we were all from Missouri, we say "Show me" when we are confronted with anything that is unknown or that doesn't fit into our preferred ways of knowing. Before accepting something as true we demand proof through experimental designs that can be replicated time and time again. This empirical approach to understanding the world is of great importance in our modern world. Yet some aspects of human experience do not lend themselves to being understood by logic and rational thought. Intuition, instinct, feelings, imagination, mystery, faith, love, religious experience, spiritual beliefs, art, and the stirrings of the soul—where do these fit into a model of knowledge that honors only what we can readily observe or measure?

Many behavioral psychologists, for example, write about mother-infant attachment as being a result of "operant conditioning." That is to say, behaviors that are rewarded will be strengthened while those that are punished will not be repeated. According to this view, infants become attached to their mothers because mothers continually reinforce them with food. This theory cannot accommodate, though, the idea that something occurs in a mother-infant relationship that reenacts an ancient biological theme and is transcendent and transpersonal:[1] that the mother-infant bond is cemented through instinct, is part of our genetic human heritage and, dare I say it, love. Ask a new mother about how operant conditioning fits into *her* feelings about her new baby and she's sure to wonder if you've gone off your rocker. She understands that it is impossible to quantify or measure love.

In graduate school I worked with a professor who once told me that "grief is the absence of reinforcement." He is a highly respected, well-published behavioral psychologist who has contributed enormously to many areas of our understanding of human behavior. He is a good and decent man, but I knew from his statement that he had never grieved. Neither grief nor love can be understood by the hard, cold lines of a quantitative chart or by statistical analysis. Take heed of what Hamlet told Horatio: "There are more things in heaven and earth . . . than are dreamt of in your philosophy." My friend Sam and I were in my kitchen discussing the finer points of an odd little kitchen gadget that allows you to bake a whole chicken so that it is standing up. Why anyone would want to do this, I'm not sure! Sam said he had never seen anything like it, and the words that came to mind were what his ninety-year-old grandmother would say when confronted by such mysteries. "What I don't know would make a whole 'nother world."

Reality includes a great deal that cannot be perceived through our senses. My dog routinely hears sounds and smells odors that I cannot. Some creatures, such as cats and farm animals, appear to have an accurate if uncanny ability to predict earthquakes in advance of the most sophisticated technical equipment. Sea mammals can feel vibrations in the water over long distances and precisely detect the direction and distance of a moving object. Snakes perceive visual information in infrared ranges and bats hear sounds at ultrasonic levels that are outside of our human sensory abilities. We cannot taste, touch, smell, see, or hear gravity and yet gravity certainly exists. Likewise, what we are aware of about ourselves represents only a tiny fraction of our total Self.

Think about icebergs. The part of the iceberg that can be seen represents only a fraction of its whole; about ninety percent of the mass of Arctic icebergs is submerged. It is not the tip of the iceberg that sinks ships, for what we can see we can navigate around. It is the part of the iceberg that is *under* the surface of the water that creates danger.

What we know about ourselves is the tip of the iceberg. And like the iceberg, the part of the Self that we do *not* know is the part that sinks ships, that causes us to feel and behave in certain ways that defy logic and reason. Understanding what lies beneath the surface of our conscious self (our ego) requires looking deeply inside, but most of us are not prepared for this introspective quest. We may feel like strangers in a strange land when we begin the task of uncovering aspects of ourselves that have been hidden beneath the surface.

And yet it is necessary to look into these depths, this underworld, to open the dark, unconscious parts of ourselves to the light of awareness. In order to become whole, to move ahead on the path of individuation, we have to understand and take responsibility for *all* that we are. At midlife, the Self is demanding to be known. The Self, as the regulating center of the psyche and the archetype of wholeness, is pushing forth within each of us. It is like a seed that is planted and then strives to break the bounds of soil, to release itself into the air and blossom into whatever is in its nature to become. So it is with the Self. Underlying psychological and spiritual forces are creating an internal combustion between the parts of ourselves that we know and those that are demanding to be known.

This chapter will focus on the ways in which the Self is pressing for expression in our lives by looking at the persona/shadow, the anima/animus, and the inferior/superior functions and their effects on both our inner life and our outer relationships. By allowing ourselves to hold on to the dynamic tension of these opposing forces, though finding this balance can be a painful and difficult task, a new consciousness can emerge and the midlife journey can begin to offer its greatest rewards.

Stripping Away the Mask

In ancient Greece, actors wore masks that designated certain characters. They called these masks *personae* (from the Latin for "mask"), and a specific mask would always represent the same character. Jung adopted this word, "persona," to refer to the part of ourselves that we present to the outside world. The social mask that we put on for others to see is a primary way in which we adapt to society—it allows us to conform to the roles that we play in our relationships and culture. Although in Jungian psychology a great emphasis is placed on the inner life and the unconscious aspects of the psyche, understanding our external relationships and the ways in which we are perceived via our persona is also important to the task of individuation at midlife. As psychotherapist and writer Robert Hopcke points out, "All of human life is not lived in the depths. As vital as the movements of the unconscious are to human existence, conscious awareness and the quality of day-to-day living will never be displaced as legitimate and necessary components of human wholeness."[2]

Responding to each other through the use of these social masks allows conversation and commerce to flow easily from one person to another. The persona, then, is a useful and necessary link that we develop between each other; it regulates our relationships, avoids the need for continuous explanations and social introductions, and allows us to function smoothly as a society.

In the course of growing up, each of us creates a persona in order to adapt to the expectations of our parents, teachers, religion, and culture. Society lets us know very early in life that certain traits are desirable while others are not, and we learn to integrate the "positive" traits into our persona: most of us want to be seen by others as caring, intelligent, honest, generous, courageous, loving, and successful people. Society also lets us know that certain behaviors are approved of in girls and not boys, and vice versa. And so we begin to incorporate these positive characteristics into our sense of who we are and who we want others to think we are. W. Brugh Joy aptly calls this the "New Year's Resolution Self."

When people do not play their expected social roles, we are likely to have strong opinions about it. Think about some of the various personae that exist in our society: the good mother, the doctor, the President, the minister, the starving artist, the businesswoman, the athlete. Imagine entering a doctor's office to be greeted with the sounds of loud rock 'n' roll music. On the floor of the office are orange and blue beanbag chairs, and posters of James Dean cover the walls; the receptionist is wearing raggedy blue jean shorts and a bathing suit top. Finally, a door opens and the doctor comes in. He is wearing a Grateful Dead mustard-stained T-shirt, plaid shorts, and long hair pulled back in a ponytail. Many people would find some reason to leave this doctor's office and it wouldn't matter if he had just won the Nobel Prize for Medicine or was the kindest, most competent doctor in the world. He doesn't fit the persona we have for a doctor, and it is unlikely that he would build a very successful practice in spite of his skills. We have specific expectations for what we will find in a doctor's office.

But in spite of the social fluidity that results from these agreed-upon masks that we all wear, there are some negative effects that can come from the persona. One common negative effect is *inflexibility*. That is, we define our persona in such a way that we can never let go of it. We find that we always have to behave to conform to certain role expectations, even though the circumstances may demand a different response.

Barry is a commander in the Navy. He graduated at the top of his class at the U.S. Naval Academy and has made his professional career in the military. He has risen in rank very quickly, has always earned exceptional evaluations, and has been described by his superiors as a "real Navy man." One of the reasons Barry has been so successful in military life is his strong allegiance to the model of following orders and carrying them out to the best of his abilities. He understands that in combat there is no time for discussion or for following one's own ideas. What matters is precise and efficient compliance with what his commanding officer dictates. As long as Barry stays on his ship he is likely to continue to be successful. But his persona is rigid and inflexible. He has two teenage children who resent his dictatorial ways with them. He cannot discuss their own ideas about life or listen to their opinions; instead he gives them orders to follow. He is in constant conflict with his seventeen-year-old son, who refuses, among many other things, to answer the telephone at their home with "Commander so-and-so's quarters," as Barry has insisted he do. "This is not somebody's quarters," his son yells, "it's our home." Barry's inflexible adaptation to his persona is costing him close and warm relationships with his children and creating daily conflict in his family.

A healthy persona is one that remains flexible, one that can adapt to changing circumstances and relationships. The deference to authority that makes Barry a successful naval officer is not appropriate to interacting with and relating to his wife and children. He has a difficult time understanding this because he has been so heavily rewarded for these autocratic behaviors in his professional life.

Another common problem arises when we attempt to present a face to the world that does not reflect the reality of our lives or our real personality. Sandra grew up in a small rural community. Her mother died when Sandra was twelve. Her father was a coal miner. The family was very poor and Sandra, being the oldest, had many responsibilities in caring for her younger siblings. In addition to taking care of the younger children and the housework, Sandra was responsible for maintaining a large garden. Often the family would survive on the vegetables that she grew there.

Rather than being proud of how hard she and her family worked, Sandra has always been ashamed of her humble origins. When asked where she is from, Sandra names a large city about two hundred miles from where she actually grew up, a rural area known for its coal mines and poverty. When she was twenty she married a good man who worked hard for a living. Her husband's income allows them to live a better economic life than she had known. They own a home in a comfortable middle-class neighborhood, always have food on the table, and have enough money for some extra things like travel and vacations. But Sandra is not satisfied. She insists that they buy the best of everything. She drives an expensive automobile and will only wear the most costly designer clothes. To meet Sandra you would think that she has a great deal of money. But in reality, her need to conform to this persona has put the family in constant debt. She and her husband argue often about money and her spending habits. As long as Sandra continues to adhere to the persona of the "wealthy woman," she will continue to create problems for herself and her marriage. Her persona doesn't fit the realities of her life.

This failure to adapt our persona, our "outer self," to the realities of our life or personality occurs often. Sometimes these inconsistencies are clear, as in the case of Sandra, but often they are more subtle. We are encouraged to adapt to certain social and family expectations even when they do not fit who we are inside.

Timothy's life is another example of assuming a persona that doesn't fit reality. Timothy was raised in a very wealthy family. His parents had grown up with money and a great deal of education and exposure to culture. From the time he was very young, Timothy lived in a very conservative boarding school. When home with his family, he remembers, he would sit at the dinner table as servants waited to bring the next course. The family was so concerned with manners and appearances that even the toddlers knew which fork to use for their salad. All the children were expected to learn to play music, since that was part of what the parents considered a cultured life. Of all the children, Timothy had the greatest natural musical talent and he was expected to excel in this field. His parents hired a music professor from a prestigious conservatory to tutor him in the piano during the summer and other vacations from school. The professor trained him in the classics and Timothy remembers his teacher smacking his hands with a ruler when he hit a wrong note or attempted to improvise on a piece of music. When I met Timothy he was an adult and had not played the piano in more than fifteen years. He refused to even have a piano in his home. When I asked him if he missed the music in his life tears filled his eyes. "Yes," he said, "but I always wanted to play jazz."

Timothy's natural disposition, his personality, is looser and more spontaneous than those of his mother and father. His parents thought they were being generous and supportive by providing him with what they believed to be the best opportunity to learn music. But no one was listening to what he wanted. No one seemed to notice that his musical instincts were to improvise. Timothy has lived half his life conforming to a certain persona: an upper-class, highly educated connoisseur of classical music and literature. In fact, Timothy would probably be happier playing piano with a jazz group in a cafe. That is the kind of music that touches his soul. Timothy also has begun to understand that the way he has given up his music is a metaphor for other ways in which he has left his real self behind. He has sacrificed the most authentic parts of himself in order to live up to a certain persona.

Like Timothy, Jim has spent all of his life living up to expectations and roles that don't reflect his own inner needs and desires. While he was in his teens he was aware of his strong attraction to other boys. Mustering enormous courage, he revealed these feelings to his parents, his minister, and the girl he was dating. He was told that it was "just a phase" and that if only he would pray hard enough the terrible, sinful feelings would pass. He recommitted to his church, had a born-again experience at twenty-two, and married the woman he had been dating. Over the years he became more and more rigid and conservative in his religious beliefs. It was as if he knew deep inside that the only way to repress his strong homosexual feelings was to keep a very tight lid on his whole life. In his late thirties he began to experience a profound depression punctuated by severe anxiety attacks that on the surface seemed to have no cause. He was successful in his career, he cared deeply for his wife, and his children were healthy. He began to wake up screaming in the night and although he couldn't remember many details from his dreams he was always aware that "someone was chasing me." During this period Jim made several suicide attempts by taking large quantities of an antianxiety drug that had been prescribed for him. One of these attempts was almost fatal. "I remember waking up in the emergency room and wishing that I had died," he said. "I knew at that moment what I had to do. The feelings that I had in my teens, my attraction to men, was not just a phase. I have always known that my real sexual and emotional preference is for men. Over the years I have avoided having any kind of relationship with men. Since getting married I can't even say I've had a close male friend." Jim's religious views were less spiritual than they were an adherence to an inflexible set of rules that could not tolerate even the idea of a gay relationship. Believing fervently in this code of behavior protected Jim from the awareness of his own homosexual leanings. He was almost forty years old before he began the task of looking inside and trying to discover who he is.

Conforming to social expectations and to a persona that doesn't adequately reflect our deep inner self is like going through life wearing shoes that are too tight. It is possible to function in shoes that are too tight: you can get through life and do most of the things that are expected of you. In too tight shoes you can walk . . . but you can't dance. And at midlife, the soul is demanding to dance.

My mother was a beautiful, creative woman who, I believe, was stuck in a persona that didn't allow for the full expression of her creativity or eccentricity. She married my father after graduation from high school and quickly adapted to the role of homemaker/mother, which was one of the few acceptable roles for women in the 1950s. Both my parents were good, hardworking people who performed the gender roles that were expected of them. But my mother, feeling the constriction of her social role, was significantly depressed and anxious for much of her life. This translated into a strong need to control others and persuade them to conform to the ways that she felt things should be done. Like many women of her time, she identified herself solely as a wife and mother. When my brother and I left home to go to college and begin our own adult lives she was lost without the constant caring for children that had defined her for so long. She continued to try and live her life through ours, which, of course, led to conflict and arguments.

After my mother's death I was sitting with her sisters, reminiscing about her. My Aunt Jean told me about the time my mother and her girlfriend had decided to run away from home, when they were about fifteen. They were caught by a neighbor as they were preparing to roller-skate to Hollywood. I learned that my mother had always been "dramatic" and loved the sparkle and glitter of movies. I wondered who she might have become had she completed that teenage quest and arrived with scorching wheels at the corner of Hollywood and Vine. I wondered how she might have been different had she been able to dance.

Although a great deal has changed in gender role expectations in the past two decades, many people still define themselves on the basis of a limited number of prescribed social roles. The persona can create difficulties when one identifies with it too closely, for this limits the realization of one's unknown and unutilized potential. As in the case of Timothy, he sacrificed his own creativity and pleasure in music to become who he was "supposed" to be. Jim has lived half his life in the closet, conforming to a persona that does not reflect his own deepest urgings. My mother never learned that there was more to being a woman than just her role as wife and mother. Karen Horney, the great neo-Freudian psychoanalyst, called this strict adherence to what we are supposed to be the "tyranny of the should."[3] We ask, "Who should I be?" and, "What should I do with my life?" We would be better served by asking instead, "Who *am* I?" and, "What do I *want* to do with my life?"

We like to believe that the idealized self, the persona, we show to the world is really all there is to us. It seems safer that way. We can identify so completely with our roles in life that we seldom even wonder about who else we might be under all those social expectations. But there are several dangers in this kind of attitude. First, when we so completely identify with the role(s) we play in life, we neglect other aspects of ourselves that could bring pleasure and meaning to our lives. And secondly, we have great difficulties in adjusting to the inevitable changes that occur when a certain role wears thin or runs out.

Gary was a very successful businessman, a vice president of a major corporation, who always reported feeling happy and having a great sense of purpose about his life. At age fifty-five he was "retired" from the company he had worked for his whole professional life. The company told him that they were sorry to have to let him go but they were being purchased by a large foreign corporation that was making major changes in upper management. To be disappointed or angry at this turn of events is understandable, but Gary tried to kill himself. His identification with his persona, the "successful businessman," was so complete that he felt he had nothing left to live for when that role was denied him.

Carol felt desperate and suicidal when her youngest daughter left for college. "I feel like I've reached my peak and everything is downhill from here," she said. Like my own mother, her self-definition as a mother was so all-encompassing that she felt there was nothing left to live for, since her children didn't need her in the same ways that they had in the past. Many women at midlife find themselves in this difficult situation. We speak of the empty-nest syndrome but fail to fully understand the powerful sense of loss that occurs when a life role changes dramatically.

Like Gary and Carol, Bill was a normal, well-adjusted person until his role in life changed. On the *very day* that Bill retired from the Air Force he experienced a panic attack of such power that he ended up in a hospital emergency room believing he was having a heart attack. The doctors there gave him a thorough examination, including an EKG, and told him that his heart was in fine shape. At the time of this panic attack Bill was forty-three years old, in good health and with lots of options for a second career. "I should be feeling happy," he said. "I've got a good retirement from the Air Force so now I have the time to do work that I can really enjoy and not have to worry about how long it might take to reach an income level that can support my family." Nevertheless, he had defined himself so completely as an Air Force officer that without that aspect of his persona he had serious questions about his own identity. This inner conflict expressed itself, as it so often does, in physical symptoms that could not be ignored.

Change in our life roles is inevitable. This is especially true at midlife, when, for many, children are growing up and away; when we may have peaked professionally and all the big promotions are going to younger colleagues. The truth is that children do grow up and leave home. Healthy parents raise their children to do exactly that. We will retire from our jobs one day or no longer be able to perform them. Thus we are in danger of coming apart when we define ourselves completely on the basis of our persona.

We like to believe that the self we show to the world is uniquely us, but, as Jung points out, the persona "feigns individuality" and is "nothing real: it is a compromise between the individual and society."[4] The development of the persona is one of the tasks of the first half of life. During this part of our lives we are served by defining our roles with others and in society as they allow us to create relationships, nurture a family, build a career, and contribute to society. *But the energy that has gone into the construction and maintenance of the persona is often at the expense of knowing anything about our inner reality.* Many of us are unaware that there is anything else to us besides this "public" self that has come to define us.

At midlife we begin to sense that there is more to us than just the face we have shown to the world. One woman described herself as feeling like she lived in an "eggshell." It covered her up, she said, but it felt very fragile. If the persona is just that eggshell, then what has happened to the rest of our human characteristics? What has happened to the qualities that are not seen as quite so acceptable? Where are the parts of us that might be considered totally unacceptable or even reprehensible? What about the positive and valuable characteristics that are unexpressed in our life? How can we possibly be whole without those lost parts of ourselves?

The Shadow Knows

Have you ever said, "I don't know what came over me," or, "I just wasn't myself," when you felt or behaved in some way that seemed unlike you? If so, who were you? Who was behaving in your place? All that is set aside, repressed, or unrecognized, all that is banished from our persona is within us still. Jung calls this unconscious and unknown part of ourselves the "shadow" and it contains all that we think we are not. The shadow contains anger, sexuality, and the darker aspects of human nature to be sure. But it also holds spontaneity, joy, and unrealized creative fires. It is only through the integration of the shadow into our conscious awareness that we can become whole and begin to live as the full and complete human beings that we were born to be. By midlife we have repressed a great deal of our personality into the realm of the unconscious, into the shadow. At midlife the shadow is demanding expression.

In order to function, all societies must teach their young ones the rules and codes of their culture. Society couldn't function without restricting certain kinds of behaviors among its members. Yet through this process of socialization we learn that certain natural human feelings, like sexuality and aggression, are not acceptable, and they are therefore shunted off into the unconscious. Very few families teach the healthy expression of anger, for example. We do not say, "It's okay to be angry but it is not okay to hit." Instead we say, "How can you behave like that to your little sister? You're bad. Go to your room." In large part, we do not teach children that there are healthy ways of expressing their sexuality. Instead we don't talk about sex with our children, thereby conveying the idea that the subject is taboo and untouchable. "Behave yourself," teachers say to children. In order to fit in, in order not to be sent to the principal's office, we learn to be still, docile, and quiet in our classrooms. "The sky isn't supposed to be orange," the critics admonish child artists. And so we learn: the sky is to be colored blue, we will sit in our seats, we will not express anger, and we will place our sexual instincts in some very remote corner of ourselves.

The poet Robert Bly writes about the shadow as the "long bag we drag behind us."

> When we were one or two years old we had what we might call a 360-degree personality. Energy radiated out from all parts of our body and all parts of our psyche. A child running is a living globe of energy. We had a ball of energy, all right; but one day we noticed that our parents didn't like certain parts of that ball. They said things like: "Can't you be still?" Or "It isn't nice to try and kill your brother." Behind us we have an invisible bag, and the part of us our parents don't like, we, to keep our parents' love, put in the bag. By the time we go to school our bag is quite large. Then our teachers have their say: "Good children don't get angry over such little things." So we take our anger and put it in the bag. By the time my brother and I were twelve in Madison, Minnesota, we were known as "the nice Bly boys." Our bags were already a mile long.[5]

Many other human characteristics which we are taught not to express get routinely dumped into the shadow: jealousy, lust, greed, and selfishness. Depending upon the values of our immediate family, our community, and our religion, we may place positive human characteristics, such as creativity, spontaneity, compassion, and tolerance, into the shadow as well. While Freud originally described the unconscious as containing only the "negative" or dark side of human nature, Jung recognized the shadow as holding everything that was unlived in an individual's life. Therefore, to Jung, there is gold in that dark place. Jung wrote, "If it has been believed hitherto that the human shadow was the source of all evil, it can now be ascertained on closer investigation that [it] does not consist only of morally reprehensible tendencies, but also displays a number of good qualities, such as normal instincts, appropriate reactions, realistic insights, creative impulses, etc."[6] But just because these are placed into the unconscious doesn't mean that they cease to exist. They are still there, still a part of us, in all their uncontained wildness, just below the surface.

My Uncle Art is a big, powerful man. He was raised in a poor family with a strong work ethic and utilitarian views about life. He was born male in an era when men were to exhibit only stoicism and strength. When he grew up, married, and had children, he supported his family by working as a fireman in a large metropolitan area that is one of the roughest cities in New Jersey. Everything about his persona said, "I am tough. Don't mess with me." I can remember taking big family vacations as a child with all of my relatives. After being sent to bed for the night my cousins and I would leap from bed to bed, hide from each other, and then suddenly jump out making the others scream like banshees. Our parents would call up to us to go to sleep. They would threaten and cajole. They would send my father or my Uncle George to deal with us. We would feign sleep and then, as soon as we could hear their departing footsteps, begin our games again. After about an hour of this our mothers would call out, "We're sending Uncle Art up." Immediately we would run for our beds. "Please don't send Uncle Art up. We're going to sleep now," we'd plead. We only knew my uncle's persona. In all the years that we were "threatened" by my uncle I never once saw him raise a hand to any of the kids, never even heard him yell at anyone. He didn't need to. It was only when I was older that I began to see my uncle's persona for what it was—a facade, a toughness that he had developed over the years. In fact, I came to know him as a very emotional person and someone who later in my life expressed those emotions with real tenderness. I remember when I finally saw through my uncle's persona. I told my mother that I had discovered that Uncle Art was really like a big strong teddy bear; that he was very sweet and helpful to me. My mother looked at me and said, "Of course." She had known all along that his persona was just that. It is often easier to see what is in the shadow of another than in our own.

In order to be a whole human being we need *all* of our human characteristics: our anger, our sexuality, all the glorious and, yes, the repugnant aspects of our humanity. Vulnerability, emotional expressiveness, creativity, softness, compassion, and playfulness, all the beautiful and life-enhancing parts of the Self that have not been given expression in our own personality, live in the shadow side by side with the darker aspects of human nature.

At midlife unconscious, shadow material erupts into our life. The emergence of the shadow is important in that it is the psyche's attempt to bring greater balance to one's personality. Yet this process requires knowing that there is more to us than the pleasant and perfectly appropriate self we show to the world at large. It means accepting our full humanity with all of its wrinkles and warts. But even more than that, it means coming to love those neglected parts of ourselves as elements of our own authenticity and humanity. The poet Rainer Maria Rilke wrote: "Perhaps all the dragons of our lives / are princesses who are only waiting to / see us once, beautiful and brave. / Perhaps everything terrible is / in its deepest being something / that needs our love."[7]

We are, and have always been, aware that there is more to us than meets the eye. Yet if we cannot love those neglected parts of ourselves, we cannot expect anyone else to. We go through life protecting ourselves. We have a sense that if anyone really, truly knew us they would see that we are not as good as we might first appear to be. This keeps us from a deep knowledge of our inner self and prevents authentic intimacy with other people. It keeps us defended and careful. We meet each other through a veil of untruth. Like one-dimensional characters, we playact through life instead of really living it.

It takes enormous energy to maintain aspects of ourselves in the shadow. We must be constantly on guard, making certain that nothing sneaks out, making sure that no one can see our dark parts. If we could free our psychic energy from the role of keeping watch, imagine the energy we would be able to spend on real intimacy, creativity, heartfelt compassion, and love.

When the contents of the shadow remain unconscious to us, we see them all around us in other people. We project our own dark side onto others, always seeing in their lives what we cannot acknowledge in our own. I was sitting in the kitchen with a friend when she looked out the window. "Ack! There goes Mary Smith again. She's on her way to another meeting. She's got to be in charge of everything. She's on the PTA council, the neighborhood citizens' group; now I hear that she's thinking about running for the school board. I can't stand her. She's got to be in charge of everything." My friend had so much emotion about something that had nothing to do with her that I knew she was projecting her own need for power onto her overextended neighbor. In fact, my friend can be a very controlling person in her own quiet, backdoor kind of way. If you were to ask her if she liked the idea of being in charge or having power she would quickly deny it. Yet here she was with a huge emotional response to someone else's behavior that was, essentially, none of her business.

At midlife the Self is pushing us toward wholeness. We know that the time we have left to move toward this goal is limited. A great deal of our psychic and spiritual energy is being, consciously or unconsciously, focused on this task. So what are we to do? Do we just sit back and let the shadow emerge or erupt, as the case may be? What happens to our lives? What happens to our families and neighborhoods? Do we run over our old life with all the animal force of these repressed energies?

The answer to these questions for our own life will be determined by the level of consciousness that we are willing to work for. From the examples in chapter 1, it is easy to see that some individuals allowed the shadow to erupt like a volcano, throwing their lives into chaos and crisis. Others attempted to become conscious of what was happening in their lives and were able to contain the pressures of the emerging shadow.

Earlier I brought up the story of Colleen. Pregnant at the age of sixteen, she married a man who made the military his career. She spent the greatest part of her young adult life raising her children, caring for their home, and playing the role of a military officer's wife. When I met Colleen her youngest child was preparing to leave for college. At this time she suffered what she called a "breakdown." She had been working part-time at an upscale West Coast advertising agency and was becoming increasingly attracted to some of the younger, creative people she worked with there. They were full of life. Her marriage, in fact her whole life, seemed dull and stale. She began to go to happy hour with these younger people on Friday nights. Her husband didn't mind; he was glad that she was making friends at her job. She began to stay out later and later with her new crowd, continuing to party with them long after happy hour was over. When she began to come home well after midnight, her husband became angry. He was concerned about her driving home intoxicated. They began to fight about her behavior. She accused him of being overly controlling and finally expressed the resentment that she had held so long about his career and the frequent moves. "I've lived my whole life for what you wanted. I've never had a life of my own," she would scream at him. One night the police called her husband. Colleen had been arrested along with a number of her friends in a cocaine bust.

By the time of her arrest Colleen had developed a serious cocaine habit, her marriage was in shambles, and her children were furious with her. Colleen's story is a good example of the power of the shadow. All her life she had been timid, tightly controlled, and excessively concerned with everyone else's needs, never taking time to explore her own needs or achieve her own goals. Now at forty-three she had become totally self-absorbed and was making unhealthy, even dangerous choices that affected her life and her family. Colleen, at this point, was possessed by her shadow. Her life was being completely overwhelmed by unconscious forces.

Colleen's story may seem extreme, and it is easy to believe that something like this doesn't happen to "normal" people. But up until this point in her life, Colleen lived a very ordinary life. You know people like Colleen. Perhaps you are like her in some ways yourself.

In midlife many people simply feel that they are "not themselves." Many will experience the power of the unconscious force of their emerging shadow in less dramatic ways than Colleen. Consider the woman or man engaged in an extramarital affair against all better judgment. Imagine people who have spent a lifetime building a career and now can barely drag themselves into work. At midlife many people are engaged in a deep inner struggle between the conflicting demands of what is expected of them and the dark stirrings of their shadow selves.

What then are we to do? If we do not honor the shadow and the unlived parts of ourselves we cannot move toward individuation. Furthermore, we are spending enormous amounts of psychic energy to control and imprison these impulses and desires.

On the other hand, we cannot individually or collectively allow ourselves to be overrun by these darker parts of the psyche. We cannot all abandon our careers, relationships, places in society, or outward persona. We cannot act out the dark side of our natures and live ethically and morally sound lives. To do so would cause our culture to come apart at its seams, and our individual lives, ones that we have worked hard to establish, would be destroyed. How is it possible to satisfy the powerful, competing demands of the persona and the shadow? And why is this such a critical issue at midlife?

Holding the Tension of the Opposites

At midlife we are deeply involved in a drama between opposites of profound proportions. Certainly, there can be no greater opposites than the face we show to the world and the dark aspects of the unconscious shadow. But it is precisely the conflict between these opposites that offers an opportunity to form a new identity, one that can incorporate aspects of ourselves that were repressed and unlived during the first half of life. We are on the threshold of a transformation and we are reaching out for greater depth and meaning. We are struggling to acknowledge parts of ourselves that have been ignored for thirty, forty, fifty years or more. We are attempting to know ourselves in new and important ways. But in order to move toward who we are becoming we have to let go, if only for an instant, of who we have been.

It is this space, between what we have been and what we will become, that is the most terrifying. It is what the mystic Christians referred to as the "night sea journey." Others have called it the "descent into hell." This netherworld is a place where a person's sense of identity is suspended, where there is no longer the same clear sense of "I" that has been a lifelong companion up until now. Deeply felt loss, nostalgia, grief, and mourning accompany us through this passage. Anxiety, depression, disillusionment, disappointment, and feelings of hopelessness are borne without any sense of a foundation being in place.

There is, at this point, a tremendous desire to put an end to this process. We yearn to return to the safety of our previous life. This is understandable, for the psychological pain of this liminal place can be overwhelming. In addition, we live in a culture that does not honor inner work, and instead, insists on defining goals and moving swiftly toward them. "Just make a decision and stick to it," "When are you going to get over this?" we are told and often tell ourselves. We think that we should choose between staying in a marriage or leaving it for someone else; that we should learn to be happy with our career or just go in and quit our jobs; that we should continue to believe what we have always believed or simply find something else that we can believe in, and quickly.

But movement from this place is not so easy. We are not deciding whether to buy the Toyota van or the Ford Explorer. Nothing in our life has prepared us for the momentous nature of the choices we are facing. We feel stuck in the middle. That is why so many people in midlife describe it as being "torn apart" or "split in half." Analyst and author Murray Stein refers to this process as "floating." During the initial, steepest descent of my own midlife passage I called it a "riptide."

Riptides occur when two opposing currents meet; it is a natural collision of opposites. These currents create a swirling action that forms channels. When a wave recedes, water rushes through that outgoing channel with great power and speed. If you love the ocean, as I do, you quickly learn that riptides are to be respected because they can drag even the strongest swimmer out past the breakers in a heartbeat. The natural impulse is to swim as hard as you can back toward the shore. But when you are caught in a riptide this is the worst thing you can do. You cannot overpower this natural force. Even very competent swimmers drown by trying to fight the force of moving water that is taking them out to sea.

Instead, a riptide demands surrender. If you simply float, taking care only to keep your head above water, the riptide will take you out about fifteen hundred feet or so, and only then can you begin to swim parallel to the shore and find your way back. We are used to being in control of our lives, but a riptide teaches that sometimes it is necessary to "go with the flow." Not knowing where you will end up and feeling helpless in the face of the power of forces that are much stronger than you are terrifying experiences. Surviving a riptide demands trust in your own ability to keep your head above the water and trust in the natural force of the event to take you only so far away from shore.

In the midlife passage it is necessary to trust in the integrity of your own inner process, the wisdom of the Self, and your own strength. As with a riptide, it is necessary to believe that the emerging intrapsychic forces will take you only so far from shore.

Jung called his own midlife transition an "encounter with the unconscious." He wrote: "I frequently imagined a steep descent. I even made several attempts to get to the very bottom. The first time I reached, as it were, a depth of about a thousand feet; the next time I found myself at the edge of a cosmic abyss. It was like a voyage to the moon, or a descent into an empty space. First came the image of a crater, and I had the feeling that I was in the land of the dead. The atmosphere was that of the other world."[8]

This image of a descent and passage through a dark, frightening threshold into a sphere of rebirth and change abounds in mythological literature from all human cultures: Dante's visitations through the circles of hell, Jonah in the belly of the whale, Kore-Persephone's departure to the underworld, Inanna's descent to the netherworld, Celtic hero Finn MacCool's being swallowed by a monster, the Inuit story of Raven darting into the gullet of a whale-cow, and knights in shining armor entering the lairs of dragons. All human societies have incorporated the process of descent and rebirth into their stories and mythologies. Yet we continue to think of these parables as purely fictional: we will never have to slay dragons or find our way out of the innards of some great beast. Midlife brings a crashing halt to this arrogance. In midlife many of us find ourselves exactly there . . . in the belly of the whale. All our past tactics for solving problems, making decisions, and pursuing goals seem weak and inadequate in the face of the terror and the power of the unconscious forces that threaten to overwhelm us.

The answer to the conflict between the opposing demands of the persona, representing collective expectations, and the more individualized, often quite primitive needs of the shadow lies in *compromise*. The answer becomes not the one or the other but a third alternative. We need not quit our job or stay shackled to it as we have before. We need not have an affair or continue in a mediocre, stagnant relationship. We need not continue to believe in the world as we always have. Jung wrote, "Out of the collision of opposites the unconscious psyche always creates a third thing of an irrational nature, which the conscious mind neither expects nor understands. It presents itself in a form that is neither a straight 'yes' nor a straight 'no.' "[9]

This third thing, the new and previously unknown alternative, is a result of a growing awareness of the shadow and its contents. Jung referred to this psychic function that arises from the tension and conflict between consciousness and the unconscious as the *transcendent function,* and recognized it as a natural aspect of the self-regulating nature of the psyche. It is the synthesis between a thesis and its antithesis (or opposite) and it is a building block toward real psychological growth. Students of philosophy will recognize something of Hegel's dialectic in this idea.

The conflict between the demands of the conscious mind (ego) and the unconscious (shadow) generates a profound psychological tension that is charged with energy, pain, and psychological symptoms such as depression and anxiety. Holding this tension is an agonizing task and many people cannot contain the feelings of being "split in two" and the internal chaos that can be experienced. And yet this is *exactly* what the psyche demands in order to move toward a higher level of self-knowledge, consciousness, and individuation.

Most important, this state of embracing both conscious and unconscious forces, or *holding the tension of the opposites,* requires that unconscious needs and demands become conscious. We can begin to allow light to enter the darkness. We can move toward a greater awareness of the shadow side, integrate this into our understanding of ourselves, and begin to take full responsibility for it. Jung wrote, "The stirring up of conflict is a Luciferian virtue in the true sense of the word. Conflict engenders fire, the fire of affects and emotions, and like every other fire it has two aspects, that of combustion and that of creating light."[10]

Barbara was similar to Colleen in that she had married young and defined herself almost exclusively as a wife and mother. She, too, began to feel unhappy, unfulfilled, and restless when her children began to leave home. "I wondered what I would do with the rest of my life. I didn't have a single idea about how I would spend my days." Barbara said that she loved Ted, her husband, but the marriage had become routine. They spent far more time in front of the television together than in conversation or any other kind of shared activities. Their sexual relationship had become infrequent and predictable. For the first time in her life, Barbara felt depressed. "I had no energy. I didn't care if I got out of bed in the morning. I'd tell myself, 'Who cares if I've gotten all the laundry done today?' 'Who cares if I've got dinner on the table this evening?' The kids are all going their own ways. I'm never even sure who will be here for dinner." One morning, Barbara became terrified of her strong urge to get in the car and just keep driving. "I thought I was going crazy. I found myself talking to myself when I was alone. It was like an argument going on inside of me."

Unlike Colleen, Barbara began to listen to her internal dialogue, to try to understand what was going on inside of her. She began to write down her feelings in a diary, something she hadn't done since she was a young girl. She began to pray. She opened up to a close woman friend and discovered, to her great comfort, that her friend had been having similar feelings. "Just to hear Marge say that she understood was the most amazing thing. I didn't feel quite so alone or crazy." Barbara and Marge made an agreement to talk at least once a week about what was going on with each of them.

Barbara had always been aware that she wanted to be an artist. She was talented, even as a young child, and was encouraged by her teachers to pursue art as a career. She was studying fine arts in college when she became pregnant. She opted to marry Ted and drop out of college as soon as her baby was born, but she continued to paint and draw when she had a little free time. She never had any great plans to show or sell her work but enjoyed the process of creating images on canvas. At midlife, as her children were leaving home and as she was questioning what she wanted for the rest of her life, her paintings began to change. She told me that she knew something important was happening to her then. "I had always painted on small canvases, never larger than five inches by seven, the kind you could buy ready-made from an artists' supply store." Barbara had always painted landscapes with neat, precise strokes on these small canvases. "I always used a muted purple or brown color scheme," she said.

Barbara's restlessness could no longer be contained in the small spaces she had allotted for her artistic expression. She asked Ted to move some of his woodworking equipment to one side of their garage so that she could have the rest for a "studio." Barbara began to paint on huge canvases. "I bought the canvas by the roll and nailed it up to the inside wall of the garage." She painted in vibrant, primary colors—gone were the small, controlled strokes of her tiny landscapes. "One day I found myself using bright red house paint and putting it on with a sponge mop," she laughed.

Barbara's painting became an important way to express the conflict and the "voices" that were arguing inside her head. She understood this process as a metaphor for what was going on in her life. "I never really let myself break loose. I was always trying to be the perfect wife and mother. My kids used to tell me I had the 'Donna Reed syndrome' because I always tried to make a perfect home like on a fifties TV show."

Barbara began to talk openly with her husband. She was surprised to find out that he, too, was feeling bored and dissatisfied with his life and their marriage. They moved the television out of their bedroom, signed up for country line dancing lessons, and agreed to spend at least some time each day talking together. They began to make fundamental changes in their relationship. Barbara continued to work with her journal and pursue a deeper understanding of her inner world through meditation.

"I'm not saying that the changes we've made have solved all the problems," Barbara said. "I still feel confused and unsure about what the rest of my life will be like. But I do know that I still love Ted after almost twenty-eight years of marriage and I know that he loves me. I have also come to realize that nothing good will happen if I just blame him for the boredom that we've shared. I'm responsible for it too."

Barbara has been successfully holding the tension of the opposites. She is allowing herself to become more aware of her own needs, inner strivings, and contributions to the problems in her marriage and her life. She is opening up to the wilder, more expressive parts of herself that had been sacrificed in order to maintain her persona as the "perfect wife and mother." But unlike Colleen, she is containing the emergence of her shadow in ways that are healthy for her and her family. The last time I spoke with Barbara she was in the middle of a nine-week course in scuba diving. Barbara is letting light into the darkness.

Barbara's story illustrates the power of holding the tension of the opposites. She has developed ways that help her contain the frightening thoughts and depression that are so frequent at midlife. Yet she has been willing to explore the feelings rather than try to alleviate them immediately by making decisions that will cause them to go away. This process is a slow one and many people are tempted to make quick, often rash decisions in order to feel better quickly. It is understandable that we just want to get back to "normal," to honor only the persona and to disregard the shadow. But to give in to all the unconscious urgings of the shadow will threaten our whole way of life. It takes courage to stand in the middle of the fray.

And yet this is exactly what we must do. We cannot "control" the shadow by simply pretending that it does not exist. In fact, the more we banish parts of our true selves into the shadow, the more power we give to them. These repressed parts of the Self build up steam and energy when they are denied any expression. This is something that I've called the "volcano syndrome." For, like a volcano building up energy under the surface of the earth, repressed shadow material is storing energy and will, at some point, explode into one's life.

I often ask clients if they understand the function of a dam. "Yes," they will say, "it is to hold things back." But that is not correct. A dam's purpose is to control the flow. Every dam is equipped with a series of valves that allow for the safe passage of water and energy through it. Without the controlled release of water through the dam, eventually the pressure of the water building up in the reservoir will inevitably break the dam apart. We have no control over the amount of water that is filling the reservoir, and at some point one drop of water too many will threaten the integrity of the dam—it will threaten to break apart and flood our homes and those of our friends and neighbors. In the dam that is the metaphor for the emergence of the shadow, consciousness is the valve system that allows for the healthy, controlled regulation of energy.

The dam is ready to break apart for many people at midlife. Their lives are so out of balance, so unconscious, that hanging on to the center feels almost impossible. And holding the tension of the opposites is more difficult when the discrepancy between our conscious and unconscious selves, between the persona and the shadow, is extreme. Jung wrote that "the brighter the light the darker the shadow." The more out of balance one's personality is in one direction, the greater the shift to the other direction when the unconscious emerges. Jung borrowed the term *enantiodromia* from Heracleitus, a pre-Socratic Greek philosopher, to describe this idea. That word, from the Latin for "running counter to," means that sooner or later everything turns into, or is seen to be identical with, its opposite.[11]

As we look at our own lives we can begin to understand the ways in which we have lived without balance. We can begin to look at ourselves honestly and with compassion as the first step on our journey toward wholeness. This requires courage, containment, and perhaps most of all, patience. The process of coming home to our true Self demands a great deal of painstaking work over a long period of time. And yet, if our individual destinies are to be fulfilled, it is this new consciousness and self-knowledge that give life its sense of purpose and meaning. By recognizing our shadow we begin, perhaps for the first time, to see the "other," the parts of ourselves that have long been ignored in favor of who we always thought we were. This is the place where a new self-awareness is formed. It is where consciousness and the beginning of enlightenment emerge.

Inner and Outer Marriage and Relationship

Yin-Yang: The Inner Marriage Between Masculine and Feminine

Androgyny, derived from the Greek words *andros* meaning "man" and *gynos,* for "woman," refers to the idea that everyone's personality contains both masculine and feminine characteristics. But we could easily refer to what we think of as the dualism feminine/masculine by other names, by Yin-Yang, right brain/left brain, or Eros/Logos, for example. Many present-day Jungian analysts continue to refer to these polarities with the terms "feminine and masculine," even though these words are more emotionally charged than some of the others, because this is how these aspects of the psyche are presented in dreams.

According to Jungians and Taoists, the "feminine" refers to human characteristics that are receptive, yielding, intuitive, holistic, related, connected, emotional, spatial, nonverbal, and nontemporal. The "masculine" includes characteristics such as analytical, symbolic, abstract, temporal, rational, logical, independent, and linear. A quick perusal of these adjectives allows one to see immediately that in our culture, for both men and women, the masculine principle is overly developed. We are a society that values analytical, logical, rational thinking rather than intuition. We are not a society that values emotional, deeply connected ways of relating to one another. The feminine—in this society, and in both women and men—is undervalued and underdeveloped. Thus we tend to value thinking over feeling, reason over intuition, independence over connectedness, goal achievement over process, science over art, aggression over surrender, and light over darkness.

The Chinese Taoist work *I Ching,* or *Book of Changes,* describes characteristics associated with the Yin-Yang (or feminine/masculine) dualism:[12]

YIN	YANG
Feminine	Masculine
Negative	Positive
Moon	Sun
Darkness	Light
Yielding	Aggressive
Left Side	Right Side
Warm	Cold
Autumn	Spring
Winter	Summer
Unconscious	Conscious
Right Brain	Left Brain
Emotion	Reason

☯ The classic Chinese emblem of Yin-Yang represents harmony between dualities such as good and evil, summer and winter, birth and death, earth and heaven, and male (Yang) and female (Yin). Each lobe of the circle contains a spot of the opposite color, reminding us that "every half of a dualistic pair contains something of its opposite within its heart."[13] The Yin-Yang symbol reminds us that there is masculine in women and feminine in men, and most important that *only when there is balance between these pairs of opposites can there be wholeness and harmony.*

Every human being is endowed with contrasting, but potentially harmonic, tendencies and energies that we have labeled "masculine" and "feminine." Like the Yin-Yang which holds something of the "other" in each lobe of the circle, every man has an internal, unconscious feminine aspect (which Jung called *anima*) and every woman has an internal, unconscious masculine aspect (called *animus.*) Jung derived these terms from the Latin *animare,* which means "to enliven." The conscious integration of the contrasexual aspect of the psyche is necessary for an "enlivened," spirited, soulful life.

Think about how we become stuck in our gender roles and exclusive identifications with only masculine or feminine characteristics. Although a great deal has changed in how we define these terms in twentieth-century America, we can still see everyday examples of men and women who are overdeveloped in one area and underdeveloped in the other. Many men suffer problems connecting with and expressing feelings. The gender role for men includes a John Wayne stoicism that often keeps them emotionally and spiritually separated even from the people they love most. On the other hand, many women who have not integrated their internal masculine aspects become overly dependent and unable to stand up for themselves.

We have only to look at human infants of both genders to understand the harmony that is obvious when the psychological aspects of the masculine and feminine are fully integrated. Healthy infants cry when they feel like it, express love, and, at the same time, assertively demand that their needs be met; they then go off to independently explore their new universe. Although there are clearly some biologically based differences between males and females, distinctions between infants, with regard to the masculine and feminine principles, are less dependent on their gender than on their individual personalities and temperaments.

Understanding the inner masculine and feminine is important in comprehending the changes that occur in midlife, for the anima and animus are powerful psychological forces that directly affect our everyday behavior and our relationship with ourselves and others. In fact, Jung described the anima and animus as archetypes. As discussed in Chapter Two, archetypes are inherited "predispositions" that are present in all human beings in much the same way that a bird comes into the world with the inborn behavior pattern to migrate, though the specifics of how and where that migration will occur may have to be learned. Archetypes, these natural blueprints, are present in every human being regardless of culture, race, geography, or the historical time in which an individual may live. A useful metaphor for understanding archetypes is to imagine a dry riverbed. Just as a riverbed creates the form and direction that water will follow, so do the archetypes set the path for psychic energy (which Jung termed *libido*) as it flows. To Jung the archetypes of anima and animus are present in all human beings. Although the specific shapes of these predispositions and expectations have changed over time (e.g., as a result of changing expectations of what it means to be a man or to be a woman), these inner masculine and feminine energies continue to exist as they always have.

Jung also speaks of the anima and animus as "complexes." Complexes are closely related to archetypes in that they are "personifications" of archetypes. A complex is an emotionally charged group of ideas or images, and the primary means through which archetypes express themselves in the personal psyche. Complexes are like partial personalities that feel as if they are beyond our conscious control. Jung described them as "psychic entities which are outside the control of the conscious mind. They have been split off from consciousness and lead a separate existence in the dark realm of the unconscious, being at all times ready to hinder or reinforce conscious functioning."[14]

The most important thing to recognize here is that both complexes and archetypes are (1) *unconscious,* (2) charged with emotion or *affect,* and (3) relatively *autonomous.* They often feel like they are "not us." Although they are unconscious they exert dramatic influences on our feelings and behavior. The anima and animus are not just dry, theoretical concepts about the human psyche, but have vivid and direct effects on our feelings, behaviors, and relationships.

The relationship between Susan and her live-in boyfriend, Justin, provides a good example of a complex as well as of a woman out of touch with her inner masculine energy. Susan's father abandoned the family shortly after she was born, leaving her mother without any income and with three small children to raise. Her mother became seriously depressed, and although she was able to take care of Susan's physical needs, she had very little left to offer her in terms of emotional support or maternal nurturance. Susan's mother turned increasingly to alcohol to numb the psychological pain that she was experiencing. In short, because of her depression, alcoholism, and the need to earn a living to support her children, Susan's mother wasn't really able to meet the normal demands of her baby.

Susan has been described by Justin (and by other men who have been in relationships with her) as extremely "needy." She demands a great deal of attention and is supersensitive to anything that remotely smacks of abandonment. Justin is a devoted lover, has never given her any reason to distrust him, and spends almost all of his free time with her. Occasionally, though, he has an offer to go away for a golf weekend with some of his male friends. Whenever this issue comes up in their relationship, Susan creates an enormous emotional scene. She screams at Justin and sobs for days. She tells him that he has never loved her and that she can't trust him anymore. He pleads for her to understand: he only wants to go away overnight with his friends for a golf outing. The more Susan clings to him and tries to prevent him from going away, the more disgusted Justin becomes. "I tell myself that I don't need this in my life," he says. "I know that she's being totally irrational. She behaves like a two-year-old throwing a tantrum." Eventually, Susan's behavior is quite likely to force Justin to leave the relationship. Any reasonable person would be put off by this display of insecurity and childishness. In fact, Susan is setting herself up to be abandoned. When this happens, as it surely will, then it will reinforce her belief that people will abandon you, so it is useless and dangerous to trust them in the first place. In fact, this has happened in several previous relationships.

Susan has a serious abandonment complex, or perhaps it is more accurate to say that a complex has Susan. In addition, she has not consciously integrated any of her inner masculine energy. Untempered by the independence and logic of a healthy animus and completely disconnected from the more powerful aspects of the feminine, she has become whiny, frightened, emotional to the point of extreme sentimentality, and desperate to be loved. She projects her psychological needs for masculine energy onto Justin, making unreasonable demands on him to prove that she is lovable and protected, and her behavior is destroying their relationship. As long as she is unconscious as to why she feels so abandoned and terrified when her lover wants to spend a little time apart from her, she will continue to respond in the same way.

While the anima and animus are archetypal, innate, and part of our human psychological endowment, they are shaped, to a large extent, by our personal experiences with people of the opposite sex (especially our parents and other significant people in our immediate environment). Early experiences, like Susan's abandonment by her father and her lack of appropriate mothering, will color all of our relationships throughout our lives as long as they are unconscious. The more unconscious they remain, the greater the effect they will have. They will determine our attractions and attachments to others.

The Self desires wholeness, and through the dialectic of opposites it attempts to move toward this psychological position. Just as the psyche devotes great energy to integrating the shadow and the persona, especially at midlife, it attempts to integrate the "masculine" and "feminine" energies within the individual. Jung considered both the confrontation of the persona and the shadow and that with the anima or animus to be the two central tasks for the middle part of life. The psychological processes required for these collisions of opposites were not for the young (or faint of heart), for they require a certain maturity and considerable courage.

The Outer Marriage or Relationship

In addition to our relationship to our inner Self, our outer relationships are deeply affected by our inner psychological and spiritual changes in midlife. The emergence of unconscious material can create chaos in our primary relationship, whether it be heterosexual, gay or lesbian, traditional marriages or nontraditional commitments. There are few marriages or relationships that are not under great strain during the midlife transition. In fact, for many people, severe relationship problems, separation, or divorce may be the *initial* warning signal of a midlife crisis.

Relationships, like many other elements of our lives, are often entered into and maintained by strong unconscious forces that are uprooted at midlife. It is not uncommon to hear people say of their partner at midlife, "She's not who I thought she was," or "He's not the man I married." In fact, they probably never were. For we project many of our unconscious desires and fantasies onto our romantic partner, and just as it is possible to have a one-sided, incomplete view of oneself, we often have these same distorted views toward our spouse or partner. In order to truly understand our relationship we must look at its unconscious aspects.

Our anima and animus are built-in anticipations that each sex has for the other and create our "idealized" view of our partner. As anyone who has fallen in love can attest, when the anima or animus is activated it packs a major jolt of electricity. We experience the feeling of falling in love when we encounter someone who embodies important aspects of our own unconscious anima or animus.[15]

Janet and Eli met at a party in their neighborhood. Janet was recently divorced but Eli was married with two young children. Within three months of their meeting, Eli had left his wife and moved in with Janet. "I never intended to fall in love with a married man," she said. "I think it's wrong to do that. I was sour on the whole idea of commitment and marriage anyway. But I fell in love with him the moment we met. I don't understand it. My friends think I'm crazy, and some are very judgmental about the fact that he was married." Janet has experienced a great deal of guilt over the fact that Eli left his family and moved in with her. In her own words she described herself as becoming "instantly addicted" to him. Janet's attraction to Eli was so intense and immediate that she circumvented her own ethical views in order to be with him.

Janet's experience is a powerful example of what it means to be "taken over by an autonomous complex." To be sure, we will not project this powerful unconscious part of ourselves onto just anyone. We need to find someone who is close enough to our own inner anima or animus image, someone who can provide a good hook for our projection and can hold it, at least temporarily. Therapist John Sanford refers to the unconscious forces of a man's anima and a woman's animus as the "invisible partners" in a relationship.[16]

Through our projections, we fall in love with the Fairy Princess or Prince Charming, a god or goddess. He or she is beyond human comprehension, can do no wrong, and is the most perfect example of the species to walk the face of the earth. Of course, underneath all of our projections of romantic perfection lies an ordinary human being just like ourselves. James Hollis notes that if all the Top Forty tunes about love were merged into one, their lyrics would say: " 'I was miserable until you came into my life and then everything felt brand new and we were on top of the world until you changed and we lost what we had and you moved away and now I am miserable and will never love again until the next time.' What varies is the gender of the singer and the presence or not of a guitar."[17]

Over time, however, and certainly by midlife, our projections have a hard time maintaining themselves in the face of the reality of the real live human person with whom we have a relationship. He may be Prince Charming but he snores like crazy. She may indeed be the Fairy Princess but she has become assertive about expressing her needs instead of always being at the Prince's beck and call. Fairy tales have difficulty in maintaining their glittering shape when one is confronted with changing dirty baby diapers or running through a hardware store to find a replacement part for the pipe that has just exploded behind the washing machine.

One of the truths about the projections that go on in relationships is that we tend to project the most undeveloped aspects of ourselves, which accounts for the old maxim that "opposites attract." For example, if we have a hard time expressing emotions, then we are likely to be attracted to a partner who is very emotional—even to the point of sentimentality or oversensitivity. If we have a difficult time accepting our own ambition, we are likely to be attracted to an ambitious mate. Often we are drawn to a person who represents characteristics that appear to be lacking in us. The thirteenth-century poet and Sufi mystic Rumi beautifully describes the soul's search for missing parts of the Self through the projection of the unconscious onto the beloved:

The minute I heard my first love story
I started looking for you, not knowing
how blind that was.
Lovers don't finally meet somewhere
They're in each other all along.[18]

The following example illustrates how we project the undeveloped aspects of ourselves onto a partner. It is important to remember that projection is a psychological process that occurs when we see some vital yet unconscious aspects of our personality in someone else, and this can occur in all kinds of relationships.

Al and Barry are a gay couple who have lived together in a monogamous relationship for seventeen years. Both are in their middle forties. Al is outgoing, spontaneous, extroverted, emotional, and very successful in his career as a salesman. Barry is several years younger, introverted, extremely responsible, very logical, and quite fearful that his lifestyle may be exposed in the small city they live in. Barry was raised in a very conservative church and has experienced a great deal of conflict between his religious views and his gay lifestyle.

At an unconscious level Al is holding all of the extroversion, feelings, and spontaneity for both of them. Completely out of touch with his own inner introversion and more responsible "adult" side, Al often complains that Barry is "too quiet, controlled, and rigid." "Barry can never do anything without planning it for months in advance. He never wants to do anything with our friends unless I beg him to," Al says. Barry, on the other hand, is always the one who gets the bills paid on time and makes most of the major financial decisions. Barry is disconnected from his own spontaneity, playfulness, and extroversion. When he sees this lost part of himself reflected in Al he gets angry and charges that Al is "always playing, never thinking about all the decisions that have to be made, and is not very responsible about money or saving for the future. He's never very rational about anything. He would much rather be out and about, spending time with our friends." While this unconscious arrangement may get the bills paid on time, it precludes any need for Al to uncover the more introverted, introspective, responsible side of his personality or for Barry to experience the more extroverted, playful qualities of his. Neither can move toward individuation and wholeness without recognizing and becoming conscious of these lost, deeply repressed aspects of the Self. By midlife, the differences in their personalities and the underlying demands of the Self toward expression have created serious conflicts for this couple.

We make many agreements and contracts throughout our lives and, particularly, with our partner or spouse. Some of these agreements are conscious and evident. For example, one person in a relationship may enjoy cooking, while the other might prefer to work in the garden and yard. A couple may verbally agree upon these "contracts," or, more often, they may just fall into certain patterns and roles.

These roles, which are very apparent in traditional relationships, make daily life flow smoothly. It is not necessary to discuss who will do what tasks each and every day. But there is danger in the inflexibility with which most of our roles are defined. For example, if I am the one always in charge of the cooking, I limit my abilities and knowledge about gardening. My father called me several weeks after my mother died with an important question: "How do you cook a baked potato?" I was amazed that this man, a successful businessman and land developer who created multimillion-dollar projects, could be so dense as not to know how to make a baked potato. The reality of his life, however, was that for forty-seven years my mother had been in charge of baked potatos. There had been no need for him to learn how to cook one.

The conscious contracts and roles we fall into usually create fewer problems than do the unconscious ones. Just as we may divide up responsibilities around the house, we may divide up important human characteristics for the sake of making things easy. For example, one partner in a relationship may be more emotionally expressive than the other. It seems logical then that this person will be the one who maintains the connections to family and friends. The other partner may "contain" all of the creativity. He or she will have new ways of looking at things and novel solutions to the issues of the relationship. *Together* we make a whole person.

At midlife the psyche will no longer tolerate our attempt to achieve wholeness through our relationship with another. We can no longer allow our independence, strength, compassion, creativity, humor, or any other human characteristic that is rightfully ours to be expressed by anyone else. At midlife psychological energy is directed toward taking full responsibility for our own development. We will have to look at and be responsible for our own movement toward self-realization and individuation.

Because we are attracted to people who, through our projections, personify unconscious and unlived aspects of our own personality we will discover that the thing that attracted us to someone in the beginning of a relationship will be the very same thing we most dislike if our projections are not withdrawn. For example, a woman may fall in love with a man because he is strong and takes charge. She admires this because she does not see herself as having either quality. Later on in the relationship, as the Self is demanding that she become conscious of her own strength and ability to take charge of her life, she begins to hate the fact that he is so "controlling." She may begin to claim that his strength is no longer so appealing, that it takes the form of stoicism: "He never talks about his feelings."

Anthony and Deborah were married when they were both twenty-one years old. They had been going together since they were sixteen; neither had ever dated anyone else. Anthony was drawn to Deborah even as a teenager because she was "not like other girls." He saw her as independent and having a mind of her own, but still she was sweet-natured and very supportive of his goals and ambitions.

Deborah loved the fact that Anthony had dreams and plans for the future. He was a hard worker and she knew that he would attain his goals. He was strong and steady, honest, and made decisions quickly and easily. She loved those things about him.

Anthony had established a manufacturing business early in their marriage while Deborah completed college and earned a degree in library science. During the course of the marriage Anthony traveled a great deal. His overseas contracts sometimes required that he be away from home for months at a time. Deborah proved to be quite independent and while Anthony was overseas she took full responsibility for raising their three children, working at a community college library, and taking care of their home and finances. In fact, Anthony often joked that he never even saw the paycheck his office deposited into their account.

When they were both in their mid-forties Anthony merged his company with a foreign competitor. The business decision was a profitable one for both companies and it also created significant changes in the way Anthony ran his business. He no longer had to travel overseas for extended periods; he now worked from nine to five and returned home every evening. Initially, both Anthony and Deborah were excited about the prospect of spending more time together. Their children were grown and were living on their own or attending college away from their hometown.

Shortly after this change in routine Anthony and Deborah began to argue. The arguments reached such a level that they discussed separation. "She's changed. She's not the sweet, supportive woman I married. I can't believe how controlling she is," Anthony complained. "I married him because he seemed to appreciate my independent personality. Now he's acting the way most men seem to. He just jumps in and changes the ways I've been doing things for more than twenty years," said Deborah.

What is clear is that Anthony and Deborah will have to find new ways of relating if their marriage is to continue. The relationship which served both of them well for over twenty years must be adjusted to their present roles. At midlife many couples discover that their relationship will have to adjust to the new realities of their lives. In order to establish an authentic, mature intimacy it is necessary to understand and come to know our partner, and this requires letting go of our projections and unrealistic expectations for what a relationship can be.

Real intimacy, which I take to mean "knowing and being known," is related to the Latin root *inter,* meaning "within." And as Thomas Moore writes, "In our intimate relationships, the 'most within' dimensions of ourselves and the other are engaged."[19] True intimacy requires the honest awareness of our partner as a unique, though imperfect, being. When we are being real we open our heart to full love and acceptance of our lover's true humanity, not an idealized version of what a human being can or should be.

Real intimacy, mature love, then, is only possible when we withdraw our unconscious projections and allow ourselves to love another without the veil of idealized expectations, without the comfort of fairy tales. Each partner must take full responsibility for the development of him- or herself. Each of us must be the pilot on the path of our own individuation, for no relationship with another person can be any better than our relationship with ourselves. At midlife, we can no longer afford the free ride. We can no longer accept that any aspect of ourselves will be lived out by someone else.

The Rise of the Inferior Function

Allison and Beth were good friends and co-workers for many years. They were both bright and creative but would constantly get into arguments when they were working on a project together. Allison was organized, structured, and methodical in her approach to completing a task. Beth took pieces of this and pieces of that, seeming to move in a hundred directions at the same time. During an all-nighter at the office, surrounded by mounds of paper and half-empty Styrofoam coffee cups, Allison threw up her hands and said, "You're making me crazy jetting from one thing to another. Can't you just stick to one thing and finish it before you start on another part of this report?!" "Of course not," Beth replied. "I'm a Gemini."

Since the beginning of time human beings have attempted to devise systems to "type" the different temperaments and personalities of our species. From the ancient Oriental system of astrology (based on the location of stars and planets at the moment of birth) to the physiological typology of Greek medicine (based on the designations for the secretions of the body) to the Sufi enneagram system (based on nine personality types associated with a specific, ingrained driving force), scholars have tried to codify and understand how people can see the same world in such fundamentally different ways.

Among Jung's major contributions to mainstream psychology are his ideas regarding *psychological types*. Jung attempted to describe individualized but predictable ways in which people see the world. His ideas of psychological types provide an interesting and comprehensive approach to understanding how two people can see the same world so differently. These concepts about individual differences present both positive and negative aspects of each of the psychological types. It is important to remember that no one approach to the world is better than any other.

Jung's theories in this area developed out of his long experience of observing, analyzing, and understanding significant differences among individuals. His ideas are complex and can be confusing when we are first introduced to them, but they are important to understand. At midlife we will experience very different ways of looking at the world than has been our custom.

Jung observed *two basic attitudes* among people. One he called *extroverted,* in which the individual's psychological focus tends to be directed away from him- or herself toward objects in the outer world. The second he called *introverted,* in which the individual's psychological energy tends to be directed from objects in the outer world into him- or herself. These terms, which have entered our everyday language and which most people understand, originated with Jung.

An extroverted individual is normally characterized by an outgoing, sociable, candid, and accommodating nature that adapts easily to social situations. He or she is a "people person," someone who enjoys making new friends and seems to become energized by spending time with other people. An introverted individual, on the other hand, would be described as reflective, solitary, quiet, and introspective. Introverts generally prefer to spend time alone or with a few people rather than with a large group. They are drawn to the inner world of ideas rather than to the world of people and things. Unlike extroverts, introverted people seem to become depleted of energy when they spend a great deal of time with others. It is not that introverts are "party poopers," but rather, they easily get pooped by the party.

Extroversion and introversion can be thought of as representing end points on a continuum rather than discrete categories of behavior or attitude. It is important to understand that no one is purely extroverted or introverted: we all embrace some elements of each. Research has shown that in the general American population about seventy-five percent of people describe themselves as extroverts and only twenty-five percent as introverts.[20] Western societies, and particularly the United States, seem to reinforce the outgoing, gregarious, sociable temperament of the extrovert. People who prefer to spend time alone may be viewed as unfriendly, distant, or self-absorbed. This is not true of all cultures, however. Many Eastern cultures expect and reward more solitary, meditative pursuits. In these societies an extrovert may be seen as overbearing, loud, and hyperactive.

Jung was open to the idea that the preference for an introverted or extroverted attitude may be "inborn." But whether we are born with these predispositions or not, it is clear that they develop and become stronger with use. Our families and social and cultural environments reinforce certain ways of behaving and experiencing the world which greatly influence whatever our innate tendencies may be.

In addition to these attitude types, extroversion and introversion, Jung also described ways in which people differ in the capacity and ability to perceive the world through *thinking versus feeling* and *intuition versus sensation.*[21] Each of us tends to develop certain ways of seeing the world more strongly and underdevelop others. For example, some individuals will predominately use the process of thinking to understand the world or make decisions, while others will use feelings to answer the same questions. The psychological functions that are the most developed in an individual are referred to as the "primary" or "superior" functions, compared to the less developed functions, which are called "secondary" or "inferior." "Superior" and "inferior" in this case do not mean better or worse; these terms only describe which function is *more highly developed* or *less developed.* For example, we are likely to automatically use our primary or superior function because it comes naturally to us; thus our primary or superior function is probably the one that we are most conscious of. In contrast, our inferior (or secondary) function is the least differentiated, the least used, and generally, the most unconscious.

Just like the shadow and the anima/animus, our inferior function, though unconscious, exerts strong influences on our behavior, feelings, and decisions. Behaving like an autonomous complex, the inferior function "secretly and mischievously influences the superior function most of all, just as the latter represses the former most strongly."[22] To the extent that a person is too highly developed on one side, the inferior function becomes correspondingly difficult and powerful. Just as with the shadow and the anima/animus, we will project those undeveloped aspects of ourselves on someone else.

Knowledge about our inferior function tells us precisely what aspects of the Self we need to develop. Jung was very aware that he was an intuitive thinking type. His own development was sparse in sensation and in feeling. In order to develop these aspects of himself he made concerted efforts to spend time in activities that would honor his inferior sensation function. Especially in his later life he cooked, painted, and sculpted. At his home in Bollingen, at the upper Lake of Zurich in Switzerland, he built a tower of stone with his own hands that he hoped would reflect his "innermost thoughts and knowledge." Jung was wise enough to know that individuation for him, as for all of us, required the development of his inferior, unconscious parts. It was not by accident that he built his tower and other stone buildings himself, reveling in the feel of the stones. Chiseling and cutting and shaping were both symbolic and concrete acts that connected Jung to his dormant sensation function.

As we have seen with the shadow and the anima/animus, at midlife the less developed parts of the Self are crying out for our attention. And they will create enough internal turmoil and symptoms to be heard.

About six months prior to what I now can see as the initiation into my midlife passage, I began to relate differently to people, especially to my friends. I turned down social invitations that I would have jumped at in the past. I found myself listening more, when I was with people, and talking much less. I took long walks alone on the beach when in the past I would have rather been with a large group of people, talking, laughing, and singing. Actually, I wasn't even entirely aware of what I was doing. My friend Judy came over one night and asked me what was wrong. I didn't know what she was talking about at the time—I think I mumbled something about being tired and overworked. She was concerned that I was upset or angry with her because I didn't seem to have much time to spend with her or much to say when I did.

It was months later that I began to understand what was happening to me. I found myself thinking about how I had always related to other people. For most of my life I have been a quintessential extrovert. My Irish Catholic extended family is loving, close, and filled mostly with extroverts. Our family gatherings, to an introverted person, must seem like a chaotic din.

In my immediate family it was impossible to be an introvert. To pull away from the group was something that made my mother uncomfortable. To want to spend time alone meant that you were angry or physically ill. I remember pretending to have a headache so that I could go to my room to read or just spend some time alone. As I was being propelled into my own midlife passage an old memory of something I loved to do when I was about eight years old came to the surface.

We lived in a neighborhood that bordered on a woods with a small creek running through it. I would get up early in the morning. My mother would make a peanut butter and jelly sandwich for me, and I would fill a small thermos with juice or water. I'd pack this lunch into my red knapsack with a little book about identifying different kinds of birds and one about identifying bugs. I had a pair of binoculars that were made for a child—now I believe that the lens was a little piece of Plexiglas that didn't even enlarge anything. Nevertheless, these were the things I packed up for the day. I would walk through the neighborhood and past the Sawtells' house to the place behind their yard where I would stand at the edge of the woods.

I always looked around carefully to make sure that no one could see me, especially my brother and his friends. For here at the edge of the woods I no longer walked. I galloped. Pretending to be riding a big "tea-colored" horse, I would gallop across the pine straw and cones, down across the rocks at the edge of the creek. I can remember vividly the sound my feet made as they hit the ground. I knew that it *was* the sound of hooves. I would finally get to a place where the trees parted and I could hear the sound of birds overhead. I would dismount (of course, I tied my invisible reins to a tree so my horse wouldn't run away), take out my books and binoculars, and spend the better part of the morning identifying the birds I observed and comparing them with the pictures in my book.

In the midst of my midlife crisis, I began to wonder about that introverted little girl who had such pleasure spending time alone. As I grew up, there became less and less room for her in my life. But now she was demanding to be heard. Since I didn't listen, didn't even remember she existed, she began, on her own, a slow but steady withdrawal from my friends.

I take better care of her now. I knows that she needs some time each day to spend writing, reading, walking, playing music, meditating, or just being alone. When I do choose to spend time with others I am conscious of wanting to spend quality time with people who are important to me. Like the seven-hundred-year-old monk who advised Indiana Jones to "choose wisely" when he was attempting to select the Holy Grail from thousands of imposters, I am choosing more wisely how I will spend my time. I try harder to find balance between being with people and spending time alone. I am more aware of the need to structure opportunities for expression for the parts of me that are not so well developed. I am learning to honor my inferior functions. It is a critical task for transformation at midlife.

. . .

This chapter has emphasized the importance of the *integration of opposites* as stepping stones on the path to individuation. In order to be whole we must claim the parts of ourselves that have been neglected, prohibited, and repressed and integrate (from the Latin *integrare,* "to make complete and whole") them into our conscious life. Nature and the Self are demanding this integration, harmony, and wholeness.

This spiral path of opposites drawing together into a union and creating new forms over and over again is the way to our own deepest meaning. What has been in the dark is now illuminated. It is this psychic energy that drives us toward our own true inner nature . . . toward authentic self-knowledge and self-realization. Learning through the difficulties of midlife can be the single greatest opportunity for transformation, wisdom, depth of personality, and joy in life's second half.

At midlife we also know that the time left for this momentous work is running out.

CHAPTER 4

Losses and Confronting Death

But meanwhile it is flying,
irretrievable time is flying.
VIRGIL, *GEORGICS,* NO. 3, 1, 284.

FROM MY OFFICE WINDOW I look out onto a small pond that fills and empties with the high and low tides of the Chesapeake Bay. I set out food there for three species of ducks, some of the craftiest squirrels ever to leap from a tree, and seventeen types of birds, including a red-cockaded woodpecker, which a forest ranger friend cannot believe because only four or five have ever been sighted in Virginia. Nevertheless, she pecks at the square of suet that I place there for her. Ducks waddle up a short hill from the water to gulp the cracked corn that I throw on the ground for them. Most of these creatures have become comfortable with my presence and will stay and eat while I sit close by and write my treatment notes.

Mulberry trees, southern pine, dogwood, elm, and oak trees surround us in this quiet spot. The robins especially grow round on the big purple-red mulberries, and although we humans end up tracking scarlet down the carpets in our hallway and search for parking spots that are not in the trees' direct line of fire, all the birds get fat and happy during the spring. Yesterday, which was rainy and gray, the small possumhaw tree looked almost dead. Its skinny limbs seemed brittle and dry. Today, the end of each branch sports a tiny bud that in a week or less will begin to bulge and become green. It happened last year about this time and the year before that. I'm confident it will happen again next spring.

One of the female mallards has made her nest under a small tree near the entrance to our building. I expect that very shortly the pond will be filled with baby ducklings, just as it was a year ago. Last year at this time, one mother duck hatched eleven fluffy little ducklings. Though normally she guzzled the corn I put out, she now stood there like a sentinel watching over her little ones while they ate. Over the course of a few days, her brood diminished from eleven to eight and then finally to five. I wondered how this dutiful new mother experienced those losses here in the same place where I have been grieving over the death of my own mother. Did she feel the same deep pain at the disappearance of more than half her brood? No outward signs of any such grief showed in her bearing. Instead her eyes were peeled for intruders, and I have no doubt that she would have heroically defended what was left of her family.

Most of us live our lives as if change were an interloper, something that goes against the way things are supposed to be. We expect life to remain static, stable, and predictable. Many of us live as if we will never have to let go of anything. We will never become ill, face the loss of an important relationship, lose loved ones to death, start over again in our career, or suffer the loss of material possessions or financial security. But to look at the way Mother Earth heralds the seasons is to understand that change *is* the natural order of things. It is only our arrogance and insistence that things stay the same that keep us from this full realization.

I am blessed to have a number of very good, close friends. Many of us have known each other for fifteen, twenty years, or longer and so we have lived a great deal of our adult lives together. Several years ago my mother died a month after the mother of one of my best friends. Another friend lost a brother to AIDS within weeks of my own mother's death. Earlier that same year, my friend Judy was diagnosed with breast cancer, as was my good friend Kay's mother. "When is this going to end?" one of my friends asked. "We've had so many losses."

Although it was a reasonable question, I remember thinking that the answer could only be "never." We are a group of friends in our late thirties, forties, and fifties; our parents are in their late fifties, sixties, seventies, and beyond. What do we expect from life?

In midlife, it becomes possible to comprehend that impermanence is the true nature of our world and reality. Our notion of a permanent, unchanging universe is a myth held by the ego, which wants to grasp and hold on to everything that is of value to it. But regardless of the desires of our ego, midlife holds the crashing realization that everything in our lives is subject to change. The Buddha said:

> *This existence of ours is as transient as autumn clouds.*
> *To watch the birth and death of beings is like looking at the movements of a dance.*
> *A lifetime is like a flash of lightning in the sky,*
> *Rushing by, like a torrent down a steep mountain.*[1]

At midlife, time does feel as if it rushes by in a torrent. We are observers to and participants in the changes that surround us, and many of these changes are hard to take. Our false belief in permanence is the "rickety foundation," as Sogyal Rinpoche points out, upon which we construct our lives.[2]

I vividly remember the exact moment when I looked at my parents and noticed, for the first time, that they were aging. We had just moved into a new house on the Outer Banks of North Carolina and they had come to help us get organized after the move. I was a month short of my fortieth birthday as I stood in front of the house and watched them drive up. They honked their horn, pulled into the driveway, and jumped out to greet me. Because of my move and other obligations I hadn't been to visit them in six months. Although we spoke weekly by phone I was not prepared for the unfamiliar faces that I saw in front of me. I couldn't imagine how they had changed so much in such a short time. Perhaps it is like visiting friends with children. They grow and change so much in a short time that you are knocked over when you see them, while the parents, who see them mature in gradual increments, don't notice how much they've grown.

I realize now that this was an early indication of the realities of the second half of life for me, though I didn't know it at the time. I remember the chill that came over me as a new awareness of my parents' mortality rose to my consciousness. I wondered if I would be prepared for the losses that would inevitably come.

For several years I conducted group therapy in a psychiatric hospital. Since it was a private hospital, the majority of the inpatients were people who were having some kind of crisis in their lives; they were not people with long-term chronic psychiatric illnesses, but for the most part functioned at work and in relationships. Most were hospitalized because life had become too much for them. They were admitted into the psychiatric unit with diagnoses of depression, anxiety disorders, and substance abuse. Very often their entry into the hospital was precipitated by a major loss of some kind. Many were there because a spouse or partner had left them, some because they had lost a job, others because someone they loved had died. I was struck by how many people were unprepared for the unavoidable realities of life.

Rose reported that she had always been depressed. "I can't ever really remember being happy, but I get by," she noted on her intake form. As the oldest child of three, Rose was expected to take care of her younger brothers and sisters while her parents worked. She continued in her role as caretaker to the family long after she married and had children of her own. Shortly after her father's death, her mother was diagnosed with Alzheimer's disease. Rose rearranged her schedule to make dinner for her mother every night and take care of all the housekeeping chores. As her mother's condition deteriorated, Rose took the responsibility for placing her mother in a nursing home. While the other siblings continued to visit on weekends, Rose went to see her mother every day after work. Several years later, her mother had lost all ability to recognize Rose or other family members. Finally, after years of living in this shadowy world, her mother died. Rose planned an elaborate funeral. All of the extended family and most of the members of their small town came to the service. Afterwards many people came to Rose's house with plates of food and flowers to offer their condolences to the family. After everyone had left, Rose put away the extra food, washed the few remaining dishes, closed and locked the doors, and went upstairs, where she took an almost fatal dose of the medications that had been prescribed for her anxiety and depression. Her sister called because she had left her purse at Rose's house. Failing to get an answer on the phone and knowing that Rose was at home, she let herself in with her key and found Rose unconscious on the bed.

"I can't stand the pain," Rose replied when asked why she had attempted suicide. She said that she couldn't live with the emptiness, loss, and grief she was feeling. Rose was fifty-six when her mother died. Her mother was ninety-one. I knew that it was normal and healthy for Rose to grieve over her mother's death, regardless of the fact that her mother had lived a long life. But I wondered what Rose expected from life. Had she believed that she would never have to say good-bye to her mother?

I have come to the conclusion that one of the secrets to understanding life is knowing that eventually we will have to lose everything that has been important to us. We don't have to be "bad" or make poor choices. All we have to do is live long enough. These "necessary losses," as Judith Viorst has called them, often arrive fast and furious during midlife. While everything is changing, as it always has been, there is a new awareness of how quickly things are moving along.

"I remember looking in the mirror one day and, suddenly, without any warning, I realized that I looked just like my mother," said Carol. One day, while she was putting on her makeup in the same mirror that she had used for more than twenty-five years, the discovery of her own aging body hit home. I smiled as she told me this. I remembered meeting a friend of a friend at a Christmas party about four years ago. He was a well-known hairstylist in the area and commented that he very much liked the "evenness" of the frosting job on my hair. He wanted to know who my hair colorist was. Since I've never had my hair frosted, I was at a loss for an answer. Mumbling something about "frosting by life itself," I made a beeline for a bathroom mirror. Recognizing our own gray hair, wrinkles, or an uncanny resemblance to our own mother or father somehow seems worse when it's initially pointed out by strangers.

We are flesh and blood, and despite all the analogies to computers and machines that we use to describe ourselves ("I need to recharge my battery." "Whew, I've run out of gas." "That's just the way I've been programmed."), our bodies age. Cells die, hair grays, and wrinkles form. No amount of Oil of Olay can forestall the reality of living in a time-limited human body.

Many see a new health consciousness as a hallmark of the baby bommer generation that is now entering midlife, and it is true that many people in midlife are in the best health they have ever experienced. Some have always lived according to good health practices; others have had a wake-up call in the form of a serious illness and responded by changing lifelong habits. Still others have simply made decisions to take better care of their health because of a new awareness of the importance of diet, exercise, attitudes, or stress reduction techniques. With the escalating base of knowledge about health, we have tremendous opportunities to make good choices about how we will live, more than any other generation before us. New research has documented the intimate relationship between attitudes and behavior and the neurological and immunological systems,[3] convincingly demonstrating that how we view life and react to it has a great deal of influence on the processes of health and aging. But while we do have a great deal of control over our health and longevity, we do not control the ultimate long-term outcome. We are dying, and even if we live to be a hundred and twenty and continue to run marathons until our last day, death is our destiny.

Most of us do not want to let go of the illusion that life can stay the way we want it to. We allow attachments to things and people that cannot be permanent. Hold a coin in your hand with your fist tightly clenched and the palm of your hand facing down. If you relax your grip, you will drop and lose what you are clinging to. In fact, it takes energy and concentration to cling to the coin. But you can also hold the coin by letting go. You can turn your hand over so that it faces the sky. Release your grip and the coin rests on your open palm. It is in letting go of our attachments that we can learn to accept impermanence and still relish life. In fact, it is only through a growing awareness of impermanence and the release of what we are grasping that we can come to treasure and fully live our lives.

Debbie was in a position in life that required letting go of many things that had come to define her. She was in a relationship that did not satisfy her, though she truly cared for her partner of many years. At the same time, she needed to make critical decisions about completing a certification program if she was to stay with her present career. But that would require a major disruption of her daily life and a move to another city. She had put off making decisions about these important life issues for more than two years. "I know what I need to do," she said, "but I just can't seem to let go."

A good friend of Debbie's was turning fifty and wanted nothing more than to try skydiving as a way of welcoming in this new decade. None of their other friends were ripe for the experience, but Debbie agreed to try it. I'm not sure why anyone would willingly jump out of a perfectly good airplane, but I understood that Debbie saw this as some kind of challenge that must be met. Debbie and her friend spent the better part of a day training for their adventure. They were instructed by expert skydivers and had to demonstrate that they knew what they were to do before the actual dive. Equipment was checked and rechecked. The pilot reviewed the preflight inspection, and they were off.

Hearts pumping with anticipation, they sat in the back of the small plane waiting for it to reach jump altitude. Several people jumped before Debbie and she could see them floating off from the plane, seeming to just hang spread-eagled in the air. She watched her classmates as their colorful parachutes opened up and they glided toward a big circle drawn on a grassy field. Finally, it was Debbie's turn. She climbed out on the metal step and inched her way toward the end of the wing. Her instructor gave the thumbs-up signal to release her grip and fall away from the plane, but Debbie wouldn't let go. The instructor gave the signal again. Debbie still wouldn't let go. The wind currents wouldn't allow her to retrace her steps and get back into the plane and the plane couldn't land with her hanging on the wing: she had to jump. The instructor, looking a bit frazzled and as if the next signal would be accompanied by some kind of attempt to swat her off the wing, gave the signal again. She had reached the point of no return. She had no choice but to let go, and she finally dropped from the plane according to the instructions she had learned. By now the plane was slightly past the large grassy field with its clearly marked target and Debbie landed in some very tall trees. Unhurt but dangling from her parachute, Debbie had more than three hours to reflect on her experience while the skydiving team worked to find a way to cut her free without letting her plummet to the ground.

"I'm certain that my fingerprints will be etched into that plane wing forever," she said. "If I had let go when I should have I would have landed with the others in the big field, where a van would have picked me up with a bottle of champagne. Instead I spent three hours hanging from a tree!" The metaphorical meaning of this experience as it applied to other issues in her life was not lost on Debbie. "While I was hanging there I just kept saying over and over to myself—'When it's time to let go, it's time to let go.' "

Frank worked for a large national corporation for twenty-five years. Over that time he had progressed up the ranks and had a high-paying job as a corporate executive. At fifty, he could not conceive of doing anything else with his life. He was happy in his work, felt creatively challenged by it, and enjoyed the excellent income that he earned. Several years before, the company had begun to downsize its executive ranks. He watched as many colleagues were let go. "It was clear that the decision to reduce the operating expense of management was the real reason that people were being fired. Some of the people that went first were some of the best assets to the company. It didn't seem to follow any rhyme or reason. I could understand letting go of deadwood but not executives who were productive and helping the company be profitable," Frank said. After almost three years of watching the changes in the company's management team, Frank was told that he was being "riffed." He was shocked and disheartened. "For some reason I never really believed that it could happen to me. I've been hardworking, loyal, productive. But then I realized that so were lots of people that had been let go almost two years before me. I could kick myself for being so unaware. If I had started to look for something else two years ago, I might be in a better position today. As it is now, I'm competing with bunches of my colleagues for the few jobs that are at the same level as the one I've had for more than half my life." Frank didn't know when to let go. Instead he held tightly to the illusion that his career was somehow magically safeguarded in spite of all the evidence to the contrary.

Generations in the past could usually consider their work or career environment as relatively permanent. We may understand that we cannot control many things in our lives, but most of us have grown up believing that if we worked hard, demonstrated loyalty, and were team players, we could be assured of working for one company throughout our career. When we reached sixty-five we would receive a reasonable pension and be given a gold watch at a nice luncheon held in our honor. But this is no longer true.

A recent survey by the American Management Association showed that forty-seven percent of its eight thousand member organizations had reduced their management staffs during the previous twelve months. High-paying blue-collar industrial jobs are increasingly lost to automation and low-wage offshore competition. Two thirds of Americans surveyed believed that job security was getting worse and that this was a long-term trend.[4] The evidence supports the opinions expressed in this survey: many of these jobs are gone forever. In the last decade, the largest companies in the United States have *eliminated* 4.7 million positions, or one quarter of their workforce, according to a firm that tracks statistics on U.S. businesses.[5]

While some new jobs are being created, they are often low-paying service jobs. For example, one study found that of two thousand workers released by RJR Nabisco, seventy-two percent found new jobs—but at salaries that averaged only forty-seven percent of their previous pay.[6] Lowering one's standard of living often takes a deep cut into self-esteem and can be a difficult change for anyone to experience. For someone in midlife with a mortgage, college tuition payments, and a certain style of life, this kind of loss is often devastating.

The loss of an important relationship at any time in life can ravage the soul, but at midlife these losses often require surrendering other important aspects of life as well. Arlene knows only too well how the loss of a relationship can plunge one's whole life into turmoil. She was shocked when her husband came home one day and told her that he wanted a divorce. They had been married for thirty-one years, and although she was aware that things hadn't been great during the past ten years, she had no idea that he was so miserable in the marriage that he wanted to be out of it. "He says he's just not happy and that's all he says," she said, tears rolling down her cheeks. Her husband moved out into an apartment "while we 'work out the details,' as he calls it." She is angry and hurt that he can appear to be so casual about ending a relationship that has been her primary self-definition for more than half her life. She is also afraid of the future. Her entire emotional and financial security has been based on her marriage, and now she will be on her own. "I've never been the one responsible for earning the money in our family. I've always worked but my primary job was to raise our children and keep our home." Her husband, a successful businessman, is begrudgingly working out a separation agreement with her and continually reminds her of how "financially generous" he is being. He appears to have no awareness that she participated as an equal partner in the way they divided responsibilities during their marriage. After the separation and divorce she will step down to a greatly diminished standard of living. She is moving out of their home, her neighborhood, and the social group that has been her environment. She is deeply concerned that at fifty-three, with no clear job skills and a scattered employment history that meandered its way around the births of her children, she is not going to be able to find a job. Most important, though, she is heartbroken and grieving. Regardless of how her husband seems to be treating her, she still maintains that he is, and has always been, the love of her life.

The end of a relationship may be second only to the death of a loved one in its capacity to wrench life apart and create deep and agonizing grief. Whether we are in a traditional relationship like Arlene's or a less conventional one; whether we are the one leaving or the one being left, severing these important connections has the power to carve out a piece of the soul. It is, as Linda McGonigal writes, like a death.

A lover's sudden leaving
like death
shrouds underpinnings
of reality

rapes the heart of trust.
The secrets and their lies
undress the soul,
pluck stars from the sky
and make constellations
meaningless.[7]

Some of the losses of midlife are not as dramatic as the death of a parent, the need to begin a whole new career, the end of a relationship through separation/divorce, or the departure of children to begin their own adult lives. Many of the changes are more subtle and difficult to pinpoint because they center on the loss of opportunities that were once important to us. The sense of fear and loss that accompanies the letting go of dreams that will never be is best described by the German word *torschlusspanik,* defined as "panic at the thought that a door between oneself and life's opportunities has shut." Marion Woodman notes that "words enter a language when they are needed, and torschlusspanik has arrived."[8]

Everyone knew that Dave was a football fanatic and didn't dare call him on Sunday afternoons or Monday nights when he was glued to the television watching the NFL games. He earned his living as a long-distance truck driver, which required him to spend long hours on the road. Unwilling to miss important games, he had equipped his rig with an expensive high-range radio that let him pick up broadcasts across great distances. Dave had played football in high school and had been something of a local celebrity when he was named to a national all-American team. It was expected that he would earn a college scholarship and maybe even play in the pros. But he wasn't able to keep up academically in college, and he found himself a small fish in a big pond as a football player at the state university. After four semesters he was dropped from the team. He quit college and looked for a job. But his love for the game of football never diminished.

"I got very depressed on New Year's Day watching the Rose Bowl," he said. "I suddenly realized that I was old enough to be the father of these kids. I felt like there was nothing much left to look forward to." Although he had known for a long time that he was never going to play professional football, that knowledge seemed to be more intellectual than emotional. On this New Year's Day he knew it in the pit of his stomach. Without any rites of passage into the middle part of life, Dave felt alone and "stupid" for having such feelings of loss. But many of us at midlife will experience a subtle but significant grief for the roads not taken: the relationship or marriage that didn't work out, the baby that was never born, the career that never happened, the dreams that will never be realized.

Buddhists believe that these losses and the changes in our bodies are examples of what they call "little deaths" or "little impermanences." Dealing with these disappointments and accompaning grief serves as a learning experience that prepares us for our greatest loss: the loss of the ego through our physical death. The universe gives us many opportunities, usually very painful ones, to become strong and spiritually enlightened as we head down the path that leads to our destiny. By the middle part of life, most of us have experienced numerous "little impermanences," and thus we have had opportunities to develop a very different perspective on loss and death than we had in our younger years. Howell Raines writes: "As I navigated through the final shoals of the passage to middle age, I came to see that the acceptance of my own mortality was the final and indispensable issue for me, that indeed it was hardly worth going to the trouble of having a midlife crisis equal to the name if you were not going to figure out how to be comfortable in the embrace of what Mr. Hemingway called 'that old whore death.' "[9] But death and the promise of rebirth are part of life, and are intimately and ultimately woven together in the great drama of earthly existence.

Many cultures have personified the archetype of life-death-life through folklore and myth, as evidenced in the story of Skeleton Woman, told among the Inuit people of North America. In this story, a woman has displeased her father, who has thrown her into the sea from a high bluff. Fish have eaten her flesh away and her skeleton has been thrown about and tumbled by the currents of the sea.

One day a fisherman drifts far from his home shores and throws his line into waters that the locals know to be haunted. His hook catches the bones of Skeleton Woman. Thinking he has caught a big fish, the fisherman is elated. But when he turns to see what he has brought up—Skeleton Woman caught on the bow of his kayak—he is terrified. He knocks her off with his oar and begins to paddle as quickly as he can toward shore. But Skeleton Woman, tangled in his line, is dragged along.

When the fisherman reaches the shore he grabs his fishing pole and runs like the wind. Still caught up in his line, Skeleton Woman is pulled behind him. The fisherman finally reaches his house and runs inside. As he lights his lamp he can see Skeleton Woman lying in a heap. There in the golden light, the man feels a sudden sense of kindness for her and begins to untangle her bones. Finally he dresses her in warm furs.

The man soon falls asleep in the warmth of his bed and during the night tears shimmer in his eyes. Skeleton Woman is very thirsty so she crawls over to the sleeping man and drinks his tears. The tears begin to flow like a river, and all night long Skeleton Woman drinks. She lies down next to him, reaches inside him and takes out his heart. She begins to bang on it as if it were a drum. The more she drums, the more her body begins to fill out with flesh. The more she sings, the more flesh and blood she becomes. She returns the heart to the man's body and wraps around him for the rest of the night. When they awaken, she and the fisherman run away together. They are fed forever after by the creatures she had come to know when she lived in the water.

Like many traditional stories of Native Americans and other cultures that live close to the earth, the myth of Skeleton Woman represents the potent connections between life and death. Clarissa Pinkola Estes relates a beautiful version of this powerful myth, among others, in her book *Women Who Run With the Wolves.*[10] She writes, "As we see in the tale, if one wishes to be fed for life, one must face and develop a relationship with the Life/Death/Life nature. . . . Rather than seeing the archetypes of Death and Life as opposites, they must be held together as the left and right side of a single thought."[11]

In nature the life-death-rebirth cycle is clear as we watch flash fires ignited by lightning level the praries. It may appear that all life is gone, lost to the ravages of flame and smoke, but within days, tiny green shoots begin to poke above the surface of the soil. Mother Earth has cleared the land for new life. Even in my garden I sense the seasons and the cycle of life-death-life. Perennials planted in my yard years ago go through their seasonal life span: a new green shoot, a blooming tulip, soon gone, but the bulb below the soil holds all the necessary ingredients for repeating the cycle again next spring.

In Western culture, we have lost sight of the relationship between life and death. We generally fail to appreciate that the boundary of death gives a sense of purpose and meaning to our life. Too often, the awareness of death can cause us to live with a sense of hopelessness: "I'm just going to die anyway, why bother with anything?" "Death," wrote Jung, "is a fearful piece of brutality; there is no use pretending otherwise. It is brutal not only as a physical event, but far more so psychically: a human being is torn away from us and what remains is the icy stillness of death. There no longer exists any hope of a relationship, for all the bridges have been smashed at one blow. Those who deserve a long life are cut off in the prime of their years, and good-for-nothings live to a ripe old age. This is a cruel reality which we have no right to sidestep. The actual experience of the cruelty and wantonness of death can so embitter us that we conclude there is no merciful God, no justice, and no kindness."[12]

On the other hand, the awareness of death can push us to dance with life, to grab it with all the gusto we can. We can live every day in the moment, learn to love without hesitation, become aware of what is truly important to us, and experience ourselves as part of a great cosmic plan. Death is the natural companion to life. Jung continues, "From another point of view, however, death appears as a joyful event. In the light of eternity it is a wedding, a *mysterium coniunctionis*. The soul attains, as it were, its missing half, it achieves wholeness."[13]

Ancient peoples believed that death does not jump out and snatch us away—instead it *meets* us according to our destiny. Death in this view is like a midwife helping us through a passage to the next life. In these cultures, as Stephen Levine writes, "death brings the whole tribe or family together in celebration and acknowledgment of the continual changing nature of life. During these celebrations, often a deeply spiritual context for this passing allows many to have profound experiences of their own true nature. For these societies, death is a continual opportunity to let go of the illusions of life, to see it as it is, and open in love to all about."[14] When we allow the reality and inevitability of death to accompany us in life, we can begin to look at others, no matter how different they may be from us, and know that our human destiny is the same. By letting death into our consciousness, we can begin to have true, heartfelt compassion for one another and to understand what Crazy Horse meant when he said, "Today is a good day to die, for all the things of my life are present."[15]

Kyle has been HIV-positive for more than fourteen years and has learned to live with the specter of death in his life. He has lost a brother and many, many friends, most of whom were in their thirties, to AIDS. "I believe that life is a gift from God, and my gift to God is what I do with it," Kyle says. "I realize that each day is going to be what I make it. Last week I went from having terrible night sweats and nausea, from the medications that I'm taking, to giving a talk in the morning to a group of students." Kyle is very aware that death is always present and that there has been a change in the way people die from AIDS. "In the past, before drug treatments for AIDS, people were sick for a long time and lived for years with illness. Now with AZT and other drugs the quality of life has increased, but when people do finally get sick they die in a few weeks instead of years. I know that, statistically, my time was up a long time ago. I could be dead in two weeks if I were to get sick. I know that.

"I really am honest with people at this point in my life. I say what I need to say to people. I've always been gregarious and had a strong sense of compassion, but I don't want to waste time now. I express many loving, tender feelings to people who are important to me that I might not have in the past. I used to put things off with kind of an 'I'll get around to it' attitude. Now I'm moved to call my friends or family and tell them that I love them. I also guard my time very jealously. I spend my time with people that I want to be with—my priorities are clear to me.

"I used to be a pretty controlling son of a gun," Kyle says with a smile. "Now, I'm much more aware of how much of my life is out of my hands. Life and death are part of the same process. But right now I'm alive and I'm going to live every day." Kyle's sense of spiritual destiny and his acceptance of his own fate hasn't created a lack of motivation or direction. He participates in clinical trials that are examining the effects of new medications and treatments for AIDS. He continues to work actively with disturbed teenagers and puts a great deal of energy into AIDS service organizations.

"My values have changed," he says. Now, he is much more content with less. "I find that I don't need as many things as I did before. I'll still get a passion for some things and then I'll do my best to acquire them, like this old house that my partner and I bought." They had purchased a "handyman's special," an old house that needed major renovations but was in a lovely neighborhood with big trees and sidewalks. "I forgot how much fun it was to take something that looked so terrible," Kyle says, referring to the kitchen, "and make it into something beautiful and functional. I've given life to this house that didn't have life in it before."

Kyle had many of the construction skills that were necessary to "put his house in order," as he says. "As I was working in this house I remembered a lot of the things that my grandfather had taught me that I didn't know I had." The newly planted shrubs that line the brick walkway are a testament to his love and care. "Yesterday, I worked in the sun and was so happy with planting and mulching. I could see how just this little change really made a difference. I am much more content to enjoy each moment, and I thought to myself—'This is living.' "[16]

Like other pandemics throughout history, AIDS has brought a brutal new awareness to our generation—that death is not reserved for the very old. While we have always known this intellectually, the loss of so many people in the prime of their lives emotionally drives this point home. The following fairy tale, "Godfather Death," reminds us that death is a companion throughout our lives and that it can touch anyone at any time.

> A poor man and his wife had their thirteenth child and did not know whom to choose as a godfather. They had exhausted all their family and friends with their first twelve children, so they took off along the road to find someone who would be willing to be godfather to their new son. They ventured out and met God along the way. "Who are you?" the man asked. "I am God. Poor man, I pity you and I will hold your child at its christening, and will take charge of it and make it happy on earth." The man replied, "I do not desire you to be godfather. You give to the rich, and leave the poor to hunger. You are not always fair."
>
> The man and his wife continued on their way and met the Devil. "What do you seek? If you will take me as a godfather for your child, I will give him gold in plenty and all the joys of the world as well, for I am the Devil." "I do not desire to have you as a godfather," the man replied, "for you deceive men and lead them astray."
>
> They went onward and Death came striding up with withered legs and said, "Take me as godfather. I am Death and I make all equal." The man thought for a moment and said, "You are the right one, you take from the rich as well as the poor without distinction; you shall be godfather." Death appeared at the christening as he had promised and stood godfather in quite the usual way. "I will make your child rich and famous, for he who has me for a friend can lack nothing," Death told the man.
>
> When the boy had grown up, his godfather appeared to him, led him into a forest, and showed him an herb which grew there. He said, "Now you will receive your godfather's present. I will make you a celebrated physician. When you are called to see a patient, I will always appear to you. If I stand by the head of the patient you may say with confidence that you will make him well again, and if you give him this herb he will recover; but if I stand by the patient's feet, he is mine, and

you must say that all remedies are in vain, and that no physician in the world can save him. Beware of using the herb against my will, or it might fare ill with you."

In a short time the man had become the most famous physician in the world. He was known far and wide for his wisdom: his ability to heal the sick or to proclaim, "There is nothing in the world that will make this patient well." One day he was summoned to the bedside of the King, who was very ill with fever. As the physician went into the King's bedroom he saw Death standing at the foot of the bed and knew that no herb could save him. "If I could but cheat Death for once," thought the physician. "He is sure to take it ill if I do but, as I am his godson, he will shut one eye; I will risk it." Quickly, the physician spun the King around on the bed so that now Death was standing at his head. He gave the King the herb and the King recovered and grew healthy again.

Death grabbed the physician and was dark and angry. He said, "You have betrayed me; this time I will pardon it, as you are my godson; but if you venture it again, it will cost you your neck, for I will take you yourself away with me."

Soon afterwards the King's daughter fell into the same severe illness. She was his only child and the King wept day and night. He sent out a proclamation that whoever could rescue her from death should be her husband and inherit the crown. The physician raced to the Princess's bedside. He saw her great beauty and immediately fell in love with her. He imagined becoming her husband and living happily with all the riches of the kingdom. But he saw Death standing at the foot of the bed. He was so infatuated that he failed to see Death casting angry glances on him, raising his hand in the air, and threatening him with his scrawny fist. He turned the Princess around in the bed so that now Death stood at her head. Then he gave her some of the herb and instantly she recovered.

Death was enraged. He seized the physician and led him into a cave below the Earth where thousands of candles burned in countless rows. Some were large, some medium-sized, and others small. Some were burning brightly while others sputtered as the flame disappeared into hot wax. Every instant some were extinguished and others burned brightly so that the flames seemed to leap in perpetual change. "See," said Death, "these are the lights of men's lives." The physician looked

> carefully and asked, "Those big candles, the ones burning so brightly, they are the candles of newborn children, are they not? And those small, sputtering ones, they are the candles for very old people, is that not true?" Death replied, "Some of the small, sputtering candles belong to very old people and some to little children. Some of the big candles brightly burning belong to newborn babes but some belong to very old people."
>
> "Show me the light of my life," the physician said. He thought it would be very tall and burning brightly, for he was a young man with much to live for. Death pointed to a little end which was threatening to go out and said: "Behold, it is there."
>
> "Dear Godfather," said the horrified physician, "light a new one for me; do it for love of me that I might enjoy my life, be King, and husband to the beautiful Princess."
>
> "I cannot," answered Death. "A candle must go out before a new one is lighted." With that the candle went out and the physician fell to the ground in the hands of Death.[17]

Like the physician in "Godfather Death," we expect that life will conform to our ideas as to what is fair and right. We like to believe that if we are relatively young and take care of our health, we will be protected from death and loss. Honoring our bodies by taking care of ourselves and avoiding risks that we are unprepared to take are good ideas. But to believe that we can insulate ourselves from our ultimate destiny is illusionary. We do not control our lives in the ways most of us have been conditioned to think.

Death remains a fearsome enemy for most of us in Western culture. Our hospitals and nursing homes are filled with people who are kept alive through their attachment to tubes, respirators, and all kinds of machines that attempt to take the place of failing organs. More health care dollars are spent in the last six months of most people's lives than in their entire earlier lives. We investigate all manner of approaches to stave off death, including freezing ourselves (or even just our heads) so that we can be resurrected at some future time when science will have found the cure for what it was that "killed" us. But in spite of all our attempts to cheat death, it is the natural and inevitable transition from life. Yeats laments the reality of death and its continuing presence throughout our lives when he writes: "Consume my heart away; sick with desire/and fastened to a dying animal."[18]

At midlife we are increasingly aware of our own destined meeting with death, how we are inexorably attached to this dying animal. What youth allows us to deny can no longer be pushed from consciousness. In fact, it is this new awareness of death that differentiates the midlife transition from every other transition that is experienced throughout life. A constant recurring theme of the midlife crisis is the fear that accompanies the understanding that time is running out.[19] Even in a culture as devoid of initiation rites as ours is, we do have rituals that help us to understand and integrate life's meaning at major crossroads. We celebrate at weddings, graduations, bar mitzvahs, and baptisms. We grieve together at wakes and funerals. At midlife there are no rituals, no cultural reinforcements that provide any support or protection from the terror that is so frequently experienced. We are alone as the reality of human life and our own mortality crashes into consciousness. In an attempt to provide some form of containment for the awesome psychological and physical symptoms that accompany the realization of our own fate, some hospitals have opened "midlife crisis units,"[20] as if this passage were a sickness that needed to be cured. The sterile hospital unit offers a poor substitute for a mystical ritual initiation conducted around a blazing fire, under a full moon and with the full tribe present.

Most of us live with an explicit need for control over the events of our lives, and indeed, our society teaches us this from an early age. We want to be the masters of our own fate, set our own course, plan and direct our own future. While this philosophy has some value in it, it fails to account for our destiny as determined by forces much larger than ourselves. Western culture does not leave much room for the powerful influences of fate, destiny, luck, chance, or limits in our lives. In truth, we are like sailors ultimately driven by prevailing winds and tides over which we have no control. But we can learn about our boat. We can understand more about its structure and how it responds to the wind and current. We can learn to tack. June Singer writes, "In learning to sail you do not change the current of the water nor do you have any effect on the wind, but you learn to hoist your sail and turn it this way and that to utilize the greater forces which surround you. By understanding them, you become one with them, and in doing so are able to find your own direction—so long as it is in harmony with, and does not try to oppose, the greater forces in being."[21]

"Why me? Why now? It's not fair," we may cry when we learn that something in life has not worked out for us. Yet life is not always fair, and we cannot always control our fate. But perhaps we can learn that while we are subject to our own destiny and the powers of the universe, we are not entirely helpless. We can determine how we will respond to the challenges that confront us.

Like Job, we question why God/nature/the universe allows such suffering when we have done nothing wrong. In the Bible story, Job is a successful man who is "blameless and upright." He worships God and is thankful for his riches: seven thousand sheep, three thousand camels, five hundred yoke of oxen, five hundred donkeys, many servants, seven strong sons and three beautiful daughters. He has every bounty that life can bestow, until one day Satan comes to Yahweh with a wager. Satan notices that it is easy for Job to honor and fear God, be upright and blameless, and turn away from evil because he has everything. Satan wagers that Job would turn away from God if things weren't so perfect in his life. Yahweh agrees to let Satan test Job.

Soon after, a messenger reports to Job that the oxen and donkeys have been carried off by Sabeans and all the servants have been killed. Even as he speaks, another messenger relates that the fire of God has fallen from heaven and burned up the sheep and the servants. Another messenger arrives and announces that the Chaldeans have stolen the camels and killed all the servants. Before he can finish, another messenger says, "Your sons and daughters were eating and drinking wine in their eldest brother's house when suddenly a great wind came across the desert, struck the four corners of the house, and it fell on the young people, and they are dead."

Then Job arises, shaves his head, tears his robe, and falls to the ground and prays. He says, "Naked I came from my mother's womb, and naked shall I return there; the Lord gave and the Lord has taken away; blessed be the name of the Lord." In all this Job does not sin or charge God with wrongdoing.

The next day Satan comes again before Yahweh. Yahweh says, "Have you considered my servant Job? There is no one like him on the earth, a blameless and upright man who fears God and turns away from evil. He still persists in his integrity although thou incited me against him, to destroy him for no reason." Satan answers the Lord, "Skin for skin! All that people have they will give to save their lives. But stretch out your hand now and touch his bone and his flesh, and he will curse you to your face." The Lord says to Satan, "Very well, he is in your power; only spare his life." So Satan goes out and inflicts terrible sores on Job from the crown of his head to the sole of his foot.

"Why is this happening to me?" Job calls out to God. Job wants answers. He is not an evil man and has never done anything to deserve all the horrors that are raining down on his life. What is the justification for this kind of treatment by the Lord? Three counselors arrive who tell Job that he should stop his questioning. He should just submit to the will of the Lord because in some way or another he had it coming. They urge him to admit this, and that although he may not understand it, God is just. But Job refuses to do this. He continues his questioning, maintaining his integrity, as he puts it.

Elihu, a much younger man, comes before Job and tells him that he is angry at Job because Job justified himself rather than God. He is angry at the three counselors, because they had found no answer though they declared Job wrong. Elihu rebukes Job, proclaims God's justice, condemns Job's self-righteousness, and exalts God's goodness and majesty. Finally God appears out of the whirlwind to answer Job directly, basically saying, "Who are you to question me? Look at all my grandeur." With that, Job is humbled and quietly accepts his situation.

God then gives back to Job twice as much as he had before. All his brothers and sisters and all who had known him formerly came to break bread with him. The Lord blesses the latter days of Job, giving him many thousands of sheep, camels, oxen, and donkeys. He has an additional seven sons and three daughters. After this Job lives a hundred and forty years and sees four generations of his children and his children's children. And Job dies, "an old man, and full of days."[22]

To Jung, the story of Job represents a powerful archetype and a central myth in Judeo-Christian cultures.[23] Who has not asked the question, "Why me? Why is this happening?" when confronted by illness, accidents, or the loss of a loved one? How do we account for the loss associated with a stillborn baby or an infant who dies from SIDS? How do we make sense of the twenty thousand Third World children who die daily from malnutrition and dysentery? What can we possibly believe to account for innocent people falling victim to acts of violence? How do we understand the suffering of people who are born with or stricken with terrible disabilities? How do we accept the death of a friend or loved one who is young and in the prime of life? How do we live with the knowledge that we will inevitably give up this life and die?

We suffer because we are human, and no one is immune. Death is the great equalizer and our common human destiny. We exist in an uncontrolled cycle of birth and death, this illusionary ocean of suffering that the Buddhists call *samsara.* Even Job, with his great wealth and his trusting relationship to God, was not spared the realities of our human existence. But suffering and loss allow us to recognize our strongest connection to each other, to God, and to the joy and mystery of life itself. C. S. Lewis, coming from a distinctly Christian perspective but echoing Eastern spiritual views, presents the idea that suffering gives us an opportunity to more fully know God and our own destiny. Knowing that all will eventually have to be surrendered and that our present happiness will never be enough to make us blessed, Lewis writes, "All this must fall from them in the end, and that if they have not learned to know Him they will be wretched. And therefore He troubles them, warning them in advance of an insufficiency that one day they will have to discover."[24]

If there is a single word that captures the essence of a conscious passage through midlife and all the losses now and yet to come, it is most probably "humility." But it is precisely this perspective of anguish that gives birth to new consciousness. As the poet Roethke so eloquently states, "In a dark time the eye begins to see."[25]

Sogyal Rinpoche relates a story of a young woman who was grief-stricken at the death of her firstborn child. The woman searched the countryside, begging for a medicine that could restore the life of her baby. She met a wise man who told her to ask the Buddha.

She went to the Buddha and told him what had happened. Listening with infinite compassion, the Buddha said gently, "There is only one way to heal your affliction. Bring me back a mustard seed from a house that has never known death."

The woman went off in search of the mustard seed. She stopped at the first house she came to and said, "I have been told by the Buddha to return with a mustard seed from a house that has never known death."

"Many people have died in this house," she was told. She went to the next house. "There have been countless deaths in our family," she heard again. She went to houses of the rich and houses of the poor. She went to every house in the city, until she realized that the Buddha's condition could never be fulfilled.

She said good-bye for the last time to the body of her beloved child and returned to see the Buddha. "Did you bring the mustard seed?" he asked.

"No," she said. "I understand the lesson you are teaching me. Grief made me blind and I thought that I was the only one that had suffered at the hands of death."

"Why have you come back?" asked the Buddha.

"I want to know the truth of what death is and what lies beyond it. Is there anything in me that will not die?" the woman asked.

The Buddha began to teach her: "There is only one law in the universe that never changes, and that is that all things change and all things are impermanent. The death of your child has helped you to see that. Your pain has opened your heart to the truth. I will show it to you."

The woman knelt at the Buddha's feet and followed his teachings for the rest of her life. Near the end of it, it is said, she attained enlightenment.[26]

The recognition that suffering and loss are part of the great impermanence of the universe can cause us, as a wise man once told me, to become "bitter or better." We can curse the darkness and ask "Why me, Lord?" or we can open our hearts to our human experience and allow the full bright light of compassion to reaffirm our relationships to others and to life.

The Hasidic Jews have a story about the Sorrow Tree: On Judgment Day, each person will be invited to hang all of his own miseries on the Tree of Sorrows. Each person will then be permitted to walk about the tree and take a good look at everyone else's miseries in order to select a set he likes better. According to Hasidic legend, each person then freely selects his own personal set of sorrows once again.[27]

Suffering has greater meaning when we understand it as part of the experience of being human and recognize that pain presents opportunities for wisdom, compassion, and the emergence of the Self. Helen Keller, the great humanitarian who lived through such deprivation, wrote: "Character cannot be developed in ease and quiet. Only through experience of trial and suffering can the soul be strengthened, vision cleared, ambition inspired and success achieved."

Jung believed that suffering without meaning, not suffering itself, was the real scourge of human life. When we come to understand that we are all part of a world of which suffering is a part, we can better understand how to grow through that pain. Jung wrote, "The world into which we are born is brutal and cruel, and at the same time, one of divine beauty. Which element we think outweighs the other, whether meaningless or meaning, is a matter of temperament. If meaninglessness were absolutely preponderant, the meaningfulness of life would vanish to an increasing degree with each step in our development. But that is—or seems to me—not the case. Probably, as in all metaphysical questions, both are true: Life is—or has—meaning and meaninglessness. I cherish the anxious hope that meaning will preponderate and win the battle."[28]

Psychiatrist and writer Viktor Frankl survived the horrors of Auschwitz and other Nazi concentration camps without sacrificing his grace and compassion. In the midst of unspeakable atrocities and dehumanization he spoke gently to his fellow prisoners about human dignity and the many opportunities of giving meaning to one's life. He wrote, "We must never forget that we may also find meaning in life even when confronted with a hopeless situation, when facing a fate that cannot be changed. For what then matters is to bear witness to the uniquely human potential at its best, which is to transform a personal tragedy into a triumph, to turn one's predicament into a human achievement. When we are no longer able to change a situation—just think of an incurable disease such as inoperable cancer—we are challenged to change ourselves."[29] Frankl was very fond of quoting Nietzsche: "He who has a *why* to live can bear with almost any *how*."[30]

Ondrea and Stephen Levine have taught a great deal about suffering, death, and the opportunities for transformation and soul-work that accompany these times in our lives. They describe their experiences of working with Hazel, a very difficult hospital patient whom the nurses called a "real bitch on wheels." She verbally abused the nursing staff and physicians with nasty comments and complaints. Her anger and despair had turned her into a critical, shrewish woman who could not be pleased. Because she was so difficult to be with, the nursing staff would finish their work and leave her room as quickly as possible. Her adult children, having been subjected to her abuse and control for so many years, would not visit her. She was dying alone and in great pain.

Her isolation and pain increased, until one night she could no longer stand the pain in her back and legs or "the pain of her unlived life." "She had never felt so alone or helpless. Feeling death approach, she remembered herself as a youngster, open and hungry for the world. She saw how she had closed down over the years. With a deep sigh she let the helplessness wash over her and, exhausted, unable to fight another moment, she surrendered, she let go and 'died into her life,' into the moment. She began to sense, quite beyond reason, that she was somehow not alone in her suffering. She felt what she later called 'the ten thousand in pain.' She began to experience all the other beings who at that very moment were lying in that same bed of agony. At first there arose the experience of herself as a brown-skinned woman, breasts slack from malnutrition, lying on her side, a starving child suckling at her empty breast, spine and legs twisted in pain, the musculature contracted from starvation and disease. For an instant, she became this Ethiopian woman with this same pain in the back and legs and hips, lying on her side, dying in the mud. Then there arose the experience of an Eskimo woman lying on her side dying during childbirth, tremendous pain in her back, hips, legs and dying the same death. Then her experience became that of a woman in a twisted car wreckage, her back and legs broken, slowly dying alone by the side of a deserted road. Image after image arose of the 'ten thousand in pain.' She experienced herself as a youth with yellowed skin curled upon his side on a dirty mattress, dying of hepatitis in a junky flat, as an old woman with grayish skin dying of old age—each with the same pain in the lower back and legs. She saw herself as a woman, her lower back crushed by a rockfall, dying by the banks of a river alone, bereft of the touch of another human being. She saw herself dying of cholera, as an Asian mother with an ill child in a thatched hut. She was dying beside the others."

This experience left Hazel transformed. "The pain was beyond my bearing. I couldn't stand it any longer and something broke. Maybe it was my heart. But I saw it wasn't just *my* pain, it was *the* pain. It wasn't just my life, it was all life. It was life itself." In the days that followed, Hazel opened her heart to all the others in pain in the hospital. She asked her children for forgiveness and they forgave. She began to ask about others she had met in the hospital. The nurses began to come to visit on their breaks because the room was being transformed by love. Stephen Levine writes, "Her room became a place of healing, of finished business, of universal care. Some weeks later, a few days before she died, someone brought her a picture of Jesus as the Good Shepherd lovingly surrounded by children and animals. And this woman, whose life had been one of hardness and isolation, looked at the picture and said with her voice cracking, 'Oh Jesus, have mercy on them, forgive them, they are only children.' Hazel's was one of the most remarkable healings we have ever seen." Hazel died surrounded by her children and grandchildren in a room filled with warmth and love.[31]

Without knowing it, Hazel had experienced the practice of *tonglen,* which in Tibetan means "giving and receiving." Tonglen opens a person to the truth of the suffering others. It unblocks the heart and allows for the full awareness of the loving, expansive radiance of one's true nature. This compassionate oneness with others bridges the gap of pain and suffering and replaces it with an enlightened understanding of the human experience. "No other practice," writes Sogyal Rinpoche, "is as effective in destroying the self-grasping, self-cherishing, self-absorption of the ego, which is the root of all our suffering and the root of all hard-heartedness."[32]

Peggy had lived a rather sheltered life in spite of her professional work as a technician in a busy inner-city emergency room. She traveled each day from her small apartment in the suburbs to the "inferno," as she called the ER. She was a competent worker and made it a point never to get too emotionally involved with the patients that passed through the doors of the hospital. "We see an awful lot of stupid, useless pain and suffering here: teenagers shot in the course of robberies or gang violence, women who have been beaten bloody by husbands or boyfriends, victims of drunk drivers, kids that have been physically battered by alcoholic, drug-abusing parents." In spite of her professionalism, Peggy saw her work as "just a job" and was no longer in touch with the earlier sense of idealism and caring that had led her into a career in the medical field.

Peggy's world was turned upside down by the very sudden, totally unexpected death of her mother from a heart attack. Relatively young and with no health problems, her mother had suddenly fallen over in her kitchen and died shortly after being taken to the emergency unit of a local hospital. A neighbor called Peggy at work and told her what had happened. Peggy raced to her mother's side but she had already died. "I can't even describe the sense of emptiness or the extreme physical pain that I felt that day," Peggy said as tears rolled down her cheeks.

A few weeks after her mother's death, Peggy was back at work in the emergency room. She had just assisted in the unsuccessful resuscitation of an older man who had been brought to the hospital with congestive heart failure. The nursing staff called the man's son and informed him that his father had been brought to the hospital by ambulance and that it was imperative that he come quickly. The nursing coordinator asked Peggy to keep an eye out for the man's son. She was to meet him and escort him through the busy waiting room of the ER into a small room that served as a chapel. Peggy knew only that the son was African-American, in his mid-thirties, and worked for the electric power company as a lineman.

Moments later she saw a tall, heavyset black man rushing down the hallway toward the emergency room. She knew that it was the son since he looked the right age and was wearing navy-blue coveralls with the logo of the power company on the front pocket. He had a pained and frightened look on his face as she guided him to the makeshift chapel. "Where is my father?" he asked. Peggy knew that notification of death was really the job of the nurse coordinator but she also knew that his question needed an answer now. "I'm sorry," she said quietly. He put his head into his hands and began to sob. "Here was this huge, strong-looking man crying his eyes out," Peggy remembers. "I sat next to him and put my arm on his shoulder and could suddenly feel exactly what he was feeling. It had only been two weeks since I had lost my mother in an almost identical way. I cannot even explain how deeply I felt his pain." In spite of Peggy's excessive sense of "professionalism," she felt her eyes fill with tears. "We just sat there, in total silence, holding on to each other. I think that he understood that I knew how he was feeling. It was a most extraordinary circumstance, as if suddenly our hearts were completely open to one another. Two perfect strangers who couldn't have been more different were totally connected. I can't really explain how powerful it felt." Peggy had experienced pure compassion. Their shared experience of loss overcame all the differences of gender, race, and class that so often separate us from our common humanity. Peggy had experienced tonglen.

The staggering dimensions of the losses that we will experience throughout our lives can blind us to the magnificent gifts that lie directly alongside them. Just as midlife can be a time of letting go and endings, it can be a time of new beginnings. Many people are discovering that changes in their career path at midlife open vast new horizons. New opportunities can abound if we keep our eyes open to them. Many others are discovering that they are becoming healthier and more beautiful or handsome as life sculpts their faces into ones of character and grace. Still others are finding that there are many simpler joys in life than the acquisition of material things. Those who do take pleasure in the material world find great release in recognizing the difference between *preferring* nice things and *needing* them. Some of us may even learn not to grasp at impermanence. While many relationships are under fire at midlife, others are transforming into true intimacy, companionship, and love. Many people are experiencing deep spiritual feelings, new directions, and an enlightened awareness as to their own natures. It is impossible to have a consciousness of death without at least asking, "Is there anything after death?" A new, vibrant relationship with God and the universe is often the result of our seeking.

Sogyal Rinpoche humorously remarks on our overly large investment in the ego and this life to the exclusion of our spiritual life in all eternity:

"It is like spending all your time and money to decorate a hotel room that you will only be staying in for a short time."[33] At midlife, we can make great progress toward nurturing our eternal, spiritual self. We may begin to experience a greater depth in our understanding of our own soul and its ultimate journey.

To accept life as impermanent and death as inevitable does not mean that our attention must focus only on loss and endings. The life energy in living things is powerful and doesn't easily surrender to the forces that threaten it. Look at the way grass and weeds, seeking light and life, will manage to grow through even the smallest crack in the sidewalk. Research increasingly documents spectacular recoveries from what appear to be terminal illnesses in many different kinds of people.[34] Whether these "spontaneous remissions" reflect the action of some undetermined neuropeptide, sheer acts of will and belief, or miracles may not yet be clear. But what is evident is the awesome power behind the will to live. As Beth Neilsen Chapman sings, "Life holds on given the slightest chance."

By the same token, to accept death as part of life does not mean that we will not grieve deeply for our losses. I can still remember the excruciating pain that accompanied the full awareness that my mother was dying of leukemia. My mother and our family had known for months that there was nothing further the doctors could offer to extend her life. All they could do was order blood transfusions and medications to ease her pain. One day while I was listening to a song that was very special to my mother, the reality of her imminent death broke through my denial. I felt as if I had been punched in my stomach. I doubled over and sobbed until I couldn't breathe. The pain was physical as well as emotional and spiritual. My own beliefs in the life-death-rebirth journey or the eternal continuity of my mother's soul did not prevent the suffering or grief that I experienced. I didn't want her to leave.

My friend Barbara and her family suffer along with her dad, Milt, as he fights to recover from cancer that has metastasized to his liver. Barbara has a strong spiritual sense and a deep faith in life after death. She and I feel a strong connection at this point in our lives, as my own father is battling a serious illness. We talk often about how we are getting through the sheer pain of our realities. Barb wrote to me, "I accept, in a rebel sort of way, that there are some things that I will never understand. I will even experience them, yet will be unable to really define my own experience. I see this in my grief over my dad's illness. Why do I grieve so desperately? It is not my fear of death at the core of these emotions, nor is it my reluctance to change. I don't deny these elements but they are not the driving force behind my pain. The driving force is my love for my dad. I love him so much, and can't stand that he will not be there to see my son graduate from high school or that he will not be there at family gatherings, behind the bar smiling and extending his affections. I simply love him and don't want a life without him in it. The emotion and experience I can't define is love. No matter how hard you try to make sense of the 'life-cycle' thing and no matter how well a person may have come to terms with that, it does not stop the pain."

Barbara and I have come to the understanding that love is transcendent, more powerful than death itself. "It's that thought that is getting me through the day," she says. And in the midst of grieving we still live in each day: shuttling kids to baseball practice, writing, preparing dinner, talking with friends. Though some days, we've agreed, are best met with a wad of Kleenex in our pockets.

At midlife we are being asked to hold the tension of the opposites, to be in the dialectic of living fully while knowing that death and loss are inevitable. If we open our consciousness to both of these awarenesses at once we allow the Self and the ego to enter into a critical dialogue. We can become increasingly aware of the joy of life, honor our true Self, and evaluate and act on our priorities with wisdom. We can come closer to knowing who we really are. There is enlightenment in the old New England saying "Farm like you'll live forever, and live like you'll die tomorrow." It is only in accepting loss and death that we may truly learn to live. In so doing, we will discover that the ways in which we live the second half of life may be far richer than the ways in which we journeyed through the first half. It is possible to live life with greater joy, intimacy with others, passion, and wisdom. It is through loss and change that we allow the Self, our soul, to blossom and become aware of the ego as a relatively small aspect of who we are. Since we will lose everything eventually, it only makes sense to live life to the fullest, to take each day and each relationship as the blessing that it is. In *Letters to a Young Poet* Rilke wrote, "Be patient toward all that is unsolved in your heart and try to love the questions themselves like locked rooms and like books that are written in a very foreign tongue. Do not now seek the answers, which cannot be given you because you would not be able to live them. And the point is, to live everything. Live the questions now. Perhaps you will then gradually, without knowing it, live along some distant day into the answer."[35]

My good friend Kathy experienced great changes as she moved into her middle forties. She decided to go on an Outward Bound adventure to get closer to nature and to her own inner self. Part of her experience there included the completion of a ropes course during which she had to walk across a narrow beam that was about a hundred feet high ("I think it was really nine hundred feet high," she said). The Outward Bound programs are very safety-conscious, so she was outfitted with a harness that would prevent her from being injured if she fell. But the harness would allow her to fall a good way before it stopped her. Knowing that she couldn't be killed or seriously hurt was some comfort, but Kathy has a particular fear of heights and falling. If she fell she would have to go through the terrifying feelings of the fall itself.

She approached the beam with extreme caution, heart pounding, and wondering what she had gotten herself into. As she stepped out onto the beam she suddenly realized that she was walking this beam in the same way that she approached life. She was reserved, controlled, confined. "I realized that I was trying to make myself smaller. My arms were folded and pressed against my chest. I was almost huddled over trying to reduce my height. I was scared to death and wishing that it was over." She knew that if this beam were on the ground she could walk it with ease. It was the fear of falling that kept her frozen and restricted.

She suddenly recognized how fear paralyzed her, kept her tight and terrified, and prevented her from moving forward with confidence and grace. "I couldn't bear the way I was doing this," she told me. This flash of awareness caused her to act with courage she didn't know she possessed. She jumped.

The harness caught her and she climbed back to restart the course. Watching her campmates tentatively and fearfully step their way across the beam, she knew that this next time across would be different for her. As her turn came she realized that she was no longer afraid. She had already faced her demons, her fears, and had found courage and power in doing so.

Kathy looked down from the top of the ropes course and then across to the landing that was her destination. She took a deep, deliberate breath and stepped out onto the beam. This was the same path that had caused such terror in her just moments earlier. This time as she moved across the beam—she danced.

CHAPTER 5

Entering the Chrysalis

You darkness, that I come from,
I love you more than all the fires
that fence in the world,
for the fire makes
a circle of light for everyone,
and then no one outside learns of you.

RAINER MARIA RILKE, "A BOOK FOR THE HOURS OF PRAYER"[1]

FOR NINE DAYS in March 1984, Mary Kay Blakely lived in the hushed cocoon of a coma. Given only a fifty-fifty chance of survival, she watched from a silent womb, unable to communicate even simple ideas or feelings. She had no choice but to descend into the unknown recesses of her own inner life. It was a journey that would change her forever.

A series of turbulent shifts and changes had arrived in Mary Kay's life, often at breathtaking speed, just prior to her physical breakdown. She labored to meet the demands of raising two young sons and maintaining her career as a writer, journalist, and lecturer. Her work required frequent travel from Michigan to New York, where she juggled both her assignments and a relationship with her lover, Larry. Her recent divorce had left her feeling confused and guilt-ridden. She found herself taking on a great deal of responsibility for the pain of her ex-husband, a man she cared for and loved but, for many reasons, could no longer remain married to. In order to make life easier for her children, and so they could maintain a close relationship with their father, she had recently moved from Fort Wayne to Ann Arbor. But this relocation required leaving a strong support system of close women friends. Serious financial problems were a constant source of stress and anxiety. Her eldest and much beloved brother had recently committed suicide after a lifetime of manic illness. Hardly giving herself time to grieve, she carried her brother's journals and notes with her in an effort to understand what had happened.

Ten years prior to her coma, Mary Kay had been diagnosed with an autoimmune disorder of her lungs, sarcoidosis, which had recently flared up, necessitating an open-lung biopsy. The exploratory surgery left her with an external tube inserted between her ribs, designed to drain her lungs. The autoimmune disease ravaging her body caused problems in other systems, and she developed diabetes mellitus for which regular injections of insulin were required. In spite of her weariness and debilitated physical condition she continued to press forward with all the responsibilities that had come to define her life. "The habit of ignoring subtle pain began in my Catholic girlhood, no doubt, during my thorough training as a young martyr. Suffering in silence was thought to benefit the souls in purgatory, and I imagined the longer I waited to see a doctor, the more souls I could spring."

As she boarded a plane to New York, ignoring the flu symptoms she was experiencing, she collapsed with a thud on top of her luggage in the narrow aisle. "Are you all right?" the stewardess asked. " 'I'm fine.' A Blakely, even when felled to the floor with an arrow sticking between her ribs, responds to all queries about her person with, 'Don't worry about me. I'm fine,' " she wrote.

Within several days, her "flu" symptoms had escalated to serious proportions and she was rushed to the hospital in an ambulance. Teetering between life and death, Mary Kay floated above the world she knew, tethered to life only by some fragile, invisible thread. Unable to speak or communicate in any way, she spent the next nine days on a solitary inner journey.

In the stillness of her coma and through her private underworld passage, Mary Kay Blakely emerged transformed. She wrote, "I had the unshakable feeling that however much I reapplied myself to life it would never be quite the same. I thought I wasn't really supposed to be here. I had been scheduled for death but—like other important deadlines I'd missed—I didn't make it. The years ahead of me seemed like pure gifts, unearned bonuses to spend however I liked. I felt radically altered by my nine-day sleep, a passionate psychological journey that uncovered old, unextinguished yearnings.

After awakening on March 31, I gradually discovered that the life planned by the woman I had been no longer fit the woman I'd become."[2]

Mary Kay Blakely's engaging and humorous account of her breakdown and breakthrough is recounted in her book *Wake Me When It's Over.* It was one of the first books I read and reread when my own life came tumbling down around me in 1989. Although I didn't have to cope with and survive the serious physical illness she did, I knew that I was experiencing a death of sorts. I wondered if there would be anything like a resurrection.

All living things go through cycles of growth and change, though; perhaps the most startling and spectacular example of this is the metamorphosis of the pudgy, creeping caterpillar into the magnificent, airborne butterfly. Caterpillars spend almost their entire lives feeding and growing. With skin incapable of stretching, the caterpillar accommodates its expanding girth and length by shedding or molting its skin. The final molt produces the *chrysalis,* or pupa, a stage at which the caterpillar comes to a rest and does not feed. Hanging from a tree, inside the chrysalis, the caterpillar begins to dissolve and create the fluids that will become the wings and body of the butterfly. Unlike the gradual changes that mark the transition from juvenile to adult in grasshoppers, humans, and most other species of animals, the caterpillar, signaled by ancient, predetermined hormonal and chemical cues, begins a total meltdown. The world inside the chrysalis becomes a kind of cater-butter stew. When the adult is fully and finally formed, the skin of the chrysalis splits open and the butterfly crawls out. It pumps fluids from its swollen body into its shrunken wings and begins to fly.[3]

In ancient Greece the word for soul, *psyche,* was often illustrated and described as a butterfly. The transformation from caterpillar to chrysalis to butterfly is an apt metaphor for what is happening in midlife. The striking transformation and radical changes in human beings who allow themselves to experience this psychological chrysalis are just as remarkable as those of our insect relatives. And the process of change is often experienced as a kind of melting down and dissolving of what was.

In applying the metaphor of the chrysalis to midlife there are four considerations that should be understood:

1. We have to sacrifice the caterpillar in order to transform into a butterfly. We have to let go of who we believed ourselves to be in order to know ourselves for who we really are.

2. The process within the chrysalis is one of isolation and solitude. It is a withdrawal from our normal mode of interacting with the world.
3. The process is one of slow gestation. It can be neither hurried nor circumvented.
4. The time in which we are psychologically and spiritually in the chrysalis offers an opening, a doorway, through which we can more clearly touch the Divine, transpersonal, and nonrational aspects of being.

Sacrifice

At midlife, the part of ourselves that we have known, the caterpillar, is in essence disintegrating. We are stepping into the abyss without a clue as to where we will emerge from it. As in the separation aspect of the Hero's Journey, we are leaving behind what we have known ourselves to be and all the safe and predictable containers for that reality. Marion Woodman writes, "Life as we have known it is over. No longer who we were, we know not who we may become."[4]

The emergence of the butterfly requires, absolutely demands, the sacrifice of the caterpillar. *Sacrifice* is derived from the Latin *sacrificium* and means the forfeiting of something of importance in the service of receiving something of even greater value. The word literally means "to make holy." From the psychological point of view, sacrifice means giving up the illusions and dependencies of childhood to reenter the world as an adult who can understand the realities of the human experience. It is the emergence of the light of consciousness from the darkness. This transformation requires letting go of old beliefs and self-evaluations.

Like the caterpillar's biological triggers to enter the chrysalis, adolescence is initiated by surging hormones that set in motion behaviors and instincts directed toward the developmental accomplishments necessary for the first half of life. Midlife, on the other hand, is not as biologically based. Instead the process of individuation is inaugurated by compelling psychological and spiritual forces. Entering the chrysalis is evidence of a deliberate, though unconscious, cooperation with the urge toward individuation and it is required for growth of the personality and an expansion of consciousness. It is based on the deeply felt need for meaning and wholeness.

Unlike the caterpillar whose entrance into the chrysalis is cued and exquisitely timed by complex chemical-releasing mechanisms, our initiation into the chrysalis may begin suddenly or gradually. Often some kind of loss launches our descent—a divorce or loss of relationship, the death of a loved one, termination from a job, the diagnosis of a serious illness. Just as often, however, there is no apparent cause—nothing out of the ordinary appears to have happened. But regardless of the nature of the onset, the initiate experiences a pervading sense of loss and dread. Murray Stein suggests that the experience includes "moody and nostalgic periods of grieving for some vaguely felt absence, a keen and growing sense of life's limits, attacks of panic about one's own death, and exercises in rationalization and denial."[5]

In the months before my fortieth birthday I thought the world was my oyster. I was living in a nice house on the edge of the ocean, starting a new job, in a loving relationship, and surrounded by good, close friends. If I had been asked to sacrifice anything in my life, I would have refused. But I wasn't asked.

I didn't know how unaware I really was about life and myself. I knew very little about who I was because I had never really looked. I believed that I was exactly who I appeared to be. I believed that if you were a good person and worked hard, you could make your life into whatever you wanted it to be. In spite of being a relatively caring and decent person I had the arrogance to believe that I could control all the important things about my life. Looking back now, more than six years later, I can see all the signs that said something was brewing, something was about to change, but I didn't have a clue at the time. I did know that I was compelled to read and reread a novel that I had always loved. My house is filled with books but I kept returning to this one. I would finish it and immediately start reading it again. I joined a women's reading group and when it was my turn to select a book to discuss, I once again chose *Praisesong for the Widow.*[6]

Paule Marshall's magnificent novel tells the story of Avey Johnson, a black, middle-aged, middle-class widow "given to hats, gloves and pearls." Avey, a supervisor at the Department of Motor Vehicles, has long since put her past behind her. She has lost sight of her own culture, her history, and her true nature in the service of an uninspired but safe middle-class life. She goes on a Caribbean cruise with two friends but early in the trip she is disturbed by a deeply felt sense of panic and troubling dreams.

> As a rule she seldom dreamed. Or if she did, whatever occurred in her sleep was always conveniently forgotten by the time she awoke.

> . . . And then three nights ago the old habit returned. Tired after a long day spent ashore on Martinique, during which she and her companions had traveled overland for hours to visit the volcano, Mount Pelee, she had gone to bed early that evening, only to find herself confronted the moment she dropped off to sleep by her great-aunt Cuney. The old woman, who had really been her father's great-aunt, was someone Avey Johnson couldn't remember ever having dreamed of before. She had scarcely thought of her in years. Yet there she had been in her sleep, standing waiting for her on the road that led over to the Landing.[7]

In the dream she is a little girl spending August with her aunt on Tatem Island, just across from Beaufort on the South Carolina Tidewater. Aunt Cuney, having been expelled from her own church for crossing her feet—dancing, the preacher said—had made the Landing her religion. The Landing, her aunt had told her, was where the slave ships had brought the Ibo people into South Carolina:

> And the minute those Ibos was brought on shore they just stopped, my gran' said, and taken a look around. A good long look. Not saying a word. Just studying the place real good. Just taking their time and studying on it. . . . And when they got through sizing up the place real good and seen what was to come, they turned, my gran' said, and looked at the white folks what brought 'em here. . . . They just turned and walked on back down the edge of the river here. Every las' man, woman and chile. And they wasn't taking they time no more. They had seen what they had seen and those Ibos was stepping! And they didn't bother getting back into the small boats drawed up here—boats take too much time. They just kept walking right on out over the river . . . Now you wouldna thought they'd of got very far seeing as it was water they was walking on. Besides they had all that iron on 'em. Iron on they ankles and they wrists and fastened 'round they necks like a dog collar. Nuff iron to sink an army . . . When they realized there wasn't nothing between them and home but some water and that wasn't giving 'em no trouble they got so tickled they started into singing.

Three nights earlier, her Aunt Cuney had appeared in Avey's dreams and beckoned her:

> Did she really expect her to go walking over to the Landing dressed as she was? In the new spring suit she had just put on to wear to the annual luncheon at the Statler . . . With her hat and gloves on? And her fur stole draped over her arm? Avey Johnson could have laughed, the idea was so ridiculous. That obstacle course of scrub, rock and rough grass leading down from the cotton field would make quick work of her stockings, and the open-toed patent-leather pumps she was wearing for the first time would never survive that mud flat which had once been a rice field.[8]

In a panic, and feeling her life beginning to unravel, she packs her bags in the middle of the night and leaves her friends at the next port of call. Avey Johnson enters into the chrysalis, separated from her friends and sacrificing all her ideas about who she is:

> She felt like someone in a bad dream who discovers that the street along which they are fleeing is not straight as they had believed, but circular, and that it has been leading them all the while back to the place they were seeking to escape. . . . Under her hat brim, Avey Johnson's eyes again had the wide frightened look of someone given to visions that were beyond her comprehension; and in the midst of the tropical heat she found she was shivering.[9]

Like my initiation into the chrysalis and that of the fictional Avey Johnson, Marion Woodman was suddenly plunged from an ordinary life into the abyss:

> I was in early midlife at the time. I had almost everything middle-class culture could offer—beautiful house, fine husband, excellent teaching position. I expected life to go on into prosperous middle age, reaching its climax in my well-earned, well-respected golden years. I had no reason to doubt that my mother country would continue to care for me: my monthly check was always deposited in the bank by my school board; income tax and pension deductions were automatic; sick leave was ready for any emergency. I had it made."[10]

Marion Woodman wrote that she was drawn to visit India by a romantic vision of the East—the Taj Mahal by moonlight, the holy men, the ivory palaces. But what she found there was herself, though it took many years to fully understand what she had learned. Touched by the sheer humanity, the chaos, the suffering, and the mingling of opposites surrounding her, she could feel her beliefs about life crashing in around her. ("The perfume of jasmine mixed with the stench of urine, the blaze of red silk mixed with the flies in a baby's eyes; the sweetness of a sitar in a summer night mixed with the screams of a beaten dog—all juxtaposed amid exotic textures and tastes, foreign and unfathomable."[11]) "Gone forever," she wrote, "was the world I had lived in. Without consciously knowing what had happened, I had sacrificed my former system of values, my sentimental understanding of life and love. In less than a week I had been forced to surrender my need to control."[12]

Like the butterfly whose birth depends upon the caterpillar's destined destruction within the chrysalis, the Self is born to awareness from the destruction taking place in this dark, interior space. In this process of birthing, it is not wise to underestimate the pain that accompanies the dissolution of the former false self, for when we surrender all of our illusions, we may feel that we are stripped to the bone. Paule Marshall shows us the power and pain inherent in the process of letting go of our false self as she follows Avey Johnson across a rough channel between Grenada and the island of Carriacou. Avey has reluctantly agreed to attend a festival honoring the ancestors, and the only way to get there is by boat. Here Marshall provides a vivid description of the agonizing, wrenching process of surrender to the Self:

> The women next to Avey Johnson on the bench took one look at her stricken eyes, at the hand clapped over her mouth, and were instantly on their feet. As if she weighed no more than the child she had been in her dream they quickly stood her up—after first snatching away the hat and pocketbook from her lap—turned her around between them and quickly put her to kneel on the bench with her head over the railing. All this they managed to do just seconds before the swollen waves that could be seen charging the schooner from all directions over a wide area of the sea sent it reeling and pitching again, and her entire insides erupted. . . . She vomited in long loud agonizing gushes. As each seizure began her head reared back and her body became stiff and upright on the bench . . . the paroxysms repeated themselves with almost no time in between for her to breathe . . . she would try clearing her

> head, try catching her breath. But before she could do either the nausea would seize her again, bringing her body stiffly upright and her head wrenching back.[13]

The process of transformation, as we let go of what was in order to usher in what can be, is agonizing. In the midst of the stripping pain we can easily lose sight of the fact that we are struggling for the incandescent beauty and perspective of the butterfly. Without the realization of what we are becoming, the enormous losses of what we appear to be letting go of can be overwhelming, frightening, and foreign. My friend Alice, who experienced a profound transformation in midlife, and I have referred to the process as being "snatched." Neither of us ruled out the possibility that aliens had taken over and snatched our brains and personalities while we continued to look like "normal" human beings going about the business of daily life.

The internal work that is going on within the chrysalis requires looking honestly at ourselves and our lives. Unencumbered by our habitual defenses, our shadow and other unconscious material rush to the surface of awareness. If we are to be reborn it is necessary to let go of our false assumptions about ourselves. Something has to die. If we are to experience the grace and the flight of the butterfly we have to let got of the anchors which keep us moored to our illusions. We have to let go of what my friend Ruth calls "ancient shit."

Many of us have lived our lives carrying old wounds and hurts that were inflicted long ago. We live our present and will enter our future with the same old expectations, values, and self-evaluations that we have carried with us for all of our lives unless we make a conscious decision to leave them behind. We recite the same scripts, play the same tapes over and over, until we can't tell what is real from what we have been told is real.

Jason was raised by a mother who had become angry and bitter about life and relationships. She had been brought up in a cold, unaffectionate home with parents who were unable to express any kind of warmth or emotional nurturance. She married at an early age just to get out of the house. She was wildly in love and believed that this love would last forever. But things didn't work out that way; she was abandoned by her husband when her child was only three. Jason was constantly told that men were terrible, unfaithful, and disgusting creatures. "You can never trust anyone," was the message he had heard from the time he was just a baby. After four failed marriages, Jason entered midlife convinced that, just as he had always believed, his mother must be right. Relationships don't work and you can't trust anyone.

At forty-six, Jason met Carrie, a woman in her early thirties, and fell in love. Carrie was as different from his ex-wives as anyone could be. She was a free spirit who was passionate about life and was madly in love with Jason. "For the first time in my life I think that I'm really in love," Jason said. "I don't want this relationship to end up like my other marriages. I'm terrified of losing her."

After dating for more than six months, Jason asked Carrie to live with him. She agreed but let it be known, in no uncertain terms, that she wanted to be married. He agreed and they planned a wedding for September, eight months away. "As soon as I moved in everything changed," Carrie said. "He keeps coming up with reasons that our relationship can't work. He's too much older than I am. He's got a lousy track record with marriage. I don't know what I want, he says. He's driving me away."

Jason has set in motion a self-fulfilling prophecy. Because he doesn't believe that relationships can work, he is bound and determined to prove it. Because he accepts that men are "terrible, unfaithful, and disgusting," he cannot embrace a reality that allows him to truly love faithfully. Such a low creature doesn't deserve happiness in relationships. To Jason, these beliefs are entirely unconscious, and if you asked him, he would have told you that he was very much in love with Carrie but that "she didn't know what she wanted." The problem here was not Carrie. She appeared to know exactly what she wanted. She wanted to marry Jason and seemed to be capable of a deeply loving relationship with him.

When Carrie finally left him because he couldn't allow the development of a true relationship with her, Jason was devastated. This was his initiation into the chrysalis: "I began to question everything about how I've lived my life. I finally saw my mother as a bitter woman who refused to move on with her life. She wanted to make my life as miserable as hers had been. I am enraged. I can't even talk to her on the phone because I'm afraid I'll go nuts on her and never stop screaming."

Anger is often a passage point on the journey to healing. Jason has every right to feel angry. He was shortchanged. Like the rest of us, he expected the archetypal mother who was healthy and strong, able to protect and nurture him, able to help him understand that some people can be trusted and others may not be. Instead, he was born to a human being with her own wounds . . . just like the rest of us. His mother was unable to give to him what had never been given to her.

Development over a lifetime depends upon the successful integration of previous stages of growth. Psychoanalyst Erik Erikson,[14] who has detailed the structural stages of human growth from infancy to old age, posits that the failure to navigate the tasks and goals at these earlier stages of development creates a psychological "weak link," a kind of Achilles' heel of the psyche. Just as a crystal will break along its fault line when dropped, we can expect to experience the resurgence of incompletely resolved developmental stages during the midlife transition.

Jason never learned the truth about trust versus mistrust. Because of what he was taught, and then came to believe, he has failed to develop the ability to discern trusthworthiness from untrustworthiness. Instead, he operates under the assumption that no one is to be trusted, and so he has lived his life behind his defenses, which allow him to cut and run whenever a relationship becomes difficult. A critical task for Jason is to come to a new understanding of what it means to trust, to sharpen his skills of discrimination in order to identify the signs and signals that indicate whether or not trust is warranted in a particular person or situation. Inside the chrysalis, he must also experience his anger at having been denied the opportunity to learn the truth about life. After passing through and honoring his anger, he must also forgive his mother. The path to enlightenment does not sidestep the human emotions that are real and unexpressed. In his case, Jason has been carrying enormous rage all his life, a rage that has been unconsciously projected on his wives and lovers and has poisoned all of his relationships with women. He finds himself stuck in the middle between his rage and his pity. "My mother did the best she could," he says. In holding the tension of the opposites, he can come to realize that both his anger and his compassion are real. Jason will have moved to a higher level of consciousness when he can come to terms with both of these emotions. In this dialectic, he may move toward forgiveness and a new awareness that he is now responsible for his own decisions and his own life.

Even in the absence of a challenging family history such as Jason's, there is still much letting go and forgiving that must take place within the chrysalis. All of us, even those from relatively healthy, "good enough," and intact families, have grown up in a culture that demands conformity to many illusionary beliefs and perceptions. We are taught that certain prescribed ways of living our lives are "good," while all others are "bad." Chained to demands of perfectionism and in the absence of an unconditional love of self and others, we experience an inner emptiness that often defies words. For many, a sense of community is something that exists only in the black-and-white memories of sitcoms from the fifties. The development of our ego allows our initial sense of connection to the universe to recede into the unconscious, and thus many of us walk through life with a deeply felt sense of alienation from each other and the world of our own spiritual nature. We are, collectively, suffering the "loss of soul" that Thomas Moore writes about so eloquently. At midlife we know that there is something missing and begin to ask anew, "Who am I?"

The poet David Whyte captures the silence of that question and the transformation that is the possibility of the chrysalis in "Tilicho Lake":

In this high place
it is as simple as this,
leave everything you know behind.

Step toward the cold surface,
say the old prayer of rough love
and open both arms.

Those who come with empty hands
will stare into the lake astonished,
there, in the cold light
reflecting pure snow

the true shape of your own face.[15]

Solitude

I had many dreams during the early, initiation phase of my journey. One, in particular, is as vivid today as any other important waking experience of my life:

I have left a shopping center–like building that appears to be deserted—it is like a mall that has been closed for the night. There are no cars or people that I can see. I'm not sure how I got there, since I have no transportation home—wherever that is. I walk up a steep hill and find a road. It is snowing now and the trees are covered with ice. They are translucent. Everything is white and cold. Snow is falling at a blinding rate. I shiver and can only see a long road stretched ahead of me. It meanders through this forest of crystal trees. I look both ways down the road, hoping to see the headlights of a car or anything that suggests that other people may be around, but nothing moves. The full white moon is my only source of light. I begin to walk up the road. I'm scared to death, alone and trembling.

This dream initiated my entrance into the chrysalis. None of the ways I had learned to live my life or see myself would ever work again. Nothing I had known prepared me for this silent and solitary place. I knew that I was dying. I was dissolving.

As a society, we are particularly uncomfortable with the solitude and isolation that surround us in the dark confines of the chrysalis. Our medical and psychotherapeutic communities generally reinforce the idea that we should never feel bad, sad, or alone, that these feelings are pathologies that should be treated with medication, just as we would use an antibiotic for an infection. More than 4.5 million Americans have taken the antidepressant Prozac since its introduction in 1987;[16] and while Prozac and related drugs certainly have a place in the treatment of chronic and debilitating depression, they are often prescribed to avoid problems of living and to take the edge off the suffering that is evoked in the chrysalis. But if we cannot experience the full gestational growth that lies within, how can we emerge transformed? "Modern psychotherapists, including myself, have taken as their criterion of emotional maturity the capacity of the individual to make mature relationships on equal terms. With few exceptions, psychotherapists have omitted to consider the fact that the capacity to be alone is also an aspect of emotional maturity," states analyst and writer Anthony Storr.[17]

Thomas Moore reminds us that there was a time when human beings had a very different understanding of human suffering, the need for solitude, and "depression." Moore notes that the "soul presents itself in a variety of colors, including all the shades of gray, blue, and black. To care for the soul, we must observe the full range of all its colorings, and resist the temptation to approve only of white, red, and orange—the brilliant colors. . . . In a society that is defended against the tragic sense of life, depression will appear as an enemy, an unredeemable malady; yet in such a society, devoted to light, depression, in compensation, will be unusually strong."[18] The ancients understood that melancholy and sadness were natural aspects of human life and identified with the Roman god Saturn. To be depressed was to be "touched by Saturn."

I rather like the idea that sometimes our sadness and unhappiness are the natural result of understanding the reality of the human experience. I like that we can see our darker moods as connected to the rest of the cosmos, as in being touched by Saturn. As a culture, we have allowed our normal human experiences to become pathologized by an overly zealous desire to never feel bad. But I suspect that when we can finally eradicate the "negative" human feelings, we will have succeeded in wiping out *all feelings* along with those that cause us distress.

Have we become such a feel-good society that we cannot tolerate the normal vicissitudes of human emotion? What do we expect it to feel like when we are letting go of what we have believed ourselves to be? How can we ever know the truth about life and ourselves if we cannot bear to look clearly and without the protection of our illusions?

In our culture introspection has the nasty reputation of being evidence of narcissism, self-absorption, and selfishness. "Just do something," "Stop wallowing in this," we're told. There is a powerful and dangerous tendency to distrust what happens in silence. And yet it is often in this "space between thoughts" that we can most clearly see ourselves.

The Buddhists speak of the intermediate states between life and rebirth, the series of constantly changing transitional realities, as *bardos*.[19] It is in these particularly powerful moments when the possibilities for enlightenment, self-knowledge, and consciousness are heightened. Sogyal Rinpoche writes: "I think of a bardo as being like a moment when you step toward the edge of precipice; such a moment, for example, is when a master introduces a disciple to the essential, original and innermost nature of his or her mind."[20]

This is the domain of the chrysalis. Metamorphosis demands the quiet, silent womb of the chrysalis—we must surrender into solitude. This can be quite a challenge for many people who are frightened or uncomfortable with the idea of being alone with themselves. And yet silence and solitude offer replenishment for the soul and a dispensation from the madding crowd. Writer May Sarton beautifully illustrates the power of aloneness in many of her poems and journals. In *Journal of a Solitude* she writes: "Here I am alone for the first time in weeks, to take up my 'real' life again at last. That is what is strange—that friends, even passionate love, are not my real life unless there is time alone in which to explore and to discover what is happening or has happened. Without the interruptions, nourishing and maddening, this life would become arid. Yet I taste it fully only when I am alone here and the house and I resume old conversations."[21]

But many of us live without breathing space or quiet moments when the Self may whisper its wisdom to our ears alone. Thomas Moore notes, "A common symptom of modern life is that there is no time for thought, or even for letting impressions of a day sink in. Yet it is only when the world enters the heart that it can be made into soul. The vessel in which soul-making takes place is an inner container scooped out by reflection and wonder."[22]

Poet Nancy Wood, in a book for young readers, proclaims the beauty and wonder of solitude in a poem that calls to those of us in midlife as well:

Do not be afraid to embrace the arms
of loneliness.
Do not be concerned with the thorns
of solitude.
Why worry that you will miss something?
Learn to be at home with yourself
without a hand to hold.
Learn to endure isolation
with only the stars for friends.
Happiness
comes from understanding unity.
Love
arrives on the footprints of your fear.
Beauty
arises from the ashes of despair.
Solitude
brings the clarity of still waters.
Wisdom
completes the circle of your dreams.[23]

Shortly after I began my journey into the chrysalis at midlife, I was presented with an opportunity to go spelunking with a good friend and a group of other therapists. I have always been terrified of closed-in spaces and my initial reaction was to say "Thanks but no thanks." I would have been far more comfortable with white-water rafting, hiking, sea kayaking, maybe even bungee jumping. But something inside of me knew that the cave was a synchronous expression of what was happening internally in my life. I agreed to go and wrote about it in my journal:

> I'm not certain as to why I agreed to go into a cave. Perhaps it was the chance to spend some time with other women psychotherapists and get to know them in a place and time where we weren't being therapists. Maybe it was because Kathy asked me to go and I wanted to know her better. Maybe both of those are true, but I think it is really because I knew in some deep and uncharted place that it was important for me to go.
>
> I've always been afraid of closed-in spaces. Perhaps they are a metaphor for something? I only know that my greatest fear was what would happen inside of me. I was afraid that I would panic beyond all recognition and go sailing completely off the abyss. I don't think that I was really afraid that the cave would close in on me. It would have been incredible arrogance to think that after 6 million years of holding steady with changes marked by millennia, not moments, this cave would choose the few hours when I would be inside to come tumbling down. I think I was only a little afraid of that. Mostly though I was afraid that I would have to experience the terror of my own fear. I wouldn't wear caving overalls as everyone else did. I thought that would add just another dimension of feeling trapped and locked in. I wasn't even sure that I would go in. I packed a book in my knapsack in case I opted to sit outside for several hours and wait for my companions to come out of the cave.

After some major anxiety attacks and soothing words from Tim, one of our guides, I descended toward the opening. Thousands of bees guarded the entrance. They were the least of my worries. I could run screaming from them in the open air if I had to. No problem. Getting past the bees was a cakewalk. We sat in a wide opening. It was dark, but the sun streaming in from the giant mouth of the cave gave plenty of light. Not bad, I thought. Room to move and stretch out. We were instructed in cave safety, the importance of leaving everything just as we found it, checking out batteries. Light is the most important thing in a cave. Without it even the most seasoned spelunker would become completely lost and in a very dangerous situation.

My greatest fear was that we would have to squeeze through small spaces where I couldn't see in front of me or move around, and our initial entrance into the cave itself was through a small space that confirmed that fear. I asked to go next to last, since our guides would lead and end the party. I remembered how my cousin Artie had freaked out in a fun house in Asbury Park when we were kids. There was a long line behind and suddenly he absolutely would not go one step farther. He screamed and refused. The whole line of people had to back out of that fun house through its narrow, twisty, black hallways. It would be better if I had to ask only one person to crawl backward rather than the whole group.

I remember the sound of my caving helmet knocking every second against the roof of this long tunnel. I wanted more room. Six million years of geological evolution can be unbending, though, so I continued to crawl. I could see a shadow of the woman in front of me as the tunnel became even narrower:

> My heart was pounding and I felt the familiar surge of anxiety that I had lived with for such a long time. The air was thick and close. I felt like I couldn't breathe. That's not true. The air was clear and cool and perfectly odorless. We crawled for sixty feet. I know that because I asked. It felt more like six thousand feet. I could see a black opening ahead of me. As I approached I saw the small head lamps of my friends moving around. They had arrived in the first "room." Sliding from the crawlway, I found myself sitting on the dirt. I looked around. Everything was brown, with massive stalactites and stalagmites creating huge formations. It was like a Gothic cathedral. I could see sparkling chips in the rock as I moved my light across the walls.
>
> We sat in a circle and one by one turned out our lights. I have never seen a blacker black than at that moment. We sat quietly. I began to feel my fear leaving me. It just vanished as if it were draining out of me into that solid rock floor. Facing one's fears has an enormous capacity to heal the place that is terrified. That's when I knew that I wouldn't be afraid again in this cave. I felt a sense of safety and great comfort in that rock room. I could see greenish-white glowing lights around the heads of each of my companions. Neither alarmed nor confused, I knew that these were not the head lamps that we each wore, since no one had yet turned them back on. Instead, I believed the glow was a bit of the light from each of our souls. I

> thought clearly of the people that I love and sent each of them some of that light. I wept.

There in that limestone chrysalis I felt the strong, courageous feeling that comes from confronting dragons. But more than that, I felt completely connected to the people in my life, to my fellow travelers, and to all of life. Sitting on the cool hard surface of the cave floor, I could sense the vibrational energy of the earth itself and feel the presence of the Great Mother. Like the initiates in the Eleusinian rites of ancient Greece, I could sense my own destiny of Maiden-Mother-Crone.[24] There in that earth-womb, I wondered what other magical, mystical rituals may have been conducted on that very spot by native people who understood, better than I, the process of life-death-rebirth that I was experiencing. In a culture devoid of ritual to help in the critical transitions of our lives, I had found my symbol.

Gestation

In my opinion, nothing in the world is better to eat than a fresh vine-ripened tomato sandwich with lots of salt and pepper. Every year I plant a variety of species in little square-foot gardens in my backyard. Supersonics, Best Boys, Early Girls, beefsteak, are all given their spots in the sun. I rig up some tomato cages, hoping that the seedlings grow big enough to need some support to hold the weight of the blossoming plants and their bountiful—if I'm lucky—cash crop. I have some control over the growth of these plants: I can water, weed, mulch, protect them from cutworms and an unexpected frost, and trim back the suckers when they appear. But no matter how I might crave the sweet juicy harvest, I will have to wait until July, assuming everything goes well, for these little plants to bear fruit.

Our society is not well prepared for the slow maturation that is the nature of gestational changes. Instead we want things to happen now. If we want some material possession we whip out our credit card to pay for it. Our world has become so busy and rushed that there is barely time to prepare and eat a meal. Instead we drive through fast-food restaurants and gulp our lunch on the run. We exercise our body in twenty-minute segments of accelerated aerobics or in wrestling with some exercise machine. Only a few follow the advice that Ficino gave more than five hundred years ago when he suggested, "You should walk as often as possible among plants that have a wonderful aroma, spending a considerable amount of time every day among such things."[25]

Our telephones, pagers, cellular devices, faxes, and modems span the world with words and ideas digitized for instant communication to almost anyone, almost anywhere. We can step on a jet in any city and within hours land in any place in the world. While all this technology in the service of rapid communication and speed has its place, in fact offers many wonderful possibilities for bridging distance between people, it is not the only pace at which the world or human beings can or should operate. One thing is for certain: it is not the way in which the Self becomes known in the inner space of the chrysalis.

The movement toward transformation at midlife is neither rapid nor linear. Just as the seasons change gradually, gently one into the next, just as daytime merges through dusk into night, the world of the chrysalis operates in a growing, maturational way. Like the distillation of gold from base matter, the *prima materia* or *massa confusa,* in the laboratory of the alchemist, the changes that occur within the chrysalis adhere to an internally determined time frame.

Howell Raines correctly observed the gestational nature of the midlife transition when he wrote, "If you contemplate such a trip, I guess it is time to let you in on a tasty little secret. To the degree that the term 'midlife crisis' implies brevity, it is a trick. Gail Sheehy was much closer to the truth when she wrote about a 'passage.' It cranks up somewhere between the ages of thirty-eight and forty-five, and in a really intense midlife crisis, which is the only kind worth having, you should count on five years of steadily intensifying anxiety or depression or some satanic combination of emotional torment."[26] I'm not certain that the midlife transition always takes place specifically in a five-year period, as Howell Raines asserts, though I do agree that the process of the chrysalis is best measured in years and not in days or months. The full development of the Self, however, will take a lifetime, and the goal of individuation is a possibility up until our last breath.

At midlife, though, many people don't believe that they can bear the uncertainty and anguish of this liminal place, and instead, look for ways to hurry things up. We wouldn't even think to scream *"Bloom!"* at the plants that we hope will grow. We would never look at a friend laid up in a full body cast and shout *"Heal!"* Though we may have to hold back the urge, we don't look at the silliness of our teenager and bellow *"Grow up."* We understand that blooming, healing, and emerging from adolescence are maturational processes that take time, operate under their own laws, and cannot be rushed. Certainly, we can take steps to help things along, but for the most part we must simply "let it be." At midlife, however, the urge to reclaim the lost parts of the Self and end the agonizing uncertainty of this birthing process often expresses itself as an addiction, an avoidance of the real issues, or, quite often, an impulse to action. Although the integration of unconscious aspects of the Self may ultimately require real, and often dramatic, changes of circumstances, concrete change is not the goal of the midlife passage. It is instead a time for introspection, reflection, integration, and imagination.

Until now in our lives we have been successful in solving problems by making decisions and taking action. So of course we are easily seduced into following the path that has proven itself worthy in the past. If I'm unhappy in my marriage, I should have an affair or get a divorce. If my work no longer offers any deep sense of satisfaction, I must need another job.

Kevin came to my office for help because he felt like he was "going crazy." He had never been to a counselor or therapist before in his life and did not believe there was anything in therapy that could help him: "My wife says that I've become impossible to live with and she insisted that I go to therapy." At forty-seven, Kevin had become increasingly dissatisfied with his life, his work, his marriage, and everything else he could think of. During the past year he had had one brief affair, changed his job, bought a speedboat and a new car (red, of course, is always the color of the midlife crisis car). He reported a great unhappiness but he was quick to point out that he "wasn't depressed." After all, he noted, "I get up every day and go to work. I spend time with my wife and friends. I'm active in a boating club and am out on the water almost every weekend."

Although Kevin did admit that he was feeling "empty" and not himself, his symptoms could be somewhat avoided by maintaining his extremely active life. If he just kept busy enough he might be able to avoid his soul's promptings for growth. In spite of the fact that Kevin was a very hard worker in almost every aspect of his life, he was unwilling to expend any effort in the process of therapy.

"Keeping a journal can be an important way to begin to look at what you are really feeling," I suggested. "I don't have time for that," he replied.

"One of the most direct ways to understand what is going on inside of you is by paying attention to and working with your dreams," I said. "I don't really think that dreams mean anything. Besides, I never remember them," he countered.

"Keeping some paper and pen or a small tape recorder on your nightstand can help you to record your dreams as soon as you wake up, and when you begin to notice your dreams you are more likely to remember more of them," I said. "Geez, I don't have time for that in the morning. I'm rushing around as it is," he said.

Kevin had no real interest in doing any kind of inner work. He just wanted to feel better and get on with his life. He refused, albeit in a passive-aggressive way, to learn anything about himself or what was happening inside. He wanted to be cured and he expected me to share some esoteric wisdom that would mysteriously make him feel better. In the absence of that magic he continued to take rash, unconscious actions in all the aspects of his life that appeared to be related to his unhappiness.

After several sessions that I'm certain were frustrating for him, he called and canceled his next appointment. "I'll be out of town for a few weeks and I'll call to reschedule when I return," he told my secretary. I knew that this was the last I would see of Kevin until his symptoms escalated in their severity. He was being driven to make changes, and was likely to have another affair or change his job yet again. He was not responding to his wake-up call.

Kevin is not alone in his desire to feel better and to end his pain quickly. This approach to dealing with the crossroads of life's journey is reflected in our medical and psychotherapeutic communities. In recent years the health insurance industry has decided that the goal of psychotherapy should be to relieve symptoms as quickly as possible, usually by medication and straightforward, short-term, behavioral interventions. While both have their place as therapeutic techniques, neither is up to the task of creating a safe place for the very real crisis and pain that are part of the midlife transition. One remaining available form of assistance is rapidly becoming a thing of the past. Managed-care's short-term limits on psychotherapy (usually six to eight sessions), the destruction of confidentiality, the lack of respect for a therapeutic relationship, and the insistence upon medication as the primary focus of treatment have become the norm. Managed-care organizations operate from a preapproved list of providers, and then dictate which therapist an individual may work with in order to have a portion of the cost reimbursed by health insurance. We have departed from understanding the process of psychotherapy and analysis as dependent upon a relationship—what Jung referred to as a *temenos,* a sacred, protected space. Instead we are in the age of the "industrialization" of psychotherapy, where it is mostly viewed as "irrelevant."[27]

The long-term effects of these changes are not yet known. But reporter Gregory Dennis writes that "this abrupt change in the availability of psychotherapy will surprise and anger the many Americans who view the profession as part of everyday life. An estimated 16 million people receive some form of mental-health assistance in the United States each year. Polls show that nearly one in four Americans have consulted a mental-health professional, while four out of five believe that therapy is at least occasionally helpful for personal problems."[28] Dennis's article notes, "Long-term therapy is becoming like opera. Both are extremely enjoyable for the participants. Both are signs of an advanced culture. And neither is reimbursable by third-party payers."

It might be the case that psychotherapy, for all but those suffering severe chronic mental illness, should never have been considered a traditional "medical" intervention, and thus reimbursable by health insurance, in the first place. Therapy from the Greek *therapeia,* means "nursing." The protective chrysalis of psychotherapy that is needed at midlife is not about making life free of all problems or alleviating all of our symptoms before we understand their meaning and symbolic value. Instead it is about containment. The chrysalis is the crucible for growth of the personality and the emergence of the Self. It gives birth to and cultivates a sense of meaning in one's life, and heralds an awakening to both life's suffering and its richness.

The Transpersonal

Less than a month after my mother died, I went to the quiet space out by the pond during a short break in my schedule. I was feeling particularly tearful and sad. The grief of the loss of my mother was very present and strong. I sat quietly and wished that I could have some sign that she was safe and out of pain. I wanted some confirmation that her spirit continued on in some form; at this time of great loss my faith was feeling unsteady and tenuous. Suddenly the tops of the trees across the pond began to shake as a great flock of mourning doves rose into the air. They flew overhead and circled around three times directly over the spot where I was sitting.

I felt a strong sense of wonder, and knowing that doves are symbols of both peace and love, I felt comforted. The logical, left-brained part of me considered this just a random act, a chance occurrence that the birds had chosen this moment to take flight. But another, deeper part of me felt a resonance with the spirit of my mother and an awesome sense of connection to her. I felt both consoled and in the presence of grace.

This experience of correlation between some inner thought or feeling and some outer event, or "meaningful coincidence," Jung called *synchronicity*.[29] He defined it as an "acausal connecting principle," a mysterious connection between the material world and the personal psyche, which he postulated, were only different forms of energy. Though he had alluded to the ideas behind synchronicity in earlier lectures and writings, Jung coalesced his ideas on the phenomenon in the latter part of his life (he was in his seventies in 1952 when he first published his thoughts on this subject). Jung's theory of synchronicity, sparked by his interest in Albert Einstein's theory of relativity and the pioneering contributions to modern physics by Niels Bohr and Wolfgang Pauli, was way ahead of its time.

Jung's efforts to describe and communicate about the phenomenon of synchronicity did not meet with a great deal of success. This was partially a function of the abstract and elusive nature of the concept itself. Secondly, the idea that there can be meaningful connections between two events that are not linked by cause and effect runs completely counter to logical, rational thought processes. Nevertheless, Jung considered the idea to be of utmost importance and experienced a number of synchronistic events in his own life.

During the time that Jung was developing his ideas on synchronicity, he had a dream about a well-fortified, golden castle. He painted the image of a mandala with a golden castle in the center. He writes, "I was impressed by the form and choice of colors, which seemed to me Chinese, although there was nothing outwardly Chinese about it. Yet that was how it affected me." A short time later he received a letter from his friend Richard Wilhelm, who enclosed a Taoist-alchemical manuscript called *The Secret of the Golden Flower*. Wilhelm was requesting that Jung write a commentary on the text.

Jung wrote, "I devoured the manuscript at once, for the text gave me undreamed-of confirmation of my ideas about the mandala and the circumambulation of the center. That was the first event which broke through my isolation. I became aware of an affinity, I could establish ties with something and someone. In remembrance of this coincidence, this synchronicity, I wrote underneath the picture which had made so Chinese an impression upon me: 'In 1928, when I was painting this picture, showing the golden, well-fortified castle, Richard Wilhelm in Frankfurt sent me the thousand-year-old text on the yellow castle, the germ of the immortal body.' "[30]

The reality of synchronicity is clearly illustrated through another of Jung's experiences. He was working with a patient, a woman who "always knew better about everything," and who was making very poor progress in her analysis. Jung writes, "After several fruitless attempts to sweeten her rationalism with a somewhat more human understanding, I had to confine myself to the hope that something unexpected and irrational would turn up, something that would burst the intellectual retort into which she had sealed herself. Well, I was sitting opposite her one day with my back to the window, listening to her flow of rhetoric. She had an impressive dream the night before, in which someone had given her a golden scarab—a costly piece of jewelry. While she was telling me this dream, I heard something behind me gently tapping on the window. I turned around and saw that it was a fairly large flying insect that was knocking against the window-pane from outside in the obvious effort to get into the dark room. This seemed to me very strange. I opened the window immediately and caught the insect in the air as it flew in. It was a scarabaeid beetle, whose gold-green color most nearly resembles that of a golden scarab. I handed the beetle to my patient with the words, 'Here is your scarab.' This experience punctured the desired hole in her rationalism and broke the ice of her intellectual resistance. The treatment could now be continued with satisfactory results."[31]

One can only imagine how Jung's patient felt as he handed her this beetle, so like the one in the dream she was describing. The fact that the scarab is an Egyptian symbol of transformation or rebirth only adds icing to the cake, in my view. The phenomenon of synchronicity is always experienced at a deeply emotional level. It is the kind of event that makes the hair on your arms stand up. It can feel eerie (my friend Paul, who actively pursues and welcomes inner wisdom, still says it sometimes "creeps him out") because it doesn't follow the pattern of how things are supposed to work in our logical world.

Jung described three types of synchronicity, which Jean Shinoda Bolen elaborates on in her book *The Tao of Psychology*:[32]

1. There is a coincidence between mental content (which could be a thought or feeling) and an outer event.
2. A person has a dream or a vision, which coincides with an event that is taking place at a distance (and is later verified).
3. A person has an image (as a dream, vision, or premonition) about something that will happen in the future, which then does occur.

We are constantly immersed in synchronistic happenings, but we mostly fail to recognize them because so much of our energy is devoted to dealing with our mundane life. Our five senses work very well in this arena, and there is scarcely a reason to think that we might need any other sensory abilities to get through the day. But when we are in the chrysalis, when we are emotionally open with new psychic energy flowing through our hearts, we are more likely to notice these meaningful coincidences in our lives. We open ourselves to the dimension of the transpersonal—that is, the parts of our nature that are beyond *(trans)* our ordinary, limited, personal self. It is in this mystical realm that we experience the Divine in our lives.

Jesus uses the metaphor of light, a description of consciousness, in many places in the Gospels when speaking directly to people who are asking to know Him more clearly. "His followers said, 'Show us the place where you are, for we must seek it.' He said to them, 'Whoever has ears should hear. There is light within a person of light, and it shines on the whole world. If it does not shine, it is dark.' "[33] In another passage, Jesus declares that the kingdom of God is already a present reality: "His followers said to him, 'When will the kingdom come?' 'It will not come by watching for it. It will not be said, "Look here it is," or "Look, there it is." Rather, the father's kingdom is spread out upon the earth, and people do not see it.' "[34] Jesus' teachings, as expressed here, show that human beings are already contained in and surrounded by the universal energy of God. These teachings are consistent with the major Eastern mystical and religious points of view. Although each religion names the experience differently, all refer to the phenomenon in which all things are related and aspects of the One. In Hinduism, the god Krishna instructs that all events around us are part of the same ultimate reality, called *Brahman*. Buddhists speak of the mystical experience of awakening to *acintya,* where all elements are as one. Zen stresses *satori* or the experience of enlightenment in which we can experience a mystical awareness of the Buddha nature of all things: We are an integrated aspect of everything that is. Confucianism and Taoism speak of *Tao,* an inexpressible inner essence of everything that has been named: God. Tao is "beginningless, incomprehensible, indescribable, an ever-transforming essence of all things, unifying and underlying the numerous gods and goddesses that are worshipped."[35]

Synchronicity may be just one expression of our spiritual independence of time and space. Just as light has been discovered to be both a wave and a particle, there are aspects of the psyche that are related to the mundane world as we know it through our senses, and other parts that are not restricted to these dimensions. Lao Tzu in the *Tao te Ching* writes:

Close your mouth,
block off your senses,
blunt your sharpness,
untie your knots,
soften your glare,
settle your dust.
This is the primal identity.[36]

My father was sixty-six years old when my mother died. They had been partners in life for forty-seven years and her death left him completely vulnerable. He had taken care of her, had been with her every moment as she wasted away from the deteriorating effects of her leukemia. Very shortly after her death he announced that he was going to Ireland. This was a trip that my parents had planned to take together, but over the years, between one thing and another, they had never gone. Both of my parents are singularly Irish (my mother's name was Mary Catherine Bernadette). My mother's parents and my paternal grandfather were all first-generation Americans, but my father's mother was born and raised in Ireland. She immigrated to the United States as a girl of sixteen when her older sister, who had gone to America several years earlier, was able to send enough money for her passage to New York. I knew how important this trip was to my father, but I was concerned about his being alone with his grief and driving down unfamiliar country roads in the dark. I suggested that he wait until the spring, when Ireland is green and beautiful, instead of going during this gray November, when it would be chilly and damp. I was hoping he would wait until one or another of our family could accompany him. But he insisted that this was the time and that his grief was quite portable. He could simply take it with him. On more like a pilgrimage than a trip, he left with a one-way ticket to Dublin, carrying with him my mother's rosary beads and a picture of his mother, both of which he wanted to bury near Galway Bay. With a promise to return before my Aunt Teresa and Uncle George's family Christmas party about six weeks off, he boarded a plane at Dulles Airport and left for the country of his ancestors.

With no itinerary and no particular plan of action, he arrived in Ireland. After landing at Shannon Airport he went to get a room at Fitzgerald's across from Bunratty Castle. The hotel had no vacancies, so he asked the young woman at the front desk if she could recommend a bed-and-breakfast. He wanted to meet and stay with local people rather than stay at inns and hotels that catered to tourists, anyway. "Yes, there are some good bed-and-breakfasts in Bunratty," the young woman replied. "I recommend that you stay at Mary Kelly's. She has a wonderful B-and-B." My father was stunned by her reply. My mother's maiden name was Mary Kelly.

Two days later he rented a car and started driving toward the west. He found the small country roads to be poorly marked and wasn't certain that he was heading in the right direction to get to the Salt Hill area of County Galway before dark. Along the way and in a cold, soaking rain, he picked up a young man, a musician, who was hitchhiking along the road. My father is not in the habit of giving rides to strangers but, he later assured me, in Ireland everyone does. Besides, he was lost and this fellow was sure to have a better idea of how to get to Salt Hill than he did. They rode together for several hours, talking along the way about music and Irish politics. By now the rain had stopped, the sun had set, and a full moon filled the sky. Along this little country road the young man said that he had reached his destination, a house about half a mile up a hill. He thanked my dad for the ride as he climbed over a low stone fence that separated the road from the long hill up to the house. "Take the right-hand road," he said as he smiled, winked, then disappeared behind the wall. My father looked at the crossroads in front of him. The right-hand sign was marked "Kilmarnock Road to Salt Hill." In the bright moonlight he could see that the young man had dropped a small gold earring on the road, and raced to the wall to give it to him. "It was just a heartbeat later," my father says as he tells this story. "Even if he ran at full speed, he couldn't have gotten up to that house in the few seconds I was looking at that sign. And I could see clearly all the way up to the house; there was a full moon and it was very bright. But he was nowhere to be seen."

A week or so later, back in Dublin, my father searched for family documents at the Hall of Records. There he found the birth certificate for his mother issued almost a century earlier. Mary Geraghity, Kilmarnock Road, County Galway, Ireland, 1897.

Unable to explain how the young musician could have simply disappeared behind a four-foot wall, and the strange coincidence of being directed toward the same road that led to the place where his mother had been born ninety-five years earlier, my logical, rational businessman of a father simply concluded that he had been in the presence of an angel.

The Butterfly

At a certain moment, as the butterly forms from the caterpillar gruel of the chrysalis, it is possible to discern the shape of its features through the pupal shell. Robert Michael Pyle captures the moment in words both scientific and wondrous: "Black-and-white eyespots on rich brown wings, antennae, great round eyes. At last the mummy case burst open and the long-folded legs, antennae and proboscis sprang forth like watchsprings unloosed. I was alarmed at the sight of the wings—all wet and crumpled and tiny. But the insect clung to the now-paled and empty case on its withered leaf, it began to wave the wings gently and pump the fluid from its swollen abdomen into their veins. The wings expanded, and in an hour or so they had assumed their true shape and the crisp condition necessary for flight. The butterfly stretched its tongue, linked the two halves together, and coiled it safely between its furry palpi. A drop of reddish fluid came out of the tip of the abdomen. It was ready to go."[37]

This "bloodletting," the last symbolic act of the sacrifice involved in its metamorphosis, often occurs during the first flight of the butterfly. After releasing the cumbersome earthbound body of the caterpillar, it moves toward the future as a different being than the one that began its life cycle. Nature has provided the ingredients for survival by increasing its versatility, adaptability, and ability to cope with the demands of the insect environment.

Similarly, the first half of life makes its own demands on human beings. As we pass through childhood and adolescence, we are molded by our family and the values of our society into individuals who will carry forward the ideals of our tribe or culture and create a new generation of progeny to carry on after we are gone. Most societies are so completely aware of the emerging and new demands of the adolescent/young adult, that initiation rites are a universal part of the passage from childhood to adulthood. Whether an adolescent celebrates a bar mitzvah, sets forth on a vision quest, slays his first animal, or has her skin tattooed with tribal symbols, these ceremonies leave no doubt in the mind of the initiate that the link to childhood has been definitively, and often painfully, severed.

As young adults we direct our energy toward our survival without the containment of childhood and our family of origin. At this point we are driven to the creation and nurturance of the next generation of the species. Both survival and procreation are strongly driven by biology, and in the human case, these take the form of establishing a job or career, preparing a foundation of financial and social security, and, for the majority of people, marriage, reproduction, and parenting children. The ruling archetypes for this period of life have to do with erotic love, bonding, and parenthood for the most part. A sense of personal identity is necessary and critical for these things to take place, and in general, we develop a self-definition that highlights our strengths and minimizes our weaknesses. Our sense of who we are and our role in society allows us to focus our attention on the accomplishment of these necessary aspects of life's first half. The intensity of a deep inner life, the emergence of the Self, and the pursuit of meaning are not developmental necessities at this time. In fact, undue attention to these things may preclude the successful accomplishment of more immediate maturational requirements.

Jung believed that the emergence of the Self and the longing for meaning could actually serve neurotic purposes if embarked on too early in one's life. They may serve as a defense against the necessary developmental tasks of the young adult: his or her cultural adaption and the full consolidation of identity. Furthermore, the numinous power of what is revealed through the consciousness of the Self must be supported by a strong sense of ego-identity. This ego strength is a necessary container for the powers that are unleashed through a heightened awareness of the Self, and in its absence, inflation and even psychosis are distinct possibilities. *The successful completion of the developmental challenges of the first half of life prepares us for the realities of the midlife passage.* A certain level of maturity, responsibility, and experience is required to traverse the abyss and resurrection of the chrysalis. Jung recognized the need for this psychological and experimental preparation for the tasks of midlife, and wrote: "Anyone who is destined to descend into a deep pit had better set about it with all the necessary precautions rather than risk falling into the hole backwards."[38]

Recognizing that certain kinds of wisdom, bodies of knowledge, and social roles should only be undertaken during life's second half, some cultures prohibit these among their younger members. In fact, in more "primitive" societies older people are almost always the custodians of the laws and mysteries of the tribe. For example, studying the Kabbalah, a collection of texts that contain Jewish mystical thought, is limited to people who have reached the age of forty, have been married, or have raised one child to the age of twelve. One must have reached the "Householder Stage" in Hinduism in order to study the body of knowledge that constitutes their mystical and spiritual teachings. Many ancient cultures restricted the practice of shamanism to women who have passed through menopause because they, unlike younger women, "held the wise blood inside."[39] In many societies the mystical healing and spiritual powers of shamans are limited to members of the group who are in their middle years. The !Kung tribe of Africa and the Maori of New Zealand limit the role of medicine men and women to those who are middle-aged and older. The Kirghiz of Afghanistan believe that a true healer must be at least thirty years of age.[40]

Interestingly, shamanic initiations or "creative illnesses" quite often take the form of the midlife transformation within the chrysalis. The themes of a descent to the underworld filled with pain and destruction, followed by life-death-rebirth and the endowment of the initiate with potent healing powers, form a common cultural myth throughout the world. The alchemists, whom Jung admired and studied, wrote about the process of transformation of lead into gold. Jung considered this an excellent metaphor for the psychological process of midlife, and in fact, it is quite similar to shamanic initiation. In alchemy, the first step is the black phase *(negredo),* during which everything is broken down to its primary elements. This is followed by the white phase *(albedo)*, which involves the purification of these primary elements. Finally there is the red phase *(rubedo),* which involves reclaiming passion. Psychiatrist and writer Allan Chinen concludes, "Alchemy thus offers a dramatic metaphor for midlife. The transmutation of base elements like lead into noble metals like gold reflects the challenge of the middle years:

to transform the dark side of life—jealousy, death, and suffering—into the wisdom and generativity of maturity."[41]

Jung was well aware that this alchemical transformation was not for the young, and he recognized that the life cycle and life span of most species revolved around their biological development and the reproduction of the next generation. It was this awareness that initiated his questing into the meaning and purpose behind life's second half. He wrote, "A human being would certainly not grow to be seventy or eighty years old if this longevity had no meaning for the species. The afternoon of life must have significance of its own and cannot be merely a pitiful appendage of life's morning."[42]

Jung posits that the function of the second half of life is to sustain the culture and provide repositories of wisdom through the fullest expression of our humanity as we move through the process of individuation. The Self desires an inner integration; we want to move toward wholeness and unity within ourselves. Through the rigors of this journey we emerge transformed and capable of contributing in new ways to our community, and the world. In Jung's view the midlife transition is seen as a normal, appropriate, and necessary part of adult development. Jung writes: "This is what happens very frequently about the midday of life, in this wise our miraculous human nature enforces the transition that leads from the first half of life to the second. It is a metamorphosis from a state in which man is only a tool of instinctive nature, to another in which he is no longer a tool, but himself: a transformation of nature into culture, of instinct into spirit."[43]

The passage through midlife and the process of aging are guided by a very different archetype than the hero of our youth. A powerful archetypal image in midlife is that of the Wise Old Man. This psychic personification Jung identified as spirit, especially as known through wisdom and knowledge, Logos in its many forms. The qualities of this archetypal form include knowledge, reflection, insight, wisdom, cleverness, and intuition. The archetype operates equally for both men and women, and is experienced as a guide and instructor. Merlin of the Arthurian legends represents the Wise Old Man archetype. In a more contemporary vein we can look to Obe Won Ben Kenobi and Yoda as they instruct Luke Skywalker in the Star Wars trilogy of films. As these characters demonstrate, the archetype depends upon knowledge and a ripened wisdom gathered from experience and living life.

Like Jung, psychiatrist Erik Erikson felt that a certain level of maturity must be reached before an individual can establish a sense of *generativity*, which he described as "the concern in establishing and guiding the next generation . . . the concept is meant to include such more popular synonyms as productivity and creativity."[44] Unless the individual recognizes and acts on this responsibility, he or she falls into a pervading sense of stagnation, boredom, and interpersonal impoverishment. At midlife, we are on the cusp of becoming the elders of our tribe and as such have a set of tasks and opportunities that are quite different from the ones of our youth. To Erikson, the accomplishment of the developmental task of generativity versus stagnation is what adds a sense of meaning and purpose to one's life.

Viktor Frankl writes, "One should not search for an abstract meaning of life. Everyone has his own specific vocation or mission in life to carry out a concrete assignment which demands fulfillment."[45] Frankl believed that human beings experience meaningfulness in their lives when they create a work or a deed rather than explore the idea of meaning in the closed confines of the psyche alone. He liked to say, "Live as if you were living already for the second time and as if you had acted the first time as wrongly as you are about to act now."[46] He was calling for a set of values that incorporates the idea of action as well as generativity.

Following her transformational experience on the small Caribbean island off the coast of Grenada, Paule Marshall's character Avey Johnson has truly come home to herself. She cannot return to the life she left, because it no longer exists: she has been changed, transformed into another person. Like the caterpillar's meltdown in the chrysalis, the old Avey exists no more. She realizes that she must return to her history, her own sense of self and who she is. This decision, however, will not just take the form of new insight. Instead it will manifest itself in a will and a wisdom to live that new understanding and to teach those values to younger people.

> Each summer [Avey Johnson] would ask that her two grandsons be sent to spend time with her in Tatem, especially the youngest one, who had known the value of a dime-store xylophone. If forced to, she would be as tyrannical in demanding that they be sent as her great-aunt had been with her. . . .
>
> And at least twice a week in the later afternoon, when the juniper trees around Tatem began sending out their cool and stately shadows, she would lead them, grandchildren and visitors alike, in a troop over to the Landing.
>
> "It was here that they brought them," she would begin—as had

been ordained. "They took them out of the boats right here where we're standing. . . ."[47]

The emergence of the Self, like the novel vantage point of the airborne butterfly, fills us with a heretofore unknown point of view. We may experience a new humility as a result of the stripping away of our arrogance, pride, and egocentricity, but with it a new appreciation of our own intrinsic worth and the contributions we can offer in the creation of a better world. We are developing character and grace. Our sense of alienation is replaced with a deeply felt empathy for other people and for all of life. At midlife we are opening our hearts and souls to the unconditional love of self, other human beings, and life itself. With that power, we can begin to let go of our need for negative judgments and the demands for perfection instead of truth in ourselves and others. Stripped of our arrogance and illusions, we can more easily feel the connection with the humanity of others, no matter how different from us they may appear to be. Mother Teresa noted: "In this life we cannot do great things. We can only do small things with great love." And this compassion will be expressed in a newfound sensitivity to life and reflected in a greater sense of gentleness and patience. Meaningfulness itself is always initiated through love. "Love," wrote Frankl, "is the only way to grasp another human being in the innermost core of his personality."[48]

As we sense our belonging to the human tribe and to all of life, we may discover or rediscover our relationship to some higher power, some transpersonal force that we may call God. Having faced the trial by fire, we may look to the future, and all its inherent pain and loss, with a newfound courage and fearlessness. Even death itself does not appear such a threat now that who we believed ourself to be has been dissolved, certainly a death of sorts, in the darkness of the chrysalis. Most people at midlife find new comfort and conviction that some form of spirit life surrounds and follows our temporal human existence, though these concepts may vary greatly from person to person. Jung believed in God so strongly that over the front door of his home near Kusnacht in Switzerland he had engraved, *Vocatus atque non vocatus, Deus aderit* ("Called or not called, God will be there").

Having been in the quiet, solitary space of the chrysalis, so integral a part of the midlife passage, many people report an awakening in their sensory perceptions as they emerge: colors are brighter, sounds clearer, aromas more distinct. "It is like everything was turned up a notch," was the way that one of my clients described it. Emily Dickinson simply wrote: "Then Sunrise kissed my Chrysalis—And I stood up—and lived—"[49] Through this opening up to sensation we discover that life is vested with soul and purpose in its daily little moments. Meaning is not limited only to grand schemes or felt only by those who win the Nobel Peace Prize, write the great American novel, or find a cure for cancer or AIDS. Meaning is derived by living life in each moment with genuineness and depth. Thomas Moore recognizes this when he writes, "When you look closely at the image of soulfulness, you see that it is tied to life in all its particulars—good food, satisfying conversation, genuine friends, and experiences that stay in the memory and touch the heart."[50]

I can hardly remember what the source of my happiness or sense of meaning was before I turned forty. But I do know that my life now is filled with enormous riches, and I'm struck by how simple most of them are. Blessed with a wealth of good friends, many of whom live on the Outer Banks of North Carolina, I find myself there more often than not on weekends. Early in the morning I will make a cup of Earl Grey decaffeinated tea and head toward the beach just after sunrise. My favorite companion, our yellow lab Dorothy, is beside herself as she sees the leash come off its hook. She is a true lover of sand and water and knows that in just a few minutes she will have the full freedom to experience both. She quivers and shakes, emitting a high-pitched whining sound before we cross the one street between our house and the ocean. As we round the sea oats and sand dunes that offer at least a little protection for the old salt-worn cottages, she can contain herself no longer. By now she is hooting and hollering and, in spite of her status as a shaky graduate of obedience school, she pulls at the lead and I am in a desert Iditarod, being pulled over the top of the dune and hoping that the hot tea will mostly splash away from my hand.

The beach at this time of day, and especially in the fall, is usually deserted. I may see a few fisherwomen or men or an occasional jogger, but generally there is just the broad expanse of white sand and the ocean in one of its many moods. On some mornings, especially when the wind is out of the northeast, the water will be choppy and dark. On other days there is barely a wave, the water is blue-green, and pelicans are doing their straight-down dive, hunting for breakfast.

At the top of the dune I release Dorothy from her restraint and she takes off toward the water. I am awed by her grace and speed (she is the fastest dog I have ever seen run on sand, with the exception of a young greyhound we encountered once in Virginia Beach). She leaps into the water and dodges the waves with such abandon and delight that I cannot keep my eyes off her. In these moments, I am fully content and happy. I feel a deep sense of connection with Dorothy and everything around me. I have learned, during this middle part of my life, to take meaning where I find it, and I'm finding it more often these days in small moments that touch my heart.

Transformation at midlife demands the letting go of all our illusions and false beliefs, but it is only when we accomplish this that we become free to see the world as it really is. During this passage many people discover, as I did, that life holds beauty, enrichment, and happiness in everyday experience, often coupled with a newfound sense of imagination, creativity, exploration, adventure, and spontaneity in appreciating what is around us. Many of the world's most notable talents who have given us the most remarkable expressions of soul in music, art, and literature began this part of their journey following an immersion in the chrysalis and moving on to the second half of life.

There is much yet to do. Life's afternoon is just beginning. The Self is continuing its emergent path toward individuation and actualization. And the journey will be infinitely richer and more authentic if we follow a path with heart. Sorcerer Don Juan, in his teachings to Carlos Castaneda, put it this way: "Look at every path closely and deliberately. Try it as many times as you think necessary. Then ask yourself and yourself alone one question. This question is one that only a very old man asks. My benefactor told me about it once when I was young and my blood was too vigorous for me to understand it. Now I do understand it. I will tell you what it is: Does this path have a heart? If it does, the path is good. If it doesn't it is of no use."[51]

Introduction to Section Two: Strategies for Growth in Midlife

How is it possible to follow a path with heart in a society that does not or cannot embrace the reality of one's inner life? How is it possible to experience ourselves as part of a great cosmic plan when our attentions are constantly focused on the mundane realities of our everyday life? Our materialism, rationalism, determinism, and pragmatism argue strongly against the need for any kind of understanding of or connection to the life of the Self and the soul.

Following a path with heart means to live one's individual life following the measured steps of one's own internal drummer, with consciousness, wisdom, commitment, courage, compassion, and love. It requires facing the realities of life's second half and all its pain and possibility with what Don Juan and Jack Kornfield, among others, call a "warrior's spirit."[1] The assumptions about ourselves and the nature of reality that we must question are so fundamental to our understanding of the world that to alter them requires a "paradigm shift"[2] in our consciousness, a major change in the way we think about ourselves, our possibilities, and meaning in our life. At midlife, nothing less is being asked of us than that we question all of the beliefs that seemed to hold true during the first half of our life.

The development of our full, authentic personality, the process of individuation, is the natural inclination and tendency for all living things. Jung understood the universal nature of this process when he wrote, "Individuation is an expression of that biological process—simple or complicated as the case may be—by which every living thing becomes what it was destined to become from the beginning."[3] But while it may appear that we can simply sit back and let our personality, wisdom, and consciousness expand and grow, this is not true. The conscious experience of individuation, of self-knowing, *requires our active participation.*

The great Sufi master Hazrat Inayat Khan, who introduced many important teachings to the West in the early twentieth century, offers an excellent metaphor for the necessity of our conscious contributions to the development of our personality and of our task of individuation. Noting that the "art of personality" fulfills the purpose of life and that we are all born with a personality, he wrote, "But even a diamond must be cut. It has the light in it, yet cutting is required: it cannot show that glow and that brilliancy before it has been cut. The same thing applies to personality."[4]

Whether the midlife passage is simply a life event that must be endured or becomes an exhilarating opportunity for change and enlightenment will be determined by our attitudes toward it and our willingness to participate in our own growth. This book does not pretend to tell you what to do or how to do it—your journey is uniquely your own and no one can describe or define for you what shape your diamond will take as you refine it. But there are some tools that are helpful in the process of cutting and polishing the raw stone into one of brilliance and light. Drawn from a variety of cultural traditions and repositories of wisdom, the approaches to a path with heart that are described in the following chapters are offered simply as *tools* that can help you to make the most of the midlife passage.

While there are many, many roads to consciousness and growth of the authentic Self, I have chosen to include the following approaches because they are applicable to our daily lives. Suggestions and exercises at the end of each chapter provide specific recommendations for integrating these ideas into one's life.

Chapter 6 discusses the importance of relationships in our lives and their power in supporting and nourishing the midlife journey. All forms of relationships, including those with spouses, lovers, family, friends, and community, provide external containers for the critical changes that occur at midlife.

Chapter 7 provides an overview of the importance of dreams and dreamwork as a direct path to the unconscious and to a better understanding of the promptings of the Self at midlife.

Chapter 8 argues for the importance of creative expression of the midlife experience. Issues regarding work and vocation are included.

Chapter 9 emphasizes the importance of introspection, reflection, and "beingness." It discusses the importance of meditation and prayer at midlife.

Chapter 10 discusses a new appreciation of our physical selves. Honoring the body, caring for it, and understanding the language of its symptoms are especially important during the midlife transition.

Chapter 11 is written expressly for people interested in understanding and helping a loved one through the midlife passage.

Finally, Chapter 12 offers some concluding thoughts about the importance of heightened consciousness at midlife, the need to reintegrate the instincts and other lost qualities of the Self, and the power of consciousness to change not only ourselves but the world and universe in which we live. Transformation at midlife offers unparalleled opportunities for a rich, meaningful second half of life.

CHAPTER 6

Building Containers, Healing Relationships, and Finding Our Neighbors

The day will come when, after harnessing the winds, the tides, and gravitation, we shall harness for God the energies of love. And on that day, for the second time in the history of the world, man will have discovered fire.

PIERRE TEILHARD DE CHARDIN, *THE EVOLUTION OF CHASTITY*, 1972[1]

I REMEMBER what a joy it was to participate in producing a concert of the internationally renowned group Sweet Honey in the Rock at a small church in Washington, D.C., in 1981. The five African-American women who make up this a cappella quintet blend their voices with such power that I was certain, on that night, that the spire of the church was going to shoot off into the starry night like a rocket. "We have ignition," I thought as the church began to pulsate with the vibrations and rhythms of people clapping and swaying to the energy of the music. Having been raised in the rock 'n' roll generation, I was far more accustomed to blasting music generated by walls of speakers and electric guitars. I was astonished at the strength of the sound that was being created only by the voices of these women and a few hand-held percussion instruments.

More than a decade later I attended a workshop conducted by Dr. Ysaye Barnwell at the Common Boundary Conference in Crystal City, Virginia, in 1993. The title of the workshop was intriguing: "The Power of a Vocal Community."[2] In addition to her work in speech pathology and her interests in computer technology, Ysaye Barnwell is also an actress, singer, arranger, and composer. Most important, as a member of Sweet Honey in the Rock since 1979, she was one of the women who had almost blown the top off that church twelve years earlier.

The room in Crystal City was filled with a wide spectrum of people: men and women, old and young (with many of us in between), black, white, and Asian. With the exception of one man who I later learned was a cantor in a synagogue and one woman who often sang in a choir, none of us were experienced singers. But the conference program said that no auditions or prerequisites, other than a willingness to participate, were necessary.

The first things we learned in the workshop were some very simple parts to an African rhythmic chant. "Doom ba, doom ba do ba, doom ba do ba," some of us sang, as new elements were being introduced: "Clang, clang, clang," "Be dat doom da, be dat doom da," "Doom down down down, gadegadega." We were told that we could select any part we wanted. If we normally sang high but always wanted to sing bass, we were invited to do so. If we were normally at the lower end of the register but had our hearts set on singing soprano, we were to go right ahead. We were, however, collectively responsible for all the parts. We could not abandon our part unless it was being carried out by someone else.

We warmed up our pipes, but the result was a mushy, disharmonious mess of a song. "Oh," Ysaye Barnwell said with a sly smile. "I didn't give you the rest of the instructions yet." She emphasized the importance of clear vision of one another: we needed to see what the others were doing. Most important, she said, we had to learn to listen. Because when we understood the whole song, we would hear, from what others were singing, exactly where we should be in our own part. We were to listen to the cutting sound that is often a part of these polyrhythmic songs; we were to listen to the person next to us and to the overall sound.

She taught us how songs from African traditions, as well as a great deal of Eastern music, were organic. They were a reflection of the way that art and soul is experienced in everyday life. People sing these songs as they work in fields, prepare dinner, tend to children, or craft objects from clay or metal. Art, in these cultures, is not restricted to something to be hung on a museum wall or placed on a shelf. Music is not something written down and practiced until the performance is perfect, as is the case with most Western and European traditions. Instead a song or rhythm naturally emerges and is changed with the addition of each new voice. Most songs create their sound through the integration and weaving of the different parts into a whole. Only rarely does any one voice carry the melody: instead melody is created by the blending of the different parts. In this combination of polyrhythms a singular and mysterious sound is created. "It is the sound where nobody is singing. This is the sound that you hear, the thing that you experience, when everything comes together perfectly," Ysaye Barnwell told us. This sound is created, she explained, only when everything is in correct relationship to everything else. "That is the magic, the deepest thing that could happen. And that is what we listen for." We needn't worry about it, she said. We would hear it. We would feel it. What she was talking about would become absolutely clear to us.

We began singing again, starting roughly as before, but we had some new approaches this time. We knew we had to listen, and we were expecting that somewhere amid this confusion of sound we would find that magic center, the "total coordination" that would be that place where nobody was singing.

After just a moment or two, as we followed our new instructions, our song started to change. We began to feel a certain confidence in singing our parts and were less distracted by the different sounds coming from other parts of the room. In fact, we were beginning to hear our relationship to those other parts. It was possible to discern the exact sound, coming from the group of people across from us, that signaled our group to begin our part. And then we came to the enchanted part, as Ysaye Barnwell had said we would. Magical and stirring, this was the moment when we were singing in perfect relationship to each other. I could see it from the faces of my fellow singers. People were smiling and singing louder, and more than a few of us had tears in our eyes. Everyone could feel the rhythm that was no longer just coming from our voices but from our souls. Less than half an hour before, we had entered the room as strangers; now, we were joined in a deeply intimate experience. The music, coming only from our human voices, created beauty and union out of our different parts. That wondrous sound, in fact, *depended* upon the diversity of our individual rhythms. The idea of being one with everything that is, despite our differences, was no longer an abstract spiritual or philosophical principle. We were living it, singing it, and everyone knew that we were in the midst of something magical and mysterious.

My experience in Ysaye Barnwell's workshop has stayed with me—I think of it almost every day. Without having to use words, she produced a powerful metaphor for the idea of a human *container*. The word "container"—which comes from the Latin *continere,* meaning "to hold together, enclose or restrain"—while used in everyday language to refer to jars, bottles, or boxes, is rarely used to describe the kind of surrounding environment that we need in order to live as human beings. Jung used the idea of the container and the contained in his reflections on the unconscious roles that so often emerge in marriage. I am using the word here to refer to relationships of all types, as well as behaviors and beliefs that have the power to enclose us, surround us, and hold us together. The path to oneself does not occur in a vacuum. These relationships are the vessels in which our process of individuation will be carried out at midlife. Eleanor Bertine, an early proponent of Jungian thought in the United States, captured the critical importance of human relationships in the individuation process. She wrote: "It is possible to develop a certain amount of consciousness in relation to things and inanimate nature, and even more in relation to animals, where feeling may be strongly touched. But only another human being can constellate so many sides of ourselves, can react so pointedly, and can bring to consciousness so much of which we had been unaware."[3]

As social animals, human beings require a sense of belonging to a family, group, or community. Abraham Maslow, in his early work, discussed a hierarchy of human needs. To Maslow, after our most basic needs are met—food and shelter, protection from wild animals and the environment—human beings must satisfy their needs for love, affiliation, acceptance, and belonging.[4] This sense of belonging is not about "fitting in," conforming, or moving up some invisible but strongly felt social ladder; it is instead the deep, resonating sense that we are part of a group that surrounds us and holds us with love. Without it, we wander and question our own sense of identity and worth. Psychoanalyst and writer Rollo May simply says, "Man needs relations with other people in order to orient himself."[5] From a biological and evolutionary point of view, human beings are more like dogs and wolves than solitary animals like most of the big cats. Human infants are born in a more helpless state than any other life-form on the earth, and we remain relatively helpless creatures. We could not protect ourselves or survive without the surrounding presence of our tribe.

A sense of oneself as contained by the human energy of love and compassion is psychologically and spiritually necessary throughout our lives. The concept of romantic love, love touched by Eros, is one important expression of love—but it is only one form of it. Jung wrote: "The unrelated human being lacks wholeness, for he can achieve wholeness only through the soul, and the soul cannot exist without its other side, which is always found in a 'You.' "[6]

We may become particularly aware of our lack of meaningful, intimate relationships and containment at times of loss or sorrow. At certain times in our lives, and many of these will occur in midlife, we are pushed to the edge of emotional experience only to realize that we have been working without a net.

"Please spend some time with Sarah this morning if you can," I was asked by one of the nurses at the hospital. I could see that Sarah was sitting quietly in the empty group room looking out the window. Her demeanor was one of sadness and she gently tore at a tissue in her hands. Sarah was a fifty-five-year-old woman who had been admitted to the hospital the night before with a diagnosis of major depression.

I introduced myself and asked if we could talk a little. "Certainly," she replied, and turned toward me.

"Why are you here?" I asked her. She looked back out the window and I saw tears fill her eyes. "I'm depressed. I have no interest in anything. I don't want to get out of bed in the morning. I cry all day long, it seems. I don't feel like I have anything to live for. My children thought that I needed to be in a hospital and my doctor agreed."

"How long have you been feeling this way?" I asked.

"Since October fourteenth," she replied, with such precision and certainty that I almost fell out of my chair. Most people will answer this question with, "I don't really know," "I've always felt depressed," or offer some vague time frame for the onset of their symptoms.

"Did anything in particular happen on October fourteenth?" I asked.

"Of course. I'm not normally like this. My husband died on October fourteenth."

I interviewed Sarah toward the end of November, just six weeks after her husband of almost forty years had died suddenly. Her reaction of sadness and her lack of enthusiasm for life seemed to me to be normal expressions of the grief that she was understandably feeling after a loss of such magnitude. Yet here she was in a psychiatric hospital taking antidepressant medication as if she had an illness.

"Tell me about your husband," I asked her. She brightened immediately. "He was my best friend," she began. She talked almost nonstop for more than an hour and a half, telling stories of how they had met and what kind of man he was. He had been a great practical joker and she shared with me many of his zany pranks on the family. "This was the time of year that we both loved," she said as she began to sob, "Christmas was always a big deal in our family and our children who live in California and Colorado always come home with our grandchildren. He always made special presents for everyone in the family. I just don't know how I will be able to even get through Christmas. I miss him so much."

Sarah had lived through the gut-wrenching death of someone she deeply loved, a kind of loss commonly experienced during the midlife transition. Her grief was completely understandable and could have been experienced quite differently had she been surrounded by comforting people and loved ones, by a container that would have allowed her to live through her sorrow as a normal part of living as a human being. But Sarah had no close friends and was not involved with any community groups or church. Her own parents had died years before, as had most of her older siblings. Her own children lived thousands of miles away. She had no support system, no surrounding sense of others to share her enormous burden: she was not contained.

A few years after meeting Sarah, I was to understand her pain more deeply as my own life was met with the loss of someone I loved dearly. I can still clearly remember the night my mother died. She had been struggling with the terrible effects of leukemia for more than two years, but our family had been able to keep her at home until four o'clock one afternoon when it became clear that she was in the very last stage of her life's journey. My father, brother, and I decided that we needed the help of the hospice group that had been so generous to my family. We consulted with them and listened closely to their suggestions. After much reflection we resolved that we needed to place my mother in a hospice bed at the hospital. We knew that she would be surrounded there by knowledgeable people who could help us care for her and could evaluate and administer medications for the management of any pain she might feel.

An ambulance delivered my mother to the hospice. By this time, she was in a comalike state and unable to communicate. Nevertheless, we continued to talk with her, rub her back, and stroke her hair. I pulled up a chair and read aloud to her from a book that I knew she would have enjoyed. My brother Jim and his children came into the room. At fifteen, Matthew had the outer look of a young man. He was determined to be an adult during all this pain and turmoil, helping where he could. But behind his blue eyes, I could see the same deep sadness and fear that we were all experiencing. Katelyn, only nine and usually a bundle of energy, quietly came to my side and took my hand. The door opened and I saw the familiar faces of my aunts and uncles: my mother's sisters, Teresa and Jeannie, and their husbands, George and Art, more like brothers to my mom than in-laws. No words were spoken. None that I can remember anyway. They went to my mother's side whispering their love and holding her. We formed a circle around her bed, holding each other's hands, and said the rosary in quiet voices.

After midnight my aunts, uncles, and I returned to my parents' home. We planned to sleep for a few hours if we could, shower, and return early in the morning. My brother returned to his home a few miles away. My father stayed at the hospital, saying he would call if there was any change. At this point, we all knew that it was simply a matter of waiting, but we did not know whether my mother's death would be hours or days away. At three-thirty in the morning, the phone rang and I jumped to answer it already knowing that it would be my father. He said quietly, "Your mother's gone." I told him that Jim and I were leaving for the hospital immediately. My brother picked up the phone on the first ring. "I'll be right there," he said, without even asking who it was. It was a clear, starry November night with a full harvest moon in the sky. We held hands as we drove back to the hospital. I felt comforted and protected just sitting next to my brother, though neither of us said a word.

The next few days were a blur of old familiar faces: my family; good friends from out of town, most of whom had never known my mother; my mother's best friend, Fran; some cousins and relations I see only a few times a year at holiday gatherings. And there were strangers: friends and colleagues of my brother or father, neighbors of my parents whom I had never met. My large extended family descended on Fairfax County en masse. My cousins with their partners and their children rented rooms at local hotels, ran errands, played in the backyard with their young children, who were all decked out in Sunday dresses or tiny suits and ties. Some sat quietly and looked at photographs of earlier days of our family. After my mother's funeral, we went back to my brother and sister-in-law's house. There was sadness and many tears amid the sounds of little children playing, people joking and telling old stories about my mother and her sisters and brothers growing up. There was both life and loss surrounding us. In spite of my aching grief, I knew that I was safe and contained in the energy of the love that filled the house that day. Teilhard de Chardin once wrote that "love is the most universal, the most tremendous and the most mysterious of the cosmic forces."[7] At this moment, I fully understood the mystery and the power of love.

Sarah, at the psychiatric hospital, and I both suffered important losses through death of someone that we loved deeply. And yet we had very different responses. I do not think that I am any wiser or stronger than Sarah, but I did have something that she did not. Unlike Sarah, I had the surrounding containment of love and connection to people to whom I "belonged." But whether or not one has the advantage of durable ties to one's biological family it is essential to belong to some kind of tribe.

The soul of a family, whether related by blood, by the attachments of the heart, or by the sense of belonging to a neighborhood or community, is best expressed in the daily vernacular by the sound of a familiar voice, the touch of a hand, a mutual history and stories, or the sharing of a cup of coffee and crying and laughing together. Thomas Moore writes about the importance of *feeling* our connections with other people: "The family the soul wants is a felt network of relationship, an evocation of a certain kind of interconnection that grounds, roots and nestles. This connectedness doesn't have to be perfect or whole in order to do its business and give its gifts, but it has to be able to stir the imagination and move the emotions in a way that is particular to family."[8]

Each of us makes decisions about what kind of containers we are willing to create in and around our lives. We decide how we will participate in life and serve as containers for other people. Midlife sees our inner world surrounded by the chrysalis, but each of us must also continue to live in an external world during this transformational process, participating in relationships of all types. What we expect of the world is most often what we get. Each of us bears the full responsibility for determining how we will live and how we will meet the realities of our life. We ourselves decide whether we will love and forgive or carry bitterness and anger. We decide whether we will open our hearts to the great human drama or close ourselves off and, instead, inhabit a narrow life devoid of love and authentic relationship. At midlife we can, and usually must, redefine what our containers will be. Some of the most important ones throughout our lives include our marriage or primary relationship, family, friends, neighborhood, and community.

Marriage and Partnership

Victor was shaking and tearful when he told his wife that he wanted a divorce. After a twenty-six-year marriage that had the normal ups and downs of any relationship, he had come to the conclusion that while he cared about and loved his wife, he was no longer "in love" with her. This developing sense of the difference between being "in love" and "loving" became the rationale behind Victor's attraction to a woman with whom he works. Although he has not betrayed his marital vows by infidelity, Victor can't imagine living the rest of his life without the excitement or the passion he feels for this other woman. The conflict that Victor describes, feeling love for a spouse or partner but no longer experiencing the feeling of being "in love," is so frequent at midlife that it has become a stereotypical part of the midlife crisis. But these internal clashes about our marriages or primary relationships are more than just stereotypes. They evoke great anxiety, depression, fear, and pain in the people who experience them. The fact that they are common or "typical" at midlife in no way diminishes the real suffering they cause.

Marital conflict, boredom or ennui, affairs, separation, and divorce are common throughout the life cycle of adults, but they occur with the greatest frequency at midlife and often serve as a primary impetus to the psychological changes of the middle passage. What happens at midlife that causes so many people to want to leave the companionship and stability of a long-term relationship for the adventure and emotional roller coaster of being newly "in love" with someone else? What is the state of many relationships as we enter into the midlife transition? Is it possible to depend on our primary relationship as a container that will see us through the rest of our lives?

Maintaining a long-term, loving relationship requires standing up to both biological processes and the enormous power of that which is unconscious in us. As one writer, Robert Wright, put it: "The good news is that human beings are designed to fall in love. The bad news is that they aren't designed to stay there."[9] Evolutionary psychology suggests that adultery or falling out of love with a long-term mate is "natural" for both men and women. Wright continues, "It is similarly natural to find some attractive colleague superior on all counts to the sorry wreck of a spouse you're saddled with. When we see a couple celebrate a golden anniversary, one apt reaction is the famous remark about a dog walking on two legs: the point is not that the feat was done well but that it was done at all."[10]

According to the ethological views of evolutionary psychology, our shifting attitudes toward our mate are dependent upon the process of natural selection which reinforces behaviors that help spread genes and thus improve the variability and survivability of our species. Research on the human endocrine system and the powerful effects of neurotransmitters on behavior has suggested that "falling in love" is a specific biological as well as psychological experience. Changes in levels of serotonin, dopamine, and phenylethylamine (PEA) have dramatic effects on our limbic system (the area of the brain thought to contain the "pleasure center") and these neurotransmitters are increasingly being identified as having a powerful role in attraction and "love."[11] Could it be that long-term relationships create a kind of drug-induced tolerance or habituation in our attraction to our mate/lover over time? If so, is it inevitable that all relationships must break apart at some point or that the partners must endure a passionless, empty marriage that holds together only for the sake of children or external social and financial reasons?

We have embraced the concept of romantic love with such fervor that it is easy to forget that this notion is a relatively new phenomenon in Western culture. Although passionate, romantic love is a natural human experience—it has been evidenced throughout the ages and is described in the earliest writings of humankind[12]—the ideal of romantic love as the basis for a marital commitment has only been a part of our value system since the Middle Ages. Prior to that time, most marriages were arranged according to the prevailing norms of their larger culture. As Jungian analyst and writer Robert Johnson points out, modern romantic love is based on symbols of idealism and fantasy. Johnson writes, "Its model was the brave knight who worshipped a fair lady as his inspiration, the symbol of all beauty and perfection, the ideal that moved him to be noble, spiritual, refined and high-minded. In our time we have mixed courtly love into our sexual relationships and marriages, but we still hold the medieval belief that true love has to be the ecstatic adoration of a man or woman who carries, for us, the image of perfection."[13]

This notion of love as ideal and perfect contains the principles of chivalry, which value bravery, honor, gallantry, purity, and courtesy. It is important to remember that this ideal and spiritual love was, in its clearest sense, asexual and highly romanticized. The bold knight carrying his lady's flag in battle is an archetypal image that doesn't leave any room for the realities of relationship or life together. It cannot accommodate the daily life of a couple raising children, paying bills, coming home from work exhausted, and still needing to cook dinner or mow the lawn. At midlife, especially, it cannot hold the reality of an aging knight and princess. Even in the absence of infidelity, separation, or divorce, at midlife many marriages suffer from a deeply felt boredom and staleness. A cartoon in a recent issue of the *New Yorker* emphasizes the ennui that characterizes many marriages at midlife. The drawing shows a husband and wife sitting in separate chairs, oblivious to each other, reading magazines. "Did we ever go through with that divorce we were talking about?" he says to her.[14] Many people long for the drama, the romantic vision, of relationships that is played out *ad nauseam* on our movie and television screens. We easily forget that these dramas are created in Hollywood and are imaginary and invented instances of "ideal love." For the most part, they fail to include real-life human experience.

When we "fall in love," we see the object of our affection as perfect and numinous, perhaps even worthy of our worship. Our beloved is not a human being, after all—we are caught in a web of magical proportions.

Romantic love has became the religion of Western culture. Instead of exploring our own inner lives and recognizing the need for an individual, spiritual relationship with our Self and the Divine, we too often imagine the Divine to be located in physical people—in the object of our love. Robert Johnson, focusing on a man's projection on his lady love, writes, " 'True love' was not the ordinary human love between husband and wife but rather the worship of a feminine saviour, a mediator between God and man, who waited in the sky to welcome the 'pure' with a holy kiss and lead him or her into the Realm of Light. By contrast with this 'pure' love, ordinary human sexuality and marriage were bestial and unspiritual."[15]

Because our beloved is far more a function of our own projections and illusions than a real human being, we can find ourselves "falling in love" with almost anyone who has enough characteristics, or "hooks," that can hold our projection, even if only for a short time. Our friends may shake their heads and wonder, "What does he see in her?" We may wonder about our friends and the "choices" they make when they are stung by Aphrodite and fall in love even at great sacrifice to their existing reality and relationships. Carson McCullers understood the truth of soul-projections in love when she wrote about it in *The Ballad of the Sad Café:* "The most outlandish people can be the stimulus for love. The preacher can love a fallen woman.

The beloved may be treacherous; greasy-headed and given to evil habits. Yes, and the lover may see this as clearly as anyone else—but that does not affect the evolution of his love one whit. A most mediocre person can be the object of a love that is wild, extravagant, and beautiful as the poison lilies of the swamp. A good woman may be the stimulus for a love both violent and debased, or a jabbering madwoman may bring about in the soul of someone a tender and simple idyll therefore the value and quality of any love is determined by the lover himself."[16]

Understanding and taking responsibility for our projections is a critical task of self-development. We project our needs, beliefs, and unexpressed aspects of the Self onto our expectations for parents, children, kin, neighbors, and even strangers. Projections affect *all* of our relationships with other people and are not limited only to those directed toward our beloved. But the sheer power of the archetypal images for romantic love demands that our unconscious projections for the beloved be played out on the main stage, the center ring, of our experience.

Through the projections we make on our beloved we are, psychologically, seeking our own lost soul. If there is to be any hope for the longevity of our primary relationship it is necessary to withdraw our projections. *The work of individuation and understanding our own soul is an inner process and not an outer one.* The psychological and spiritual demands of midlife require that we take on the responsibilities of maturity and stop depending on our partner to live out for us the aspects of our humanity that we are not living for ourselves. Understanding and becoming conscious of the realities of our romantic relationships then becomes a psychological path toward the recognition and experience of one's own internal feminine (anima for men) or the internal masculine (animus for women). In this view, our primary relationship becomes the alchemical *vas,* a crucible in which our path to individuation can take place.

When we withdraw the projections of our soul-image from our spouse or partner we can begin, perhaps for the first time, to see him or her as a real human being. By becoming conscious of our own projections we can cease comparing our real-life spouse or partner to the chivalrous ideal that we believed we fell in love with. And once we have done so, we will understand that our beloved simply reflected back to us a deep longing for our own soul.

The withdrawal of our projections, or what in psychological terminology is called *integration,* is not an easy or all-in-one process. We do not simply get up one day and withdraw our unconscious projections, just as we do not develop wisdom or individuate in a single step. Marie-Louise von Franz, a prolific and brilliant Jungian analyst and writer, likens the process to peeling back the layers of an onion. She writes, "Integration in modern psychology is a remarkable and complicated process in which a hitherto unconscious psychic content is brought repeatedly into the view of the conscious ego and recognized as belonging to its own personality. In this process this content is changed in its functioning and effects."[17]

Von Franz discusses five stages of projection and their withdrawal in her thought-provoking, though difficult book, *Projection and Re-collection in Jungian Psychology*. In the first stage of projection, an individual believes that an unconscious inner experience is, in truth, an outer experience. For example, a person truly accepts that the beloved is perfect in every way. In the second stage, there is a realization, usually a very gradual one, of the disparity between the projected image and the reality of the other person. Von Franz notes that a "differentiation" now takes place. The projections begin to wear thin and the true human limitations of our beloved become clearer to us. In the third stage, we must bring this discrepancy to consciousness and acknowledge the disparity between the projection and the reality. In the fourth stage, we must conclude that we were originally in error about the beloved, that we were under "illusion." Finally, in the fifth stage, consciousness requires that the lover search for the origins of the projected energy with him- or herself. Von Franz rightly observes the unsettling realization that comes with the withdrawal of projections on the beloved: "One would have to reflect on how such an overpowering, extremely real, and awesome experience could suddenly become nothing but self-deception."

But in spite of the difficulties associated with the withdrawal of projections, it is necessary for the health and well-being of our relationships. Projections cannot be expected to go on indefinitely, and so long as we are bound to illusions about our beloved, we will find reasons to disparage the relationship without ever understanding what part of ourselves has been projected. The failure to withdraw our projections accounts for the observation that many relationships end with as much passionate anger as they begin with passionate love. Jung wrote, "Every normal person of our time, who is not reflective beyond the average, is bound to his environment by a whole system of projections. So long as all goes well, he is totally unaware of the compulsive, i.e., 'magical' or 'mystical' character of these relationships. So long as the libido can use these projections as agreeable and convenient bridges to the world, they will alleviate life in a positive way. But as soon as the libido wants to strike out on another path, and for this purpose begins running back along the previous bridges of projection, they will work as the greatest hindrances it is possible to imagine, for they effectively prevent any real detachment from the former object. We then witness the characteristic phenomenon of a person trying to devalue the former object as much as possible in order to detach his libido from it."[18]

The withdrawal of projections and the process of taking responsibility for our feelings rather than projecting onto another the contents of our own inner lives are not just part of a theoretical idea about midlife and relationships. They have real and vital applications to the quality of our everyday interactions and to the durability of our primary relationship over time. Daryl Sharp, a Jungian analyst and writer, describes in his typically humorous way the form that honest relationships take when we withdraw our projections and are finally conscious of who our beloved really is. When we find conflict or problems in our relationships, he advises, we must look at our own participation rather than blaming our partner. He writes, "You work on a relationship by shutting your mouth when you are ready to explode. By not inflicting your affect on the other person. By quietly leaving the battlefield and tearing your hair out. By asking yourself—not your partner—what complex in you was activated, and to what end. The proper question is not, 'Why is he or she doing that to me' or 'Who do they think they are?' but rather, 'Why am I acting in this way?—Who do *I* think they are?' And more: 'What does this say about my psychology? What can I do about it? That is how you establish a container, a personal temenos. Instead of accusing the other person—'You're driving me crazy'—you say to yourself, 'I feel I'm being driven crazy—where, in me, is that coming from?' It is true that a strong emotion sometimes needs to be expressed, because it comes not from a complex but from genuine feeling. This is a fine line to recognize, and that's another value in having a container. You can tell the difference if you have something to slosh things around in. And then you can speak from the heart. . . . On the whole you work on a relationship by keeping your mood to yourself and examining it. You neither bottle up the emotion nor allow it to poison the relationship."[19]

The withdrawing of projections is a difficult and painful process, as we must let go of blaming others for our problems and relinquish our naive hope that salvation from the distressing realities of life will come from another person. We will not be saved but can only save ourselves. The awareness of this truth is a precondition, an absolute requirement, for maturation and individuation at midlife. James Hollis observes, "For every inner child, riddled with fear and looking for rescue from the adult world, there is an adult potentially able to take responsibility for that child. By rendering the contents of the projections conscious, one has taken a large step toward emancipation from childhood."[20] As we come to really know ourselves we will be crossing through the frightening terrain of the shadowlands as well as that of the light. But the process is essential, not only for our process of individuation but also for the creation of authentic relationships, for we can never have a better relationship with another person than the one we have with ourself.

By withdrawing our projections and taking responsibility for our own soul-work, we may discover truly awe-inspiring, authentic love. While our partner may not be the Prince or Princess, we are very likely to find that he or she does embody wondrous *human* qualities, such as nurturance, compassion, responsibility, fidelity, intelligence, courage, humor, and kindness. We may discover that there is great capacity for genuine relationship when we are stripped of our unconscious need for perfection and illusion. We may begin to live the love that the poet Rilke describes when he writes, "Love consists in this, that two solitudes protect, and touch, and salute each other."[21]

Family

The infrastructure of the human family includes the roles for a mother, a father, and children. As a basic form of human relationship, families provide shelter, emotional and physical security, guidance, and love, although cultures throughout the world vary greatly in the expression of these needs. At midlife, the container that is our family includes both the family to which we were born *(family of orientation)* and the family we have created with our partner/spouse *(family of procreation)*. But while many people have been raised in families that provided for their psychological and spiritual needs as young and growing human beings, many others have not. The powerful process of change at midlife often includes the upheaval of the repressed wounds that we have been carrying for a lifetime; and we are certain to meet the ghosts of our past as we explore the terrain of the unconscious at midlife. But even relatively stable, loving families are influenced by the unconsciousness and distorted values of our culture. In fact, in a patriarchal culture such as ours, which has relegated the feminine principle—the Yin—to our collective shadow, one may argue that even the best, most psychologically healthy families are not up to the task of providing for all the needs of a human being. One thing is for certain: that in a dysfunctional culture all families are dysfunctional in some ways. Certainly some families are better able to provide the kind of psychological and spiritual intimacy, love, and support necessary to contain the sacred human need for belonging, while others fail miserably at these tasks. But at midlife, regardless of the relative health of our family of origin, there is a need to look back, to understand where we came from and how we are contained by our family. We will ask the questions: Who is (or was) my family? What kind of container does this family provide in my life? What did I learn about myself and the world as I grew up?

Ellen was raised in an extremely disturbed family, though on the surface they appeared to be normal and happy, raising children in the 1950s. Although the extent of dysfunction, pathology, and cruelty in Ellen's family is not the norm, her story shows clearly how the past may accompany us through our lives. After a devastating series of losses in midlife, Ellen attempted suicide by swallowing hundreds of pills and then slashing her wrists. After her suicide attempt, images of the past surfaced every night in her dreams. She vividly recalled her mother's physical and verbal abuse of her and her sisters. Her mother would constantly tell Ellen and her two sisters that she hated them and wished they had never been born. On many occasions her mother would scream that she couldn't take it anymore and was leaving. She would then hide in the cellar while the children frantically called out for her and stood by the window waiting for her return. Ellen's mother had died several years earlier, and, by Ellen's own admission, she had never grieved for her.

Ellen's father had also been physically and verbally abusive to his children. "I hate him," she says simply. He is now in his nineties; a series of strokes have left him without the ability to recognize her or communicate. She has not visited him in years. She knows that her father will die before too long but rightly understands that "nothing will really change when he's gone."

Ellen has been carrying severe and painful wounds from her childhood experiences. She knows this intellectually and understands why she has been unable to create strong bonds of intimacy with anyone except her children.

"I knew that I didn't want to be like my parents with my own children. When I was a teenager I made a list of the terrible things they did to us and promised myself that I'd never to do any of those things. I was going to be a very different kind of parent to my kids." Ellen kept that vow with her three daughters. But now her children are grown up and moving on with their lives. Ellen, having been through four marriages, feels alone and "abandoned." Describing a "lump" in her chest and stomach and startled from sleep by terrifying dream images, she says "I can't think of why I should go on."

Ellen's childhood experiences were brutal and sorrowful. Now at midlife, with the exception of her relationships with her children, she is uncontained by any sense of belonging to a family. She travels through life burdened by the slow, dark vibrations of her anger and rage, unconsciously projecting this lack of faith in family onto every potential relationship. Ellen's dysfunctional family continues to influence her present and, undoubtedly, her future.

Our family of origin sets a foundation for how we will see the world and react to it. No other species' offspring have such a long term of dependency on their parents. Because they are unable to care for themselves for so long, biological families have multiple and continuous opportunities to teach them. If we have a relatively healthy family, we will receive a good dose of ego strength and self-value and will be capable of forming relationships with others that are based upon love and mutual respect. Being raised in an abusive or severely impaired family restricts our growth and leaves us with psychological and spiritual wounds. Carson McCullers perceived how the past reflects itself in our present when she wrote, "But the hearts of small children are delicate organs. A cruel beginning in this world can twist them into curious shapes. The heart of a hurt child can shrink so that forever afterward it is hard and pitted as the seed of a peach. Or again, the heart of such a child may fester and swell until it is a misery to carry within the body, easily chafed and hurt by the most ordinary things."[22]

Ellen's family experiences produced a house made of straw as her only containment, barely up to the task of providing shelter in good times. When the winds of change and loss blow in life, as they surely will and especially at midlife, her straw house will offer no protection at all. As long as she remains unconscious of the full extent of her rage and is unable to work through her anger, she will be a pawn of her past. She will continue to believe that she is not worthy of being treated with respect and love. Like a heat-seeking missile, she will be drawn to relationships that reinforce her deeply felt sense of unworthiness and shame. Ellen must rebuild for herself a new container, a new protection that allows her to feel a sense of love and belonging to other human beings. She must experience her anger and rage consciously and then grow past them. She must stop blaming her parents for all that is wrong with her life and begin to take responsibility for her future from this point on. As difficult and improbable as it may seem, Ellen's goals must include forgiveness.

Just as we make projections onto our beloved, we may also place an enormous unconscious burden on our families. Failing to see our families as made up of real, mortal human beings, we may find them sorely lacking when compared to our ideal of a family. The powerful influence of the archetypes is part of these inborn expectations, and two of the most powerful of these archetypes are those for Mother and Father. We were born into the world with an instinctive expectation of what our parents will be to us.

The archetype of Mother, which is contained in all human beings, holds primordial images of chthonic Earth Mothers, fertility goddesses, Sky Mothers and Dark Mothers. We expect Gaia, Anu, Demeter, Kali Ma, Ishtar, the Virgin Mary, and all manner of the feminine and the power of Eros, creation, protection, bounty, selflessness, and infinite nurturance. We are born expecting the feminine side of the Divine to be our mother. Erich Neumann, whose book *The Great Mother: An Analysis of the Archetype* remains the classic work on this subject, observes: "When analytical psychology speaks of the primordial image or archetype of the Great Mother, it is referring, not to any concrete image existing in space and time, but to an inward image at work in the human psyche. The symbolic expression of this psychic phenomenon is to be found in the figures of the Great Goddess represented in the myths and artistic creations of mankind."[23]

We expect our own human mother to embrace the characteristics of the inhuman, divine Great Mother as they are represented in our unconscious: a round, large-breasted woman who can envelop us in her loving arms and protect us with unimaginable power. Like the earth itself, she can give us anything and everything that we need.

But we are not born to the Goddess. We are, instead, birthed by human, mortal women who cannot possibly live up to our archetypal expectations. It is certainly the case that some mothers can provide adequate or "good enough" mothering to children, while others, carrying their own wounds, cannot fulfill even the most basic requirements. Kathie Carlson writes of the long-term injuries that we live with when our mothers have not been able to provide for our basic needs: "We end up disappointed in our mothers, hurt, angry, blaming, needy, raging, yet unable to let go of our need for them. We feel starved emotionally and try to cover that over. We feel terrified of becoming like our mothers and vow to be different with our children. We end up estranged from our mothers and estranged from ourselves. We carry around an unhealed child, a sense of woundedness and of longing that seems to have nowhere to go."[24]

Why is it that while some women are better mothers than others, no human mother can live up to the ideal of our expectations? For three thousand years our culture has venerated the masculine (Yang) way of perceiving the world. This imbalanced adoration of a rational, individualistic set of values has denigrated and reviled the feminine. More than a thousand years before the common era, patriarchy extended its powerful hand and affected all aspects of human life requiring structures of hierarchy, submission, and domination. The infanticide of female infants in many parts of India and China as well as the more subtle expressions of the devaluation of women in more "advanced" societies give concrete evidence to ways in which patriarchy has suppressed the feminine. Riane Eisler, in her book *The Chalice and the Blade,* notes that the powers of patriarchy extend even to our transcendent beliefs about the nature of God. She writes: "A male-dominated and generally hierarchic social structure has historically been reflected and maintained by a male-dominated religious pantheon and by religious doctrines in which the subordination of women is said to be divinely ordained."[25]

In fact, that so many women have been unable to provide adequate mothering is more understandable than how others have been able to be "good enough" mothers under the misguided cultural values that surround our families. The poet Adrienne Rich expresses the annihilation of the feminine and the creation in us of an unhealed, "wildly unmothered" place when she writes: "The woman I needed to call my mother was silenced before I was born."[26] But even this insight into the ways our mothers were shaped by their own experiences and cultures cannot prevent our unconscious, emotional comparison with the ideal, with the archetype that we instinctively expect.

Just as we anticipate the Goddess as our mother, the archetype for the Father has been defined through centuries of belief about the masculine. Expecting a Zeus or a mythical king, we meet instead a masculinity that has been castrated by patriarchy and untempered by the compensating and balancing energies of the feminine. The early stages of twentieth-century feminism drew unfortunate parallels between masculinity and patriarchy, but it is important to keep in mind that they are not the same thing. The masculine, like the feminine, is an inner energy, a form of consciousness. It is what Jung called Logos, and it incorporates judgment, discrimination, reason, and a will to action. Since the dawn of patriarchy, we have not culturally or individually experienced a healthy, authentic masculinity. It has been relegated to the same dark underworld as the feminine by the insistence on power as the overriding force in patriarchal cultures.

Just as we have archetypal expectations for the Mother, we expect the Father to embody the wisdom of Logos, to protect us with an enormous strength, and to hold us as he points toward the horizon and teaches us to navigate by the stars. In every culture the role of husband and father includes the support and protection of the wife and children and provides the masculine linkage to the rest of the community. But as Robert Bly points out in his aptly titled article "The Hunger for the King in a Time with No Father," we are living in a time when "there is not enough father."[27]

In our contemporary society, more than forty percent of American households have no father present. This is a dramatic change in our families: in 1950 less than six percent of children grew up without a father in the home. While the long-term, intergenerational effects of the father's absence on sons and daughters cannot yet be fully known, research has shown that children growing up without fathers are five times more likely to be poor, twice as likely to drop out of high school, and more likely to end up in foster care or juvenile detention facilities. Daughters are three times more likely to bear children out of wedlock, and sons are more likely to become unemployed, break the law, and be uninvolved with their own children when they become fathers themselves.[28]

Patriarchy has taken its toll on all aspects of our families and, as Bly points out, "we see in each succeeding generation less bonding between fathers and their children, with catastrophic results."[29] Unlike the agricultural society that allowed sons and daughters to work side by side with parents in the fields, fathers (and most mothers) commute to distant factories and offices in the pursuit of the American Dream. Bly continues: "But in most families today, the sons and daughters receive, when the father returns home at six, an irritable mood and that is all. The successful father brings home a manic mood, the unsuccessful father depression. What does the son receive? A bad disposition, springing from powerlessness and despair mingled with long-standing shame and the numbness peculiar to those who hate their jobs. Fathers in earlier times could often break through their own defective dispositions by teaching rope making, fishing, post-hole digging, grain cutting, drumming, harness making, animal care, even singing and storytelling."[30]

The days when families spent time around a hearth in conversation seem to have been replaced by an age of silent disconnection around the glowing screen of our television sets. One recent study showed that parents spent 38.5 minutes per week in meaningful conversation with their children. Meanwhile, at least one television set in the typical American household is in use an average of seven hours and 34 minutes a day.[31] How can the soul of relationship be honored when it is ignored and considered insignificant?

Relationships between siblings appear to have been relegated to controlling the "sibling rivalry" that so many families seem to expect children to express. But sibling relationships offer a unique connection because of the shared history. Of all the members of a family, siblings who are close in age have an opportunity for an intimate relationship capable of lasting a lifetime, outliving relationships with grandparents and parents. With the exception of our own children, brothers and sisters will be the family members who can provide solid containment and deep intimacy for our entire lives.

Kinship networks or extended family, prevalent in almost all societies though in greatly varied forms, fulfill critical psychological needs for nurturance and support. But these important relationships are, for many people, absent from our contemporary culture. Writer and futurist Alvin Toffler observed that small nuclear families whose mobility allowed them to follow jobs replaced larger, extended families as economic production shifted from the field to the factory. "Burdened with elderly relatives, the sick, the handicapped, and a large brood of children, the extended family was anything but mobile. Gradually and painfully, therefore, family structure began to change. Torn apart by the migration to the cities, battered by economic storms, families stripped themselves of unwanted relatives, grew smaller, more mobile and more suited to the needs of the new techno-sphere."[32] Some sociologists do not agree that extended families ever really lived up to our idealized view (e.g., *The Waltons*) of these family networks, even in preindustrial Western societies. Regardless of how and when family structure may have changed or how idyllic these extended families really were, close relationships with grandparents, aunts, uncles, nieces, nephews, and cousins have become inconsequential to many American families.[33] For example, Lillian Rubin's research on friendship and kinship revealed that only eight percent of those interviewed even mentioned aunts, uncles, or cousins when asked to describe their family relationships. Fewer still referred to these relationships as "significant."[34]

Many people speak of the demise of the American family, and there is strong evidence that they are right. A return to "traditional" values has become the watchword of the far right and the Christian Coalition, but unfortunately, their call for a return to the values of the past suggests the restoration of patriarchal dogma: rigid role definitions for men and women, inflexibility, unquestioning deference to authority, intolerance, structured beliefs, and the subordination of the feminine. But these are the values that have set us on our descent to begin with. There is nothing to return to. Instead families can attempt to embrace unconditional love and tolerance while continuing to teach and embody loyalty, discipline, kindness, responsibility, courage, and compassion.

The deep and far-reaching turmoil of the midlife transition requires a container of family that can hold our "craziness," and changes with love and compassion. We must not forget the terror and confusion that emerge from the deep confines of the unconscious as the Self attempts to assert itself. "The experience of the Middle Passage is not unlike awakening to find that one is alone on a pitching ship, with no port in sight,"[35] James Hollis writes; and the container of family becomes, during these darkest hours, a reminder that, while there may not be a port in sight, there can be beacons to help us navigate our way home.

Thomas Moore comes closest to describing what we need as the container of family, whether we define family as our blood relations or those people attached to our heart and soul. He writes, "The soul needs a felt experience of family, whether we are children getting most of our family experience at home, or adults looking for a family in the workplace or neighborhood. In the extended sense, 'family' is no mere metaphor, but a particular way of relating that can take many different forms. It always provides a fundamental relatedness that doesn't depend upon attraction or compatibility. . . . When we hope that our nation can hold together as a family, or that the family of nations can live in peace, these are not metaphors, but rather the expressions of a profound need of the soul for a special grounded way of relating that offers deep, unconditional, and lasting security."[36]

Friends

Ralph Waldo Emerson wrote a treatise on friendship in 1841 that still has the capacity to stir the soul. In his essay, Emerson captures the sacredness of friendship by describing it as a gift from God and a "masterpiece of nature." He writes, "I do not wish to treat friendships daintily, but with the roughest courage. When they are real, they are not glass threads or frostwork, but the solidest things we know."[37]

My friend Judy understood that this is so shortly after she was diagnosed with breast cancer in her mid-forties. Her doctors were encouraging and optimistic about a full recovery following a lumpectomy of the tumor. She would need to follow this surgery, however, with chemotherapy and then radiation treatments. Judy lives in a small town in North Carolina and would have to travel about two hours to Virginia Beach to receive treatments. She knew that the trip to the cancer center would be fine but had concerns about the two-hour drive home: she had been cautioned that radiation therapy would be likely to leave her feeling exhausted and nauseous for at least a few days afterwards. Within hours of learning of the situation, more than a dozen friends were in her living room with a calendar and their work schedules. Quickly and efficiently this group of people who love Judy had worked out a system of drivers so that she could be chauffeured to each and every treatment session. Judy was deeply touched by the overwhelming love and grateful for all the support that she received. One of her friends, surprised by her reaction, asked simply, "What did you expect us to do, Judy? We're your friends."

Al had been diagnosed with end-state renal disease and was told that he needed to begin kidney dialysis three times a week. The doctors evaluated his condition and determined that he was in good health, except for his failing kidneys, and a good candidate for a transplant. Luckily, Al had an identical twin brother who would be an ideal organ donor since at the time of his diagnosis, kidney transplantation was in its infancy and donor organs from cadavers were a risky business, highly prone to rejection. Al's twin felt compassion for him but reluctantly refused. He had great fear that kidney disease might run in the family and he might someday need both of his kidneys. In spite of the medical information showing that Al's kidney problem was caused by a viral infection and not genetic, his brother would not consider it. Al then turned to his two other siblings, who refused to discuss the subject and thought he was "selfish" for putting them in the difficult position of turning him down. But Al did have one willing organ donor—his best friend, Jerry. They had been best friends since they lived next door to each other as very young children. How their friendship had thrived was in itself something of a mystery. Their childhood neighborhood was newly integrated racially in the middle 1950s and the area was permeated by both prejudice and violence. Al is white and Jerry is black, but even as children they said, "Who cares?" Throughout the years, they had remained in close touch and often spent time together fishing and helping each other out with household projects. They had been good friends through all the ups and downs of their lives: Jerry was his friend's biggest supporter during Al's difficult divorce; Al acted as job placement specialist, résumé writer, counselor, and general helpmate following Jerry's job layoff and unemployment that lasted almost a year. Medical tests showed that Jerry could not be a kidney donor—they weren't even the same blood type. But it was Jerry who was willing to donate his kidney, not Al's biological family, and it was he who accompanied Al to his dialysis appointments. Years later, when Al did finally receive a kidney transplant, it was Jerry who kept the round-the-clock vigil at Al's bedside during the initial, critical hours following the surgery.

More mysterious than relationships between family and kinfolk, friendships have no formal role in our systems of human connection. There are no a priori expectations about who will become our friend, no clearly defined rules or systems upon which these relationships are based. With only one word for a myriad of different kinds of relationships we emphasize our relative cultural ignorance about the power of friendship. In fact, the word "friend" fails to distingush between the relationships that are transient and superficial (people we may occasionally do things with) and those that will last a lifetime, that are truly attached at the heart. Judith Viorst makes a start in distinguishing the many levels of friendship in a chapter of her book *Necessary Losses* titled: "Convenience Friends and Historical Friends and Crossroads and Cross-Generational Friends and Friends Who Come When You Call at Two in the Morning."[38]

Anthropologists and sociologists use the term "fictive kin" to describe the kind of friends who become part of an extended family network though they are not related by blood, marriage, or adoption.[39] These people seem to me to be the class of friends Viorst is describing as "friends who come when you call at two in the morning." They are the types of friendships that are described in the stories about Judy and Al and Jerry—not a luxury in life but a necessary part of the container that must surround us if we are to live fully.

Research has shown that a lack of friends can create physical problems and emotional voids. Depression, anxiety, sleep disorders, headaches, cardiovascular disease, and numerous other stress-related illnesses have been demonstrated to correspond strongly to a lack of social support.[40] A lack of friends can create loneliness and isolation even among people who are happily married. In old age, friends have been reported to be more important in reducing depression and maintaining a high level of morale than are grandchildren. The emotional support of friends and the link they create to the outside world are considered to be the major form of social support for recently divorced women. Close friends are critical to our well-being throughout our lives.[41]

The archetypal images of Ruth and Naomi, Artemis and Apollo, Philemon and Baucis, Butch Cassidy and the Sundance Kid, all speak to the power of friendship to evoke our sense of loyalty, kinship, and love. Like the Velveteen Rabbit, who becomes real through the love of a little boy who has cherished him through thick and thin, even when his fur was rubbed bare and he looked like hell, our true friends love us and stand by us, no matter what. The loyalty and nonjudgment that seem to characterize true friendship have the power to allow us to be real, to be ourselves. Words like "trust," "respect," "understanding," and "acceptance" are often used to describe the deepest kinds of friendships. It is perhaps in true friendship that we have the clearest glimpse of our own authentic Self beneath the persona and the posturing that we so often use as a shield in other relationships. Emerson wrote, "A friend is a person with whom I may be sincere. Before him, I may think aloud. I am arrived at last in the presence of a man so real and equal that I may drop even those undermost garments of dissimulation, courtesy and second thought, which men never put off, and may deal with him with the simplicity and wholeness with which one chemical atom meets another."[42]

In a more contemporary vein, Lillian Rubin in her book *Just Friends* makes a critical point about the freedom to be our true selves through the support of friendships and their special significance at transitional points in our lives such as midlife. She writes: "Whether child or adult, it is friends who provide a reference outside the family against which to measure and judge ourselves; who help us during passages that require our separation and individuation; who support us as we adapt to new roles and new rules; who heal the hurts and make good the deficits of other relationships in our lives; who offer the place and encouragement for the development of parts of self that, for whatever reasons, are inaccessible in the family context. It's with friends that we test our sense of self-in-the-world, that our often inchoate, intuitive unarticulated vision of the possibilities of a self-yet-to-become finds expression."[43]

Ellen, described earlier in this chapter, credits her women friends with nothing less than keeping her alive. Following her suicide attempt, they rallied to her support and encouraged her to find new meaning in her life. Without any reminders from her, they remembered the anniversary date of her attempt to take her own life. On that day a year later, this group of friends took her out to lunch and gave her a special gift. The attached card read simply, "We love you. We're glad that you're here with us."

True friendship touches the soul. Aristotle defined it as "a single soul dwelling in two bodies,"[44] while another writer has called friendship a sacrament in which there is a pure "transfusion of grace."[45] Mary Wollstonecraft simply concluded, "The most holy bond of society is friendship."[46] Thomas Moore sees friendship as critical to the work and expression of the soul: "If the body is in pain, one of the first things to look for is infection; if the soul is in pain, we might look for lack of friendship."[47] The poet Rumi speaks eloquently of the containment offered by authentic friendship: "Friend, our closeness is this: Anywhere you put your foot, feel me in the firmness under you."[48]

Released from some of the archetypal expectations of family and kin, friends have an opportunity to love each other unconditionally. We are, after all, not required to be friends. Less judgmental than many kin relationships, and often cleared of some of the most troubling projections, friends are more likely to be able to accept our dark side, our warts and less than honorable traits, along with the more positive aspects of the persona that we show to the world. Perhaps it is in friendship that we can be most ourselves and know that we can be loved anyway. At midlife, when we aren't sure ourselves of who we really are, the love and containment of friends offers strength, support, and an opportunity to know how much we are loved.

But to fully understand the relationship between friendship and unconditional love, it may be necessary to reach beyond the human species to our four-legged, winged, slithering, swimming brethren. The creatures that share our homes and lives offer friendship and unconditional love in great abundance. The power of our friendship with animals has long been understood by our species. Human beings have had animals as companions for more than thirty thousand years. Research has shown that more than half of all households in Britain and North America include pets as part of the family. They bring out our ability to love and be loved. Their undying loyalty, their unadulterated reverence for us contribute to our sense of well-being and self-esteem. While dogs and cats are the most popular companion animals throughout the world, birds, rabbits, snakes, fish, and all manner of creatures can fulfill this role.

Companion animals, especially dogs and more recently small monkeys, have served as guides and helpers for people who suffer from physical disabilities. The image of the Saint Bernard carrying a small barrel of brandy under its chin to rescue fallen skiers along alpine trails has given way to the contemporary picture of urban search-and-rescue dogs gingerly pawing their way through the rubble of disaster sites. But they continue to serve us with the skill of their senses, their waggling joy in our company, and their undying loyalty and love.

So closely did most Native American people see their relationship to other species that most of their languages did not include a word for "animal." There were, of course, words for particular types of animals: Bear, Eagle, Wolf, Raven, Deer, Frog, Butterfly, Hawk. But these words were descriptions of a particular type of creature. There was no word for "animal" because there was no sense that they existed as a separate class of being. They were a part of a sacred unity, a part of "all our relations." Native tribes understood how much animals had to teach human beings, and shamans could communicate directly with them in order to understand their healing power and wisdom.[49]

Recent research has shown that people who live with pets report fewer cases of depression, have lower blood pressure, and may even live longer. Studies with geriatric populations have shown that pets increase a sense of well-being, facilitate socialization, and help to break the sense of isolation and loneliness. Similar results have been found by introducing animals into homes for mentally retarded people and into prisons.[50] One study, investigating the effects of social isolation on the death rates of patients hospitalized for severe heart disease, looked at a wide variety of social support indicators. These researchers found that the presence of a pet was the strongest social predictor of survival at one year after hospitalization. This finding was true for the entire sample, including people who had many other forms of social support, including happy marriages.[51]

Expressing our love to animals allows for the creation of a container of powerful proportions. That they also take loving care of us is entirely clear to me. During a time of tremendous loss and stress in my life, I would fall into bed night after night exhausted. Bone-weary and too tired to sleep, I would lie wide awake staring at the ceiling. After a few minutes I could hear the quiet footsteps of our cat, Agatha, as she jumped from some dark windowsill and padded down the hall to the bedroom. She would curl herself into a ball and sit on my chest. I could feel the gentle vibration of her purring and my tight muscles would begin to relax. I always told her that she was like a little, four-legged massage therapist.

Dogs, of course, with a very different energy from their feline relations', are generally more expressive of their full measure of unconditional love. Regardless of whether I have had a successful day or been a total failure, Dorothy, my sweet yellow lab, greets me at the door each day with wide-eyed delight that I am home. When I have been grieving, she curls up beside me and silently comforts me. In the weeks before my mother's death, my mother would stroke Dorothy's soft ears for hours while Dorothy lay quietly beside her. Marie-Louise von Franz, on observing the love, understanding, and connections between humans and dogs wrote, "Of all the animals, the dog is the most completely adapted to man, is the most responsive to his moods, copies him, and understands what is expected of him. He is the essence of relationship."[52]

That animals can surround us with the most loving container is emphasized in Walt Whitman's "Song of Myself":

I think I could turn and live with animals, they are so placid and self-contain'd,
I stand and look at them long and long.
They do not sweat and whine about their condition,
They do not lie awake in the dark and weep for their sins,
They do not make me sick discussing their duty to God,
Not one is dissatisfied, not one is demented with the mania of owning things,
Not one kneels to another, nor to his kind that lived thousands of years ago,
Not one is respectable or unhappy over the whole earth.
So they show their relations to me and I accept them,
They bring me tokens of myself, they evince them plainly in their possession.[53]

Good friends are necessary for the fullest expression of the depth and complexity of the human experience. Understanding friendship as a universal need helps us to feel a sense of belonging in the world. Even in our darkest moments, friends reassure us of our value, providing a clear reflection of our inherent lovability. One writer observes that friendship is "an aspect of an organic reality as natural and as necessary for our human thriving as sunshine and fresh air. It is best understood as a part of the great chain of humanness, the substance that links us together in the same family."[54] Good friends become flesh-and-blood representations of the numinous and deeply emotional sense of being one with all of life. They serve as sacred containers throughout life and especially during life's transitions, such as midlife. As such, friendships are both necessary to the life of the soul and to what links us to the divine. Emerson wrote, "Happy is the house that shelters a friend! It might well be built, like a festal bower or arch, to entertain him a single day. Happier, if he know the solemnity of that relation, and honor its law! . . . I who alone am, I who see nothing in nature whose existence I can affirm with equal evidence to my own, behold now the semblance of my being in all its height, variety and curiosity reiterated in a foreign form; so that a friend may well be reckoned the masterpiece of nature."[55]

Neighborhood, Community, Planet—Our Corners of the Cosmos

Modern culture has created a world in which most of the human containers that have been provided by neighborhood or community have fallen apart. Our fast-paced, technological world has been more committed to speed and productivity than to the nurturance of human relationships. And yet our neighborhoods and communities are the largest containers, the macroenvironments, in which we will attempt to navigate the midlife transition. But looking carefully at the world in which we will experience our process of individuation may cause a deep shiver to run down some of our spines.

The sustaining of community has become much more complicated in our highly technological world. We have experienced what sociologists call a "culture lag," meaning that technology and knowledge have advanced at a logarithmic speed while our human evolution, both individually and culturally, in coping with these changes is moving forward arithmetically. That is, we haven't yet caught up psychologically or collectively with the realities of our changing world. Alvin Toffler describes our present reality as the "Third Wave." The First Wave of civilization, which began ten thousand years ago when our previously nomadic ancestors began to put down roots and develop agriculture, was the beginning of a felt sense of neighborhood or community. The Second Wave, touched off by the Industrial Revolution, dramatically altered the way we had lived for thousands of years. Lasting only three hundred years or so, the Second Wave has given way to even more rapid and profound social changes. More than fifteen years ago, Toffler wrote: "A new civilization is emerging in our lives, and blind men everywhere are trying to suppress it. This new civilization brings with it new family styles; changed ways of working, loving, living; a new economy; new political conflicts; and beyond all this an altered consciousness as well. Pieces of this new civilization exist today. Millions are already attuning their lives to the rhythms of tomorrow. Others, terrified of the future, are engaged in a desperate, futile flight into the past and are trying to restore the dying world that gave them birth."[56]

In the past—or the Second Wave, as Toffler would call it—neighborhoods and communities could be defined more simply. I recall learning one sociological definition of neighborhood: A neighborhood consisted of the homes and businesses that could be reached without crossing a major street. With this operational definition, and the social realities of the time in which it was used, one could be relatively certain that one's neighborhood would consist of people much like oneself in terms of race, economic class, education, political attitudes, and so forth.

Yet today, small local shops where people bought merchandise from people they had come to know over years have been transformed into anonymous megacenters that require a map to find a picture hanger or a notebook. In many cities and towns, our schools, once centers of learning and imagination, have become war zones. Today, more than fifty-seven percent of all schools are equipped with metal detectors to prevent children from bringing guns in. Our modern society has neglected our adolescents in failing to provide forms of initiation or transformation from childhood to adulthood. Without the containers of intergenerational values and the guidance and support of extended family and community, young teenage girls, trying to bridge the transition into womanhood, give birth to infants they cannot possibly care for emotionally or financially. Adolescent boys, in search of manhood and without examples of how it should be expressed in healthy and prosocial ways, develop their own rites of passage, mainly derived from the violent heroes of film and television. Without any leadership from the generation before them, these young men act out an unrestrained masculinity that reflects itself in allegiance to gangs and participation in reckless, violent, and life-threatening behaviors.

The older members of our society, those people whose life experience and knowledge in other times and cultures would have made them revered as "elders" and community leaders, have been relegated to nursing homes and retirement communities. Many families seem to have no choice about how they will care for their older members. The economic realities of their lives do not leave room for the careful tending of elderly people who may need help with everyday tasks.

As a society, we have watched our leaders fall from grace, abuse their positions, and betray our trust by a seemingly limitless lust for power and money. It has become difficult, and perhaps naive, to continue to place our faith in institutions that are supposed to provide the stable infrastructure of a complex society. During our lifetime we have watched as a president of the United States resigned in dishonor, senators and congressional representatives are regularly brought before ethics committees, and religious leaders are led off to jail in handcuffs for bilking their loyal congregations. To many, our churches have become "big businesses," more interested in the state of our wallets than the state of our souls. Professional athletes and celebrities, the closest thing our society has to heroes, routinely make the news for drug abuse or violent behavior, including rape and murder. Savings and loan executives live off their hidden assets while taxpayers pick up the tab for their greed and dishonesty. Insider traders walk away from our judicial system with a slap on the wrist, while ordinary people try to pick up their lives after the devastation of huge financial losses brought about by these white-collar con men.

In our global, transient society children grow up, get jobs, and move far from the hearth of original families. Even our architecture gives testimony to the changing face of our communities. Increasing drug abuse and violence cause us to live in tightly guarded enclaves that we call our homes. Gone are the wide wraparound porches with the swing and the comfortable wicker just waiting for a friend or neighbor to drop by for some iced tea or a cup of coffee. The old sense of neighborhood as a place where we knew people well and depended upon each other with few exceptions has given way to tracts of homes and apartments that are connected only by their geographical relationship. Thomas Moore, reflecting on this loss of soul and relationship in our communities, writes: "It isn't easy in modern culture to cultivate friendships, not only because life is so fast and busy, but also because many of the values that at one time sustained friendships have waned . . . A soulful activity like friendship requires a soulful ambience: a neighborhood of stores, porches and safe walkways where people can see and get to know one another."[57]

Living a soulful, deeply loving, and connected life is extremely challenging in our modern world. Fear, paranoia, and lack of trust accompany us as we go about our daily lives. But our world, to a large extent, will be perceived and defined by how we *choose* to view it.

A number of years ago I was impressed by two photographs in a newspaper laid out on the front page, one next to the other. I was living in southwestern Virginia at a time when our community experienced a sudden, major flood. The city was effectively closed down for days and several people lost their lives crossing small bridges that suddenly gave out underneath them. It was a frightening experience for all of us. The two photographs in the newspaper that week showed the best and worst of human nature. One photo pictured several people wearing ski masks navigating a small boat through the flooded stores of the downtown area. These were looters who were stealing from local merchants at a time when many would already be suffering irreparable losses from water damage. The second picture, taken the same day, showed a group of people, some standing up to their chests in rushing, muddy water, passing cats and dogs over their heads. They were saving the lives of the animals that had been stranded at the SPCA. The photograph portrayed a range of human beings: male/female, white/black, old/young (including some small children). United only in their desire to rescue these helpless victims of the flood, they acted with compassion and mercy.

The presence of grace and love can have immediate, inexplicable effects on negativity, selfishness, and violence, which are reflections of a will to power. Jung reflects on the tension of opposites in the two forces of love and power when he writes: "Where love reigns, there is no will to power; and where the will to power is paramount, love is lacking. The one is but the shadow of the other."[58]

Many of us read about or watched on the news the story of a young American boy, Nicholas Greene, who was killed in southern Italy in 1994 while vacationing with his family. His father was driving their car when a vehicle pulled alongside and terrorists began firing automatic weapons. Mr. Greene was somehow able to escape from the terrorists, and after a harrowing drive, brought his wife and daughter to safety. But bullets had already pierced the car and ten-year-old Nicholas, asleep in the backseat, was shot several times. He did not survive.

In spite of their deep sorrow at the random and purposeless loss of their son, the Greene family decided to donate Nicholas's organs to people who needed them in southern Italy. ABC television's *20/20* program presented a moving and emotional tribute to the humanity and grace of this family as they showed the Greenes' return to Italy to meet the people who had been given life and sight through Nicholas's heart, liver, kidneys, and corneas. A small town renamed their elementary school after Nicholas Greene as a lasting testimonial to his remarkable family's generosity and compassion.[59]

While the Greene family's story represents the human capacity for goodness in archetypal proportions, countless smaller acts occur every day in our lives which reflect the presence of kindness and love in the world. The playfulness and care given to young children and infants with AIDS by students at Old Dominion University certainly challenges the stereotype that today's young people, those of Generation X, are cynical and only driven by money. And there is the woman who is dying of breast cancer but puts the little energy she has left after her radiation treatments to collecting signatures on a petition asking the government to pay attention to the striking number of women affected by this disease. "It's too late for me," she says, "but if I can help someone else, then that's what I'm going to do." Most of us are not familiar with Christiana Noble, who grew up an orphan on the streets of Ireland. She established a foundation that provides shelter, food, and mothering for thousands of Vietnamese children abandoned by their families to the streets of Ho Chi Minh City.

At one time I worked with a young video-and-film production company struggling to get by financially. One morning I walked into the building to find a note pinned to the inside of an interior door. It was from a thief. "I came in through the roof," it said. "I know that most people don't ever think that they can get ripped off from that direction, but I can do it." My heart began to pound—I knew the company couldn't survive if the robber had gotten away with a video camera or other equipment: we simply didn't have the resources to replace anything. Our building was protected by a security system, but this thief was quite creative and had opened a steel plate that exited to the roof. No alarm was ever sounded. "I went downstairs and saw your desks," the note continued. "Most of you had pictures there of children or families. Then I went in the back room and saw the two kittens." One of our producers had found two tiny abandoned kittens in the alley just a few days before—we had made a bed for them, bought food and toys, and had posted some signs around the area seeking good homes for them. "I decided that I just couldn't take anything from people that would take care of little kittens." The intruder then drew a detailed plan of how he had entered through the roof, and added suggestions as to how to prevent anyone from doing it again. I was thunderstruck at how a small amount of soulfulness—pictures of children and tending to abandoned kittens—had made such a dramatic impact on a thief. We promptly named the kittens Cagney and Lacy since they had been such exceptional watchcats.

Even in the seemingly impersonal world of cyberspace, soul and love have a place. Fifth-graders communicate with entomologists and each other throughout the United States and Canada about the migration of the monarch butterfly: they take to the fields, spot the beautiful winged creatures, and report back to the rest of the group through their computer modems. After the San Francisco earthquake in 1990, one could find messages from frightened people asking about friends and relatives whose fates were unknown, and in the days before telephone communications were restored it was not uncommon for anxious relatives to find comforting messages from complete strangers: "I walked over to the address that you gave. I saw your sister Brenda and told her you were concerned about her safety. She is fine. No one in the family is hurt. She will call you as soon as telephone service is restored. Glad I could be of help."

Living in a global community, we now are in many ways connected more closely with each other than ever before. Decisions and behaviors enacted on a local level today have a far-reaching impact on the rest of the world, and we are more aware than ever just what our effect on other parts of the world will be, we know that decisions by legislators in South America can affect the skin cancer rates of infants born in Finland as the rain forest is destroyed and the overall weather patterns and condition of our planet are affected. Water polluted in Michigan will find its way through our rivers and oceans and eventually destroy life forms on the shores of Barbados. Al Gore provided many important examples of our global interconnectedness in his book *Earth in the Balance:* "The 600 percent increase in the amount of chlorine in the atmosphere during the last forty years has taken place not just in those countries producing the chlorofluorocarbons responsible but in the air above every country, above Antarctica, above the North Pole and the Pacific Ocean—all the way from the surface of the earth to the top of the sky."[60]

The interrelatedness of all life on our planet can be demonstrated by science and technology. That we are all interdependent and will share a common future is no longer in question. But earlier societies understood this on faith, without the tools of modern empiricism. In a letter to U.S. President Franklin Pierce in 1855, Chief Seattle wrote: "This we know: The Earth does not belong to man, man belongs to the Earth. All things are connected like to blood that connects us all. Man did not weave the web of life, he is merely a strand in it. Whatever he does to the web, he does to himself. . . . As we are part of the land, you too are part of the land. This Earth is precious to us. It is also precious to you. One thing we know: There is only one God. No man, be he Red Man or White Man, can be apart. We *are* brothers after all."[61]

For Chief Seattle and other Native Americans, this deep respect for the earth and the interconnectedness of all life was reflected in their nation of the "seven generations," which emphasized respect for previous generations and nurturance of future ones. These generations—our great-grandparents, grandparents, parents, children, grandchildren, great-grandchildren, and our own generation—were considered in every decision made in Native American tribes. Mark Gerzon writes eloquently of how concern for the well-being of the generations, as examined through the Native American tradition, reflects itself in a better world for all: "Authentic community—that is, community that honors the interdependence of all seven generations—ensures that the young are initiated by adults; that infants are tended by parents or other loving caretakers; that those in the second half are supported by others in carrying out their responsibilities; that the old are respected and their skills utilized. Authentic communities do not isolate the old in ghettos for the elderly, or warehouse the young in impersonal, understaffed child-care centers or schools that neglect them; they do not leave young mothers trapped home alone with infants, or create jobs that prevent working parents from being with their young children. Authentic communities do not place education at the bottom of their budgetary priorities and do not frighten the elderly by jeopardizing their financial support systems. Authentic multigenerational communities tend to *every* stage of the life cycle because they know that, ultimately, this is the only way they will flourish. When the community is weak or absent, we all stumble forward, lurching through the life cycle. When it runs strong, life flows with greater meaning."[62]

Belonging to and feeling the connection to other human beings and life itself is a critical part of the containment that is necessary during the midlife passage, whether expressed in the world of cyberspace or on the streets of our own neighborhood or city. The extent to which we can honor and feel our common bond with other people, and with life itself, is the extent to which we can build our communities.

The future of our neighborhoods and communities and the fate of our planet itself will be shaped and sculpted by the power of our own individual and collective consciousness. If we are truly able to celebrate the majestic diversity of life on our planet with respect and love, each one of us will contribute to the future of our world. It will be in this new, expanded consciousness that we may reach that place of mystery, that magical instant where "nobody is singing." In so doing, we may learn, as W. H. Auden wrote, to love our crooked neighbor with our own crooked heart.[63]

Concluding Thoughts on Building Containers, Healing Relationships, and Finding Our Neighbors

There are cultures and philosophies that strongly hold that there are no accidents in life, that everyone who has touched one's life whether through an intimate relationship or a casual meeting has done so for some reason. Whether mere chance or divine plan, we may never know for sure; but we have much to learn from each other and we can often learn the most from people with whom we have conflicts or differences. If we believe that everyone we meet in our life has something to teach us, then we will learn from them. Eastern philosophies understand that when the student is ready the teacher will appear.

By midlife we have often experienced many endings of relationships. Too often people we once loved and may even have had children with are now referred to bitterly as "exes." Friendships drift apart, often for no reason or because of some disagreement that couldn't easily be resolved. We refuse to forgive our parents for their mistakes. By midlife many of our containers of personal connection have rips in the places where love once was, and some of us may find ourselves surrounded by something that resembles Swiss cheese. We may sometimes feel that we live in an age of temporary and replaceable relationships. But in fact, every relationship is sacred, and while new containers can be forged, older ones can never really be supplanted. But old ones may be repaired as well. Midlife is a time of letting go of many things, but it can also be a time of reclamation. We serve our own process of growth and individuation, and honor the Self when we forgive others and ask forgiveness for ourselves. Letting go of anger, bitterness, and disappointment lightens our load as we move toward the future.

Some Thoughts and Suggestions

Marriage and Partnership

1. Begin the process of self-discovery in earnest. The emergence of the energies of the uncompleted Self at midlife—especially the shadow and the anima/animus—requires understanding our own projections on our partner or spouse. In order to do so, we must first understand our inner life and the archetypal energies and complexes that operate as autonomous or "sub"-personalities. Learn about these aspects of yourself by creating a dialogue with your inner self (the following chapter explains more about this process of "Active Imagination"). Talk to it, write it a letter, sculpt it, draw it, reflect or meditate on it. Learn to recognize these inner energies in the symbols of your dreams (I will explain how to do this in greater detail in the following chapter). I realize that it may sound strange to hear a psychologist urging you to talk to yourself, instead of thinking you are odd because you do. Nevertheless, real inner work requires an active relationship with the unconscious parts of the psyche, for this is how they become conscious.

2. Take responsibility for your own process of individuation, recognizing that while your spouse or partner can be helpful, the journey itself is yours alone. The following chapters describe some additional tools such as dreamwork, body work, creative self-expression, and keeping a journal. Don't just read about these powerful paths but integrate them into your daily life.

3. Look honestly at yourself and your relationship with your spouse or partner. Talk about your relationship, your dreams, hopes, and fears with him or her. Make a list together of the ways in which your relationship has divided up the unconscious aspects of your life together. It will probably be easy to make a list of how you've divided tasks like lawn care and cooking. But how have you parceled out thoughtfulness, initiation of activities together, keeping connections with friends and family, creativity, spirituality, ambition, and so forth? Learn more about each other. What was your partner like as a child or teenager? What are his or her biggest disappointments in life? What are his or her happiest moments? What are you projecting onto your partner or spouse? What are the negative as well as the positive projections? What is your partner or spouse living for you that you will not live for yourself? These are the questions that are asked along the inner journey.

4. A relationship is like a beautiful flower that will wither if it is not nurtured and cared for. I am always amazed when couples come to me for therapy and cannot remember when they last spent quality time alone together. How do we expect our relationships to flourish when they are deprived of the daily attentiveness of love and friendship? Take frequent walks together and talk. Eat dinner together with candles, flowers, and good music. Set out the best for each other, just as you would for friends. Take a day trip to a place that you've never seen before. Work on a project together. Enroll in a class together "just for fun." Our time, in this culture, is extremely precious. Between working, cooking, cleaning, doing errands, and spending time with children, friends, and family, there is very little time left. My Aunt Teresa, who has always been like a second mother and a great friend, shared with me some wisdom that she believes has helped to make her life full and rich. She told me that she takes a long walk at least every six months for the purpose of asking herself one question: "If I had only six months to live what would I do differently in my life?" Then she makes a determined effort to make those changes real. The answers to her questions have found her hot-air ballooning over France, traveling, driving a black hot rod like the car in *Knight Rider,* and coaching a little girls' T-ball team when she was in her sixties. Mostly, Teresa makes certain that her priorities are in order. She makes time, no matter where she may have to take it from, to nurture and celebrate the relationships and spiritual beliefs that are important in her life. Relationships, especially those with our beloved, don't prosper by wishing

and hoping. Make your relationship a priority in terms of the time and loving energy that you devote to it.

5. Say what you mean and feel. Unconscious complexes and projections thrive in the land of passive-aggressiveness. Expecting your partner to know how you feel about something ("If he or she really loved me, then he or she would know how I feel.") is unrealistic. If you are angry or hurt find a way to say so. Explore your feelings about what you are experiencing. Look honestly at what you are projecting onto someone else.

6. Practice soulfulness on a daily basis with your spouse or partner. Unexpected flowers, a card, or a carefully written note bring the healthy parts of romantic love into our everyday lives. Remember what your loved one says and likes. A woman I know was touched beyond words when her husband bought her a special book for her birthday. He remembered that she had said, months earlier, that she had always wanted to read it. This was not an expensive gift but one of memory and soul.

7. Listen to each other. An ancient bit of Persian wisdom advises us: "Look at the composition of the head of man. God has given me two shining eyes, two ears, but only one tongue, so that I may see twice, I may listen to words of wisdom twice, and speak but once."[64] Research has shown that when a couple has a conflict, often neither member is listening to the other: usually one person is formulating a response while the other is making his or her case. Resolution of differences depends upon true understanding of what the conflict is about. When in conflict ask yourself this: "What am I contributing to this problem?" The chances are excellent that you are very well aware of what your spouse or partner is contributing.

8. Make a decision to get rid of the baggage that you brought into the marriage. We all arrive on the doorsteps of a relationship with baggage from our earlier experiences in life. Some of us arrive with a couple of suitcases; others pull up with a fully loaded eighteen-wheeler. At midlife, it is past time to let go. Professional help in dealing with severe or traumatic life experiences may be necessary.

9. Some marriages simply cannot serve as containers for the individuation of the partners. Perhaps the marriage was based upon false assumptions and

solely unconscious beliefs to begin with. Perhaps you both have taken different paths and directions in life. As James Hollis points out, "One should not automatically applaud the fifty-year marriage without knowing what happened to the souls of those in the relationship. Perhaps they feared change, feared honesty, and suffered."[65] In such cases, it may be necessary to end the marriage or relationship. It is important that such decisions be made with a high level of honesty, reflection, and consciousness about the nature of the relationship. Look sincerely and deeply within yourself and at your contributions or lack of them to your marriage or partnership. Ask: "Can this relationship contain my growth, or does it stifle it and prevent the actualization of my personality?" "What changes need to be made to make this relationship healthy and authentic?" "Are those changes possible for both of us?" "Am I basing my decision to leave my relationship on a refusal to work on my inner life?" "What am I projecting and expecting this relationship to be to me?" If, with a high level of consciousness and awareness, it is clear that the relationship needs to end, then end it with love. Don't allow yourself the luxury (and unconsciousness) of rationalizing why you should leave. Don't excuse yourself by blaming your partner. Don't create a scapegoat. Maybe there is no one to blame. Instead, accept that life is filled with changes and perhaps it is you who have changed. Allow yourself to feel the energy of the love that you once felt for your spouse or partner, and accept that this love may have to change its shape. Be honest, accept responsibility for your own decisions and actions, be loving and compassionate, and don't fight about anything that could blow away in a hurricane.

Marion Woodman, in a book that I believe may have saved my life during the most treacherous crossing of my midlife passage, uses a metaphor from Dante to describe the mystery and importance of love and relationship in our lives. She writes: "It seems to me the most important thing in surrendering a close bond is sacrificing the relationship without sacrificing the love. If life is an 'opening out like a rose that can no longer keep closed,' then everything we love is an opening of a petal. When the thorns are accepted love abides. The profound relationships in our lives, whatever their outcome, have given us the riches of loving and that wealth is the only wealth that means anything in the end."[66]

Family

1. Who have you been and who are you within the context of your family? Which of your beliefs and values remain unquestioned? What kind of family mythology do you believe in? Were you assigned a family role that continues to prevent your full actualization of talent and authentic personality? Ask yourself what you continue to carry with you that keeps you from being fully alive and yourself. Write these down. Craft a story that describes your life. Write in the third person if you need some distance to see your experiences through the clear eye of objectivity.

2. Many of our problems as adults result from the complex that has lately been termed "inner child." The concept of the wounded inner child has become popular and, in many ways, oversimplified. Nevertheless, we do carry with us wounds that were inflicted years earlier, and they do affect our feelings and beliefs about ourselves as well as our expectations for relationships and life in general. It is important to understand and acknowledge the inner child that travels with you. As John Bradshaw writes: "At first, it may seem preposterous that a little child can continue to live in an adult body. But that is exactly what I'm suggesting. I believe that this neglected, wounded inner child of the past is the major source of human misery. Until we reclaim and champion that child, he will continue to act out and contaminate our adult lives.[67] Learn about this aspect of your own personality. Talk to it. Write letters, draw, paint, describe this part of yourself. Learn what it needs. Look through pictures of yourself as a child and try to remember who that child was and still is. Buy a frame and put that picture on your desk or bureau so you can remember her or him. Learn that the only person who can truly protect and love that child unconditionally is you. You are now responsible for healing and helping the injured parts of yourself. Understand that love can be seen as an abundancy or as a scarcity. This underlying belief, which is almost always the belief of the child within and is based on our early experiences, fundamentally affects our views of ourselves and the world. Which do you wish to believe? Is love parceled out in small amounts, and when it is used up is there none left? Or will there always be enough to go around? Will you get your share? Can you believe that love

is infinite and that the more you love and are able to be loved, the more there is? Accept your humanity, your shadow parts, change and grow, but learn to love yourself unconditionally.

3. Who are your parents? Who were they before they became your parents? If your mother and father are alive, talk with them. Ask them about growing up: What formed them? What were their experiences in life? Who were they as children, as teenagers, as young adults? Talk with other, older family members. Listen to what they have to say about the early life of your family. Listen to this oral history with an open heart, as if you were a stranger. Visit the places where your parents grew up, if possible. Try to understand your parents and how they came to create your family. Many therapists recommend confronting our parents with our anger, but I don't agree that this is always the best way to proceed. Most parents believe that they did "the best they could." To send them letters or confront them personally with their failings in parenting often does nothing more than create conflict and pain. Healing from the pain of past wounds is an inner process and only in rare circumstances does it need to be discussed with those family members involved. Allow yourself grief and anger at not being given what you might have needed, but see this as a starting point to greater self-awareness, not as the destination. Recognize your own expectations for what you wanted and needed but did not receive. Learn to see your parents as fallible, mortal human beings who gave you some good things and some not so good things. As an adult you must now sift through these and determine for yourself what you will retain and what you must relinquish. Begin to see your parents through the eyes of another human being and not those of a child. Forgive them.

4. If you have children of your own, look honestly at your projections on them. Do you have expectations that they can never live up to? Are you unconsciously expecting that they will live out your own unlived life? One of my clients said, referring to two very different characters from *Gone with the Wind,* "My parents could never accept that they wanted Melanie and got Scarlett." Can you accept your child, regardless of his or her age, as having the right and responsibility to live his or her own life? Can you love your children unconditionally, regardless of how they may deviate from your expectations for them? Can you—do you?—show them that love? Can you spend more quality time with them?

5. Look honestly at your relationships with your brothers and sisters, if you have any, and your extended family. Draw your family tree and reflect on the connections that remain strong and true and those that have drifted. What do you give to these relationships? Did some of them erode simply because of a lack of attention or the demands of daily life? Find new ways of nurturing these fragile tethers to the family of your blood. Make time for them in your life. Remember birthdays or special occasions and send a note, card, or small gift. Telephone for no particular reason. Don't just wait for family gatherings, like funerals and weddings, but spend some time together now when you can join in celebration of the everyday life of your family.

6. Celebrate your sense of family. Accept that no families will ever live up to the archetypal ideal of what family is supposed to be. Families are collections of people who can love and support each other; sometimes there is a relationship by blood and sometimes there is not. These families come in many shapes, sizes, and colors. Learn to appreciate the uniqueness of your own. Jane Howard's book *Families* illustrates the amazing variety of ways in which people choose and are chosen to exist in relationship to one another. Common themes of love, support, and connection seem to be at the heart of all healthy families regardless of their eccentricities from the established "norm."[68]

Friends

1. Listen gently to your friends. There is much power in simply receiving without trying to solve problems or interpret their meaning. Let your friends know, in absolute terms, that you are there for them through good times and bad. Thomas Moore observed that many friendships don't usually ask for a great deal of activity. But they do require "loyalty and presence."[69]

2. Extend loyalty by keeping confidences, even when it is not specifically asked for. Friendship requires a sense of confidentiality and trust. After all, our good friends are strong containers for aspects of ourselves that we do not reveal to other people.

3. Even though strong friendships can endure separation by time and distance, we can nurture these special bonds by phone calls, cards, notes, let-

ters, and visits. Friends of mine have a small plaque on the wall of their home. It says: "Go often down the road to thy friend's house, for weeds will choke the unused path." This is good advice.

4. Allow for the periodic waxing and waning of particular friendships. Like the many moods of the ocean, we experience changing levels of attachment and separation, especially with friends who live far away. Don't write off friends because you haven't heard from them in a while. Nurture the relationship by making contact yourself.

5. Allow your friends to make mistakes. They will not be perfect, nor will you. Be aware of unconscious projections that create unreasonable expectations for your relationship. Just as with your marriage, partnership, or family, don't expect your friends to do the inner work that you must do for yourself.

6. Learn to enjoy the unfolding intimacy of a relationship with a friend. One cannot force friendship, but with love, patience, and mutual respect deep friendships evolve over time and become what Emerson called the "solidest things we know." Like all relationships, and life itself, it is the journey, not the destination, in which friendship, love, and wisdom are best expressed.

7. Consider the companionship of animals. If you are blessed with a pet, do not neglect this relationship because of time constraints or other priorities. If you do not have a creature as part of your family, consider it. This is an important decision and must be made extremely thoughtfully. Companion animals require serious commitments of time, energy, and money that cannot be taken lightly. We must ask ourselves what we can give to these animals, and not only anticipate what they will give us. Whether you elect to have an animal as part of your family or not, learn from them. Set a bird or squirrel feeder in your yard and observe their habits, read books about animals, watch television documentaries that describe their lives. Take a quiet walk in the woods and look around you. Go on vacation to a place where you can watch whales from boats or swim in a natural setting with dolphins. Animals have the power to teach us wondrous things about our own instinctive natures. We need their medicine.

Neighborhood and Community

1. Take a good and honest look at your neighborhood and immediate community. The negative aspects are probably all too clear to you. What are the good things in your neighborhood or community? Are there neighbors involved in community activities that bring life and good energy to your immediate locale? I have observed that even in the middle of one of the roughest neighborhoods in my city, someone has planted flowers along a public walkway. I have lived in cities where demolished, crime-ridden downtown areas have been brought to new life by the will of the community. In Roanoke, Virginia, as in many other cities, I watched as our decaying inner-city neighborhood was resurrected. Shops, restaurants, small parklike areas with trees and benches, art galleries, a science museum, and an excellent theater replaced dark warehouses and dangerous streets. On Saturdays the area is filled with farmers selling fresh vegetables and colorful flowers. People feel safe there now and children play in streets that once required an armed escort. This change brought with it a new sense of community and is a testimonial to the will of people to connect to one another. Where does life exist among the difficulties in your town or neighborhood?

2. How do you contribute to your neighborhood or community? Volunteer your time for something that you deem important. Reach out to others with your talent and energy. Every week in our local paper there is a list of volunteer organizations that need help: Habitat for Humanity, Meals on Wheels, AIDS hospice programs and programs for children, the Special Olympics, soup kitchens for the homeless, libraries, hospitals, nursing homes. The list—and therefore the opportunities to help others—is endless. Human beings are happiest when we know that we have contributed, have helped someone else. Small acts of soul have the power to cut through the alienation that so many of us feel in our communities. There is a wonderful story about Karl Menninger, the psychiatrist and writer who established the Menninger Foundation in Topeka, Kansas. Dr. Menninger was asked to talk with a woman, a widow who had been depressed for many years. This was in the days when house calls were still an option, and he met her at her home. She was sitting slumped in a chair and she acknowledged that she had been extremely depressed since her husband died many years earlier. Her house was

mostly dark and quiet, as if life never entered her rooms. But Dr. Menninger noticed that there were beautiful African violets on every windowsill. He wrote the woman a prescription to regularly read her local newspaper and to send one of her African violets to someone who had experienced a significant event: the birth of a baby, a marriage, a graduation. She was, he instructed, never to let a week go by without sending at least one of the flowers to someone in her town. Within a month the woman called him and told him that she had changed dramatically. Gone was the slow depressed speech that he had heard when he visited her. She was bright and excited about the many activities she was involved in. He learned that she had done as he instructed, and each time someone received a violet they responded in kind with a note of thanks, some cookies, a visit to tell her how much they appreciated her thoughtfulness. She became known as "the violet lady," and lived the rest of her life surrounded by her new friends and neighbors.[70]

3. What attitudes and beliefs reflect themselves in your values and behaviors? Do you hold love for others, or harbor predjudices and negative judgments about people who are different from you? What are your beliefs based upon? Our feelings about others, both positive and negative, often reflect projections of our own shadow. What can you learn about yourself from your beliefs about others?

4. What do you do for the earth? Helping in small ways asserts our connection to our larger *reality*. Our global community will really change only when we each take care of our own backyard. There is a bumper sticker I have seen all over the country that says, "Think globally. Act locally." This is good advice. Honor the earth and our collective environment in small ways. Recycle your aluminum cans, newspapers, glass, and plastics. Build a wildlife refuge in your yard. Plant a tree. Help with environmental cleanup in your area. In Virginia there is a very active group of people working to clean up the Chesapeake Bay. What needs to be done in your community? Other members of our area serve on rescue teams for injured or wounded sea mammals stranded on our shores. Still others work with the science museum to count whales or seabirds for scientific research. Creatively explore ways in which you can contribute. The best-selling book *50 Simple Things YOU Can Do to Save the Earth* offers lots of specific examples. The book is dedicated to the "not-yet-born."[71]

CHAPTER 7

Dreams and Dreamwork: The Royal Road

At the time of night-prayer, as the sun slides down,
the route the senses walk on closes, the route to the invisible opens.
The angel of sleep then gathers and drives along the spirits;
just as the mountain keeper gathers his sheep on a slope.
And what amazing sights he offers to the descending sheep!
JELALUDDIN RUMI (1207–1273), SUFI POET AND MYSTIC,
"NIGHT AND SLEEP"

WESTERN CULTURE has witnessed the annihilation of dreams as sources that give meaning to life, provide a path to knowledge, and allow for encounters with the Divine. Most people totally disregard the images of wisdom and self-revelation that come to us in the night. "Dreams don't mean anything." "They're too hard to understand." "Dreams are weird." "I just ate too much pizza before I went to bed." "I never dream anyway." These are the comments that are often heard about the relevance of dreams. But these attitudes cause most of us to leave gold on our pillows as we wake to the day and go about our business.

At forty-one Laura had been feeling many of the gnawing symptoms of the midlife transition for more than a year. Though she was not in a crisis, her attitudes and feelings had been shifting in ways that she did not understand. She was feeling restless and unsettled, vaguely dissatisfied with both her work and her life in general. An avid card player, she found herself making excuses not to join her bridge club for their regular weekly games. She was also withdrawing from a group of friends who regularly got together on weekends to play tennis and cook out. She didn't have much to say to Bill, the man she was in love with and had been dating for several years.

Laura found herself crying often and for unexpected reasons, sometimes awakening with a deep sense of sadness and despondency about the day facing her. This made no sense to her. She liked her job, had a close and loving relationship with Bill, was blessed with good friends, and was in excellent health. There was nothing at all wrong in her life that she could attribute these feelings to, but she couldn't shake the sense of darkness and despair that seemed to surround her. "You're depressed, go to the doctor," her friends told her. She knew they were right but didn't understand what she could possibly be depressed about. She was afraid the doctor would offer some kind of medication to make her feel better, but she was not a believer in quick fixes and wasn't convinced that she needed a pill to get back into the swing of things.

One night Laura awoke shaken to the core. She was trembling, sobbing, and gasping for breath from a dream that was so vivid and powerful that she had to walk around the house and turn on all the lights to convince herself she had only been dreaming. Laura rarely remembered her dreams and didn't attach any importance to them. But this one was so forceful that she could recall its every detail:

> I am walking down a dark street and I'm all alone. I hear a sound coming from an alleyway to my left and I become frightened. I start to walk faster and then I see that there is a group of young men, gang-looking kinds of guys, dressed in black, and they start to follow me. Very slowly at first but as I start to walk faster so do they. I'm terrified and I start running as fast as I can, but my legs feel like rubber or like I'm in some kind of mud or quicksand. They are gaining on me and I can hear them laughing in a sinister way. I run into an old house and try to lock the door behind me but the door is made of very old wood and is mostly rotten and soft. I run to the other side of the house and discover that it is right on the oceanfront. It is very windy and the waves are huge and crashing over the deck of the house. The water splashes over my feet, so I run up some stairs that are almost caved in but I get to the next floor. The room is very narrow and the only opening is a doorway to a deck where I can see that the waves have gotten higher and higher, so I run up another flight of stairs to the very top of the house. As I'm standing and looking at the water, trying to figure out what to

> do, I see in the distance a huge wave. Like the tidal wave in *The Poseidon Adventure,* it is hundreds of times higher than this house that I'm in. I am paralyzed and can't move. The wave crashes onto the house.

Laura awoke in such terror from this dream that she believed she was "going crazy." It was at this point that she felt she needed help in understanding what was happening to her. Laura had ignored the promptings of the Self, her wake-up call to individuation and growth, which had been expressed for more than a year in the more subtle symptoms of withdrawal, sadness, and feelings of meaninglessness. A more strident, breathtaking message was inevitable, for the unconscious is not asking, it is demanding to be known. As a general rule, the more out of touch we are with our inner life, the more strongly these energies will announce themselves. In his poem "The Second Coming," Yeats evidences his understanding of the power of these forces to create turmoil and dramatic change in our lives: "Turning and turning in the widening gyre/The falcon cannot hear the falconer/Things fall apart; the centre cannot hold."[1] Very often we will hear the falconer's call; the urgings of the Self will be made conscious by the way of a dream.

Throughout life, and especially during important transitions such as midlife, dreams provide a direct pathway to the unconscious aspects of the psyche and to rich, dynamic meetings with the Self. Because dreams are so vital to our process of individuation and self-knowledge, it is important to honor their mystery and to learn from them. At midlife, especially, dreams are an indispensable tool for inner work.

In order to recognize and appreciate the powerful significance of dreams, it is important to understand what they have meant to people in other times and cultures and why they have been lost to us as a source of comfort and guidance. Through such an understanding we can better realize the importance of reclaiming the way of the dream in our own lives.

The Role of Dreams in Human Culture

Sitting around the crackling campfires of antiquity and discussing the messages that came in the night, our ancestors understood the powerful wisdom revealed to them through dreams. The Aborigines of Australia refer to the time before anyone can remember as the "dreamtime," and believe that the knowledge created and left there by those who lived before can be retrieved through dreams. The Plains Indians of North America sent adolescents on a "vision quest," in search of a dream or vision, to provide an image of a guardian spirit which would protect them for their entire lives. The Iroquois Nation shared dreams during special gatherings held every winter. In Islamic societies and in ancient Jerusalem, the interpretation of dreams was an everyday activity. The Senoi people of Malaya are known for their use of dreams in creating harmonious relationships within their culture.[2] The Native American prophet Smohalla of the Nez Percé tribe simply said, "Wisdom comes to us in dreams."[3] In most tribal societies, dreams were believed to emanate from a divine source and were given to humankind to provide enlightenment and wisdom. That dreams are sacred messages and guidance given by a loving God or higher power was and is still a belief found in all cultures throughout the world.

Classical Western traditions venerated the role of dreams as pathways to wisdom and healing as well as our human connection to the Divine. In Greece, the cult of Aesculapius, the Greek god of healing and a son of Apollo, cured illness by customary rites of purification during which a sick person would sleep in the Aesculapian temple until a significant dream occurred. References to the importance of dreams are found in Homer's *Odyssey* and Virgil's *Aeneid* as well as in the works of Plato, Socrates, Cicero, Lucretius, Artemidorus Daldianus, Pliny, and Galen. All the classical Greek thinkers, with the exception of Aristotle, believed dreams to be important paths to knowledge, messages of divine origin. Origen and Clement, educated men of the third century who founded a school in Alexandria, believed in dreams as a means of revelation. Hippocrates, the source of the Hippocratic oath and often thought of as the father of medicine, believed that dreams were among the most important methods for diagnosing illness. He theorized that the sense organs dominated during the day while the soul was passive, but that during sleep the soul produced images and impressions rather than received them. Tertullian, a Christian writing in Rome in the beginning of the third century, believed that dreams were the movement of the soul coming in contact with God or nature. He wrote in A.D. 203: "Is it not known to all the people that the dream is the most usual way that God reveals himself to man?"[4]

Buddhist, Jewish, Islamic, and Christian traditions all address dreams as containing enlightened information, instruction, or guidance that is not available in a waking state. The Pali scriptures describe half a dozen of Buddha's dreams as he opened himself to enlightenment; and it was through a dream that the Buddha's mother, Queen Maya, predicted that she had immaculately conceived a great and universal monarch. Muhammad was instructed of his divine mission in a dream. The Talmud directly states, "A dream that has not been interpreted is like a letter that has not been opened."[5] The Old Testament contains multiple instances of God speaking directly to the prophets through the language of dreams. "Hear my words: If there is a prophet among you, I the Lord make myself known to him in a vision, I speak with him in a dream" (Numbers 12:6). Joseph predicted seven years of plenty and seven years of famine for Egypt through his interpretation of Pharaoh's dream of seven fat and seven thin and ugly cows. Pharaoh was so impressed that he granted Joseph authority over the whole land (Genesis 41:17–45). Job states, "For God speaks in one way, and in two, though people do not perceive it. In a dream, in a vision of the night, when deep sleep falls on mortals, while they slumber on their beds, then he opens their ears and terrifies them with warnings."[6] In the New Testament, Joseph accepts Mary's pregnancy as of divine origin, is instructed to flee into Egypt and then instructed to return, all on the basis of God speaking to him through dreams (see Matthew 1:20–21, 24; 2:12–13, 19–22).[7]

Dreams, like myths, played a central role in the psychological and spiritual lives of our ancestors, acting as an important pathway to understanding God and the promptings of the Self. Between the earliest dawn of human consciousness and our beliefs today, though, the importance of dreams in Western traditions has eroded almost completely. Our insistence on rationalism as the only way in which to view the world has left little room for the symbolic and mythological worlds of the spirit, rendering our inner life, and its expression through dreams, meaningless. But like our ancestors, we too have access to the power of dreams. Dreaming is, after all, a universal experience, a part of our human inheritance that transcends all of the differences between us.

Freud and Jung—Reclaiming the Dream

The early twentieth century evidenced a "paradigm shift" in the way human beings understood the world and the nature of reality. New discoveries in physics by Albert Einstein, Niels Bohr, and Wolfgang Pauli, among others, extended human knowledge about the nature of matter and demonstrated that Newton's laws, while applicable to the large-scale world, did not hold in the subatomic realm. The turn of the century was associated with an emerging intellectual environment that questioned the fundamental philosophies of rationalistic Western society as applied to science, based heavily as they were on the theories of Newton and the philosophy of Descartes. This challenging period created an opportunity for very different speculations on the nature of reality and of the human mind.

In 1899 Sigmund Freud completed his major work, *The Interpretation of Dreams* (published in 1900), in which he reclaimed the importance of dreams in understanding human beings. In *Patterns of Dreaming,* Jungian analyst and writer James Hall aptly describes Freud's bold contribution to the understanding of human psychology: "Freud's significant and lasting achievement was to recapture the sense of personal meaning of the dream for the dreamer, a perspective that had been lost with the decline of the Aesculapian sanctuaries."[8]

Although Freud later slightly modified his theory of dreams as it was elaborated in 1899, his basic belief was that dreams serve to camouflage underlying instinctive impulses. In order to understand his views on dreams, it is necessary to know something about his views of the personality. In his theory's simplest form, Freud hypothesized three basic structures of the personality: the *id,* the *ego,* and the *superego.* The id contains the drives and instincts of the biological needs of the body. It is interested only in its own fulfillment; thus Freud referred to this aspect of personality as following the "pleasure principle." The ego is a kind of executive director, an administrator of the "reality principle," which oversees the desires of the id and allows a person to postpone immediate gratification. The superego is an introjected image of the dominant parent and contains the cultural ideals for behavior as determined by the surrounding social environment.

Freud believed that the fundamental energy in man is sexual libido, which is always pushing to express itself in pleasure and gratification. However, the superego will not allow for this wanton display of instinctive urges and so represses them into the unconscious. This dynamic tension between the instinctive strivings of the id and the repressive, controlling nature of the superego is important to understand because it provides the basis for Freud's beliefs about the nature of dreams, which he referred to as the "Royal Road to the Unconscious." Dreams became, to Freud, the compromise between these two opposing forces of the id and the superego. Dreams express the disguised instinctual strivings that are the forbidden wishes of the superego. To Freud, dreams have both manifest and latent content: the manifest content is what the dream appears to be about, while the latent content is what it is actually about. To understand the meaning of the dream, Freud theorized, it is necessary to go beyond the manifest content to the latent content. The bottom line, to Freud, was that dreams serve to prevent certain unacceptable aspects of the personality from being known to consciousness. They preserve sleep so that the underlying anxiety of the internal conflict between the id and the superego will not be brought into awareness.[9]

Freud's *Interpretation of Dreams,* published when he was forty-three years old, was not initially well received by the medical community, but it was read by an eager, young Swiss doctor. Carl Jung wrote: "As early as 1900 I had read Freud's *The Interpretation of Dreams.* I had laid the book aside at the time, because I did not yet grasp it. At the age of twenty-five I lacked the experience to appreciate Freud's theories. Such experience did not come until later. In 1903 I once more took up *The Interpretation of Dreams* and discovered how it linked to my own ideas."[10] Jung was drawn to Freud's work because his own research with the word association test had demonstrated that some process of repression did operate in the human psyche. However, Jung disagreed completely with Freud about the nature of what psychic material was being repressed. Freud had written that all repressed psychological material was due to some kind of sexual trauma or sexual energy. This did not fit with Jung's observations that the libido, or energy of the psyche, contained much more than just sexual energy. Jung saw libido as natural appetites, a life force that included sexual desires but also contained the psychic and spiritual energy of human beings. Freud's views on dreams did not fit Jung's perceptions of his patients, nor did it correspond with his overall philosophy of the human psyche and the spiritual nature of man.

These conflicting theoretical views about the nature of dreams were one of the many radical differences between these two influential men. The philosophical divisions between Freud and Jung later proved to be so overwhelming and irresoluble that they eventually led to a painful parting of the ways. This was after more than a decade of intellectual and personal friendship and in spite of the fact that Freud had designated Jung as his "crown prince" of the psychoanalytic movement.[11]

Jung fervently believed that dreams did not exist to disguise aspects of the personality or realities of one's life from consciousness; rather they were functions of the dynamic Self as it moved *toward* consciousness and wholeness. The purpose of dreams to Jung was to *reveal* aspects of the unconscious to the ego, not to mask them, as Freud had suggested. He wrote: "To me dreams are a part of nature, which harbors no intent to deceive, but expresses something as best it can, just as a plant grows or an animal seeks its food as best it can. These forms of life, too, have no wish to deceive our eyes."[12] Responding to Freud's theory that the actual dream images were nothing more than a facade for other repressed psychological material, Jung wrote: "The so called facade of most houses is by no means a fake or a deceptive distortion; on the contrary, it follows the plan of the building and often betrays the interior arrangement. The 'manifest' dream-picture is the dream itself and contains the whole meaning of the dream. . . . What Freud calls the 'dream-facade' is the dream's obscurity, and this is really only a projection of our own lack of understanding. We say that the dream has a false front only because we fail to see into it. We would do better to say that we are dealing with something like a text that is unintelligible not because it has a facade—a text has no facade—but simply because we cannot read it. We do not have to get behind such a text, but must first learn to read it."[13]

To Jung the manifest dream *was* the material that was striving to be known to consciousness. The fundamental difference between Freud and Jung regarding dreams is actually quite simple: To Freud, to dream of a pencil was to dream of a penis. For Jung, a dream pencil was, well, a pencil. If the psyche wanted to dream of a penis it would just go ahead and dream of one. Jung understood that the pencil in the dream symbolically represented something that the psyche was striving to understand. Thus, for Jung dreams always speak in the language of symbols, while for Freud dreams are disguises." With his emphasis on the revelation of the Self and on the symbol-making aspect in the human psyche as presented in dreams, Jung had resurrected the earliest language in which human beings had communicated with the innermost quarters of their own unconscious life and thus reclaimed an ancient path to the Divine.

Modern Sleep and Dream Research

Modern sleep and dream research has demonstrated that all human beings and all animals that have been studied do dream. Dreaming, among mammals, is as natural an activity as breathing. Anyone who has ever closely watched another person or an animal sleep has most likely observed the rapid movement of the eyes during certain stages of sleep. But scientific research into the nature of sleep and dreaming didn't really begin until the mid-fifties when Kleitman and Aserinsky demonstrated a strong relationship between rapid eye movement (REM), also referred to as paradoxical sleep (PS), and dreaming. This gave science an external variable, paving the way for investigators to look more deeply into both sleep and dreams.[14]

As research continued, science began to identify different stages of sleep and disprove the idea that sleep was a unitary experience. In fact numerous studies, including REM research and the measuring of brain-wave patterns by EEG, clearly show that what we call sleep is actually a fluctuating cycle of alternating states of consciousness and physiological phenomena such as respiration rate, heart rate, blood pressure, penile erection, change in blood levels of free fatty acids, and in neurotransmitters and hormones. In fact, brain-wave measurements during REM sleep, and thus during dreaming, appear to more closely resemble measurement of a waking state than those of other stages of sleep.[15] The evidence that REM and non-REM sleep are quite different physiological states demands that we rethink our old ideas that waking life and sleep are completely different states of consciousness.

REM sleep appears to be very important to the overall physical and psychological health of mammals. Studies have demonstrated that depriving sleeping subjects of REM sleep (and dreams) causes a disorganization of the waking personality, even though these subjects were allowed as much non-REM sleep as they wanted.[16] Modern sleep and dream research continues to provide evidence for the importance of REM sleep to the maintainence of normal biological processes. Studies suggest that sleep, and specifically REM sleep, is an important mediator of nutritional reactions, the incorporation of new behavior, the restoration of neurochemical systems in the brain, information processing, and memory storage.

There is much left to be learned about sleeping and dreaming. At this point, however, we do know that all humans and mammals (and marsupials) dream[17]; we are more likely to dream during the REM cycles of sleep; REM cycles occur approximately every ninety minutes in human beings; most people dream between five to seven dreams per night; dreams may last from a few seconds to over an hour; long sleepers (more than 6.5 hours per night) report more dreams than short sleepers; most people do dream in color; drugs, especially alcohol, interfere with REM sleep and thus with dreaming.[18] James Hall concludes his excellent review of the scientific sleep and dream literature by noting, "We are emerging from a period when waking and sleeping were considered polar opposites into a more complicated but more exciting era in which we must ask again the important questions in the light of a nonunitary conception of sleep that itself may be a precursor to deeper understanding of waking life as being composed of interacting psychological and neurological motives."[19]

Jungian Dreamwork

To Jung, dreams are a self-dramatization of the actual state of the psyche and the unconscious. They are natural and purposive and exist to help us understand our inner life. Jung very clearly described his view about the revealing nature of dreams when he wrote: "The dream is a spontaneous self-portrayal, in symbolic form, of the actual situation in the unconscious."[20] Just as an X ray or CAT scan can look into the workings and state of health of the body, dreams reveal what may be wrong and what is trying to be healed in the psyche.[21] Thus, dreams provide important, highly objective information about what is really going on inside a person, untempered by their personal beliefs about themselves or their psychological defenses. Dreams, Jung believed, do not censor, distort, or disguise. Instead they "show the inner truth and the reality of the patient as it really is: not as I conjecture it to be, and not as he would like it to be, but as it is."[22]

Though dreams contain vital information about our inner life, they are often difficult to decode. In fact, most dreams may appear to be nothing more than jumbles of bizarre situations and outlandish stories that make no sense at all. However, if we open our minds to dreams as speaking in the language of *symbols,* a whole new way of understanding them becomes accessible to us.[23]

A symbol (from the Greek *symbolon,* "token of identity") is something that represents something else by association or resemblance. It may be a term, name, picture, sound, or image that is quite familiar to us in daily life, but has connotations in addition to its obvious meaning. A symbol, to Jung, is an "intuitive idea that cannot yet be formulated in any other or better way."[24] Jung points out: "A word or an image is symbolic when it . . . has a wider 'unconscious' aspect that is never precisely defined or fully explained.

Nor can one hope to define or explain it. As the mind explores the symbol, it is led to ideas that lie beyond the grasp of reason. . . . Because there are innumerable things beyond the range of human understanding, we constantly use symbolic terms to represent concepts that we cannot define or fully comprehend. This is one reason why all religions employ symbolic language or images."[25] Jung believed that human beings spontaneously and unconsciously produce symbols and that these symbols come to us in the form of dream images and fantasies as well as art, poetic imagery, fairy tales, and myth.

Symbols, charged with emotion, meaning, and energy, have held important roles in all cultures. The Olympic torch, banners, sacred books, uniforms, medals of honor, the Star of David, crucifixes, wheels (in Eastern religions), wedding rings, colored ribbons to remember hostages, for AIDS and breast cancer awareness, and all manner of forms, sounds, and figures convey much more psychologically and spiritually than their purely rational aspects would predict. Whether we follow the adventures of noble knights riding through dark Celtic forests in quest of the Holy Grail or Luke Skywalker ceaselessly searching for the wisdom of the Force, symbols release enormous psychological and spiritual energy that propels us on our journey through life.

The overpowering emotion one feels standing before the Vietnam Veterans Memorial in Washington, D.C., evinces the numinous power of symbols. The cold black marble etched only with the thousands and thousands of names of those killed in that war says more to the human heart than all the speech makers' rhetoric can. The feelings of patriotism that fill us when we see our country's flag and hear voices raised in our national anthem are good examples of the psychological and spiritual power of symbols. Rationalism cannot describe this intuitive, emotional response and would say, instead, that a flag is only a design on a piece of cloth and an anthem only a song.

We apprehend and understand the symbols that have been part of our culture and experience. But when we encounter a new or foreign symbol we may easily dismiss it as meaningless, simply because we don't understand it. Jung told a story of a Native American who visited Europe and, upon returning home, told his friends that the Europeans worship animals, since he had seen lions, eagles, and oxen in many old churches. This traveler from North America did not know that the animals depicted are symbols of the Evangelists and are derived from the visions of Ezekiel. Dreams do not reveal their mystery in left-brain verbal or logical languages. Instead, they find their voice in the rich language of symbolism and archetypal imagery. The symbols and images of dreams predate rational concepts in the life of our species and in our individual development. In human beings, the original unit of mental functioning, the primary process, is the image. It is the fundamental language of the soul.

Artists, writers, poets, musicians, creative thinkers, and others who travel in the realm of symbols have frequently reported that the images for their work appeared to them first in dreams. Recently, the popular musician and songwriter Billy Joel reported that he first hears almost all of his music in his dreams. Billy Joel is in good musical company: Mozart, Beethoven, Wagner, and Schumann all observed that the inspiration for some of their music came from their dreams, often in the form of specific musical sounds that they would faithfully transcribe upon waking.[26] Robert Louis Stevenson stated that the central ingredients for *The Strange Case of Dr. Jekyll and Mr. Hyde* were clearly detailed in a dream after he had struggled for a long time to find a tale that would describe the dual nature of man. Other reports suggest that it was Stevenson's wife who insisted that he record his dream.[27]

Inspiration from dreams is not limited to the artists, musicians, and writers. The symbolic images of dreams have influenced scientists and inventors and all manner of "logical" thinkers, including several Nobel Prize winners. Otto Loewi proved that nerve impulses are chemically transmitted after dreaming of an experimental design that demonstrated it. Kekule von Stradonitz, the chemist who discovered the ring-shaped form of the molecular structure of benzene, first understood the form in a dream. Reportedly he dreamed of a snake biting its own tail (an ancient, archetypal image referred to as Uroboros and seen as a symbol of infinity or eternal return). Kekule is reported to have directed his colleagues in basic research by stating: "Gentlemen, learn to dream!"[28] Albert Einstein related his initial ideas about the theory of relativity to a dream he had in adolescence in which he was riding on a sled as it started moving faster and faster. He watched in amazement as the sled approached the speed of light and the stars distorted into beautiful patterns and colors. In his later life he observed that his entire career could be viewed as an extension of that dream. Niels Bohr experienced a dream that led to the formulation of his theory of atomic structure using quantum theory, for which he won the Nobel Prize for physics. Bohr dreamed of a horse race in which the marked lanes on the racetrack, within which the horses had to run, were analogous to the fixed and specific orbits that electrons travel around the nucleus of the atom. Elias Howe, dreaming of being poked by the long sharp spears of cannibals in a jungle, noticed that all the spears had small holes in the tips. This image helped him to solve the problem of thread transport when he invented the sewing machine.[29] Thomas Edison reported that an image of his dead brother came to him in his sleep with instructions on how to design the electric light bulb. While we assume that rational thought is the source of scientific advances, the evidence shows that quite often initial ideas are based on intuition and feeling rather than cold, hard facts. Often this creative intuition is first expressed in the foreign, symbolic language of dreams.

The stories of great minds that found their inspiration in dreams are fascinating. But what of the rest of us? Why do we dream every night? What is the function of dreams in our everyday world?

According to Jung, one psychological function of dreams is what he called *compensation.* By this he meant a natural process aimed at establishing or maintaining balance in the psyche. Just as the body has many mechanisms for maintaining homeostasis in temperature, blood pressure, oxygen intake, and hormonal levels, the psyche too has processes for self-regulation. Dreams often compensate for, or offset, the conscious attitudes of the dreamer, especially when those attitudes are out of touch with one's reality. Often dreams bring forth, frequently in exaggerated ways, the polar opposites of our conscious views. Compensation is then a kind of balancing of the psyche, a maintenance of equilibrium between conscious and unconscious energies.

David had recently been diagnosed with a serious illness that required what was still classified as experimental surgery. In spite of the gravity of his situation he refused to talk about any of the "scary" parts of what he was experiencing. A former Marine in his mid-fifties, David held strongly to the belief that real men don't cry or complain; they are stoic in the face of danger and don't "feel sorry for themselves." "It will be fine," he told his family. "There's nothing to worry about." His optimism went beyond a healthy, positive, hopeful attitude which can be critically important in meeting difficult situations in life. To everyone in his family, his conscious attitude seemed more like denial, a refusal to look honestly at his situation. The idea that he was repressing his real feelings about his health was supported by his family's observations that he had become increasingly irritable and short-tempered about everyday matters. His attitude about his upcoming surgery seemed to be more bravado than real courage. Several weeks prior to his surgery he reported the following dream:

> I am in a hospital and I'm looking everywhere I can for a baby that I've lost. I go into room after room but I can't find him. I get in the elevator but when the door closes I realize that the elevator is attached to the side of the building, like in fancy hotels in large cities. But there is no glass in this elevator. Just a floor that is now going down a hundred stories and it keeps gaining speed. I feel very frightened and I lie on the floor and try to hold on to the edges so I won't fall off. When I get to the bottom I get on a bus. It is a bus like in amusement parks with open sides and just a kind of handrail to hang on to. The bus starts going very fast over winding roads and then we go over a big causeway across a large body of water. I'm scared to death and I'm holding on real tight. I'm let out of the bus on a wide beach. It's dark and someone is selling tickets for passage on a big ship. I can see the ship in the distance offshore. It's dark-looking, kind of ominous. It scares me and I know I don't want to get on it. I'm told that the ship is the *Queen Elizabeth.* I tell the ticket seller that I don't want to buy a ticket and I get back on the bus. I return to the hospital where I continue to look for the baby. Then I wake up.

Even without any further interpretation of the dream and without any background in working with his dreams, David had the feeling that this was an important one. He referred to it as a "big" dream.[30] "The ship is death," he said quite simply. "It's dark and it scared me just to look at it. I'm more afraid of dying from this surgery than I've been telling anyone or even letting myself know."

David's dream is a clear example of compensation: it allowed for the conscious awareness of his underlying, unconscious fears about his health and his upcoming surgery. After his dream, he began to recognize that he could continue to be courageous and go forward with what had to be done in spite of his fears. He opened up to his wife and family about his feelings. He still did not dwell on them or feel sorry for himself, as he was so afraid of doing. Instead he began relating to himself and his family in meaningful ways. The psychic energy that had been bound up in repressing his fears of his illness and death could now be released and redirected toward the process of health and healing.

Not every dream is as clear or direct as David's, and compensation, though the most common, is not the only function of dreams. Often dreams will *complement,* or complete, the prevailing conscious position. Dreams that complement will add missing pieces to our conscious awareness when our conscious attitude is only slightly out of balance with our reality. Compensation and complementation respond to how "off course" we may be. The more out of balance we are in terms of the discrepancy between our conscious and unconscious attitudes, the more we need a major shift of direction (compensation). If we are mostly heading in the right direction but are just a little askew from our true path, the psyche will offer a more gentle, subtle reminder, putting us back on course (complementation).

Jung also wrote about dreams that may be more or less unrelated to the conscious position of the dreamer and may be neither compensatory nor complementary. Some dreams are *prospective,* or anticipatory, in that they "anticipate in the unconscious, future conscious achievements and, thus, for example, provide solutions to conflict in allegoric or symbolic form."[31] Dreams of this kind may provide an outline or plan for a solution of a particularly difficult life situation, and "may prepare the dreamer for a future attitude that may not be recognized as needed until weeks or even months after the dream. The dream can be either positive or negative in its import and, occasionally, it may foreshadow specific good fortune or catastrophe."[32] The unconscious generally knows what is going on in a person's life before there is conscious awareness. For example, most psychological crises in life, like the form that the midlife transition can often take, do not just jump out on a particular day and sandbag us. If we are aware, we often see signs and signals as to where we are heading long in advance of the actual crisis. Symbols describing our direction are often seen in dreams, though many people do not pay attention to their dreams until they are already in the midst of crisis. Jung observed that dreams "prepare, announce, or warn about certain situations often long before they actually happen. This is not necessarily a miracle or a precognition. Most crises . . . have a long incubation in the unconscious."[33]

Other dreams appear to support and coincide with the conscious attitude of the dreamer. Jung called these *parallel* dreams. They function as a kind of "cheerleader" to encourage us to continue in the direction that the conscious attitude is heading. *Traumatic* dreams, in which the dreamer feels physically or psychologically threatened, are generally neither compensating nor complementing a conscious attitude. Often seen in the wake of extremely traumatic events such as sexual abuse, rape, natural catastrophe, or war experiences, these dreams are frequently recurring. They appear to be a way of exposing the traumatized person to the stimulus memories of the event in order to reduce the emotional impact of these memories. The presence of these recurring dreams is included in the psychological definition of post-traumatic stress disorder (PTSD), which has been well documented particularly in veterans of the horrific experiences of the Vietnam War.

Jung also wrote about dreams that evidence *extrasensory perception,* though he considered them to be rare. These dreams could be either precognitive (knowing something in advance) or telepathic (knowing something that is going on in some distant place). *Prophetic* dreams foretell the accurate details of some specific but future event. Rather than describing these kinds of dreams—which toward the end of his life he referred to as "Psi phenomena"—as coming from the supernatural, Jung believed that they were more likely to be synchronistic and based upon unconscious ways of knowing that are simply not yet understood by us.

In all of these various functions of dreams, the dream material attempts to "complete" the dreamer's understanding of a situation. Contrary to a great deal of public opinion, however, no dream spends its energy telling us exactly what we already know. Every dream, even a small fragment of a dream, offers an opportunity for a greater awareness and understanding of our inner life and provides a direct experience of the guiding energies of the Self.

Working with and Understanding Dreams

Our dreams are populated by all sorts of folks, some known to us, and others who are "dream inventions," no one we recognize or have known in our lives. These may take the form of Wise Old Men, tricksters, Fairy Godmothers, Black Madonnas, heroes, or guides. They may be wild savages dancing around a sparkling bonfire or a group of high-collared Victorian ladies sipping tea. They may be male or female, old or young, foreign or everyday in their appearance. Our dream alleyways are haunted by dragons, aliens, monsters, or raging gangs that chase after us. Horses, dogs, frogs, birds, snakes, cats, elephants, our own pets, and other animals make their appearance in our nocturnal theater. Natural events like hurricanes, tornadoes, floods, fires, tidal waves, and volcanic eruptions compete with quiet spring days or walks in the woods in our dream landscape. We may find ourselves naked in the most inappropriate circumstances, taking exams that we are totally unprepared for, calling for help with no one answering, watching as our teeth fall out, plunging from all kinds of high places, or making passionate love with unknown strangers. Castles, caves, distant planets, magical foreign places where we have the power to fly, houses and apartments that we have never seen, and old vaguely remembered homes that we lived in as children provide some of the settings, the locational contexts of our dreams. We understand that dreams speak to us in the language of symbols which, like a foreign tongue, we do not easily understand. But what do they mean? How can we understand the messages from our dreams? Most important, how can we use dreams for greater self-knowledge and individuation, and greater insight into our life?

Clarissa Pinkola Estes observes that there are as many ways to look at a dream as there are dreamers, and that every culture has ideas about the source of dreams. In many Native American cultures the dream-maker is referred to as the "Shadow Catcher" or "Shadow Walker." To other people the dream-maker provides a mirror that reflects the land of the unknown back into the topside world. To still others, dreams are manifestations of the spirit world. To Jung, the archetypal Self is the source of the spontaneous symbols of dreams. Dreams serve to point out and illuminate our complexes and show us the scope and specifics of our inner life. But there is no doubt that the symbols in dreams can be confusing and unintelligible. Emerson noted that dreams present "an answer in hieroglyphics to the question we would pose."[34] Estes, in describing the source of dreams, uses the metaphor of the "Riddle Mother," from a childhood rhyme: "Riddle-dee, Riddle-dee, Riddle-dee Rakes / She leaves more behind than she ever takes."[35] The Riddle Mother will respond to anything that we ask of her but she always answers in the form of a mysterious riddle which we are charged with unraveling.

In unraveling and interpreting the hidden messages in dreams, it is best to take three important steps:[36]

1. We must have a clear understanding of the exact details of the dream.
2. We must make associations and amplifications on one or more levels: the personal, the cultural or natural, and the archetypal. Jung

wrote: "A dream is too slender a hint to be understood until it is enriched by the stuff of associations and analogy and thus amplified to the point of intelligibility."[37]

3. We must consider the amplified dream in the context of our life and the process of individuation in order to fully understand the meaning of the dream.

1. Recording Dreams

Research has shown that all people dream every night but that many do not recall their dreams in the morning. Often we may experience an initial, immediate recall of at least some of the dream images, but by the time we are on our way to the bathroom to brush our teeth, they are gone. Like smoke evaporating into the air, dream images are fragile and not able to withstand the clear light of morning. In working with dreams it is critical to write them down immediately upon awakening. Occasionally, a person may have a dream of such impact that it can be remembered long into the day, perhaps even forever, but this is very rare. Anyone who is truly interested in working with dreams will keep a pen and paper on the night table. Some people prefer speaking their dreams into a small tape recorder and that, too, is fine. The point is that dreams need to be recorded immediately if they are to be remembered.

It is important to record dreams in as much *detail* as possible. Imagine that you are writing a news story and every detail is critically important. It matters whether you were driving a blue car or a red car in the dream. It matters whether you were driving or whether someone was driving you. If you dream of a dog you should record what kind of dog it is. Is it male or female? Aggressive or docile? What color? Does it have any unusual features? Christopher Wren, the architect who designed St. Paul's Cathedral in London, observed that "God is in the details." So it is with dreams.

A man contemplating a divorce in midlife reported the following dream to me: "I am driving in a car with my wife." With so little information, the dream appeared to be of no great importance or interest. However, when he had a similar dream the following night, he wrote down that he was "in a dark blue car, an old Chevy. My wife is sitting in the backseat and I'm driving." The color and type of car reminded him of a car he had bought two years before he married. His wife hadn't liked the car at that time and castigated him for making such a poor choice. With the addition of these small details, this man better understood the dream symbol and gained insight into the long-standing critical attitude his wife had toward his choices and decisions. The details of the dream added to his awareness of his current feelings about his marriage and helped him to make a more conscious choice about whether to remain married or not.

The importance of recording details cannot be overemphasized. James Hall underscores this importance when he writes: "To say 'I dreamed of work' is like saying that the play 'Hamlet' deals with 'family relationships.'[38] The richness and meaning of dream symbols can only be uncovered by paying attention to the details.

The ultimate importance of interpreting and working with dreams is in relating them to our actual lives and using our own unconscious wisdom to become more conscious. In recording dreams, it is important to write down the date of the dream along with any initial observations as to what was going on in our outer life at that time. Keeping a dream journal of some type so that one can review past dreams is the best way to record dreams.

2. Associations and Amplifications of Dreams

The meaning of a dream's symbols can be understood only in the context of the dreamer's psyche. At first blush, the symbols of the raw dream are often confusing and make very little sense. Although Jung believed that dreams may have a transformative effect even when they are not interpreted or translated, in such cases the benefit is usually transitory or weak. Dreams release their power more often when we honor them by trying to understand their symbols and relate them to our lives. Freudian dream interpretation suggests that dreamers *make free associations* to dream images and then associations to those associations, creating a chain of successive associations that get farther and farther away from the original dream image. Jung, on the other hand, urged his patients to *stay close to the dream images themselves* because in the dream the Self, after all, is attempting to reveal, not hide, aspects of the dreamer's unconscious life. Jung was clear and adamant in his belief that the symbols of the dream, when understood, would speak for themselves.[39] He also believed that one should approach dreams with an open mind and heart, unencumbered by complicated theoretical biases or explanations. Jung felt that we should "play" with the images of dreams and allow our intuition and instinct to have a major role in understanding the symbols. "One would do well to treat every dream as though it were a totally unknown object," he wrote. "Look at it from all sides, take it in your hand, carry it about with you, let your imagination play around with it."[40]

Jung also believed that every dream can be looked at and interpreted on a number of levels. For example, dreams may be viewed from an *objective* level, where we interpret the images and people in our dreams with reference to persons or situations in our outer world. If we have a dream about a friend, for example, the dream may really have to do with our external, real-world relationship with that person. When we look at a dream from the *subjective* level, we interpret the images, persons, or situations in the dream as symbolically representing aspects of our own psyche. In this way even familiar people may represent an archetypal element of our own unconscious. Here we must ask ourselves questions such as: How would I describe that person? What do I have in common with him or her? What do I know about that person that could be symbolizing something about myself?

It is not necessary to take an either/or, subjective/objective approach to any dream. In fact, *dreams should be looked at from both an objective and subjective level,* though the Jungian approach to dreamwork assumes that there is some subjective reality in every dream. Referring to the subjective level of dreamwork and the dramatic structure that is found in so many dreams, Jung wrote: "A dream is a theater in which the dreamer is himself the scene, the player, the prompter, the producer, the author, the public and the critic."[41]

In fact, many dreams follow a classical structure of dramatic elements. Edward Whitmont and Sylvia Perera, in *Dreams, a Portal to the Source,* point out that the form of classical Greek drama most succinctly expresses the dramatic structure of the dream: exposition, peripeteia, crisis, and lysis. An understanding of the dramatic structure of a dream can often lead us to an understanding of its meaning. The setting *(exposition)* of the dream often states the theme of its psychological or symbolic focus. The development *(peripeteia)* shows possibilities, trends, and dynamics. The *crisis* is the critical point of the dream in which opposing tendencies reach their highest pitch. Finally, the *lysis* shows the way in which the dream crisis may be resolved.

Interpreting the dramatic structure of a dream can help us understand its meaning, but it is also true that we may never fully or immediately comprehend any dream. Marion Woodman acknowledges that she is only beginning to understand some of the dreams that she had more than twenty years ago.[42] But while we may not immediately and completely grasp the meaning of any given dream, we can know that we are on the right track in our interpretation of a dream when we feel that it "clicks." Often we will have a bodily response when this occurs, an "Aha!" experience that lets us know that the way we are looking at the dream resonates within us. It tells us that something in this new interpretation of the dream symbol is touching a nerve. The absence of an emotional response does not necessarily mean that an idea or interpretation is "wrong" or that it has moved down an unproductive path, but when the click happens, the dreamer knows it immediately.

When the undeciphered symbols are related to the *personal associations* of the dreamer, light begins to emerge from the darkness. Associations are ideas, images, memories, reactions, or feelings that are spontaneously connected to the symbols from the dream. Because every dreamer has his or her own personal experiences and beliefs, the symbols must be looked at from those particular perspectives. Looking at the dream from the point of view of personal associations is the first crucial step in understanding a dream's meanings.

The importance of the personal context in understanding dreams was described as early as the second century in the writings of Artemidorus. It is readily apparent in the fact that different symbols will have different meanings for different people—for example, while dung might indicate good fortune in the dream of a farmer it would not for a lawyer or a carpenter.[43] The dark blue Chevy, in the dream cited earlier, had an important meaning to the man who dreamed it, but would not have the same emotional or personal associations for someone who received a blue Chevy as a graduation present from her loving parents. Because the associations to the symbols of a dream come from the personal unconscious, it is impossible to devise a list of the meanings of dream symbols, though there are many books on the market that purport to do so. No book can tell you what your dream means—only the dreamer can truly know. Instead of opening a dream book, we must instead ask ourselves questions about the symbols. For example, if my dream includes a five- or six-year-old child, I might ask myself: What was my life like when I was that age? Is there a child of five or six who is in some way involved in my life? What is happening in my life right now that is similar to what was happening in my life at that age? What is this symbol of a child trying to tell me about my own life as it is right now?

After losing his job at a large computer company as a result of corporate downsizing, Ted was thrown into a spiral of depression and suicidal thoughts. He had worked at the company for more than twenty-five years and was hoping to retire in less than ten more. Like many people who suffer such losses in midlife, he had not anticipated anything like that ever happening to him. He said he understood that these things happen in business—the company hadn't been as profitable as it once was and the stockholders were demanding a lean and mean management structure. His company had done the best they could, he believed, in giving him a fair severance deal and providing career counseling for all those let go.

Ted was in his early fifties, with many financial obligations, and he felt hopeless about his future. In the midst of his anguish, he reported a dream in which he was sitting in the back pew of a church, when he saw a mother enter with three small children. She walked to the front of the church and sat down in the first pew and took out her hymnal. At first she sat with what appeared to be the oldest of the three children on her lap. A minute or so later the youngest child, a very tiny infant, began to scream and cry. The infant's wailing was so loud that everyone in the church got up and left except for Ted and this woman and her children. The woman picked up the child who had been sitting on her lap and threw him into the aisle of the church. She then placed the infant on her lap and began to feed it a bottle of milk. Each time the older child tried to reclaim his position on the mother's lap, she would heave him into the aisle again. Ted awakened from the dream shaking.

Ted had no knowledge of what the dream might mean. He only knew that it was upsetting to him and he didn't even want to think about it again. "How old was the boy in the dream?" I asked. Ted thought that he looked about three or four years old. "What was happening in your life at that time?" I asked. Ted said he couldn't remember anything particularly traumatic during his early childhood. "Oh," he said after a few minutes, "my sister was born when I was three." Ted's chin began to tremble and tears welled up in his eyes. "My sister was born deaf and my parents had to give her a lot of time and attention. When she was about a year old my mother took her to a special clinic in another city and was gone for almost six months, except for occasional visits on weekends. Even though my father stayed at home with my older brother and me, I felt abandoned and unimportant. After my mother and sister came back from the clinic—they weren't successful in helping my sister's deafness—I felt that my sister got all the attention from my mother. As I got older I understood that Mom had no choice.

She had to take care of my sister, who had so many problems, and I love my little sister, anyway."

"Is there anything that you may have felt at three years of age that seems in any way similar to what you are feeling now?" I asked him. Ted's tears began to flow as he described the same kind of feelings about being let go by the company that had been his container for more than half his life. He was feeling the same kind of abandonment and unimportance that he had as a very young child, around the same age as the child figure in his dream. He couldn't recognize any anger at this situation about his job because he "understood" it, just as he had "understood" that his mother had to give most of her attention to his physically disabled little sister. Ted had allowed his reason to talk him out of his feelings. But it is possible to be angry *and* to understand why something is as it is. When Ted was better able to accept his feelings and express his anger, his depression became far less intense. He was still disappointed of course at the turn of events in his life, but freed from the debilitating sense of despondency and helplessness, he was far better able to put his energy into seeking another job, and he was better able to enjoy his life during the search. More conscious of his abandonment complex, he was able to understand in new ways his own value as a person, and to come to different terms with the fact that life is not always fair but we're still allowed to have feelings about that fact. Ted's dream, like an X ray locating and identifying a physical problem, had pointed out the exact state of his unconscious, inner world. His personal amplifications of the dream images helped him to understand these symbols in the context of his own life and experience. Most important, the dream provided a kind of healing that allowed him to move on with his life with greater awareness.

Sometimes dream images cannot be understood in their personal context. In the second stage of dream amplification, the dreamer looks at the *natural and cultural associations* of the images. For example, if a dream symbol is an animal, the dreamer might consider what he or she knows about that particular kind of animal's behavior or appearance. What does that animal naturally do? Is it a predator or prey? What are its defenses? What are its physical features? What are our general cultural impressions of that animal (e.g., "blind as a bat," "smart as a fox," "a lone wolf," "stubborn as a mule")?

Like cultural experiences, natural occurrences can be looked at in terms of how they exhibit themselves and how we perceive them in the natural world. A tornado is a very different image from a gentle breeze; a flood does not contain the same energy as a flowing stream. What these natural events are like in real life can tell us much about their meaning in our dreams. The symbol of the President, in a democratic country, is different from that of a homeless man. In Western society, a dream of eating a big juicy steak at a barbecue would have one meaning, while the same dream by a person faithful to Hinduism, which considers cows to be sacred animals and never to be eaten, would have quite a different meaning. To dream of sailing in a small boat and killing a whale would have one meaning to an Inuit fisherman and quite another to the head of Greenpeace.

Dreams often serve up their symbols by playing on the language of the dreamer's culture and using metaphors, analogies, similes, allusions, overstatement and understatement (called hyperbole and litotes in poetic language). They frequently speak in puns and figures of speech. "This is going to be a long haul," one of my clients said as she discussed her process of individuation and how far she felt from any sense of wholeness. "So I'll tell you this dream I had. I'm going down a long hall . . ." The Self has access to an immense storehouse of symbols rich in meaning to describe the state of our psyche. In dreams, people find themselves "making mountains out of molehills," "at the end of their rope," "singing the blues," "too big for their britches," "letting cats out of the bag," and "hanging out their dirty laundry."

Sometimes the meaning of a dream's symbols are not clear from either personal, cultural, or natural associations. In these cases, we can look beyond the dream's personal context through the third level of dream amplification, which includes looking at the dream image in terms of its *archetypal associations.* It is at this level of amplification that dreams take on awe-inspiring meaning; this is the terrain of the "big" dreams, far more vivid, numinous, and common at midlife than during the first half of our lives. As our path toward individuation pulls us into greater contact with our inner life during the midlife transition, our dreams seem to reach more often into the deep inner core of the collective unconscious to produce their symbols. Jung observed: "A man in middle life still feels young, and age and death lie far ahead of him. At about thirty-six he passes the zenith of life, without being conscious of the meaning of this fact. If he is a man whose whole make-up and nature do not tolerate excessive unconsciousness, then the import of this moment will be forced upon him, perhaps in the form of an archetypal dream. It would be in vain for him to try to understand the dream with the help of a carefully worked out context, for it expresses itself in strange mythological forms that are not familiar to him. The dream uses collective figures because it has to express an eternal human problem that repeats itself endlessly, and not just a disturbance of personal balance."[44] The rational mind may balk at the idea that we experience dream images that have potent meanings of which we are consciously unaware, that exist for all people in all cultures. Nevertheless, the presence and power of these dreams are self-evident to anyone who has ever experienced one.

The archetypal symbols that come to us in dreams are the stuff of ancient religious traditions, cultural anthropology, folklore, fairy tales, art, esoteric philosophy, archaic practices of alchemy, astrology, and myths. Adding to an understanding of the power behind these archetypal symbols in dreams, Whitmont and Perera write about these transpersonal images: "[Archetypal symbols] represent the ways in which mankind's collective unconscious in its different cultural expressions has responded spiritually, philosophically, socially, ethically and esthetically to the grand themes of existence . . . . Through their appearance in dreams, they enable direct confrontation with the numinous, transpersonal, and ultimately unrepresentable general elements that structure human activity and consciousness—patterns of life, death, rebirth, childhood, development, sacrifice, conflict, suffering, achievement, order, relationships, separation, connection, to name but a few."[45] Archetypal images, drawn from these deep wells of wisdom and collective human experience, emerge from the Self and deposit themselves in our dreams. Joseph Campbell aptly describes the intimate relationship between the archetypal symbols of dreams and the images of great myths. He writes, "A dream is a personal experience of that deep, dark ground that is the support of our conscious lives, and a myth is the society's dream. The myth is the public dream and the dream is the private myth."[46] Jung, in fact, became aware of the archetypes through his observations that the same kinds of primordial images appeared in the dreams of modern people as in ancient myths and religions. Thus a business executive in Seattle can experience the same dream symbols as a Mongolian nomad.

During the most extreme part of my midlife crisis, I experienced a very odd dream. It was more like a still photograph than the typical moving-picture images in most dreams. An unusual symbol in a bright turquoise appeared in bas-relief against a black background. The symbol was repeated over and over clearly, like a wallpaper pattern, and was "on screen" for such a long time that I had no trouble drawing it in my dream journal when I woke up. I had no idea what the image meant in spite of searching for any personal associations or cultural meaning that could be attached to it. After a while I forgot about it.

Almost a year and a half after this dream I was browsing through a bookstore and opened up a dictionary of symbols. The book's pages naturally opened to the center, and there before my eyes was a drawing of the symbol I had seen in my dream. I was not fully able to believe what I was seeing so I bought the book and immediately upon returning home, searched through my dream journal to find the drawing I had made earlier. My drawing and the one in the symbol dictionary were almost identical. I learned that the symbol that appeared in my dream is called the Knot of Isis and among the ancient Egyptians it symbolized life and immortality. Ankh-shaped, with arms at its sides, it was a widely used amulet. Isis was the goddess of the earth and the moon, the sister-wife of Osiris and the mother of Horus. She ruled in heaven, on earth, and on and under the sea as well as in the underworld. She was called Au Set, meaning "exceeding queen" or simply "spirit." As a highly revered Egyptian goddess, Isis was associated with creation myths and the life-death-rebirth cycle. As I reviewed my dream journal and the events of my life at the time of the dream, I realized that the Knot of Isis was a perfect symbol. At that point in my midlife transition I felt like I was dying—I now know that a part of me *was* dying. Overwhelmed by letting go of what my life had been, I could see no future and was not consciously aware that there might be anything like a resurrection on the horizon. My unconscious, guided by the Self, was offering a compensation, an archetypal reminder that there is, in fact, life after death. Perhaps I found the book at a time in my life when I could better appreciate and understand the wisdom of this dream symbol as it applied to my own life.

Marie was experiencing a profound identity crisis in midlife. The wife of a prominent physician, she was generally an extroverted, upbeat woman who devoted a great deal of energy to community service and to traveling with and supporting her husband as he gave lectures throughout the country. But she had become increasingly reclusive and she described the inner "emptiness" that is so often experienced during the midlife transition. She reported a dream that confused her since she could not make any sense of the symbols. There were no personal associations that came to mind for a powerful and frightening dream image: "I dreamed that someone came from a dark shadow and cut off my hands." The image terrified her and she was concerned that it might be some kind of warning about a physical problem she was not aware of.

As a therapist I have heard dozens of women, especially those in midlife, report a similar dream in which their hands were cut off. Although not a single one of these women was familiar with it, their dreams had reached into the mythological dimension and retold the story that is known in the literature of fairy tales as "The Handless Maiden" or "The Girl Without Hands." Understanding Marie's dream by amplifying the symbol at an archetypal level provided a richness and texture to this dream symbol that would not have been possible otherwise. An awareness of how this fairy tale illuminates the heroine's journey as a reclamation and re-membering of her lost feminine energy helped Marie to understand how she had given over all her power to her relationships with men throughout her life,[47] first with her father and now with her husband. At midlife, she had "lost her grip" on her own self-identity and didn't have any strong sense of who she really was as a human being short of her definition through her roles in life, first as daughter, then as wife. Through comprehending this archetypal layer of the dream, Marie gained a great deal of insight into both her own inner life and the practical outer realities of her marriage.

Ellen experienced a powerful dream in the weeks following her suicide attempt (described in the previous chapter). She wrote down the following details of the dream in her dream journal: "I cannot tell if I am a bird or if I am watching a bird that is rising up from a swirling cloud of dust and sparks on the ground. Like a small tornado of fire and dirt. As the shape of a bird emerges, I can see that it is throwing off flames, fire, or something shiny like little slivers of glass."

Ellen could make no personal associations with the images in the dream, though she did feel that the dream represented some kind of change in her life. Just as the bird was rising from the dust, something inside of her was transforming. Although still deeply depressed by the losses that had met her head-on during her midlife transition, she could sense some newfound energy for life and made a clear and conscious decision to live.

By looking at her dream from the point of view of archetypal amplification, Ellen was able to see her inner changes more clearly. She was consciously unaware of the story of the phoenix, a universal symbol of resurrection and immortality, of death and rebirth by fire. The phoenix, the name the Greeks gave to the mythical Egyptian bird Bennu, is a symbol of the rising sun. According to the myths of many cultures, this fantastic bird constructs its own funeral pyre and lights it with the beating of its wings. It then dies by fire and remains dead for three days, rising again from its own ashes on the third day. The image of the phoenix symbolized Ellen's emergence from the self-destruction and terror that had led her to make a serious suicide attempt. Like the bird rising from the ashes, she was making new claims on her life and had been psychologically and spiritually reborn.

Discussing a dream with a trained Jungian analyst or with anyone who has an understanding of the kinds of symbols that the Self often relies upon to bring its point to consciousness can be a powerful tool, since knowledge of the mythological, alchemical, poetic, and artistic realms of human experience and culture, the repository of the universal images that fill our dreams, is necessary in order to understand a dream at the archetypal level. But dreamers can open themselves up to the vast body of knowledge that provides the imaginative symbols of the collective unconscious. Books and other sources of information can be very helpful in understanding these symbols if they are used to illuminate a dream image rather than to provide an explicit answer as to what a symbol means. This is an important point, for, as stated earlier, no book or outside source can tell a dreamer what his or her dream symbols mean. But the Self does speak in the figurative language of imagination that is included in the vast wisdom of human cultures, and people seriously interested in a deep understanding of their dreams can benefit by access to this information. There are many good symbol dictionaries that can be helpful tools, as well as numerous other sources that shed light on the human imagination.[48]

While we may speak intellectually of our process of individuation and of the importance of understanding that we are more than our persona and must integrate and make conscious the energies of the shadow or the anima/animus, dreams can show us these unconscious parts of our personality quite clearly, offering the quickest and truest path to them. While there is great individual variation and a limitless number of images that may appear in dreams, many of the major archetypal aspects of the psyche—for example the shadow, anima/animus, persona, and Self—may present themselves in somewhat predictable types of dream symbols, though they are not limited to only the forums presented in the following discussion. To look at a dream from the subjective point of view emphasizes that all the characters and other symbols in it reflect some part of the dreamer's personality. Understanding the nature of these images may give the dreamer important clues to the aspect of the psyche that the dream is trying to help the dreamer understand.

The *shadow,* all of those aspects of ourselves that we are not conscious of, most often appears in our dreams as a *figure of the same gender as the dreamer.* This includes people that we may know or have known in our waking life, but more often the shadow is represented by a dream character that is not known to us. Frequently the shadow is portrayed in very negative terms. It is the same-sex dream figure that torments us, chases us, and tries to call our attention to neglected aspects of the Self. Our shadow may manifest itself in many different guises. "The shadow can be anything," Marion Woodman observes, "in our 'holier than thou' attitude that we think we're not."[49] But the shadow also presents itself in more positive terms. After all, it is the repository of our unlived lives, and so it also contains creativity, spontaneity, courage, and many wonderful human qualities that we may have repressed. For example, animals in dreams frequently represent our unconscious instincts which have been relegated to the shadow, since instincts and intuition have been denigrated in our culture. Very often these dream animals alert us to important, positive aspects of ourselves by prompting us to ask: What is this animal like? What is its nature? What do we know of its behavior and adaption to its world?

The unconscious aspects of *anima/animus,* in both their positive and negative dimensions, are most often represented in dreams by *figures of the opposite gender to the dreamer.* These powerful autonomous energies of the psyche have retained a strong personality because they have been split off and undeveloped. In some ways the integration of the shadow is easier than that of the anima/animus. After all, the psychic material in the shadow was at one point known to us and then repressed. The anima/animus, on the other hand, has never been consciously known. In interpreting the symbolic meaning of dream images that reflect the shadow or the anima/animus, we must ask a number of questions about the characters in our dreams: How would we describe the person in the dream? What is he or she like? Where is he or she trying to lead us? How are we like or unlike this person? Some writers have suggested that most often the anima in a man will be represented in a specific female dream character, while the animus in women may more often be symbolized by a group of male characters (e.g., a gang of men). While there is no hard and fast proof of this, I have seen it quite often in women's dreams.

The *persona,* the aspect of the psyche that is the conscious outer face we show to the world, is often represented in dreams by *clothing or lack of it; makeup; masks; disguises; performing for audiences; hats, wigs, or other symbols that represent our adaption to the external world.* For example, judges may dream of gavels, carpenters of hammers and other tools, academicians of books, and so forth. Common dream motifs that refer to the persona include looking for the right clothes, looking for something else to wear, and appearing naked or inappropriately clothed for certain occasions.[50]

In dreams an encounter with the *Self,* the ordering and unifying center of the psyche, is a powerful and numinous experience. Dreams of the Self are the "big" dreams that leave us feeling as if we have had an encounter with the Divine. Even people new to working with their dreams have an emotional response to the extraordinary energy of this powerful God-image within the human soul. These dream images of Self and transformation occur often in midlife. The Self may appear in dreams as a *Wise Old Man or Wise Old Woman, or as God-images from the dreamer's own faith.* Jung wrote about his own dream encounter with an Elijah-type figure of ancient wisdom. He first appeared to Jung in a dream and Jung called him Philemon. Jung describes his dream: "There was a blue sky, like the sea, covered not by clouds but by flat brown clods of earth. It looked as if the clods were breaking apart and the blue water of the sea were becoming visible between them. But the water was the blue sky. Suddenly there appeared from the right a winged being sailing across the sky. I saw that it was an old man with the horns of a bull. He held a bunch of four keys, one of which he clutched as if he were about to open a lock. He had the wings of the kingfisher with its characteristic colors."[51]

Jung wrote that he did not at all understand this dream image, so he painted it to impress it upon his memory. While he was finishing the painting, he took a walk near his garden on the shores of the lake and encountered a dead kingfisher (a small-footed, heavy-headed, heronlike bird that perches above the water and dives headfirst to catch fish and insects). He wrote: "I was thunderstruck, for kingfishers are quite rare in the vicinity of Zürich and I have never since found a dead one. The body was recently dead—at the most two or three days—and showed no external injuries."[52] Jung felt that Philemon represented superior, though somewhat mysterious, insight and wisdom. This self image, powerful in the dream and made even more numinous by the synchronicity of finding the dead kingfisher in his garden, became to Jung "what the Indians call a Guru." He wrote: "Philemon and other figures of my fantasies brought home to me the crucial insight that there are things in the psyche which I do not produce, but which produce themselves and have their own life. Philemon represented a force which was not myself. In my fantasies I held conversations with him, and he said things which I had not consciously thought. For I observed clearly that it was he who spoke, not I. . . . He confronted me in an objective manner, and I understood that there is something in me which can say things that I do not know . . ."[53]

In addition to figures that are old and wise, the Self may also reveal itself through many other symbols. For example, a frequently reported dream includes nothing but a *disembodied voice* which addresses the dreamer directly, usually in a brief statement of great significance. Three other powerful and frequent manifestations of the Self in dreams are the images of a *Divine Child, the number 4,* and a *mandala.* The Divine Child, shown most clearly in its religious and historical context by the Christ Child, carries with it the strong presence of new beginnings; it is an image of transformation and individuation.

The number 4, which Jung called the "quarternity," may also represent the Self in dreams. In Jung's initial dream of Philemon, for example, the Wise Old Man held four keys. Four is a number that occurs frequently in mythology, folklore, literature, and ancient religious and philosophical systems. While the number 3 often represents something that is "in process," or becoming (e.g., three tasks for the hero to undertake on his or her quest is a frequent symbol in fairy tales and folk stories), the number 4 symbolizes completion and wholeness: the alchemists treated with four elements (earth, air, fire, water) and four qualities (dry, moist, hot, cold) and believed that fourness was the basic organizing principle of matter. There are four seasons, four directions (according to most Native American tribes and others), four psychological functions (thinking, feeling, sensation, and intuition), and quadruplicities (groupings of four) are found in all systems of astrology. Edward Edinger writes: "The quarternity image expresses the totality of the psyche in its structural, static, or eternal sense, whereas the trinity image expresses the totality of psychological experience in its dynamic, developmental, temporal aspect."[54]

The number 4 is often related to the image of a mandala, which Jung also believed represented the Self and wholeness in the images that are spontaneously produced in fantasies and dreams. The word *mandala* is from the Sanskrit language and means circle. This circular symbol—which is found in religious imagery from every culture, in architecture and art, sacred dances, and meditation images—may include a square or other four-sided figure. Jung wrote about this image in his autobiography: "I began to understand that the goal of psychic development is the Self. There is no linear evolution; there is only a circumambulation of the Self. Uniform development exists, at most, only at the beginning; later, everything points toward the center. This insight gave me stability, and gradually my inner peace returned. I knew that in finding the mandala as an expression of the Self I had attained what was for me the ultimate. Perhaps someone else knows more, but not I."[55] Interestingly, Jung began the spontaneous creation of mandala symbols in his dreams and drawings around 1918, as he was emerging from his own midlife transition.

Images of the Self in dreams, though in no way restricted to the examples given here, are extraordinarily powerful symbols. Katherine, a forty-three-year-old woman who had been overwhelmed by a severe psychological breakdown during midlife, came to my office in tears and said that she had been profoundly depressed for more than six months. She was extremely self-critical. She believed that she always had to be perfect, so she did not allow any room for herself to experience normal human feelings or to make mistakes. During her inner journey of midlife she had a dream in which she was sitting in a small boat, like a canoe, on a slowly moving river. She had no paddle and so could only let the river carry her to her destination. Beautiful trees and plants surrounded her on the nearby banks of this river, and at one point she could see a deer peering through the leaves. Then she heard the sound of a waterfall in the distance. At first she was afraid, but the waterfall appeared to be gentle and nonthreatening. Her boat carried her through the splashing waterfall into a realm of perfect white light where she felt totally loved and protected. She awakened from the dream with a peaceful feeling of contentment, which she said she could not adequately describe. Even uninterpreted, this dream had a dramatic and profound effect on her feelings and behavior. My secretary, on seeing her in the waiting room before her appointment, pulled me aside and asked with great surprise, "Is that Katherine?" Usually she would sit quietly in a chair, her head in her hands and her eyes downcast. She never spoke to anyone else who might be waiting there at the same time. Today, Katherine was talking with a woman who was waiting for her appointment with another therapist in my practice. She was smiling and sitting straight in her chair with a great deal of poise and confidence. She was dressed in more colorful clothes than I had ever seen her wear and was animated and alive. She attributed these powerful changes to the images she had seen in her dream.

Katherine's experience with her dream is a remarkable one. It is rare to see such sudden and observable changes following a single dream.

But the experience of the transformative Self in dreams cannot help but change us.

Amplifying the meaning of dream images by making associations at the personal, the cultural or natural, and the archetypal level can provide an understanding of the symbols that help us to comprehend our deep inner world. But these symbols are of little use unless we can discover how they pertain to our own life and our psychological and spiritual development.

3. Placing the Dream into the Context of our Lives

Dreams provide a symbolic access to the unconscious aspects of ourselves, and thus provide a direct course to self-knowledge, understanding, and growth. They allow us to understand our turbulent inner forces in order to integrate them into consciousness without being overcome by their power. John Sanford speaks of this "doling out" of the knowledge of the inner world when he writes that dreams "break up the tremendous inner forces of the Self bit by bit and enable us to integrate the unconscious gradually so that we are not overwhelmed by it. The effect of this, providing we adopt the correct attitude, is the enlargement of consciousness and the expansion of our personality."[56]

In order to fully understand and integrate the power of the dream, we need to apply its message to our life and our self-knowledge. We can ask ourselves questions: Why did I have this dream now? What in the dream brings up issues that I am currently dealing with? What conscious attitude is being compensated for by the dream? But because the ego is involved in interpreting the dream, there is a tendency, especially for people working alone with their dreams, to come to a conclusion that the dream is simply reiterating what we already know about ourselves. That is one reason why learning from our dreams is facilitated by working with an analyst, therapist, or dream group. As a general rule, if you believe that you already know what the dream seems to be saying, then you have missed its true meaning.

In looking at a dream's meaning it is best to begin with personal associations rather than the archetypal ones. In fact, there is a danger in becoming obsessed and inflated with the archetypal level because of its numinosity and power. It can be very seductive to feel ourselves in the presence of the Divine Mystery rather than to face the fact that we may be selfish or greedy. Dreams do not exist only to show us the sacred face of God; they also help us to know ourselves better in our daily lives and to relate to others in more conscious ways. They instruct us in ways to live meaningfully in the present and to embrace joyfully our life's realities. In desiring to see everything at the level of archetype, we will overlook the very real associations of the personal unconscious. James Hall notes, "There is a clear order for amplification: personal material takes precedence over cultural material, and cultural amplifications take precedence over archetypal amplifications. Thus one does not move toward the less personal areas of cultural and archetypal amplification unless the meaning of the dream does not become clear within the range of personal amplification."[57]

Dreams can often best be understood when we look at them in the context of their relationships to one another as well as in relationship to our real, external life. Jung felt that a single dream only rarely revealed its meaning to the dreamer. Dreams may recur or present the same basic themes in escalating, dramatic ways, seemingly in an attempt to get our attention. Thus a carefully kept dream journal, which includes dates of specific dreams, is a valuable tool in seeing our dreams in relationship to each other as well as in the context of our lives.

Jung believed that images from dreams could be further enhanced and understood by continuing to work with them beyond the amplification of the dream images. To fully integrate the dream symbols into consciousness, he believed, it was necessary to "carry the dream forward."

Active Imagination and Carrying the Dream Forward

Jung believed that dreams could be further understood by using one's imagination. He practiced a kind of meditation, concentrating on a dream image and allowing the psyche to spontaneously produce feelings and images. In describing Active Imagination Jung wrote, "You choose a dream, or some other fantasy-image, and concentrate on it by simply catching hold of it and looking at it . . . You then fix this image in the mind by concentrating your attention. Usually it will alter, as the mere fact of contemplating it animates it. The alterations must be carefully noted down all the time, for they reflect the psychic processes in the unconscious background, which appear in the form of images consisting of conscious memory material. In this way conscious and unconscious are united, just as a waterfall connects above and below."[58]

Active Imagination allows for a dialogue with the interior figures and symbols produced in our dream images. It is in a way like a conscious dream, one that allows us to face our unconscious inner world directly while at the same time maintaining conscious awareness. The process itself is really quite simple. In your imagination you create a dialectic between the ego and the unconscious by talking to the images and characters that presented themselves in your dream and asking questions such as, "Why have you appeared in my dream?" "What are you here to tell me?" As Robert Johnson accurately observes, "They answer back. You are startled to find out that they express radically different viewpoints from those of your conscious mind. They tell you things you never consciously knew and express thoughts that you never consciously thought."[59]

During the earliest part of my midlife crisis I had a dream in which a small catlike animal appeared from behind a bush and led me through a maze. In the dream, I felt betrayed and badly treated by someone with whom I worked. I could make no real sense of the dream because my conscious attitude about this co-worker was quite positive, and in fact, I refused to believe that there was any objective truth in the dream. We were not close friends but my colleague appeared to be an ethical and decent sort of guy. In focusing on the dream symbol of the cat by visualizing it in Active Imagination, I realized that it was a lynx. I could tell by the small tufts of fur that stuck out from the top of its ears. I sat quietly and in my imagination I asked the lynx what it was trying to say to me. There were several minutes of silence—apparently the lynx didn't have much to say—and then the lynx said very clearly and three times, "You do not yet know what you know in the dream." I wrote this down in my dream journal although, frankly, I still did not understand what it meant.

Two and a half months later I learned that my co-worker had taken a great deal of credit for work that I and others had accomplished. He had been doing this for more than a few months. In fact, he had been doing it at the time of my dream. I felt the same betrayal that I had felt in my dream. My unconscious, as is so often the case, knew important information well in advance of my consciously knowing it. Months after this dream and the betrayal by my co-worker I was browsing through the index of a book about Native American animal medicine, and noticed a section on "lynx medicine." I had not forgotten the dream or the lynx's message from my Active Imagination and was interested in knowing more. I learned that to many Native American tribes, the lynx represents the holding of secrets. I read, "It is said that if you want to find out a secret, ask Lynx medicine. Unfortunately, it is difficult to get the silent Lynx to speak. To be confronted by the powerful medicine of Lynx signifies that you do not know something about yourself or others."[60]

In addition to using Active Imagination in a dialogue between ego and unconscious we can use many other methods to better understand dream symbols. Jungian analyst and writer June Singer observes that active imagination is "an attitude toward the unconscious. It cannot be said to be a technique or even a method of coming to terms with the unconscious, because it is a different experience for each person who is able to use it. The common feature of all varieties of active imagination is its dependence upon a view of the unconscious that recognizes its contents as containing innate structures (archetypes) which inevitably define the potentialities and the limitations of the personality."[61]

Jung felt that all kinds of imaginal pursuits could help one to understand the dream symbols that are so critically important to the process of integration, individuation, and consciousness. Other cultures better understood the importance of carrying the dream forward. In the Iroquois Nation, for example, if a member of the tribe dreams of giving a feast, she will make the preparations and arrangements for hosting one when she awakens. She believes that the image was expressed in the dreams for important reasons. The interpretation and understanding of dreams is far more art than science, more in the realm of intuition and feeling than reason or sensation. Not only can we meditate on the dream image, but we can draw or paint it, as Jung frequently did, or contemplate it in other ways. All forms of artistic expression—painting, drawing, dancing, sculpting, writing, and playing music—offer paths to interacting with the dream symbols and the unconscious inner world. Any activity or ritual that brings us closer to the dream image can help us to more clearly understand its meaning.

Just about a week prior to her remarkable dream about the light behind the waterfall, Katherine had remembered another dream. In this dream, she was walking through the woods when she heard footsteps behind her. She turned and looked but no one was there. She continued on her way and heard the footsteps once more. Again she turned to find no one. When she heard the sound a third time, she turned around to see young deer behind almost every tree. They were watching her quietly with their large brown eyes. She stopped and looked at them, remarking to herself how beautiful they were.

In working with this dream, Katherine decided that she would spend some time understanding what the symbol of the deer meant. She had no personal associations or experiences with deer but perceived them to be gentle and compassionate creatures that she related to the feminine. She attempted a dialogue with one of them but did not feel that she could "get into it." She rented a documentary video about white-tailed deer and checked out a few books about them from the library. She spent an afternoon at a state park sitting quietly and waiting for one to appear. She did not see any deer that day but she did draw some in her dream journal. As she was walking around in a mall she came to a little gift shop that had a revolving display of small animal figures crafted out of pewter. As the display turned she saw several small replicas of deer. They were only a few dollars and so she bought the one that most reminded her of the soulful eyes she had seen in her dream. That night as she went to sleep, she asked the deer in her dreams to help her understand why they were in her dream and what they were there to tell her. She held the small pewter deer in her hand as she dozed off. On that night, she experienced the dream of the brilliant white light that so fundamentally changed her.

In midlife, the task before us requires us to look deeply into the well of our own unconscious life. If we are to follow the path to our authentic Self and pursue the process of individuation and wholeness we must take heed of the precious symbols that come to us during sleep. In dreams, the unconscious speaks most clearly, and if we are willing, we can have the power to hear and understand. Jung wrote in his autobiography, "Day after day we live far beyond the bounds of our consciousness; without our knowledge, the life of the unconscious is also going on with us. The more the critical reason dominates, the more impoverished life becomes; but the more of the unconscious, and the more of myth we are capable of making conscious, the more of life we integrate."[62]

The poet Rilke seizes on the power of our nocturnal meetings with the Self and their contribution to the vibrancy and passion of a life filled with self-awareness when he writes:

The man who cannot quietly close his eyes,
certain that there is vision after vision

inside, simply waiting until nighttime
to rise all around him in the darkness—
it's all over for him, he's like an old man.[63]

Some Thoughts and Suggestions

1. Make a commitment to work actively on your inner life by working with your dreams. Growth and change rarely happen without elbow grease. In order to remain fit and healthy we make regular commitments of our time and energy to physical exercise. Inner work requires the same devotion.

2. Be aware that dreaming depends, to a large extent, on the quality of our sleep. Drugs and alcohol have been shown to interfere with REM sleep and should be avoided. There is some research that demonstrates that some of the B vitamins may have a positive effect on dream recall. Review your diet to see if you are getting a proper percentage of these vitamins, which may also help in managing stress. Consult your doctor about whether taking additional B would be a healthy decision for you.

3. The psyche is very cooperative and desires consciousness. It wants to help you to know yourself. Simply saying to yourself, "I will remember my dreams tonight," before you go to sleep has a remarkably positive, though inexplicable, effect on dream recall.

4. Keep a dream journal or tape recorder by your bedside. It is very important to write down or record the dream immediately upon awakening. If you awaken in the night remembering a short dream fragment, write it down or record it in as much detail as you can. Sometimes it may be necessary simply to lie quietly with your eyes closed and let yourself remember the dream. Jumping out of bed is a very good way to lose the memory of a dream. Date your dream entries so that you can understand your dreams in a series and can refer to them later and more easily place them in the context of the events of your conscious life. It may also help to reinforce the memory of a dream by giving it a title. For example, Katherine, discussed in this chapter, titled her first dream "Deer in the Woods" and the second "White Light."

5. Work on amplification of the dream symbols. Begin to interpret your dream by writing down all of your associations with the symbols. Begin with your personal associations and ask yourself: "What does this remind me of?" "When have I experienced this before?" "Does this ring a bell?" "Is the dream best understood at the objective or subjective level?" "Does the association 'click' or resonate with me?"

Some Jungian analysts suggest that writing or recording your dream in the present tense helps to make it more real.

If you do not understand the dream at the level of personal association, consider the natural and cultural associations to the dream images. What do you know about the people, animals, or other images that were presented in your dream? Is the dream speaking in any kind of metaphorical, figurative language? Is the dream saying something that is a pun or play on words? Do the symbols make sense at this level of association? Write down all of your associations.

Some dreams can only be understood at the level of archetypal amplification. If so, what can you learn about the archetypal significance of the dream symbols? At this stage of interpretation a symbol dictionary and other sources of archetypal information are usually necessary to understand the symbol. Use these resources as food for thought rather than expecting that they will directly say what your dream symbol means. The dream must resonate within in order for us to make sense of it. Is there anything within the dramatic structure of the dream that can help you to understand it? Are any major archetypes, such as the shadow, anima/animus, persona, Self, or others, being portrayed in the structure of the dream? For example, are major characters in the dream of the same or of different sex than you? Are there images that seem to reflect the persona, the Self, or transformation itself? Allow yourself to make creative and intuitive associations. Don't get locked into the idea that your symbol must only have a single meaning. Remember that dreams are multilayered and often are best understood at many different levels of interpretation.

6. Look at your dream as part of a series. Review your dream journal and determine if there are patterns, themes, or elements common to many dreams.

7. What is the meaning of the dream in the context of your present outer life? What can you learn from the dream? How does the dream reflect the

experiences of your midlife passage? How can this knowledge be integrated into your daily experience?

8. Jungian analyst Mary Ann Mattoon suggests that we verify the dream interpretation by exposing it to the following tests as recommended by Jung[64]:

a. Does the interpretation "click"?
b. Does the interpretation "act"? That is, does it seem to create a feeling of vitality and a flow of feelings?
c. Is the interpretation confirmed (or overturned) by subsequent dreams?
d. Do the events anticipated by the interpretation occur in the dreamer's waking life?

9. Carry the dream forward with Active Imagination or by creatively giving expression to the dream images through drawing, writing, sculpting, dancing, music, or ritual. The following chapter describes some elements of the creative process and offers additional suggestions.

10. Dream interpretation is best conducted within a therapeutic relationship or a group. There is a danger for dreamers interpreting dreams on their own to conclude that the dream tells them something that they already know. We may be too close to our own dreams to understand their meaning fully. If possible, work with a Jungian analyst or a Jungian-oriented psychotherapist or become involved with a dream group. Dream groups do not have to be formally structured or run by a professional. They can simply be a group of friends who get together to discuss their dreams. Talk about your dreams with other people, perhaps members of your family. Jeremy Taylor, in his book *Dreamwork,* presents a chapter called "Twenty-one Basic Hints for Group Dream Work" that is very informative and easily understood.[65]

11. Learn more about dreams. There are many excellent books and audiotapes about Jungian approaches to dreams and dreamwork. Many are listed in the notes section of this chapter. There are chapters of the Jung Society in most major cities of the world. Often these groups, and many others, offer workshops and seminars on dreamwork. Most are inexpensive to attend and offer an opportunity to learn from major writers and thinkers in the field of dreams and dream interpretation. But remember that our own intuitive wisdom will play the major role in understanding dreams. Jung observed, "The

art of interpreting dreams cannot be learnt from books. Methods and rules are good only when we can get along without them."[66] The more familiar we become with the language of our own unique Self, the more we will correctly translate its messages and meanings. The Self offers dreams as a way toward individuation, consciousness, and self-growth. As these are the primary tasks of the midlife transition, dreams offer enormous potential in our quest for knowing ourselves deeply and honestly. They provide a direct course to our unconscious inner life and the wisdom of the Self. At midlife and throughout life, dreams attempt not to deceive but to disclose, teach, and embrace.

CHAPTER 8

Creativity: Breathing Life into the Process

In creating, the only hard thing's to begin;
A grass blade's no easier to make than an oak.
JAMES RUSSELL LOWELL, "A FABLE FOR CRITICS," 1848

BEN'S MARRIAGE did not survive the changes that midlife brought to his relationship. He and his wife, Jennifer, had led a comfortable life together that revolved around the activities of their children. Less than a year after their youngest child left home to attend college, it became obvious to both Ben and Jennifer that there was very little passion or real relationship between them. Jennifer announced that she didn't want to live the rest of her life surrounded by such "ordinary boredom." She had come into a small inheritance and become very interested in returning to graduate school. She had married Ben a month after graduating from college, had gone from her father's support to his, and wanted to know what it was like to live "on her own." Although she knew that Ben was a good father and husband, their marriage had long ago become stale and monotonous. "I feel like I'm suffocating," she told him. Her plans and desires for the second half of her life did not include marriage to Ben.

At forty-six, Ben found himself moving into a small furnished apartment while Jennifer prepared their house for sale. While searching in the basement for a box of old pots and pans that he could use until he and Jennifer divided up their possessions, he stumbled over a dusty guitar case. Without even understanding why, he put it in the pile with the rest of the things that he would take to his apartment.

Ben felt an overwhelming sadness as he finished moving his few things into his new place. Only expecting to be in the apartment for a few months, he had none of his normal diversions, no television set, no CD player. He had a small clock radio, but the reception was terrible and he wasn't used to listening to the radio except while driving to work anyway. In despair and grieving he opened the musty old guitar case. His guitar, a classic Martin, was in good shape except for the strings. They were so rusty, Ben joked that he needed a tetanus shot before playing them. With nothing better to do at the time, he drove to the mall and bought a new set. That night short phrases and chords of old, vaguely remembered songs began to come back to him: James Taylor; Crosby, Stills, Nash and Young; Joni Mitchell; Judy Collins; the Grateful Dead; the Beatles.

Ben thought about the days in which music and playing his guitar meant everything to him. He had even considered majoring in music, maybe teaching. But his family and his college adviser had urged him to major in something more solid and reliable. "Teachers make lousy money," his father said. Instead of following his instincts and interests, Ben majored in business administration and landed a very good job after graduation.

But during college he partially supported himself by playing music and singing for tips in a small bar near campus. In fact, that was where he had met Jennifer. She was a transfer student, new to the university, and he thought she was the most beautiful woman he had ever seen. She was with a group of friends, and he asked if he could join them for a beer during his break. She agreed and they hit it off at once. They went out for a late dinner, began dating immediately, and were married three years later; they had been almost inseparable ever since. That was more than twenty-seven years ago. Ben wept as he thought about his life now without Jennifer in it.

Over the next few months, Ben reclaimed a great deal of his musical dexterity. He would remember the beginning of a familiar song, and without even trying, his fingers would continue on, although he did not consciously remember how to play the song. "It felt like I just had to let my fingers do the walking," he said. He began to look forward to coming home in the evening, to relax and work on a song that he had thought about during the day. After the sale of the house, Ben bought a townhouse, and, though he now had a television and stereo, his books and familiar belong-ings around him, he continued to play his guitar in the evenings. He signed up to take guitar lessons on Saturday mornings and practiced scales and techniques he had never learned. Ben began to write songs of his own expressing his sadness about the end of his marriage. After a time, other themes began to emerge in his music as well; he began to compose songs that were not as deeply disharmonious and dark. Though Ben continued to work at his job in city government and had no intention of performing for a living or selling his songs to a publisher, the music brought a new sense of vitality, emotional expression, and enrichment to his life. Like Ben, many of us will discover that the experiences of midlife cry out for expression, for symbols, words, colors, sounds, and movements which will help to give shape and voice to our inner experiences.

By midlife, unless we are involved in the arts as a vocation, most of us have left behind the clearest expression of our unconscious inner life. By midlife, most of us have limited our encounters with art, music, writing, or dancing to being a member of the audience, sacrificing our uniqueness, our most creative voice, to the everyday realities of earning a living and taking care of our responsibilities. Most of the time we fail even to interject our own style and vision into our daily lives. But we did not start out this way.

As young children, we lived with creative energy; the life force which Jung called libido and which Dylan Thomas poetically referred to as "the force that through the green fuse drives the flower"[1] flowed freely through us. Unencumbered by the need to conform, to avoid criticism and judgment, we made up stories, wrote poetry, drew imaginary creatures, painted the sky purple, sang our own made-up songs, and accompanied these tunes on a percussion section of plastic bowls and wooden spoons. We made houses, stores, and forts from common cardboard boxes, dressed our pets up like babies, created chemistry experiments by mixing shampoo with mouthwash and Jell-O, delighted in the movement and dance of our bodies, made up rhymes where no adult would imagine them, and saw the world and our place in it as infinitely interesting and free. Life was an adventure just waiting for our individual experience of it, and absolutely no medium was exempt from our creative energies. Psychologist Howard Gardner, who has written extensively about originality and artistry, describes the preschool years as a "golden age of creativity, a time when every child sparkles with artistry."[2] One little boy, not quite two years old and in the midst of toilet training, called his grandmother to the bathroom. "Come here, Grandma!" he yelled, with his arms high over his head in a victory stance. Showing her his little turds in the toilet bowl, he announced with great flair and excitement, "I made *fish!!!*"

Just as all children naturally gravitate to the fullest expression of their own personalities and views of the world, our ancestors, throughout all observable human history, also understood the power of creative self-expression. Artistic representations of human experience abound in all forms and mediums in every culture in the world. From the exquisite sand paintings of the Navajo, the beadwork of the Lakota Sioux and the Iroquois, the delicate wood carvings of ancient China, the polyrhythmic songs and chants of African cultures, the highly stylized woven baskets of Amazon tribes to the images of God painted on the ceiling of the Sistine Chapel and the strains of an orchestra playing a symphony by Mozart, human beings have found means of symbolically and creatively expressing everything from their most deeply held sacred beliefs to their delight in the decoration of everyday objects. Recent discoveries of Paleolithic art on the limestone walls of caves near Avignon, France, reveal a highly sophisticated form of creative expression by Cro-Magnons, splendid images of a variety of animals. And these cave paintings are not rare, not limited to an unusual group of particularly creative and artistic beings. More than two hundred late–Stone Age caves with wall paintings, engravings, bas-relief decorations and sculptures have been discovered in southwestern Europe alone. Personal ornaments such as bracelets, necklaces, pendants, and beads have been found at the burial sites of these ancient ancestors. Archaeologists have retreived thousands of engraved objects and sculptures in hundreds of locations throughout Australia, southern Africa, northern Asia, and Europe. But even these discoveries, considered to be more than twenty thousand years old, do not reflect the full history of creative expression among human beings. Although most prehistorians believe that "art," as we think of it in today's terms, dates back more than forty thousand years, other researchers have found evidence for symbolism and ritual among Neanderthals dating back more than a hundred thousand years.[3] Michael Lemonick points out that "when Paleolithic people first crawled in the Chauvet cave to daub the walls with images of rhinos and bears, nearly half of all art history was already over with."[4]

What is it about creative self-expression in words, forms, and sounds that demands such attention from members of every culture? What motivated our ancestors to reflect their experiences in the symbolism of painting, sculpture, music, and decoration? Perhaps more important, what is this process of creativity? How does it express itself both in art and in everyday life? Why is it that at midlife so many people feel compelled to express themselves in ways they have never tried before, or to reclaim methods that were left behind in the service of adult responsibilities?

The English words *create* and *creative* come from the Latin *creare,* meaning "to cause to grow; to bring forth, create, or produce." The name of Ceres, the goddess of agriculture, derives from the same Latin source. Personifying the forces of creation, fertility, bountiful harvests, and deep rich earth, Ceres—known in Greece as Demeter—represents, as an archetypal energy, the naturally growing and expansive creative force within all of us. Creativity is more than an occasional good idea. It is an attitude toward life, a way of expressing inner reality by bringing it into our outer world. It incorporates innovation, new perspectives, passion, humor, playfulness, joy, and inspiration. Living a fluid creative life enriches the texture of existence, brings sensation to a new level of experience, and allows for a new understanding of our connection to the great Mystery.

In spite of all the evidence to the contrary, many of us believe that only a few individuals are blessed with strong creative ability or imagination. An early philosopher on this subject, Immanuel Kant, described creativity as a natural gift or talent which gives rise to the original and beautiful. He spoke of "spirit," in an aesthetical sense, as the animating principle of the mind, imaginative and entirely opposed to the spirit of imitation. He recognized that it was this spirit, or soul, that brought brilliance to art: A poem could be elegant and neat but without a greater depth; a conversation might be entertaining but lack soul; a man could be handsome but not contain this soulful animation. American philosopher and biologist E. W. Sinnot observed that creativity is a natural manifestation of life and that its origins are in the unconscious.[5] Abraham Maslow considered creativity to be a critical aspect of every self-actualized personality.[6] Psychotherapist Rollo May views creativity as nothing less than the "process of making or bringing into being the way we express our being."[7] As such, our creativity has the potential to enlarge our own and all human consciousness.

Yet as we grow older and begin to develop a sense of ego and a need to fit in and find approval, we begin to leave behind that pure sense of joy, adventure, and spontaneity that is part of creatively expressing ourselves. We become cautious and conforming and cease to hear the promptings of the Self as it exerts its steady push for expression. By midlife, the joy of experiencing our creative voice is sometimes only barely remembered.

Deena Metzger, a wonderful writer and teacher of writers, tells of a three-year-old girl who composed her first poem:

> Tree
> *It doesn't grow in water,*
> *it doesn't grow in sand,*
> *but in happy children's hands.*[8]

Metzger describes how the three-year-old's natural exuberance with words changed over time. She writes: "After that she didn't write a poem she liked for over twenty years. When she was three, she knew something that she then forgot and only gradually began to remember over a long period of time. When she was three, she knew the magic of words; she knew that words could create magic, that they were magic. She knew that they could create worlds, could describe worlds, explore worlds, and also be the bridge between one world and another."[9]

Barry Lane, who also teaches writing, tells of being two years old, crawling out of bed, and with a purple crayon scribbling beautiful flowers on the freshly painted white walls of his home. "They were sloppy flowers with great looping petals and long stems that curled onto the wood floor. Look at the flowers! I yelled to my mother, who was dusting in the hallway. She took two steps into the room and shouted, What are you doing? My clean white walls! Get out!"[10]

Betty Edwards, in her very popular book *Drawing on the Right Side of the Brain,* describes the process by which children express themselves in art after a short period of scribbling that begins at about one and a half years of age. Beginning with a symmetrical, circular form (a universal image drawn by all children, regardless of their culture or experience), we add blobs or dots for eyes and call it "Mommy," "Daddy," or "my dog." At the tender age of one and a half we are learning, as Edwards points out, that "a drawn symbol can stand for something out there in the environment."[11] We are expressing our own creative interpretation of our world. But around the age of nine or ten children begin to abandon art and become critical of their own drawings. A cultural expectation that drawings should be realistic, coupled with a lack of training and technique, causes most children at this age to throw up their hands in frustration, crying, "I can't draw. I hate it anyway. I don't want to do this anymore." Frequently, unthinking people will add to this sense of failure and judgment by sarcastic ("What is *that* supposed to be?") or derogatory ("That dog shouldn't be bigger than the house, should it?") remarks. Before very long we begin to lose our deeply felt connection to our spontaneous, creative inner inspiration. Pablo Picasso rightly observed "Every child is an artist. The problem is how to remain an artist once he grows up."[12]

Our creative imagination offers a direct conduit to the energies of the Self and to a deep and soulful experience of our inner life. Yet by the time we are adults, most of us have relinquished the path with heart, the one that allows for the fullest expression of this experience. We begin to truly believe the falsehood that creative expression is something reserved for "great thinkers," "inventors," or "artists." Whoever these creative people are, they are certainly not like us. But this is an illusion created by a society that separates creative expression from everyday life. Thomas Moore acknowledges the importance of seeing creativity as something accessible to all of us as we move through our daily lives. He writes, "In ordinary life creativity means making something for the soul out of every experience."[13]

Creativity and creative inspiration were considered by our ancestors to be direct messages and instructions from a divine source, the unconscious, or some power outside of our normal bounds of ego. At midlife, as we explore avenues that reveal our deepest unconscious wisdom, it is important to acknowledge creative self-expression as one of those paths. Plato, for example, describes the creative process in poetry as a kind of "divine madness" in which a human being has a direct contact to some outer muse. In *The Ion* he says, "It seems to me, the god would show us, lest we doubt, that these lovely poems are not of man or human workmanship, but are divine and from the gods, and that the poets are nothing but interpreters of the gods, each one possessed by the divinity to whom he is in bondage. And to prove this, the deity on purpose sang the loveliest of all lyrics through the most miserable poet."[14] Coleridge, in describing his method of writing poetry, observes that at least some aspects of his process were outside of his conscious control: "The poet, described in ideal perfection, brings the whole soul of man into activity, with the subordination of its faculties to each other, according to their relative worth and dignity. He diffuses a tone and spirit of unity, that blends, and (as it were) fuses, each into each, by that synthetic and magical power to which we have exclusively appropriated the name of imagination."[15]

In many cultures, art and spirituality are intimately linked as a cloud is to the sky. Some cultures even believed that once images had been drawn or carved they had a magical existence of their own. Among Australian Aborigines, for example, these images became powerful spirits in their own right and the places in which they were depicted (e.g., the walls of a cave) became sacred.[16] In Japan, the concentrated practice required of the artist is seen as a *shugyo,* or aesthetic meditation that leads to deep spiritual fulfillment, a part of a sacred path. Such creative mindfulness is considered "narrow" or "slender" enough to slip between the "thingness" of things.

The seventeenth-century Haiku master Basho, wrote, "When you are composing a verse . . . let there not be a hair's breadth separating your mind from what you write. Quickly say what is in your mind; never hesitate at that moment."[17] Michelangelo used the word *sprezzatura* to describe the "easy union of eye, hand and brain that produces a worthy human work."[18] While this sense of "mindfulness," of being at one with the creative process and the created work itself, is central to the concept of inspiration as coming from a source other than our conscious ego, there is something of the Self implanted into every creative act.

Jung recognized the numinosity of the creative experience and its relationship to the archetypes and collective unconscious. He understood that the psyche is the "womb" of all the arts and sciences, and postulated that deeply held archetypal themes of the unconscious are transformed by the artist. He wrote about the process of creative self-expression: "[Artistic works] come as it were fully arrayed into the world, as Pallas Athene sprang from the head of Zeus. These works positively force themselves upon the author; his hand is seized, his pen writes things that his mind contemplates with amazement. The work brings with it its own form; anything he wants to add is rejected, and what he himself would like to reject is thrust back at him. While his conscious mind stands amazed and empty before this phenomenon, he is overwhelmed by a flood of thoughts and images which he never intended to create and which his own will could never have brought into being. Yet in spite of himself he is forced to admit that it is his own self speaking, his own inner nature revealing itself and uttering things which he would never have entrusted to his tongue. He can only obey the apparently alien impulse within him and follow where it leads, sensing that his work is greater than himself, and wields a power which is not his and which he cannot command. Here the artist is not identical with the process of creation; he is aware that he is subordinate to his work or stands outside it, as though he were a second person; or as though a person other than himself had fallen within the magic circle of an alien will."[19] Although Jung recognized that there exists a creative process which does emerge from a conscious intent of the will, it is this sense of creativity attached to the unconscious promptings of the Self that is so important to understand in its relationship to the midlife passage.

Many people throughout all cultures and times corroborate Jung's ideas about the expression of the Self in creative endeavors. For example, poet Maya Angelou describes her approach to writing in a way that can only be understood by accepting that creativity is intimately linked to the unconscious and the Self. She describes her process by noting that she gets up early, around five-thirty or six, washes, prays, puts on some coffee, and "arranges her mind in writing order." By that she means "I tell myself how lucky I am that this morning is new, a day never seen before, that ideas will come to me which I have never consciously known." She then goes to her writing room, where she keeps a Bible, a dictionary, Roget's Thesaurus, a bottle of sherry, cigarettes, an ashtray, and several decks of playing cards. During the five or more hours she spends there daily, Angelou observes, she spends more of her time playing solitaire than writing. "It seems to me," she says, "that when my hands and small mind (a Southern Black phrase) are engaged in placing the reds on the blacks and the blacks on the reds, my working mind arranges and rearranges the characters and the plot. Finally when they are in a plausible order, I simply have to write down where they are and what they say." She also reveals that she usually wears a hat when she writes in order to keep her brains from spilling out![20]

Like Maya Angelou, the German dancer and choreographer Mary Wigman describes her experience of the creative process as being attached to the deepest part of the soul. "During the process of artistic creation, man descends into the primordial elements of life. He reverts to himself to become lost in something greater than himself, in the immediate indivisible essence of life."[21] Describing each time we sit down to write as a "new journey with no maps," Natalie Goldberg, writer and teacher, honors the basic, and sometimes primitive, place that is the wellspring of the soul's inspiration. Come to writing, she says "not with your mind and ideas, but with your whole body—your heart and gut and arms. Begin to write in the dumb awkward way an animal cries out in pain, and there you will find your intelligence, your words, your voice."[22] As one explores the thoughts and feelings of creative people, it becomes very clear that there is a universal understanding among the imaginative giants in literature, music, philosophy, and art, that the creative process itself offers an almost magical conduit from some deep inner well or from a divine energy. As we navigate the midlife passage, in particular, unleashing our own creative potential is a critical aspect of listening to our core inner wisdom and the promptings of the soul.

Julia Cameron, the author of *The Artist's Way,* notes: "Life is energy: pure, creative energy. . . . There is an underlying, in-dwelling creative force infusing all of life—including ourselves . . . When we open ourselves to our creativity, we open ourselves to the creator's creativity within us and our lives. . . . Just as blood is a fact of your physical body and nothing you invented, creativity is a fact of your spiritual body and nothing that you must invent." In her book she has assembled a particularly interesting array of creative people's comments about the deeply spiritual and unconscious process of their creativity.[23]

- "The music of *(Madame Butterfly)* was dictated to me by God; I was merely instrumental in putting it on paper and communicating it to the public."—Giacomo Puccini
- "Straightaway the ideas flow in upon me, directly from God."—Johannes Brahms
- "Inspiration may be a form of superconsciousness, or perhaps of subconsciousness—I wouldn't know. But I am sure it is the antithesis of self-consciousness."—Aaron Copland
- "The position of the artist is humble. He is essentially a channel."—Piet Mondrian
- "In the brush doing what it's doing, it will stumble on what one couldn't do by oneself."—Robert Motherwell
- "I myself do nothing. The Holy spirit accomplishes all through me."—William Blake
- "Inside you there's an artist you don't know about . . . Say yes, quickly, if you know, if you've known it from before the beginning of the universe."—Jelaluddin Rumi

Recent research in brain physiology and function suggests that creative people are accurate in describing the process of imagination and creation as being a less than conscious operation. In fact, absorption in a creative task, like many other activities such as meditation, listening to music, praying, daydreaming, and driving down the highway, induces an altered state of consciousness that is different from our ordinary waking awareness. Artists, writers, sculptors, and dancers who describe their process as being transcendent are describing a nonverbal process that occurs when the nondominant hemisphere of the brain is in charge of consciousness. In fact, an understanding of the organizational structure of the brain offers a physiological basis for some of these unconscious processes and a better understanding of the process of creativity.

The right and left hemispheres of the brain appear to hold distinctive and specialized functions in terms of their ability to process verbal versus nonverbal information. In the vast majority of right-handed people, the left hemisphere is dominant in that it processes verbal information in analytical ways. Although the specialized functions of the right hemisphere have been more elusive than those of the left, research suggests that the right brain responds to nonverbal, spatial stimuli. It is also clear that the two hemispheres hold vastly different strategies for processing information.[24]

In comparing the characteristics of the left and right brains, one is struck by the similarities of the functions of the left brain to the Jungian notions of the masculine and consciousness, and of Yang energy in Eastern thinking. The right brain, on the other hand, is associated with characteristics similar to the feminine, unconsciousness, and Yin energy. Betty Edwards in *Drawing on the Right Side of the Brain* uses some of the following adjectives to describe what she calls "L-Mode" (left brain) and "R-Mode" (right brain) characteristics:[25]

LEFT	RIGHT
Verbal	Non-Verbal
Analytic	Synthetic
Symbolic	Concrete
Abstract	Analogic
Temporal	Nontemporal
Rational	Nonrational
Digital	Spatial
Logical	Intuitive
Linear	Holistic

Given the cultural bias toward verbal and analytical ways of knowing, it is clear that our society sees greater value in the way the left brain processes the world. As we grow up we learn more and more that intelligence is equated with rational ways of seeing the world. By midlife, most of us have learned our lessons well, to the exclusion of our own intuitive and creative abilities. Understanding this bias, Roger Sperry wrote: "There appear to be two modes of thinking, verbal and nonverbal, represented rather separately in left and right hemispheres, respectively, and . . . our educational system, as well as science in general, tends to neglect the nonverbal form of intellect. What it comes down to is that modern society discriminates against the right hemisphere."[26] Arthur Koestler, writing before much of the literature on left- and right-brain functions was known, understood the need to enter into other realms in order to explore and express our deepest creative energy. He wrote: "Among all forms of mentation, verbal thinking is the most articulate, the most complex, and the most vulnerable to infectious diseases. It is liable to absorb whispered suggestions, and to incorporate them as hidden persuaders into the code. Language can become a screen which stands between the thinker and reality. This is the reason why true creativity often starts where language ends."[27]

True creativity, the ability to see things in new ways and express our own view of the world, requires a departure from our standard ways of knowing and a greater access to the perceptions of the right brain. In fully appreciating and understanding the creative process, particularly as part of a path with heart at midlife, it is also essential that we depart from the idea that the creative process is linked excessively with the arts or that some special talent is required to live creatively. In fact, true creativity is much more about our approaches to the world and our reality, than any tangible results. As Maslow and others discovered, creativity, as an attitude and intention, can be expressed in every area of human endeavor, from the development of an inspired management plan, to a strategy for feeding the homeless in our community, to climbing a mountain, to dressing in a way that pleases us, to finding a new way to fish for drum, to writing a poem, to planning a child's birthday party, to training a dog.

Allowing our creative energy to flow through us provides a richness of experience and a sense of meaning that are central goals of our midlife search, and the clearest way to live passionately and with deeply resonating soulfulness. Thomas Moore reflects on the soulful aspect as the core of the creative process when he observes: "Creativity is, foremost, being in the world soulfully, for the only thing we truly make, whether in the arts, in culture, or at home, is soul."[28] Theologian Paul Tillich concurs, stating, "Spiritual self-affirmation occurs in every moment in which man lives creatively in the various spheres of meaning. Creative, in this context, has the sense not of original creativity as performed by the genius but of living spontaneously, in action and reaction, with the contents of one's cultural life. In order to be spiritually creative one need not be what is called a creative artist or scientist or statesman, but one must be able to participate meaningfully in their original creations."[29]

Abraham Maslow observed that he had to change his original ideas about creativity when he began to study people who were psychologically healthy, mature, and self-actualizing. He wrote: "A fair proportion of my subjects, though healthy and creative in a special sense that I am going to describe, were *not* productive in the ordinary sense, nor did they have great talent or genius, nor were they poets, composers, inventors, artists or creative intellectuals."[30] Instead of assuming that all creative acts were in the domain of certain kinds of professions, he observed that creativity, as a potential, was within every individual and that creativity reflected itself in everyday, mundane activities. In one case, for example, he observed a woman who was uneducated and poor and yet brought unconventional creativity to her roles and behaviors as a homemaker and mother. He noted that although she had very little money or resources to work with, her home was always beautiful, meals were banquets, and her taste was impeccable. He wrote: "She was in all these areas original, novel, ingenious, unexpected, inventive. I just had to call her creative. I learned from her and others like her that a first-rate soup is more creative than a second-rate painting, and that, generally, cooking or parenthood or making a home could be creative while poetry need not be; it could be uncreative."[31]

By loosening the definition of creativity beyond pertaining to the arts or "special" people, we open up whole new vistas in which to express ourselves, our Self, in everyday activity. Letting our innate imagination soar in our daily lives adds spontaneity, passion, and a sense of adventure and zest to our lives. At the same time, we may discover that our old, habitual ways of doing things have contributed to a sense of mind-numbing boredom in our daily activities. At midlife, we are challenged to look at our lives from new perspectives, and if we remain open to this new energy flowing through us, no part of our life will remain unchanged. "Bring the muse into the kitchen," urged Walt Whitman.[32]

Michael had worked very hard to move up the ranks of a large men's apparel company. By midlife, he was a hotshot vice president earning a six-figure salary. But during his tenure with the company, management had changed hands several times and a bureaucratic mentality was pervading the corporation. Although he was making an excellent salary, the thrill was gone and he began to realize how unhappy he was with his work. He and his friend Arthur began to talk about starting their own business, but nothing they wished to pursue presented itself. One afternoon, while visiting a shopping mall in San Diego and searching for something to eat, they came upon a cookie shop with a line of hungry customers. "That's it!" Michael thought.

Armed with a chocolate-chip cookie recipe from Arthur's wife's great-great-grandmother and eight thousand dollars in personal savings, Michael Coles and Arthur Karp opened the Great American Cookie Co. in an Atlanta, Georgia, shopping mall. Today, the company has more than four hundred stores and annual sales of nearly $100 million.[33]

The story of Michael and Arthur's success is not an isolated one. The popular business literature abounds with similar stories in which average and everyday people guided only by an entrepreneurial spirit, an openness to opportunity, and more creativity and courage than investment money pull off striking successes in business, industry, and commerce.[34] At midlife, many people will find themselves drawn to whole new beginnings. As we hear the clock ticking, we may decide that there is simply no sense of life or passion in the work that we do. We *must* move on to something new.

Peter O'Connor, an Australian psychologist, conducted midlife research with a large sample of men. He reported that a single theme dominating all of his interviews was men's dissatisfaction with their current career or occupation, regardless of how successful they were or how much money they earned from their work. Noting that men in particular tend to draw a large part of their personal identity from their work and that midlife is a time of questioning and reworking one's sense of identity, he considered that this common theme made sense. Most of his respondents used words like "tiredness," "boredom," "depression," "lethargy," and "inertia" to characterize their feelings about their work; yet they also felt burdened, even overwhelmed with financial responsibilities, and thus often felt stuck and unable to make any changes in their work lives. Interestingly, when asked to describe the kinds of work they would rather be doing, almost all his subjects cited several specific work fantasies. These men wanted to be farmers, nurserymen, writers, or in a job in which they helped other people. Regardless of whether the men were professional or blue-collar, they were drawn to creative activities like writing or ones in which they were closer to the rhythms of nature and life.[35]

Although O'Connor's research was based on a sample of men only, there is other evidence to suggest that at midlife many women report the same kinds of dissatisfaction with the day-to-day routines of their work life. Gail Sheehy's research showed that the most unhappy women at midlife were those who felt trapped in low-paying, dead-end, jobs.[36] Stuck between deeply felt boredom and a sense of meaninglessness, and the fear of losing their boring job through downsizing, corporate takeover, or outsourcing, many men and women at midlife feel inert and powerless. Nightly complaining about how much one hates one's job is exacerbated by the profound sense that the time to do anything else may be running out. But the ways in which we earn our livings offer ripe and wondrous opportunities for creativity, and it is critical to our sense of individuation and wholeness that we follow our urges. Betty Friedan, writing about the years past midlife, recognizes the critical importance of meaningful work to a rich life when she observes, "Much research has shown that the most important predictors of vital age are *satisfying work* and *complexity of purpose*. Those who continue working at jobs that have become mindless and routine forfeit the fountain of age."[37]

In order to live creatively and fulfill the need for a passionate life that arrives on the wings of the midlife passage, many people will be drawn to making major changes in their professions. For others, though, a radical move may not be the solution; many people will instead find ways of bringing a new sense of spontaneity, creativity, and life to the work they are already doing. Mitch, the middle-aged character played by Billy Crystal in *City Slickers,* is disgusted with the meaninglessness of his work selling airtime for a New York City radio station. He is bored and exhausted with his life, his work, his family responsibilities. One year he and two friends take a vacation in which they herd cattle across the Great Plains; this provides the excitement that is lacking in their everyday lives. During the course of this adventure, Mitch faces a life-threatening experience and recognizes for the first time the importance of both his family and his job. He returns to New York with a newfound passion for his marriage and a commitment to do his job better. Like Mitch, many of us at midlife will learn to perform our work better when "better" means more creatively, joyously, and authentically.

Fortunately, we are living in a time when more and more of our employers (though certainly not all) are recognizing the importance of nurturing creativity in the workplace. John Naisbitt and Patricia Aburdene, authors of *Re-Inventing the Corporation,* write that in the "new information-rich, decentralized, global society, creativity will be increasingly valued in business.

Creativity is the corporation's competitive edge. It is the special talent that discovers the right market niche. Creativity finds that final bug in the new computer system, writes the proposal that gets the company into Saudi Arabia, redesigns the organization chart into a decentralized network, and meets the other challenges the megatrends bring."[38]

Authors Tom Peters and Nancy Austin echo these thoughts in *A Passion for Excellence,* and observe that the most innovative and successful companies are those in which people are encouraged to use their imagination and creativity.[39] Many leading companies, such as Apple Computer, ARCO, Colgate-Palmolive, DuPont, the Federal Reserve Bank, General Electric, Hewlett-Packard, IBM, ITT, NASA, Sears, Westinghouse, and Xerox, have even hired consultants to work with their management and organizational structures specifically to find new ways of encouraging creativity and innovation among their employees.[40]

But even those of us working in organizations that are supportive of imagination and innovation may not take advantage of opportunities to express our creativity. By midlife, many of us have forgotten the indescribable pleasure of allowing the creative spirit to course through us. "I'm too busy," we say. "I don't have enough time." We believe the myths that say that creativity is only for a special few. We believe that if we aren't going to come up with a product that will be excellent and marketable, there is no sense in going through the creative process. We listen too closely, it seems, to the voice inside that says, "You are wasting your time," "You're not an artist (or a writer/potter/musician/dancer/gardner . . .)." We don't want to risk looking foolish by making mistakes or not being very good at something. We compare ourselves to the greatest talents in the world, as they appear to us now, and find ourselves lacking. We demand perfection, even on our initial efforts. We do not see all the pages of manuscripts that great writers threw away, the paintings covered over by gesso to make room for a new image. We don't hear the scratchy, squeaking sounds of Yo-Yo Ma's cello before he learned his craft, or observe the hundreds of inventions that ended in the scrap heap yet paved the way for a "genius" to grace us with some new device to make our lives infinitely better. Since we do not have a chance to observe the process but only the outcomes of other people's creative activity, we assume that their art, writing, or music flowed perfectly from their brush, typewriter, or instrument. "That's not like us," we think, as we struggle with the terror of a blank canvas, mute instrument, or stark computer screen. Far too often we allow that inner voice—the critic, the censor, the editor, the naysayer, the negative mother or father complex—to stop us before we begin. We believe the left brain, the voice of reason, which tells us that any attempts to express ourselves creatively are a waste of our precious time and also bound to fail. Most of us do not even require an external critic, some envious person who disparages our efforts. By midlife, certainly, our internal critic is generally sufficiently loud and strong to keep us from trying. And so most of us effectively and tragically stop ourselves from doing what is a natural part of our human birthright.

Clarissa Pinkola Estes tells a folk story she calls "Wolfen," though the story has been found in many cultures under many names. This wondrous, deeply emotional tale metaphorically describes the process of the self-annihilation of the creative spirit: In the tale a king returns from a foreign land. As he approaches his castle he sees his favorite dog, one he has raised from a puppy—his most loyal companion—in the middle of the courtyard barking and yelping. Instead of greeting the King, the dog continues to bark excitedly. As the King nears, he sees that the dog is agitated and wild, his muzzle and whiskers covered with blood. The King hurries closer but the dog runs away from him and into the castle. Racing after the dog, through long winding hallways, the King is terrified. This is not the way his dog normally acts. "What can be wrong?" he thinks as his panic rises. The dog continues to bark in a most agitated way and runs into the nursery where the King's firstborn infant sleeps. As the King enters the room he sees the bassinet overturned. The room is silent; blood is splattered over the walls. He looks at his beloved dog, barking, snapping, out of his mind, with blood on his whiskers, and the King pulls out his sword and slays him. At that moment the child cries and the King rushes to the bassinet. There, alive and frightened, is the baby, his firstborn child, under the dead body of a wolf that had entered the castle and tried to attack him. The heroic dog had protected the baby and killed the wolf. And the King is beside himself with grief. He holds his son and weeps and weeps and weeps.[41]

This story frequently evokes a strong emotional reaction from people—I watched tears spring into the eyes of a strong man who works at a shipyard but yearns to be a writer, as he heard this story for the first time. I believe this is because the story resonates within a deep part of all of us. We are all guilty of the behavior of the King and we know it. We slay the most loyal, devoted, instinctive parts of ourselves.

Dr. Estes describes this story as one of the "critic" or the "devourer." The King, as the ego, has misidentified who has harmed whom. The wolf, as a terrible complex ("You can never do that"), has come to kill off creativity, personified as the baby in this story. Consider, Estes says, the woman who has harbored a desire to paint. She makes a small studio in her basement and begins, very slowly at first, to put her brush to canvas. Immediately, she hears the critic's voice: "This is terrible. Your work is pathetic. You are disgusting. You will never be a painter." So she burns her paintings. But like the King in the story, she has destroyed the wrong thing. Instead, she must turn on the critic. "An artist is an artist no matter what," Dr. Estes notes, "before anything is produced. It is the soul that makes them the artist. Just as each and every individual has a soul, we are artists before we have produced one single thing. But that is not the voice of the wolf. Not only must we produce but we must produce world-class phenomena. If we are a writer we must win the Pulitzer or the Nobel. If we are a painter, we must be in the American Academy of Art and the London Academy as well. If you are a sculptor you must have a foundry in Italy and on and on and on. That is the voice of the wolf. If you kill off the products, if you kill off your hopes and dreams, you are killing off the wrong thing. If you kill off that instinct to keep creating, then you have killed the wrong creature, the wrong instinct."[42]

Most of us are guilty of allowing the critic to rule our creative lives. We hold ourselves up to impossible, perfectionistic ideals. We tremble with the fear of appearing foolish or silly or, perhaps worse, totally incompetent. And yet creativity is truly connected to foolishness. We must let go of what we think we know in order to allow for the expression of what we do not yet know. In allowing this to happen, we forgo the safety of our predictable, certain reality and, as a stranger, enter into the land of the unknown. Children, perhaps our greatest teachers about creativity, know instinctively that foolishness is part of the process of self-expression, and it is when we become most like children in our innocence and openness that we will discover our creative center. Rumi writes: "A certain young man was asking around, 'I need to find a wise person. I have a problem.' A bystander said, 'There's no one with intelligence in our town except that man over there playing with the children, the one riding the stick-horse. He has keen, fiery insight and vast dignity, like the night sky, but he conceals it in the madness of child's play.' "[43]

In a way similar to the naivete of children, myths and fairy tales from all cultures abound with images of fools, "dummlings," and tricksters solving the creative challenge for the hero or the townspeople with their openness, innocence, and pure foolishness. To the ancient Greeks and Romans, Hermes, as youthful sweet-talker and thief, and Mercury, as "Quick-Silver," or shape-shifter, were considered the sources of creative and spiritual metamorphosis. The alchemists combined their names and used the term *corpus hermeticum* to describe this transformational energy.[44] In the Zen tradition, enlightened ones speak of *shoshin* or the "beginner's mind," in which the mind is "empty, free of the habits of the expert, ready to accept, to doubt, and open to all the possibilities."[45]

The archetypal image of the trickster, which we all contain in our unconscious, and its role in creativity is clearly described by William Doty. The trickster "laughs at established customs and gives us a second slantwise view of life that depicts customary everyday reality as too often cheap, banal, tawdry, undeveloped. Such views upset the going consensus definitions, trailing snickers and laughter in their wake. They cause us to experience an almost overpowering challenge to the going order, in a blitz of insight about what *else* may be possible."[46] In Native American cultures, the archetype of the trickster is often known in the form of Coyote or, among northwestern and Alaskan tribes, as Raven. In these stories, the trickster is a source of new vision and new approaches, though these characters have to go beyond the bounds of known reason and frequently have to trick, cheat, or steal in order to accomplish their task.

In the Alaskan Tlingit creation myth, for example, Raven must trick a great chief who possesses the sun, the moon, and all the stars, keeping them in a carved cedar box. Since there is no light in Raven's world, all the creatures must live in darkness. Raven understands that he must trick the Chief and all the villagers in order to steal their treasure. Turning himself into a hemlock needle, he falls into the drinking cup of the Chief's beautiful daughter, who fills it with water and drinks the needle. The daughter bears Raven as a baby, and he becomes the grandson of the great Chief, who loves him dearly and will give him whatever he wants. Raven, will not stop crying until his grandfather lets him play with the stars and the moon. As soon as he has them, Raven throws them up a smokehole and they scatter across the sky. Although the Chief is not happy about this, he loves his grandson too much to punish him. Now Raven begins to cry and cry, so hard he almost makes himself sick, until finally the Chief gives him the box containing the sun. Once he has it, Raven turns himself back into a bird and flies up the smokehole with the box. When he is far from the Chief's village he hears people speaking in the darkness and approaches them, asking if they would like to have light. No one believes him. No one can give them light, they say. But Raven opens the box and lets sunlight into the world. The people run away in fright to every corner of the world. This, says the myth, is why Raven's people are everywhere and why there are stars, the moon, and the sun, and it is no longer dark all the time.[47]

It is in this archetypal energy of the fool or the trickster that we find a direct path to our own creative source. Our clearest, purest expressions of the Self emerge when we still the voice of the critic, our rational mind, and reach down to the intuitive, childlike center that harbors our imagination. Betty Edwards, in teaching drawing as part of a creative process, writes about the importance of "tricking" the dominant, verbal left brain, which is not very good at spatial tasks like drawing, to let the more intuitive, concrete, gestaltic right hemisphere handle the job. Instead of actually seeing the subject of the drawing, the logical, rational mode of consciousness will most often draw a simple symbol for it. She has her students act as tricksters by looking at a subject and drawing it upside down or drawing the space around or between the subject(s) rather than drawing the thing itself. Since logic and reason (the left brain) can't understand these ways of looking at reality, the right hemisphere can work unencumbered by the hurrying messages of reason and is then permitted to really *see* what is there and to draw a creative representation of that subject as it really is.[48]

It might seem that the "critic," reason, or the left brain has no role to play at all in the creative process. If we just allow our deep inner sense of creativity to emerge, then we will all produce the most amazing things. While there is great truth in this as possibility, there is also value in *working* at our creative efforts. It is unlikely that we will have the ability to express ourselves fully if we have not mastered our tools. The pianist must practice her scales if she wants the freedom to express the music that is in her soul. The photographer must understand the workings and mechanics of the camera before he can use it creatively to express his vision. The dancer must patiently rehearse the same move or step over and over until it becomes instinctual and can then be integrated into the dance. The inventor will certainly find a lot of early efforts on the scrap heap before coming up with the final working creation. The potter will throw away more pots than she "throws" as she comes to understand the nature of the clay and the movement of the wheel. Natalie Goldberg writes about the importance of training and exercise in honing our creative expression. "We must keep practicing. It is not an excuse to not write and sit on the couch eating bon-

bons. We must continue to work the compost pile, enriching it and making it fertile so that something beautiful may bloom and so that our writing muscles are in good shape *to ride the universe when it moves through you*."[49]

As part of the process of creativity, we can and should look at our creative products and appraise them honestly. But this is a *separate process* from the act of creating. Analysis and opinion inserted too early in the creative process serve only to frighten the creator and deter the flow. Sometimes they bring the whole endeavor to a screeching halt. But when we have completed a work, we can and should look at our creative result and ask: "Does this work for me?" "Is this the way I want to look, sound, read, taste?" "Do I like this or not?" As Clarissa Pinkola Estes points out, this is a very different way of looking at our creative efforts. The critic can be an important part of our creative process as a reviewer and guide. It is only when the critic becomes harsh and judgmental, crying, "That is pathetic and horrible," or sees things in terms of good and bad or right and wrong that it terrorizes the childlike, creative aspect of the Self and pushes us toward inertia.

Full creative expression requires patience, work, and discipline. Igor Stravinsky, one of the greatest twentieth-century composers, did not believe that the artist is simply a pure channel for inspiration. "One had first to be a craftsman," he says. Citing Stravinsky and others, Thomas Moore writes: "Creative work can be exciting, inspiring, and godlike, but it is also quotidian, humdrum and full of anxieties, frustrations, dead ends, mistakes and failures. It can be carried on by a person who has none of the soaring Icarus wishes to abandon the dark shadows of the labyrinth in favor of the bright sunshine."[50]

Like many other aspects of the midlife passage, the creative process requires a balance of preparation and risk, of working hard at something and, at the same time, allowing for our inner muse to speak through us, a holding of the tension of opposites between polarities. Finding that balance can be a challenge.

Since the age of twelve I have wanted to be a writer. I loved the way it felt when stories poured through me into my mother's old typewriter. But as I grew older, I became more and more convinced that I could never be a writer. I was afraid to write my mind for fear of sounding silly or foolish. I didn't ever seem to make the time for the pure joy of writing a story. As I moved into a career as a psychotherapist, I published in professional journals, which gave me the false sense that I was writing; in truth, I knew that this kind of writing was mostly by formula, at least for me. Still, it kept me safely away from exploring what I really wanted to write, since it provided the illusion that I was truly allowing my creative force to express itself. As I entered midlife, I once again convinced myself that I was going to write . . . someday. So I prepared myself. I read every book I could find about writing. I took classes in creative writing. I learned to use not just one but three different word-processing programs for my computer. I was forever getting ready. When I sat down to write, terrified by the blank computer screen, I would leave my desk and spend the next several hours arranging books, or polishing the tables in my office, or using glass cleaner on my computer monitor screen, or watering plants (everything has to be just *right* in order to *write,* you know). While incubation and gestation are a part of the creative process, my procrastination was becoming ridiculous. Two years ago I attended a workshop with author and teacher Tom Bird, who gave a very succinct answer to the question "What is a writer?" "The difference between a writer and someone who wants to be a writer," he said, "is that writers write." He then proceeded with his workshop. That was all that needed to be said, like the Nike ad: "Just Do It."

Today, like so many people in midlife, I am more willing to trust my dreams and intuition. I believe that it's never too late to start and am comforted by the stories of other people who only really begin to find themselves and their creative voice in midlife. "Anyone who imagines that all fruits ripen at the same time as the strawberries knows nothing about grapes," wrote the sixteenth-century Swiss physician and alchemist Paracelsus.[51] I'm willing, more than ever before, to be a fool if necessary in order to explore the little-known parts of myself. I am seeking the awareness that will help me better understand who I am and how I can best express this emerging person. I am looking to discover wisdom and ways in which to be more vitally alive, trying to stay close to a path with heart. Today, I am learning to move through fear and inertia to allow creative energy to flow through me. The sight of a blank computer screen can still set my knees to shaking, but I read a short poem that I have taped on my wall, take a deep breath, and begin. The poem is by Rumi, the thirteenth-century Sufi mystic and poet, who began his most profound creative process in midlife, at the age of thirty-seven. It reads:

Today, like every other day, we wake up empty and scared.
Don't open the door to the study and begin reading.
Take down the dulcimer.

Let the beauty we love be what we do.
There are hundreds of ways to kneel and kiss the ground.[52]

Some Thoughts and Suggestions

1. Begin to explore your inner life by keeping a journal.[53] These daily writings become a container in which we can, in a very private way, tell ourselves what we know about what is going on inside ourselves. This exercise is even for those who do not have an urge to write, for the knowledge one gains is critical to the process of individuation and the task of wholeness. Robert Bly writes, "No one should make you feel guilty for not keeping a journal, or creating art, but such activity helps the whole world."[54] Through the ritual act of writing, we can explore our inner poet, our interior muse, without fear. Julia Cameron, in *The Artist's Way,*[55] suggests writing three handwritten, stream-of-consciousness pages every day. Calling them the "Morning Pages," she feels that they prime the psyche for the creative process. Through time, the ritual of writing will provide a powerful place to explore one's own nature and engage in dialogue with the Self. Some people enjoy the process of keeping a journal in the context of a workshop with other people. Still others relish the privacy of this intimate space. One woman, experiencing many changes and losses in midlife, recently described her journal to me as a "lifeline." Whether you keep a journal on a computer disk or in a blank book is up to you. Some people love the feel of smooth, clean paper in a beautiful bound book. It becomes, for them, a remarkable container for their deepest feelings. When one good friend of mine decided to keep a journal another friend of hers, who loved her own journals, bought a beautiful leather volume for her to begin. Each night my friend would sit down with it, but she was so intimidated by its elegance that she would become mute. Going to the junk drawer in the kitchen, she retrieved an old spiral notebook that she had started to use for a real estate class. Tearing out the pages of notes from her class left her with a place that was somehow "friendly" enough to allow her to share her thoughts and feelings. She has now gone through many spiral notebooks and uses the leather volume to make grocery lists.

2. Ask yourself two questions: "What did I most love to do when I was about ten years old or so?" and "What would I do with my time if I won a lot-

tery and was financially set for the rest of my life?" The answers to these questions will provide great insight into what the soul is asking for in life. If you discover that you have not integrated any of those activities into your life on a regular basis, you are cutting off the very stuff that feeds the Self and the soul. Perhaps your first ambition was to become a rock 'n' roll star. But now you are an accountant and earn a very good living. You have children in college and can't afford to pitch your practice, buy an old Volkswagen bus, and offer to play percussion for Grateful Dead concerts as you travel across the country. But an integrated life and moving toward wholeness *require* that you find some creative way to integrate this musical energy into your life. Take music lessons, go to concerts that feature drummers you admire, get together with other people who enjoy playing music. Gail Sheehy relates a very funny anecdote in *New Passages* in describing a woman who recovered a long-lost passion for music in midlife: "Jeannie enrolled in music school to study electric bass and drums. She now plays in a garage rock band with 18-year-old boys. She already has planned her antidote to 'hardening of the attitudes.' After 65 she plans to launch a heavy metal band called Guns and Geezers."[56] My Aunt Teresa took tap dancing lessons—something that she had always wanted to do—in her sixties. She had no ambitions to dance at Radio City Music Hall but delighted both herself and the rest of the family by tapping as she served Thanksgiving dinner one year. Explore your own inner playfulness. Embrace your own eccentricity. As George Eliot wrote, "It is never too late to be what you might have been."[57]

3. Enter into a dialogue, an Active Imagination, with the critic, those places in you that argue against the creative life. Listen carefully. The rational, critical part of your mind is active when you hear all the reasons that you can't or shouldn't allow for your playfulness, humor, or creativeness to express itself. Be alert to internal messages such as: "You don't have time for this"; "You're not really going to spend twenty-three dollars on watercolors and paper, are you?"; "People will think this is stupid or crazy, you can't learn to play the bass at forty-eight"; "You're never going to be good at this anyway, why bother?" Allow the critic to speak, learn to love that part of yourself, but do not allow it to control your efforts or frighten you away from the path with heart. Write it a letter, talk to it every day, if you must, but help this aspect of your personality understand that while you are not going to mortgage the house to buy watercolors, you are going to spend Saturday afternoons painting by the edge of the ocean.

4. Surround yourself with support for your creative process. This may be in the form of a writers' group, musicians who will play music in your basement, or friends who will hike an unexplored trail with you. Connect with people who understand your need to express yourself, by attending workshops and seminars devoted to the creative process or some aspect of it that interests you. Read some of the many books, or listen to audiotapes, that encourage your creativity. At midlife, our new foray into our creative process can be fragile, easily damaged by the external critics and naysayers. Positive energy and encouragement is catching, and, as Natalie Goldberg notes, "If you walk in the mist, you get wet."[58] Many excellent resources are listed in the notes to this chapter.

5. For the most part, turn off your TV.

CHAPTER 9

The Life of the Spirit: Prayer, Meditation, and Being

Throughout my whole life, during every moment I have lived, the world has gradually been taking on light and fire for me, until it has come to envelop me in one mass of luminosity, glowing from within . . . The purple flush of matter fading imperceptibly into the gold of spirit, to be lost finally in the incandescence of a personal universe.

PIERRE TEILHARD DE CHARDIN, *THE DIVINE MILIEU*, 1957

In May 1995, zookeepers at the San Francisco Zoo were concerned about a female snow leopard named Shin who had refused to eat for more than two weeks. A group of eleven Tibetan Buddhist monks happened to be visiting the zoo and heard about the sick leopard. Nancy Chan, spokesperson for the zoo, describes what happened: "The monks, who were on a three-month concert tour, were very interested, intrigued, by coming in to have a behind-the-scenes tour of the zoo, which they've never had before because they don't get to see animals except on video. So when they called they said, 'Do you have any animals that are unhealthy?' And we said, 'Well, you know, by the way, we have a ten-year-old snow leopard named Shin, a female, who happens to have some problems.' And they said, 'Well, where is this snow leopard from?' We said, 'Tibet.' And they said, 'Oh, we've never seen a snow leopard in real life.' "

The monks decided to give a blessing, what they called a puja, or healing chant, to the snow leopard. Nancy Chan observed that when the monks lined up outside the snow leopard's cage and began to chant, Shin "came down from her perch, she sat right in front of the mesh screen, just right against the screen really, and just watched them. . . . It was absolutely amazing. I think everybody who was there that witnessed this just felt this feeling of a blessing for all of us." The monks completed their chant and Shin, the snow leopard, walked away. Later that day, the zookeeper put food into her enclosure and she started eating again.[1]

At forty-one, Pete had resigned himself to the process of dying. Having lived with AIDS for more than ten years, he had developed a strong spiritual belief in the durability of his own soul and was not afraid. He had taken care of all the "loose ends" in his life, written a will, made arrangements for all his material possessions, and said good-bye to many of his friends. But Pete was sad and felt "incomplete" about his relationship with his younger brother, Eddie. Years of estrangement and family conflict had taken their toll. The brothers, who had been extremely close as children, had not been in contact for many years. Pete had tried repeatedly to get in touch, but Eddie would never respond to any of his offers of reconciliation. Pete recognized that any additional efforts to contact his brother would be as futile as all the others had been. Eddie knew, and had known for a long time through other family members, that Pete was very sick, that he was dying.

One night, Pete sat in front of an old black-and-white photograph of the brothers in their much younger days and prayed: "God, please let Eddie know that we need to heal our relationship and that we need to do it now." Pete believed that after his death his soul would be in a peaceful place, but that Eddie would suffer with the pain of the unfinished business between them. His prayer was more for Eddie than himself and he went to sleep that night with the contentment of knowing that there was nothing more he could do for his brother.

At six o'clock in the morning, Pete's phone rang. It was Eddie. He said that he couldn't get Pete off his mind the night before. Would it be all right if he came to see him? Eddie left his home and flew across the country to Pete's side. When Pete died about a week later, it was in Eddie's arms, and surrounded by the rest of their large family.

In June 1995, U.S. Air Force captain Scott O'Grady was ejected from his F-16 airplane after being hit by a surface-to-air missile launched by Serb troops over northern Bosnia. Trying to stay alive and undetected by the foot soldiers who were combing the area, Captain O'Grady was able to conceal himself and survive by eating leaves, grass, and ants. By catching rain in plastic bags and squeezing water out of his wet woolen socks, he obtained a minimal amount of fluid, but it was enough to keep him alive. At times, Serbian troops were as close as three feet from him, pounding the ground with their rifles in an effort to flush him out of his hiding place.

After six days of this physically excruciating, terrifying ordeal, O'Grady was able to get a radio message to fellow F-16 pilot and friend Thomas Hanford, who was flying over the area hoping for a signal that Scott might still be alive. Within hours, a daring rescue attempt was launched as a Marine Expeditionary Unit, based on a helicopter carrier in the Adriatic Sea, screamed off in a pair of huge Super Stallion helicopters to O'Grady's location. Backed up by more than forty planes, Harrier jump jets, and replacement helicopters, the rescue team watched O'Grady as he ran across an open field. He was pulled into the open door of one of the big helicopters and it carried him back to its base.

O'Grady was given a full hero's welcome at the Air Force base in Italy and then in the United States. The low-key captain gave the full measure of praise and thanks to his Air Force and Marine rescuers. They were the true heroes, he said repeatedly. In spite of his own heroism and ability to utilize his survival training, O'Grady underplayed his own responsibility for his survival and gave the greatest thanks to a higher source: "I prayed to God and asked Him for a lot of things, and He delivered throughout the entire time. . . . When I prayed for rain, He gave me rain. One time I prayed, Lord, let me at least have someone know I'm alive and maybe come rescue me. And guess what? That night T.O. (F-16 pilot Thomas O. Hanford) came up on the radio."[2]

Since the birth of human consciousness and in every culture, prayer has existed in a multitude of forms. Whether in the form of a *petition,* in which we ask for something for ourselves, or an *intercession,* in which we ask for something for someone else, or in forms of *adoration, confession, invocation, lamentation, meditation, thanksgiving, contemplation,* or *surrender,* prayer is always an attempt to communicate with some transcendent power that looks over us, loves us, and has compassion and concern for us.

Even today, with our culture's logical, empirical view of the universe, recent studies have shown that nine out of ten Americans believe in the profound power of meditation and/or prayer in their lives.[3] Like Pete, Captain O'Grady, and the Tibetan monks who chanted for Shin the snow leopard, ninety-five percent of people strongly feel that their prayers have been answered.[4] These surveys also found that as people got older, there was a greater belief in the power of prayer to positively affect emotional health.

In recent years a variety of studies has investigated the power of prayer.

Larry Dossey, a physician, and co-chair of the newly established Panel on Mind/Body Interventions at the National Institutes of Health, cites a number of these studies in his excellent and provocative book *Healing Words*. For example, the Spindrift Organization, in Salem, Oregon, has for more than ten years conducted simple laboratory experiments demonstrating the effects of prayer. In one of these experiments, a mold growing on the surface of a rice agar plate was "stressed" by immersing it in an alcohol rinse that damaged it and restricted its growth. The experimenters then divided the plate in two by placing a string across it and marking the control side A and the treated side B. Nondirected prayer, in which the petitioner makes no specific request and holds no particular outcome in mind, was then used to encourage the growth of side B, while no prayers were said for the control side, A. On side B the mold began to multiply and form concentric growth rings. No such growth was seen in the identical, but "un-prayed-for" mold on side A. In addition to demonstrating the power of prayer to inhibit or encourage the growth of various biological materials (e.g., molds, spores, soybeans, etc.), the Spindrift studies also revealed that *nondirected prayer* appeared to be quantitatively more effective than *directed* prayer ("Please let this cancer be cured").[5]

Cardiologist Randy Byrd conducted an experiment in 1984 at San Francisco General Hospital in which he assessed the effects of prayer on the health and healing of cardiac patients in a coronary intensive-care unit. In this study, a computer assigned 192 patients to an experimental (prayed-for) group and another 201 patients to a control group. The two groups were matched for age and severity of their cardiac condition. The experiment was designed as a double blind study in that neither the patients, nurses, nor doctors were aware of which group a particular patient was in. Thus any difference in the results of the study could not be attributed to the expectations of the patients (i.e., a placebo effect), the subtle (and sometimes not so subtle) influences of the experimenters, or the beliefs of the attending medical team.

The experimenters then recruited numerous clergymen and women throughout the United States from a variety of different religions and faiths. Each of the clergy was given the first names and the diagnoses of specific patients and asked to pray each day for their "beneficial healing and quick recovery," but were not given instructions on how to pray. All patients in the experimental group, none of whom were aware that they were being prayed for, were on the prayer list of five to seven people.

The results of this year-long experiment were presented at the 1985 meeting of the American Heart Association, and they were stunning. On measures including the number of antibiotics prescribed in order to control infection, the presence or absence of pulmonary edema, and whether or not a respirator (to help with breathing) was necessary, the experimental (prayed-for) group fared consistently and statistically significantly better than the un-prayed-for control group. Additionally, although the result was not statistically significant, fewer patients in the prayed-for group died compared to the control group.[6]

Other researchers, using scientifically controlled experiments, have shown powerful effects of prayer on fungi, yeast and bacteria, cells (including cancer cells), plants, animals, and humans. Some of these studies investigated the effect of prayers of highly spiritually developed psychics and healers. Other experiments looked into those of average, everyday people.[7] The results of all these studies suggest that prayer is powerful, that nondirected prayer seems to be more powerful than directed prayer, and that the force of prayer does not diminish over time or distance. If then prayer is some form of energy, as has been proposed, it is not of a type that matches our traditional theories of space-time or matter-energy. And yet it is precisely this understanding and acceptance of a relationship to the universe that transcends matter and physical form, which is at the heart of spirituality and which makes it such an important issue at midlife. June Singer observes, "There is a 'visible world' and there is an 'invisible world.' Both are real, although they are real in different ways. Both need to be recognized and experienced, and ways can and must be found to move between the two in response to the demands that life places upon us as human beings."[8] Some belief in an enduring, eternal aspect of the Self, the soul, or consciousness which is intimately and deeply connected to a larger universal force is central to all spiritual, mystical, and religious traditions. An awareness and belief in this relationship, whatever it may be, gives a profound sense of meaning to one's life. The clarification of our individual spiritual convictions is especially important during a challenging midlife passage when so many of our cherished beliefs about the world are called into question.

Discovering a sense of meaning in our lives is one of the critical tasks of the midlife transition. Jung's view of this dimension of the midlife experience highlights the importance of the development of one's spiritual nature: "Among all my patients in the second half of life—that is to say over thirty-five—there has not been one whose problem in the last resort was not that of finding a religious outlook on life."[9] At midlife we may find ourselves moving toward more profound beliefs in a realm of spirit in an attempt to provide some comfort, some way of balancing the growing awareness of our own existential neurosis and the inevitability of our own death. Or, as Jung has suggested, it may be that human beings instinctively possess a powerful, unconscious, archetypal energy toward transcendent, mythological, and metaphysical beliefs, a "natural religious function." Jung wrote, "The decisive question for man is, is he related to something infinite or not? That is the telling question of his life. Only if we know that the thing that truly matters is the infinite can we avoid fixing our attention upon futilities and upon all kinds of goals which are not of real importance. . . . In the final analysis we count for something only because of the essential we embody, and if we do not embody that, life is wasted."[10] Jung fervently believed that numerous psychological problems arose from a disregard of this fundamental spiritual need of the psyche, especially during the second half of life.

At midlife, a sense of meaning and belief in some spiritual dimension of our life may come from a fervent, unshakable faith in a traditional religious belief system. For some people, religion not only offers a shared experience of worship and ritual but may also provide a community of support, guidance, and nurturance. For others, including many of the rebellious baby boomer generation, the answers being sought may not be found in the realm of organized religion. Instead they may look to a way of knowing that, from ancient times has been called *gnosis,* a path to wisdom and transcendence that comes from the soul rather than the intellect, reason, or faith alone. On this path, spirituality is not based upon faith, nor is it necessarily religious.[11]

Development of a new consciousness, individuation, and the movement toward the realization of the Self will require at the very least the belief in the reality of an "invisible world," which Abraham Maslow referred to as an exploration of the "farther reaches of human nature." Moving forward in this journey demanded of Maslow, as it will of us, the "continuous destruction of cherished axioms, the perpetual coping with seeming paradoxes, contradictions and vagueness, and the occasional collapse around my ears of long-established, firmly believed in, and seemingly unassailable laws of psychology. Often these have turned out to be no laws at all but only rules for living in a state of mild and chronic psychopathology and fearfulness, of stunting and crippling immaturity which we don't notice because most others have this same disease that we have."[12]

Spiritual beliefs are seen as somehow separate from the rest of our life. Spirituality and religion in our culture are relegated to specific times and places in our daily schedule. We may believe that when we go to church or temple or mosque we are in touch with our spiritual self while at all other times we perceive the world and behave according to the secular values of our society. But this is our cultural distortion, for none of the major religious systems has ever suggested this dichotomy between what we believe spiritually and how we live. Like creativity, spirituality is more about attitude and intention, a prevailing worldview, than specific activities; true spiritual enlightment is about who we are and are becoming, about being rather than doing.

Eastern traditions often speak of holding awareness, a compassionate heart, and a loving energy toward all beings while we "chop wood and carry water." Coming from a Western tradition, Thomas Moore concurs when he writes: "Spirituality is seeded, germinates, sprouts and blossoms in the mundane. It is to be found and nurtured in the smallest of daily activities."[13] When we allow ourselves to experience the transpersonal in everyday life, we awaken to the sacredness in each and every moment. Meditation master and Buddhist teacher Chögyam Trungpa observed simply that "when you see ordinary situations with extraordinary insight it is like discovering a jewel in rubbish."[14] In a similar vein, Vietnamese Zen master and poet Thich Nhat Hanh reminds us that the path with heart must be embraced and actualized in our everyday existence. "Our own life is the instrument with which we experiment with truth," he writes.[15]

For many of us, the idea of living our spiritual beliefs in an earthy, everyday kind of way is an enormous challenge. Mostly this is because we race unconsciously through our lives as if the present moment doesn't even exist. So programmed are we to making preparations for the future that for most of us our consciousness is days, weeks, months, years ahead of our actual experience. Perhaps we may fear giving our full attention to the present moment because we then would have to be aware of all of our emotions; we would have to experience the full measure of our pain as well as our pleasure. But unless we do so, we may pass through our lives without ever experiencing them.

Nancy was forty-eight years old and in the midst of the challenges of the midlife transition before she discovered that she may never have actually experienced what it is like to be present at any given moment. Because of the death of her father, her mother's full-time job, and a severely mentally ill brother who required a great deal of special attention, her mother had, very reluctantly, handed over a great deal of household responsibility to Nancy when she was just twelve years old. Nancy learned to be a tireless worker and careful planner, always prepared for the future. When she was in school she was thinking about what to make for dinner. While she was eating dinner she was going over homework assignments in her head. When she was doing her homework she was considering how she would get her brother up and ready for school in the morning. After she arrived at school the next day, the whole process would repeat itself, as it did every day.

As an adult, Nancy held a management position that required long hours of work and was both physically and mentally taxing. At work, she often daydreamed about her days off when she could relax on the beach and read or talk with her friends. When her vacation finally rolled around, she would pile her luggage, beach chairs, fishing poles, and dog into the car. Excited to be away from the daily grind, she would head toward the ocean. But while her body was "relaxing" on the beach her head was back at work: "I wonder if they've taken care of that order this week." "I've *got* to paint the house this year for sure." "Oh Lord, the lawn must be looking very raggedy by now. I should have had someone in to cut it while I'm on vacation."

In midlife, Nancy finally became aware that she was wishing her life away. "I'm never where I am," she said. "I filter everything through the future."

Nancy's difficulty with staying in the present is not a bit uncommon. Her willingness to recognize it is. Most of us go through our lives without the rich experience and satisfaction of being in the present, feeling everything that is there at any given moment.

To question whether or not "we are where we are" is akin to asking ourselves whether our consciousness is attached to our body at any given moment. As it turns out, most of us are guilty of a kind of unconscious "out-of-body experience," in that our consciousness is never where we are. We're thinking of work when we're on vacation, we're dreaming of our vacation while we're at work. While we're relaxing we're thinking that we should be mowing the lawn, while we're mowing the lawn we're wishing we could be relaxing in our hammock. But this is such a common theme in our fast-paced society that we rarely see it as a problem. After all, this is what everyone does. It is the way to success.

A wonderful film, *Koyaanisqatsi,* vividly portrays how this pace and attitude toward our experience is both exhausting and inauthentic. *Koyaanisqatsi* is a Hopi word which means "life out of balance," and as the film opens, images portray, in real time, the beauty of the Bad Lands—brown, craggy mountains and fine sand blowing over smooth dunes. The clouds move slowly overhead, casting their shadows across the desert and a clear, mirror-smooth blue lake. The music, by Philip Glass, lulls us into an even greater sense of appreciation of the great beauty before us. Then slowly, almost imperceptibly, everything begins to speed up. Images of the desert give way to modern skyscrapers, factories, explosions of the land as mining operations carve into the earth. The shadows of clouds begin to move by so quickly that we can no longer recognize their shapes. We watch, stunned, both by the contrast between the natural beauty of the land and the waste and destruction wrought by human hands and by the speed at which everything is moving. Images of faces in large, crowded cities, are empty, lifeless, diminished, grim. By the end of the film we watch cars speeding by on a huge cloverleaf in an American city. It is nighttime and things are moving so quickly now that we cannot even make out the images of the cars themselves; they are simply whirling ribbons of white and red as they approach and retreat from our vantage point. The music becomes frenetic and wild. By the time the credits roll, one's heart is pounding and one experiences a sense of profound exhaustion. We can feel the grief, not just for Mother Earth but for ourselves as well. This is the way most of us live: "life out of balance." We are racing where, and for what purpose?

At midlife, if we are truly seeking a greater wisdom, a more authentic sense of who we are, a deeper sense of our spiritual connection, and are listening to the promptings of the Self, *it is necessary to live in the moment in which we are existing.* Like the space between thoughts, or a rest between two notes of music, it is in being that we, perhaps for the first time, can hear our inner rhythm and see our own clear reflection. The poet Rumi says simply and wonderfully: "Stay here, quivering with each moment, like a drop of mercury."[16]

Jack Kornfield beautifully describes the courage we need to slow down and face whatever is present in our lives. He writes: "You may have heard of 'out-of-body-experiences,' full of lights and visions. A true spiritual path demands something more challenging, what could be called an 'in-the-body-experience.' We must connect to our body, to our feelings, to our life just now, if we are to awaken."[17] By the time we are in midlife our addiction to speed and to never living in the present is strong, automatic, and hard to break. The most difficult habits to change are those that take place inside our heads, and yet this is where the most profound change can take place as well. Yaqui sorcerer Don Juan's lesson to anthropologist Carlos Castaneda in the importance of really "seeing" bears this out. "Things don't change. You change your way of looking, that's all."[18] Ram Dass notes: "When you are living in the spirit it all looks different to you."[19] In the Zen tradition, this intentional practice of awareness is referred to as "polishing the mirror," since a sparkling, clear mirror has no intrinsic bias for or against anything, but generously reflects whatever it encounters.[20] It is important to realize that every religious and spiritual practice includes some form of practice in awareness and mindfulness, whether it be through meditation, prayer, or introspection and reflection.

Shunryu Suzuki, the first Zen master to establish a Zen training monastery outside of Asia, describes the importance of meditation practice in order to live in the moment and achieve boundless compassion and *shoshin,* or beginner's mind. Zen meditation posture, in which one sits in the full lotus position with left foot on right thigh, right foot on left thigh, expresses the oneness of duality, emphasizing the idea that body and mind are both two *and* one. In this zazen posture the spine is straight, as if you are supporting the sky with your head. Hands are placed left on top of right with the middle joints of the middle fingers together and thumbs lightly touching each other. Breathing is like a "swinging door" in which you inhale the air into the inner world and exhale the air out to the outer world. In zazen, all that exists is the movement of the breathing, but there is awareness of the breathing, emphasizing that in the zazen "we must exist right here, right now." The zazen form itself, says Suzuki, is not the means to obtain the right state of mind. Rather, taking the posture itself is to have the right state of mind: being fully present in the moment.[21] In horseback riding, riders refer to a "good seat" to explain the quality of settling into the saddle and connecting to the horse. John Welwood observes that "the classic meditation posture—sitting still in an upright, balanced way—lets us ride the wild horse of the mind without losing our seat."[22]

Practiced meditation, whether it be Zen, transcendental meditation,

Yoga, deep prayer, or another form, is a powerful and significant way to relax the body and become more mindful of our experience of the moment. When practiced with discipline, meditation and prayer allow an entry into new states of awareness and nonordinary states of consciousness. In fact, meditation practices of all kinds are a very direct expression of what the Buddhist tradition refers to as "Right Mindfulness." Right Mindfulness, or attentiveness, requires the *diligent awareness* of the activities of the body *(kaya),* sensations and feelings *(vedana),* the activities of the mind *(citta)* and ideas, thoughts, conceptions and things *(dhamma).*[24]

Jon Kabat-Zinn, a clinical psychologist who has taught mindfulness training and meditation to Catholic priests, judges, health professionals, Olympic athletes, and prisoners, rightly observes that this practice is simple but not necessarily easy. "Mindfulness," he writes, "requires effort and discipline for the simple reason that the forces that work against our being mindful, namely, our habitual unawareness and automaticity, are exceedingly tenacious. They are so strong and so much out of our consciousness that an inner commitment and a certain kind of work are necessary just to keep up our attempts to capture our moments in awareness and sustain mindfulness."[24]

Practice at meditation is an important path to an increased ability to live in the present, to allow the space for the unconscious to express itself and the Self to be known. At midlife especially, this kind of practice is highly recommended. But in addition to these more formal approaches, there are other ways of achieving mindfulness. Natalie Goldberg speaks of the process of writing from the inspiration of the egoless Self, or "first thoughts," as a Zen practice of mindfulness.[25] Even the act of playing a musical instrument requires a here-and-now presence that is filled with a sense of awareness. In fact, many creative activities in the arts and in crafts, if performed in a mindful way, become excellent activities to learn how to *be* at one with the present moment.[26]

Activities that engage us physically also offer great potential for living in the moment. Athletes in every sport speak of their full participation in the moment, which is necessary for them to perform well. I remember snow skiing one winter during a time of my life that was filled with stress. Throughout the drive to the lodge, putting on equipment, and all the way up the lift to the top of the mountain, I ruminated over a problem I was having with my dissertation research. Clearly, I was not living in the present moment. In fact, in my distraction, I had chosen a run that was well beyond my skills. Once I left the top of the mountain, as I focused my concentration completely on getting over the next mogul and avoiding trees and other skiers, my worries about my dissertation completely disappeared. Instead, my entire attention was in the present terrifying, yet exhilarating moment as I struggled to get to the bottom in one piece.

Writing in the 1950s, Eugen Herrigel, in *Zen in the Art of Archery,* describes the importance of losing oneself in the shot by the "loosing" of the arrow. "This state, in which nothing definite is thought, planned, striven for, desired, or expected, which is at bottom purposeless and egoless, was called by the Master, truly 'spiritual.' It is in fact charged with spiritual awareness and is therefore also called 'right presence of mind.' "[27] Herrigel's thoughts about archery are mirrored in Timothy Gallwey's on tennis: "When a tennis player is 'on his game,' he's not thinking about how, when, or even where to hit the ball. He's not *trying* to hit the ball, and after the shot he doesn't think about how badly or how well he made contact. The ball seems to get hit through an automatic process which doesn't require thought."[28]

Experiencing nature with our full attention is also practice in mindfulness. The natural world is a container in which our instincts can be refined through attention to its unpretentious and ever-present beingness. Listen to Annie Dillard's description of watching the movements of a muskrat in the mountains of southwestern Virginia. Unable to see the animal itself, she watches the ripples upstream and the "gliding shadow on the creek's bottom." Then she follows the reflection of a cloud on Tinker Creek. "At last I stared upstream where only the deepest violet remained of the cloud, a cloud so high its underbelly still glowed feeble color reflected from a hidden sky lighted in turn by a sun halfway to China. And out of that violet, a sudden enormous black body arced over the water. I saw only a cylindrical sleekness. Head and tail, if there was a head and tail, were both submerged in cloud. I saw only one ebony fling, a headlong dive to darkness; then the waters closed, and the lights went out."[29]

Terry Tempest Williams reflects a similar immersion in the present in her remarkable book *Refuge,* which follows the rise of the Great Salt Lake during the spring when her mother was dying of ovarian cancer. "This afternoon, I have found quiet hours alone picking tomatoes. As my fingers find ripe tomatoes, red and firm, through the labyrinth of leaves, I am absorbed into the present. My garden asks nothing more of me than I am able to give. I pull tomatoes, gently placing them in the copper colander. Pulling tomatoes, pulling tomatoes. Some come easily."[30]

William Carlos Williams's poem "Thursday" captures the essence of staying in the present and is a wonderful example of his own admonition to "write about things that are close to the nose":

> *I have had my dream—like others—*
> *and it has come to nothing, so that*
> *I remain now carelessly*
> *with feet planted on the ground*
> *and look up at the sky—*
> *feeling my clothes about me,*
> *the weight of my body in my shoes,*
> *the rim of my hat, air passing in and out*
> *at my nose—and decide to dream, no more.*[31]

While most of us may not yet be able to describe our experiences with the beauty and certainty of Williams, Dillard, or Tempest Williams, we are blessed with the same sensory abilities with which to take in what is around us. Being in the present requires a reintegration, a "coming to our senses." Mindfulness demands an open awareness to sight, touch, taste, smell, and sound. Anyone who has ever walked through the woods in spring, smelling the freshness of new growth, hearing the trilling of songbirds, and seeing the mottled shadows of gently moving leaves on rich brown earth, understands the direct access our senses give us to mindfulness in the present moment. The world is truly "sense-luscious," as Diane Ackerman has described it.[32]

Native American traditions are intimately connected to here-and-now experiences of the earth. Lakota shaman Black Elk speaks eloquently of a moment of oneness, when all the senses—hearing, smell, taste, seeing, and feeling—are connected to the heart, when concentration moves from head to heart in the ever-present moment. At such a moment we can hear nature's "songs." Black Elk writes: "Even the Earth has a song. We call it Mother Earth. We call her Grandmother, and she has a song. Then the water, it has a song. The water makes beautiful sounds. The water carries the universal sounds. Now the green. This tree, every green has a song. They have a language of their own. There's a life there. You say there is a chemistry language there. So each green has a song. There's a lot of songs we don't know yet. One man could never get to know all of them."[33]

Poet Nancy Wood, in "Mother's Words," captures the beauty of the moment in nature as seen in the Native American tradition:

Why look for answers, my child,
Among the people you meet?
Why believe there is fulfillment
In your narrow life of work?
Why sacrifice the gift of loneliness
to fill up the time with diversion?
Look inside every living thing you find.
Feel the energy of rocks and leaves, hummingbirds and cactus.
Dwell for a moment in a single blade of grass.
Discover the secret of snowflakes.
In these patterns lie harmony, my child.
In harmony, the universe.[34]

Mindfulness does not require any special setting or activity. It is, instead, a decision and a dedication to experience the reality of the present moment, what has been rightly called the "precious present." We can allow for this spiritual awareness to flow through us at every single moment of our life, whether we are driving, eating, Jazzercising, gardening, singing, walking, reading, making love, dancing, listening to the songs of nature, or making widgets in a factory—as well as sitting still, inhaling into the inner world and exhaling into the outer, in zazen. As it says in *The Lazy Man's Guide to Enlightenment,* "Enlightenment doesn't care how you get there."[35]

As human beings we live a double life, with one foot in the invisible, spiritual world of the psyche and the sacred and the other in the visible, familiar, material world. We must ride along the razor's edge, or "hold the tension of the opposites," in order to work through the resistance that we all have to the full wisdom of both worlds.

The path of individuation provides a solid basis upon which our own sense of spirituality can rest. The world seems to be full of people who speak beautiful spiritual language but who seem to have never found their soul, to have never become conscious: people who may worship vigorously but have not discovered compassion for others; people who have great learning and knowledge about religious traditions or New Age mysticism but are unable to forgive; people who are strong in their own beliefs concerning God and the sacred but disrespectful of the beliefs of others. The number of wars fought on the grounds of religion and spiritual beliefs and our defilement of nature and Mother Earth resoundingly illustrate that holding spiritual beliefs and living in a spiritual way do not necessarily coincide. In fact, spirituality that is not contained in a true, vibrant sense of self can be a movement toward greater *unconsciousness* rather than the conscious wholeness of mind, body, and spirit. Gnostic teacher Monoimus says: "Abandon the search for God and the creation and other matters of a similar sort. Look for him by taking yourself as the starting point."[36]

If we hope to become more enlightened and fulfill our spiritual destiny, we must begin by dealing with our own personal psychology, our own unconsciousness, our shadow, our own "dirty laundry," as John Sanford has called it.[37] Marion Woodman tells a wonderful story of a woman who has a dream in which she is a priestess and has prepared the altar for a great celebration. She places a bouquet of roses in a center position on the altar where there is sunlight coming through the window in the shape of a cross. She tries to place the flowers in the cross-shaped sunbeam but she cannot make them fit. An old man enters and says, "Your hymns will never rise to heaven until you clean up your mess in the basement." And she says, "There is no basement in this temple. I never heard of a basement." "That's the problem," he says. "There is a basement."[38]

The spiritual quest at midlife will often take us through the basement, through the darkness of our own shadow. The process is not an easy or quick one. And it may not always be safe. Strong, durable containers of ego strength and support are necessary to handle the awesome power of a deep spiritual search and the exploration of the "invisible world." We are well advised to clean up the mess in the basement as a prerequisite. It is important to remember that psychotics drown in the very same sea in which mystics swim.

The Kfar Shaul Psychiatric Hospital in Jerusalem serves as a stabilization center for victims of the "Jerusalem syndrome." The staff at the hospital has provided safety and help for a bearded Italian dressed in a sack with cloth bags for shoes, totally oblivious to the snow outside, carrying a New Testament and claiming to be Jesus Christ; a naked man who ran with a sword through the Old City on a mission to heal the blind; an angry German man who called the police complaining that the staff at the hotel kitchen were stopping him from preparing the Last Supper. The Jerusalem syndrome has affected both Christians and Jews and is described as an "affliction of tourists who, overwhelmed by the city's intense spiritual evocations, have become convinced that they are the Saviour, or some other biblical figure, or that they have been given a special message or mandate by God."[39]

The vast majority of those of us at midlife who are searching for our spiritual beliefs are unlikely to end up in the Kfar Shaul Psychiatric Hospital, or any other psychiatric hospital for that matter. We may, however, be in danger of a type of *inflation* that can come from a glimpse, however brief, into the realm of the invisible world without the down and dirty work of making the unconscious conscious, without relinquishing an identification with the mask of the persona and becoming who we were authentically meant to be. Jung described inflation as the expansion of the personality beyond its proper limits through its identification with the persona or with an archetype. It is a psychological state in which a person feels an exaggerated sense of his or her own self-importance. "Inflation," Jung wrote, "occurs whenever people are overpowered by knowledge or some new realization. 'Knowledge puffeth up,' Paul writes to the Corinthians, for the new knowledge had turned the heads of many, as indeed constantly happens. The inflation has nothing to do with the kind of knowledge, but simply and solely with the fact that any new knowledge can so seize hold of a weak head that he no longer sees and hears anything else. He is hypnotized by it, and instantly believes he has solved the riddle of the universe. But that is equivalent to almighty self-conceit."[40]

The Greek myth of Icarus illustrates the importance of maintaining our earthbound connections, keeping one foot in the everyday, human, visible world even as we learn to soar to the heavens. According to the myth, the Cretan king Minos ordered an architect, Daedalus, to build an enclosure for the Minotaur, a half-bull, half-human monster with a penchant for gobbling up the maidens and youths whom Minos sent each year as a sacrifice. Daedalus built a labyrinth, a maze of intricate passages from which it was impossible to find an exit, to hold the dangerous Minotaur, but later Minos became enraged with Daedalus and imprisoned him within the labyrinth he himself had built. Daedalus escaped by fashioning wings from feathers and wax for himself and his son, Icarus. But in spite of his father's warnings, Icarus flew too close to the sun. The wax in the wings melted, and he was plunged into the sea and drowned while his father floated safely on currents of air to Sicily. This myth is usually interpreted to depict a rash and unconscious adventuresomeness which leads to downfall; but it is also a wonderful illustration of the dangers of inflation, of flying unprepared too close to the energy of the sacred.

A similar story is found in Native American, Zuni culture and is called "The Youth and His Eagle." It, too, describes the terrible danger that can arise from inflation and emphasizes the importance of keeping one foot in the visible world, of confronting and illuminating our own inner psychology as we seek the ineffable dimension of individuation and spirit. In this myth, told elegantly by Clarissa Pinkola Estes,[41] a young boy is charged with taking care of a cornfield. While his brothers and other relatives work the land, the boy spends all his time tending to his pet eagle. The brothers devise a plan to kill the eagle and cure him of his infatuation with the bird. But the eagle overhears their plot and determines that she must leave. The boy cannot bear the thought of being without her and demands that he accompany her. The eagle protests, saying that the boy cannot possibly live the life of an eagle. The next day the boy holds on to the strong back of the eagle and they fly away. When they arrive in the land of the eagles they are married and the elders fashion a coat of eagle feathers for the boy so that he too can fly. He is given great freedom but is told that he is not allowed to fly toward the south. After some time, the boy becomes curious about why he is not permitted to fly south, and so he does. The inhabitants of the land of the damned observe him flying there, and he and the eagles are invited to a great festival and dance. The eagles have no choice but to accept the invitation and the boy is instructed that in no case is he to smile or laugh while at this great dance. Again the boy violates the eagles' commands and the eagles take from him his coat of great and beautiful feathers. Instead he is given an old, raggedy coat of feathers and told to accompany his eagle wife into the sky. They fly very far, with the eagle wife helping him as he falters. After some time they fly over his own village. The eagle wife tears off his coat with her talons and he falls into his own unweeded field and dies.[42]

Clarissa Pinkola Estes observes that in the descent toward the Self, particularly the descent associated with midlife, there is a tendency to abandon the earthly plane in the effort to transform and transcend: our cornfields go untended while we wish to soar with the eagles. The pull toward an inflation of the ego as we undergo the process of individuation and the search for spirit should not be underestimated. It can be dangerous and can lead us into greater unconsciousness. Citing the different archetypal energies that are present at midlife as compared to our youth, James Hollis correctly observes, "Wisdom is always humbling, never inflationary. . . . The realistic thinking of midlife has as its necessary goal the righting of a balance, the restoration of a person to a humble but dignified relationship to the universe."[43]

During the initiation to my midlife journey I began to experience an overwhelming push to more deeply understand my life and my own spiritual beliefs. Spending such a great deal of time in introspection, reflection, and prayer, I began to experience a kind of inflation that I was not aware of until two events occurred. First, I had been conducting a therapy group that had a particularly large number of members, most of whom were in some form of midlife crisis and were very angry about the experiences that life had recently thrown at them. It seemed like every session was a frustrating struggle to help them focus on anything other than their rage and their "Why me?" kinds of conversation. As I was leaving the group and walking to my car, I remember a kind of holier-than-thou feeling. It was too bad they couldn't understand that life is filled with suffering, I thought. I was suffering at the moment; in fact, I felt as if I had been stripped of everything I had ever valued. I felt cut loose from my foundation, floating in space with no tether to anything that felt solid or real. But I wasn't whining about it, was I? How could they all be so unconscious? I thought. As I opened my car door another therapist, a friend, pulled into the next parking space. I closed the car door and made small talk for a few minutes. As I turned back to my car I realized that I had unconsciously thrown the keys onto the seat and reflexively locked the door. Sitting on the curb, in 90-degree heat, waiting for a locksmith to open my door for forty dollars, I repented my hubris. It was a powerful lesson, especially rich in its synchronicity, in just how unconscious (and judgmental) I, too, could be.

Later that night, the second lesson occurred. I had a dream in which I was high above the trees in a sort of lookout tower. There were all kinds of people there: black, white, Asian, Native American, men, women, old people, children. I was somehow in charge of leading them to some better place. I was pleased with myself in the dream. I felt a little like Moses. As I sat on the edge of a window and looked over this group, for which I had so much responsibility, I suddenly fell over backward from the tower. Luckily I wasn't hurt, because I fell into a huge pile of soft mud and excrement. When I wrote the dream in my journal, I was laughing so hard at my own arrogance I could barely write the words. "All right already," I said out loud. "I get it." The psyche has its own natural approach to establishing balance if we will only listen.

Since my two lessons, it has been easier to avoid being puffed up. I've understood more clearly that my life, like all our lives, will be filled with challenges, suffering, blessings, and joy. I'm working at seeing each as a lesson, as an opportunity to learn about myself and my reality as I try to keep one foot in both the visible and invisible worlds with some humility and humor. At midlife, I'm understanding that I am just one amid many souls in this human incarnation, with many blessings and many challenges and losses yet to be faced, and with no extra-special abilities or blocks along the path of individuation and spiritual seeking. I know that I'm just one among the family, awakening at my own pace, as we all will.

Some Thoughts and Suggestions

1. Make a conscious and disciplined effort to stay in the present. Be aware of the thoughts that keep you living in the past or the future. Notice where you are at the present moment. Nature is an excellent teacher; stay close to it.

2. Honestly examine the ways in which you live or do not live your spiritual beliefs. Put your beliefs into daily practice with your family, friends, neighbors, co-workers, and all living things.

3. Be vigilant for signs of inflation, negative judgments, or mean-spirited feelings toward others. Work at forgiving those toward whom you hold anger or grudges. Holding on to those feelings keeps you from the fullest experience of your own soul.

4. Look closely at dream symbols for images that guide you and keep you close to a path with heart and a relationship to your own spiritual energy.

5. Study your path. Read the great wisdom that is contained in the mystical literature, poetry, and holy books of all the great religions. Participate in workshops and seminars with other seekers.

6. Practice some form of meditation, prayer, quiet time, reflection, or introspection every day.

CHAPTER 10

Living in the Body

If anything is sacred the human body is sacred.
WALT WHITMAN, "I SING THE BODY ELECTRIC,"
LEAVES OF GRASS, 1855

OUR QUEST FOR wholeness and individuation at midlife necessarily includes a new relationship to our physical body. In fact, for many people, the initiation to the midlife passage may begin with a new awareness of our physical body, perhaps in the form of an illness or a simple change in the way we experience ourselves. We may notice that our teenage children are beginning to beat us regularly at tennis, we may experience the oftentimes profound changes brought on by menopause or midlife impotence, or we may find ourselves facing a lump in our breast or a questionable outcome on a prostate exam.

Richard, a highly regarded landscape artist in his forties, needed to awaken to the wisdom of his body in midlife. For more than half of each year he traveled to major cities throughout the country to enter his paintings in art shows. Every show required the exertion of an enormous amount of energy—painting new pictures, making slides, filling out applications, packing materials, and driving his van through the night. When he arrived at the site of a show he would unload his display tent, set it up, then work for several hours to hang his paintings so that the judges and the public could get the best look at them. Working in the sun all day, he would gobble junk food and drink coffee as he talked with potential customers about his work. At the end of each show, he would yank down his display tent, heave it onto the top of his van, and drive back through the night toward home, gulping coffee and chain-smoking cigarettes along the way.

After several weeks of this grueling schedule, Richard would *always* get sick. Sometimes an old back injury would flare up. At other times he would "catch" a particularly vigorous strain of strep throat, experience chest pains that he attributed to indigestion, or be laid out by a stomach flu that was "going around." He would complain that he was fed up with this never-ending routine. He hated spending all his time on the road, was tired of never having any time to spend with his friends, and worst of all, was beginning to detest having to paint the same kind of picture that he knew would sell. He hadn't painted anything new in as long as he could remember. He was feeling depressed and out of sorts with his life. Nevertheless, year after year he continued to exhibit his work at as many art shows as he could squeeze in.

One hot August afternoon, Richard was more than two hundred miles from home at an art show, when he fell over with a massive heart attack. He was rushed to a local hospital, and after more than three weeks in and out of a coma, he awakened. The doctors told him that they were frankly shocked that he seemed to be recovering well. The plaque in the arteries leading to his heart had created an obstruction of such magnitude, they said, that these blood vessels were operating at less than ten percent of their capacity. Hadn't he experienced any symptoms? they asked, as he was recovering from quadruple bypass surgery. Richard, who had lived his life totally out of touch with the wisdom of his body, said simply that he "really didn't think so." Richard had disregarded the clear physical and psychological summons to listen to his body. Chinese wisdom teaches that health is the natural state of all living things, and emphasizes the importance of honoring the body and preventing ill health through attention to and balancing of the vital energy that flows through us. "Treating someone who is already ill is like beginning to dig a well after you have become thirsty," they say.[1] Luckily for Richard, he has been given an opportunity at midlife to dig a new well before he becomes thirsty again, to seek balance and express self-love for his body.

Richard is not alone in his disconnection from his body. In our society many of us have divorced our mind and soul from our physical body;

we have separated spirit from matter. Early human beings understood their deeply rooted relationship to matter and the earth, for the earth provided food, shelter, clothing, and life itself. For our ancestors, the cyclical changes of the natural world—the waxing and waning of the moon, the coming of winter and the emergence of new life in the spring—mirrored the cyclic changes in the bodies of women. They observed that women and female animals give birth just as the earth gives birth to life itself and to the harvest upon which life depends. This ancient intuition about the earth as the ground of being and giver of life became imagined as a sacred female, a goddess. Symbolic images of this sacred female crafted in figures of clay and stone, and painted and scratched on the walls of caves, stress the physical aspects of life. These universal images emphasize, even exaggerate the fertility and fecundity of the human female figure with a sensuous emphasis on breasts, vulvas, vaginas, buttocks, and pregnancy.

At the beginning of human evolution, the sacred and the physical, spirit and matter, light and dark, were one. But as patriarchal religions and cultures disowned and denigrated the feminine principle we began to split matter and spirit, body and soul, into discrete and separate categories of being. All of our instinctive, natural, physical human attributes become associated with the darker, more primitive and undesirable nature of human beings. And, as psychologist Jeanne Achterberg points out, "When spirit no longer is seen to abide in matter, the reverence for what is physical departs."[2]

The psyche-soma split that is so much a part of our ingrained belief system causes many of us to be deeply unconscious about the needs of our bodies. As we have discarded our relationship to the spirit that is incarnated in matter, we have left behind a vital, earthy energy. What has replaced this is great disregard, and sometimes contempt, for our bodies. Marion Woodman writes: "The body has become the whipping post. If the person is anxious, the body is starved, gorged, drugged, intoxicated, forced to vomit, driven into exhaustion, or driven to frenzied reaction against self-destruction. When this magnificent animal attempts to send us warning signals, it is silenced with pills. Many people can listen to their cat more intelligently than they can listen to their own despised body. Because they attend to their pet in a cherishing way, it returns their love. Their body, however, may have to let out an earth-shattering scream in order to be heard at all."[3] Addictions to food, drugs, alcohol, tobacco, sex, and even to starving ourselves abound in our society. We drive our bodies beyond healthy limits by consistent self-destructive, high-powered, and stress-producing behaviors, routinely holding enormous tension in our muscles and tissues. Even those of us who behave in healthy ways often "hate" our bodies. Comparing ourselves to models, celebrities, and even to our own bodies in our younger days, we see ourselves as too fat, too thin, not pretty or handsome enough. At midlife especially, many people, comparing themselves to a youthful ideal of physical health, beauty, and sexuality, may find themselves coming up short. Although the social values that deify youth are changing to some extent, our society still believes that it is better to be young than old. Our cultural notions of attractiveness, sexuality, and health are more often found in the creamy clear complexion of youth than in the subtle laugh lines of the faces of men and women in midlife, which often express wisdom, experience, and a seasoned sensuality. "I'm the oldest sexual person on screen at the moment, which is a very odd label to be inhabiting," forty-eight-year-old actress Susan Sarandon said in a recent interview.[4]

Even those of us who are not as dissociated from our own physical reality suffer, with everyone else, from the state of our environment. Our collective befoulment of our air, water, and soil claims a physical toll on our health, longevity, and vitality. This lack of respect and caring for our world reflects the energy of our collective shadows, which fails to see matter as sacred. Contaminants surround us and create a toxic texture to our world and to each living cell in our bodies. Nell Newman, ecologist and director of Newman's Own Organics, Second Generation, a food manufacturer committed to producing high-quality organic food products, notes that American farmers are trapped on a "chemical StairMaster" in that the conventional seeds that they buy to plant have already been treated with fungicides and work best in soil that is dependent on fertilizer, pesticides, and herbicides. "Conventional farming," she notes, "is the number one source of run-off pollution, contaminating river and ground water. It's a vicious cycle. You have to keep spraying and you have to keep putting nitrogen down because your soil doesn't have anything left in it anymore."[5] Vice President Al Gore simply concludes that "there are so many distressing images of environmental destruction that sometimes it seems impossible to know how to absorb or comprehend them."[6] We do know, however, that the destruction of equilibrium and harmony at the level of the environment reverberates in the lives of each and every living thing.

Jung believed that the Judeo-Christian emphasis on the spirit led to a dramatic depreciation of the feminine principle, the body, and matter in Western cultures. In his view, the physical realm of the body is often relegated to the shadow, where it lives in unconsciousness until its symptoms symbolically alert us to the fact that something is out of balance. But to Jung, the body was as important as spirit in the realm of the psyche. In a letter written in 1935, Jung observed, "Body and spirit are to me mere aspects of the reality of the psyche . . . Body is as metaphysical as spirit."[7] Elaborating on this theme in an essay, "On the Nature of the Psyche," Jung emphasized the intimate relationship between spirit and matter, between body and soul, by noting: "Since psyche and matter are contained in one and the same world, and moreover are in continuous contact with one another and ultimately rest on irrepresentable, transcendental factors, it is not only possible but fairly probable, even, that psyche and matter are two different aspects of one and the same thing."[8]

We are both body and soul. Teilhard de Chardin deeply understood and appreciated the integration of spirit and matter as necessary for wholeness and spiritual enlightenment. "This is what I have learnt from my contact with the Earth," he wrote, "the diaphany of the divine at the heart of a glowing universe, the divine radiating from the depths of matter a-flame."[9] Jack Kornfield also emphasizes the intimate connection between spirit and matter: "I learned that if I am to live a spiritual life, I must be able to embody it in every action: in the way I stand and walk, in the way I breathe, in the care with which I eat. All my activities must be included. To live in this precious animal body on this earth is as great a part of spiritual life as anything else."[10] The poet Rumi in his typical elegant economy of language, writes: "What is the body? That shadow of a shadow of your love, that somehow contains the entire universe."[11]

In fact, evidence from both ancient traditions and modern empirical research suggests that there is a greater relationship between spirit/mind and matter than we might suspect. Our views of the body are entrenched in the same restrictive paradigm as are our concepts of matter in general—the Newtonian-Cartesian model, in which matter (including our body) is solid and immutable, like a "frozen sculpture," as Deepak Chopra has written. "Because we see and touch our bodies, carry their solid weight around with us, and bump into doors if we don't watch out, the reality of the body appears to us as primarily material—such is the bias of our world."[12] But matter is more like a river, flowing with an energy and movement; research in contemporary physics has shown that the view of reality postulated by the Newtonian-Cartesian model does not account for what happens at the subatomic level. The myth of matter as solid and unchangeable has given way to evidence, both theoretical and experimental, from quantum physics, which has demonstrated that atoms, the basic building blocks of the universe, are essentially empty. Stanislav Grof writes: "Within this new perspective of the universe, what we once perceived as the boundaries between objects and the distinctions between matter and empty space are now replaced by something new. Instead of there being discrete objects and empty spaces between them the entire universe is seen as one continuous field of varying density. In modern physics matter becomes interchangeable with energy."[13]

Ancient cultures understood the vital energy which is a part of our physical reality in ways that are only now becoming understood in an empirical way. Ancient Chinese medicine emphasizes the importance of a force called *chi* and its proper balance and flow, through the polar forces of Yin and Yang, in maintaining health and wellness. According to this tradition, the physical body is a series of energy conduits or meridians through which chi flows. Traditional Chinese medicine, often in the form of herbal remedies, chi gong, acupuncture, or acupressure, offers ways in which the energy flow is restored to an individual whose energy is out of balance. The exercise of t'ai chi ch'uan, more than twenty-three centuries old, is a daily method for moving the body in a way that facilitates the proper and healthy flow of chi throughout the body.[14]

Ancient Indian traditions describe a universal life force, an energy called *prana*. Present in every mental and physical event, prana flows directly from the spirit, enters our body through the breath, and is directed and moved by our thoughts. The traditional healing system of Ayurveda (in Sanskrit, "the science of life") emphasizes that behind our creation lies a state of pure awareness, beyond time and space. This energy, the basic force of life itself, in an effort to experience itself, creates the body out of this consciousness. Diet, exercise, breathing, and meditation are ways to encourage prana to flow freely throughout the body.[15]

Siddha and Tantric Yoga philosophies understand the life force as a physically and spiritually experienced energy of *kundalini*. Metaphorically viewed as a sleeping serpent, the kundalini energy lies coiled in an energy center or *chakra* (Sanskrit for "wheel") at the base of the spine. In traditional Yoga literature, a psychic awakening, the rising of kundalini, causes this energy to move from the base of the spine to the top of the head. As kundalini rises it awakens and energizes each of seven chakra centers.[16]

The energetic aspect of physical matter incorporated in the ideas of chi, prana, and kundalini is described in rituals and healing practices of shamans, yogis, and medicine men and women throughout all cultures. Healers and mediums throughout history have described *auras* and *halos* of light as manifestations of the energetic fields of the body: Western occult traditions refer to this phenomenon as the *etheric body* or the *fine matter body;* Rosicrucians refer to the *vital body;* the ancient Egyptians called it *ka soul,* which is the equivalent of the European idea of the *Doppelgänger,* or *double.* The father of modern medicine, Hippocrates, described similar body energies as *enormon* and the *physis.* Yaqui sorcerer Don Juan instructs Carlos Castaneda in pre-Columbian Indian wisdom and urges him to see the *strings of light* that emanate from all forms of matter. American clairvoyant and seer Edgar Cayce described the human body as being made up of *electronic vibrations.* Referring to the *dreambody* or the *subtle body,* Jungian analyst Arnold Mindell observes the difficulty which the Western mind may have in accepting these ancient views of the human body: "Conceiving of the real body as a temple for the spirit seems relatively easy. However, the reader may find it difficult to accept the concept of the dreambody as a subtle essence, aura, or radiation permeating and extending beyond the real body."[17] Nevertheless, a review of ancient healing and religious and philosophical systems lists ninety-seven separate cultures that refer to this phenomenon with ninety-seven different names.[18]

A deeper understanding of and appreciation for the light in matter allows us to come to a greater appreciation for our physical body. This new paradigm offers explanations for both physical and spiritual healing, and increases our knowledge about the relationship between our mind/thoughts and the health or illness of our body. In our quest for wholeness, individuation, and consciousness at midlife, this is a critical part of the process, for wholeness necessarily implies an integration of mind, body, and spirit. Transformation at midlife requires a "reentering" of the body with a newfound sense of its wonders and its relationship to the consciousness of the Self.

Scientific research has clearly demonstrated the relationship between psychological factors, especially symptoms such as anxiety, fear, pain, and depression, and physical illness. For example, increased levels of corticosteroid production and other endocrinological and physiological changes during periods of high stress have been linked to numerous physical manifestations and diseases, such as headaches, ulcers, muscle tension, hypertension, impotence, and Raynaud's syndrome. In fact, most medical texts suggest that anywhere from sixty to ninety percent of all diseases are related to psychological factors. A belief in the intimate relationship between mind and body would argue that all physical illness, one hundred percent, is to some degree related to the mind. The observation that physical symptoms and processes—even those controlled by the autonomic nervous system, such as blood pressure, heart rate, respiration rate, and galvanic skin response—which had previously been thought to be "automatic" and beyond our control, could be controlled through biofeedback gives further, and measurable, evidence for the ancient idea that spirit and matter are deeply connected.[19]

Recent research on the nature of neurotransmitters, peptide molecules such as interleukins, interferon, endorphins, and receptor sites has revealed that every cell in the body is capable of responding to chemical messages which were thought to exist only in the brain. In other words, there are receptors, previously thought to be "brain" receptors, on white blood cells and the cells that line the intestines—in fact, in every cell in the body. For example, research conducted by Dr. Candace Pert, a co-discoverer of endorphins with Nobelist Solomon Snyder, found that all the cells of the immune system contain receptors for various neuropeptide chemicals which control mood in the brain. These cells are also capable of producing the chemicals. This research is so compelling that Pert notes that it becomes harder and harder to think in traditional terms of a mind and a body. She perceives instead a single, integrated entity, a "bodymind."[20] These findings and others provide an opportunity for an empirically based paradigm shift. For those who revere logic and reason, these observations provide exciting evidence that breaks through our commonly held view of the universe—a "crack in the cosmic egg," as Joseph Chilton Pearce has called them.[21]

In fact, many more recent studies have confirmed and expanded on the idea that each cell in the body contains a kind of "intelligence" or consciousness. Deepak Chopra writes: "The know-how carried by neurotransmitters and neuro-peptides represented something else altogether: the winged, fleeting sentient intelligence of the mind. The wonder is that these 'intelligent' chemicals are not only made by the brain, whose function is to think, but by the immune system, whose primary role is to protect us from disease. From the standpoint of a brain chemist, this sudden expansion of messenger molecules adds a new order of complexity to his work. But for us, the discovery of a 'floating' intelligence confirms the model of the body as a river. We needed a basis for claiming that intelligence flows all through us, and now we have it."[22]

This "bodymind" intelligence flowing through the body, in each cell in fact, is part of what must be reclaimed at midlife and brought to consciousness. It can be found in listening carefully to the language of our body and in hearing and trusting our instincts. Heightened consciousness occurs when we recognize the history and memory that is embodied in our physical self—a "character armor," as Wilhelm Reich has called it, which exists as a rigid, constricted defense system that blocks the natural flow of energy through the body. A simple thought or memory of a traumatic event, for example, has the capacity to increase our blood pressure, raise our heart and respiration rates, send hundreds of chemical signals to our endocrinological and immune systems, and evoke the same kind of fear and trembling experienced during the original trauma. Even in the absence of extremely traumatic experiences, the existential abandonment, losses, and exclusion of the feminine that everyone has experienced remain, mostly unconsciously, in the memory of cellular intelligence. By midlife the dam can no longer hold for most people. After half a lifetime of not trusting our instincts and our own bodymind wisdom, it is understandable that the body may be terrified of trusting them now. And yet, as Mark Gerzon has written, "Our bodies can be our wisest teachers, our most enlightened gurus. Perhaps it is a headache or a backache, slumping shoulders or chest pain, failing eyes or constipated bowels. Almost always, hidden in our wound, is something that will enrich and deepen our lives."[23]

Regarding himself as a "Jungian surgeon," physician Bernie Siegel understands the deeply intimate relationship between the Self and its expression in the physical symptoms of the body. "What is the Self trying to get you to learn about yourself?" he asks his patients. By getting in touch with "what is happening at deep levels of consciousness, these questions can help direct you toward healing." Siegel proposes asking ourselves the following questions about our bodies' symptoms: "Do you want to live to be a hundred?" "What happened in the year or two before your illness?" "Why do you need your illness, and what benefits do you derive from it?" "What does the illness mean to you?" And he suggests, "Describe *your* disease and what *you* are experiencing."[24] Jung observed that physical symptoms, much like dreams, mirror and express the underlying Self. He wrote: "The physical disorder appears as a direct mimetic expression of the psychic situation."[25] The Self continues to press for higher consciousness at midlife and is giving us important messages in the symbolic form of physical symptoms. If we are not listening, the body will have no choice but to turn up the volume.

Rediscovering our body at midlife often requires a new level of love for this tired animal, a recommitment to health, healing, and wholeness—all words derived from the same root word as "holy." After a lifetime of abusing her body with food and self-hatred, Marion Woodman found herself passed out on the floor of her bathroom in the Ashoka Hotel in India during her midlife quest. In evocative and moving language, she describes an out-of-body experience that profoundly changed her life:

> I remember falling on the tile floor, weak from dysentery. How long I was there, I do not know. I came to consciousness on the ceiling, my spirit looking down at my body caked in dry vomit and excrement. I saw it lying there helpless, still, and then I saw it take in a breath. "Poor dummy," I thought. "Don't you know you're dead?" And mentally gave it a kick. Suddenly I remembered my little cairn terrier. "I wouldn't treat Duff that way," I thought. "I wouldn't treat a dog the way I'm treating my own body. I wonder what will become of it if I leave it here? Will they burn it? Will they send it home?" Paralyzed by the immensity of my decision—either to leave my body there or to go back into it—I saw it take in another breath. I was overcome with compassion for this dear creature lying on the floor faithfully waiting for me to return, faithfully taking in one breath after another, confident that I would not forsake it, more faithful to me than I to it.
>
> All my life I had hated my body. It was not beautiful enough. It was not thin enough. I had driven it, starved it, stuffed it, cursed it, and even now kicked it, and there it still was, trying to breathe, convinced that I would come back and take it with me, too dumb to die. And I knew the choice was mine. Most of my life I had lived outside my body, my energy disconnected from my feelings, except when I danced. Now it was my choice—either to move into my body and live my life as a human being, or to move out into what I imagined would be freedom. I saw it take another breath and there was something so infinitely innocent and trusting, so exquisitely familiar, in that movement that I chose to come down from the ceiling and move in. Together we dragged ourselves to the little bed. I did my best to take care of it. It was as if I could hear it whispering, "Rest, perturbed spirit, rest." For days, perhaps nine days, I stayed in the womb of the Ashoka.[26]

At midlife we can consciously recognize that good health and freedom from illness will determine the quality and length of our lives. We can understand that we are, in many ways, responsible for and in control of our physical health. Indeed, today we know a great deal about how to maintain physical, spiritual, and psychological health. The mounting evidence clearly confirms the intimate connection between our thoughts, consciousness, intentions, and feelings and the viability and health of every individual cell in our body. Even in circumstances of serious, potentially fatal illness, our beliefs and attitudes about our body have tremendous power to heal us. Carl Simonton and Stephanie Matthews-Simonton, early researchers in the mind-body connection, present compelling evidence for the power of personal beliefs and visualization of both disease and healing with patients suffering from life-threatening cancers, in their book *Getting Well Again.* They conclude: "We all participate in our own health through our beliefs, our feelings and our attitudes towards life, as well as in more direct ways, such as through exercise and diet. In addition, our response to medical treatment is influenced by our beliefs about the effectiveness of the treatment and by the confidence we have in the medical team."[27] Simonton's conclusions reflect those of Native American shaman Rolling Thunder, who describes the importance of thoughts and beliefs to the process of healing: "The place to start is learning how to control your thinking. If you find a harmful thought going through your head, learn how to put it out. Thoughts can be very powerful."[28] Recognizing the power of our perceptions and our thoughts in determining our own reality and health, Don Juan tells Carlos Castaneda: "The trick is in what one emphasizes. We either make ourselves miserable, or we make ourselves strong. The amount of work is the same."[29]

Just as our thoughts and beliefs affect our physical health and well-being, the inevitabilities of aging are being shown to have more to do with how we think about our expectations and convictions regarding our body and age than with any real ingrained or predetermined process. If we adhere to a belief system that assumes that aging necessarily includes a loss of health and sensory and cognitive abilities, then that is likely to be what we will experience. We may choose instead to believe that health and balance are the natural state of the body throughout the life cycle, and that while aging may be inevitable, illness and disease, which are so often a part of this process, are not. Our cultural biases and beliefs about aging are based too heavily on gerontological studies with people who are institutionalized for physical or mental illness. When we begin to study older people who are aging in their own communities, a different picture emerges. Major longitudinal studies conducted by highly regarded scientists and scholars at Duke

University and the National Institute on Aging have failed to show any inevitable or predictable physical and mental deterioration as a consequence of aging.[30] Other research has shown that our common expectations about aging and life expectancy are not backed up by facts. The data suggest that with the incorporation of good health practices, the current average life expectancy of seventy-five years may rise to ninety and one hundred years in the near future.[31] Other research suggests that ninety-nine percent of the energy and intelligence that make up our physical body is untouched by the process of aging.[32]

Many people will experience midlife and beyond with dynamic and vibrant health. Our pursuit of what Betty Friedan has called "vital age"[33] will depend, in large measure, on our attitudes, thoughts, habits, and behaviors. Consider Norman Vaughn, for example. In his much younger days, Norman was a member of the Admiral Byrd expedition which first explored the South Pole. Norman's contributions to that pioneering adventure earned him the honor of having a newly discovered mountain in the southernmost part of Antarctica named after him. Throughout his life, Norman dreamed of returning to Antarctica and climbing the mountain that bears his name—frequently beset by mighty blizzards and freezing ice storms, Mount Vaughn is a tremendous challenge even to seasoned mountain climbers. Beyond dreaming, Norman planned for this adventure. He fervently believed that he would, at some point, see the world from the top of his mountain. In spite of a long series of failed attempts due to bad weather, a plane crash that injured one of his crew members and killed some of his sled dogs, and lack of financial support for the endeavor, Norman scaled Mount Vaughn accompanied by his wife and a team of much younger climbers shortly after his eighty-eighth birthday.[34]

Understanding that chronological age and biological age are not necessarily correlated, numerous studies have shown that many people in midlife and older have been able to push the biological clock backward by decades by practicing healthy behaviors, such as eating a balanced diet that is low in fat, cholesterol, and refined sugars and high in complex carbohydrates, grains, fruits, and vegetables; engaging in regular aerobic exercise; adhering to safe sex practices; engaging in positive thinking; practicing relaxation techniques; meditating; and avoiding toxic substances such as highly processed foods, tobacco, drugs, and alcohol to excess. Terri Apter, in looking at her data from a small survey of women in midlife, observes, "Midlife—the time between 40 and 55 years of age—is now younger than anyone imagined it would be. With better health and longer life expectation, midlife becomes a turning point toward new futures."[35]

Urging those of us in midlife to strive for the freedom and dynamism of an athlete, Robert Arnot, physician and midlife athlete himself, describes some of the changes that we experience when our sedentary lifestyle gets in the way of a healthy life. Though his book is directed toward male readers, it has a great number of helpful ideas for women as well. He notes, "The twenties are your last decade of maintenance-free living. You can drink, party, stay out all night, eat trash foods, yet still pick up a sport at a moment's notice and show dazzling athletic prowess with little conditioning. But beginning in your thirties, body bits and pieces begin to fall apart. Your recovery slows after a hard Saturday and Sunday as a weekend warrior. You can't sprint as fast. Beginning at fory, the sedentary male will lose six pounds of muscle, nearly seven percent of heart function, and eight percent of lung function every ten years. Many men accept those events as an inevitable genetically programmed disintegration. Misuse and abuse are widely misinterpreted as aging. The same misfortune would befall a poorly maintained car. After 30,000 maintenance-free miles, many cars will begin to deteriorate if they are not properly cared for. Yet that same car may go to 150,000 miles if meticulously maintained."[36] Apter, Arnot, and others remind us that it is never too late to seek a higher level of health, and that although we may be in the middle part of our lives, we are in the youth of our old age. The ways in which we treat our physical body and health at this point in our lives will have a major influence on how long and how well we will live in the future.

The literature on midlife and aging is now filled with miraculous stories of people who are defying the images of aging that we have grown accustomed to. In these following excerpts from life, perhaps in our own life as well, we come to understand that midlife can be a time of great physical vibrancy, a time in which our bodies are strong and powerful and our minds clear and open.

At forty-seven, Tom maintains the same weight he did during his college running days. Always committed to staying healthy, he needed no real changes in his behavior as he entered midlife. "It's not that I'm some kind of health nut," he protests, "it's just that I feel better when I'm eating right and exercising. I have more energy." He continues to participate in twenty-six-mile marathons, and in fact, his time has actually improved over the past few years as he has had more time to devote to his training. He has no plans to stop running and says that he would like to run in Boston, "the greatest marathon of them all," when he is a hundred years old.

Reba had always believed that she would get old just like her mother and grandmother. Growing up in a small rural community in North Carolina, she had seen both of those women become very large and tired by the time they were in their thirties. Plagued with high blood pressure and heart problems, her mother and grandmother were both more than a hundred pounds overweight and spent most days watching television, too exhausted to do anything else. On Reba's forty-seventh birthday a friend, knowing how much she loved Tina Turner, gave her a copy of the autobiography *I, Tina*. Reba started reading the book that night. "In the first chapter, I realized that we had the same birthday, November 26, 1939. I looked at her picture on the cover and I thought, "No way, we can't be the same age. She looks twenty years younger and full of life." On that very day, Reba made a decision that changed her life forever. She decided that she would not follow in the footsteps of her mother and grandmother. She went to the library and read everything she could about nutrition and exercise. She began to understand why everyone in her family was overweight: all their dishes, even vegetables, were cooked in layers of fatback, and no one ever did anything physical, not even taking a walk around the block. She understood how her job as a receptionist kept her stuck in a chair all day and how she reflexively cooked everything she ate in the way she had been taught. She began to exercise regularly and totally changed her patterns of eating. Today, at fifty-six, Reba is in better physical health than she has ever been in her life. She has lost more than ninety pounds and regularly speed-walks more than ten miles a day. "I don't know what would have happened to me," she says, "if I didn't have the same birthday as Tina. But I don't think that I would feel as good or be having as much fun."

Eleanor has defied her medical prognosis and outlived her doctor's expectations by more than twenty years. Diagnosed with ovarian cancer in her early thirties, she had a complete hysterectomy followed by chemotherapy and radiation. Nevertheless, medical tests showed continued evidence of microscopic cancer cells throughout her lymph system. Her doctor informed her that she probably had less than a year to live. "I decided then and there," she says, "that I wasn't going to let that happen. I had Patty [her thirteen-year-old daughter] to think of, and I was going to be there for her until she finished high school." Patty did finish high school, and Eleanor then decided that she couldn't die until her daughter was safely and happily established in college. At college, in her second year, Patty met Jeff and they became engaged. "I realized that there was always going to be something else that I wanted to stick around for," Eleanor said with a great laugh. "First, it was that I wanted to go to Patty's wedding. Then I wanted to be around for the birth of her first child. Then I realized that Ray [Eleanor's husband] and I had never seen Europe like we had always wanted to. Every time I turn around there's something else." Today, at fifty-one, Eleanor lives a full and happy life, traveling with her husband and babysitting for her twin grandsons as her daughter continues her education in graduate school. She continues to be monitored by CAT scans and examinations of her lymphatic fluid, but there has been no further evidence of the cancer.

Midlife is a time for changing the ways we think about and honor our physical body, for understanding its importance to the quality of the rest of our lives and its relationship to spirit. There is much that we can do to affect our own health and longevity, but that is only half the story. The other reality of our lives is that much is out of our control. Although stories like those of Reba and Eleanor may suggest that everyone, through sheer acts of will and determination, can control the outcome of illness or poor health, this is not true. Many others suffering from serious illness may exhibit the same strength of spirit and hope and yet not experience a remarkable recovery or spontaneous healing. We do not yet understand all the factors at play in health and illness, and while it may be true that at some cosmic level we have determined our destiny, this does not always appear that way within our human experience. Nor does it relieve us of the suffering that comes from the loss of our physical ability and health. Midlife is a time for the recognition of this humbling fact. We cannot, and do not, consciously control every aspect of our fate. We live, as we have throughout our lives, on the fulcrum of the seesaw, holding a tension of opposites, a polarity between forces both seen and unseen. On the one hand, we have tremendous control over our physical health and longevity. On the other hand, we are participants in a grand plan that includes illness, aging, death, and moving toward some other form of consciousness. It is critical to appreciate and understand the importance of avoiding either of these two extremes—that we control everything or that we control nothing—we must instead seek a "middle path," as the Buddhists have called it, on which we can honor our own bodymind power as well as accept that there are parts of the midlife passage which reflect our destiny, our fate. Jung understood this and wrote about it after his own heart attack: "It was only after the illness that I understood how important it is to affirm one's own destiny. In this way we forge an ego that does not break down when incomprehensible things happen; an ego that endures, that endures the truth, and that is capable of coping with the world and with fate. Then to experience defeat is also to experience victory. Nothing is disturbed—neither inwardly nor outwardly, for one's own continuity has withstood the current of life and of time. But that can come to pass only when one does not meddle inquisitively with the workings of fate."[37]

Consider, for example, Roger's circumstances at midlife. Like Tom (the runner), he had always been very health-conscious and had always taken good care of his body. As he entered his early forties he began to experience some visual problems and went to see first an optometrist, thinking he needed glasses, and then an ophthalmologist. Finding no real visual problems that would account for the kinds of symptoms he was experiencing, the ophthalmologist referred him back to his family doctor, who after a series of tests sent him to a neurologist, where he was diagnosed as being in the early stages of multiple sclerosis. Today, at forty-seven, Roger must use a wheelchair to get around, and with each passing day he seems to lose more of his ability to control the muscles of his body. Nevertheless, after a prolonged period of grieving for what was happening to him, he allowed his courage and spirit to shine through and began the long process of learning to get the most he can out of his deteriorating body.

Vicky was a healthy, vigorous thirty-eight-year-old when she contracted some kind of viral infection. The doctors were never able to identify the specific virus involved, but they attributed the infection to a mosquito bite that she got while at a company picnic. The virus entered and destroyed a number of her cranial nerves and today, at forty-four, she is totally blind and experiences memory lapses of such significance that she was forced to retire from her government job and live on a modest disability stipend. Her entire life was changed by a mosquito bite. Why her? Why not any of the two hundred other people who were in the same picnic area with the same mosquito?

At forty-one, John Lescroart, a writer, took a much needed break from writing and the disappointing sales of four books. Barely able to make ends meet in spite of working two full-time jobs and squeezing his writing into the hours between six and eight-thirty A.M., discouraged by his lack of success as a self-supporting writer, and burdened by family and economic responsibilities, he went bodysurfing at Seal Beach to get his mind off things.

While there he contracted spinal meningitis from contaminated seawater and almost died. "The doctor told my wife I had two hours to live," Lescroart recalls, "which meant she would be left alone with two babies, one twenty months old and the other five months old." But John defied the doctor's prognosis and after eleven days in intensive care he recovered. The experience totally altered his views of life and his priorities. "There's something about almost dying that really clarifies things," he says. "I quit my job to devote myself full-time to writing. We moved to Davis and went into serious debt while I finished another Dismas Hardy book, *Hard Evidence.* I decided if that one didn't make some money I was out of the writing business for good." Today, at forty-seven, John is a successful and prosperous writer who has been favorably compared to John Grisham and Scott Turow.[38]

At midlife, by looking at our own lives as well as at the lives of other people, it is easier to understand that we do not dictate our fate. In fact, at this time of life we are more capable than ever of understanding the danger inherent in assuming that we control every aspect of our destiny. Such a belief creates a very false sense of power and security and can cause us to experience great guilt when things don't go exactly as we expect that they should. At midlife, we will be buffeted by many of the realities and losses of human existence; surely we do not need to see ourselves as somehow failing simply because we are living a human life. Larry Dossey reminds us of Jesus' words when he encounters a man who is blind from birth. "Rabbi, who sinned, this man, or his parents, that he was born blind?" Jesus' answer shows both illumination and compassion. "Neither this man nor his parents sinned; he was born blind so that God's works might be revealed in him."[39]

Dossey further reminds us that some of the most enlightened beings in the world still endured physical pain and suffering. All experienced the very human process of aging, illness, and death: Saint Bernadette died at age thirty-five of disseminated tuberculosis (although it is usually described as bone cancer); Suzuki Roshi, who brought Zen from Japan to the United States, died of cancer of the liver; Sri Ramana Maharishi, the most revered saint in India, died of cancer of the stomach; the Buddha himself, Siddhartha, died of food poisoning. On first discovering this account, Dossey thought, "Somehow, I'd expected a more dignified cause of death than spoiled food. . . . Sickly saints and healthy sinners show us that there is no invariable, linear, one-to-one relationship between one's level of spiritual attainment and the degree of one's physical health. It is obvious that one can attain immense spiritual heights and still get *very* sick. . . . In nature the occurrence of disease is considered a part of the natural order, not a sign of ethical, moral or spiritual weakness."[40]

Bernie Siegel, who has done more to popularize the idea of bodymind medicine and healing than almost anyone else, begins his book *Love, Medicine & Miracles* as follows: ". . . I did not write *Love, Medicine & Miracles* to make anyone feel guilty. I wanted to make people aware they were not statistics or probabilities but possibilities, that they have an opportunity or challenge, not another chance to fail."[41] I personally like to remind myself, as I move sometimes gracefully and sometimes stumbling through the midlife transition, that even the enlightened Dalai Lama wears glasses.

At midlife, we will experience physical changes that are part of our human heritage. For example, the midlife transition for women has always been closely associated with, and to some indistinguishable from, menopause. While I believe the midlife transition to be far more than just hormonal and physiological, it is clear that these changes do play a significant role in midlife. And we are really only beginning to understand them, for a number of reasons. First of all, issues specifically related to women's health have always been given short shrift in both clinical and research funding. Secondly, with an average life expectancy in the United States of forty-seven years as late as 1900, there is no large base of data and experience upon which to draw in order to understand the full range of psychological, emotional, intellectual, and physical changes associated with menopause. Thirdly, like many aspects of sexuality and the physical body, menopause, along with menstruation, has been a taboo subject until very recently. Gail Sheehy, in observing the power of this taboo, has referred to the whole phenomenon of menopause as the "Silent Passage."[42]

At its simplest level, menopause occurs anywhere from the early forties to the late fifties; the ovaries fail and there is a sudden change, a dip, in the level of the female sex hormones, estrogen and progesterone. This causes a cessation of menstruation. While some women will breeze through these changes, others will experience a variety of distressing physical, emotional, cognitive, and psychological reactions. Symptoms such as hot flashes, night sweats, insomnia, thinning hair, back pain, breast soreness, frequent or urgent urination, and loss of libido may be experienced for a decade or more. Although hormones do not create emotions, they have a strong capacity to amplify them, and during perimenopause and menopause many women report mood swings, anxiety, tiredness, and depression. Other symptoms, such as thinning and drying out of the vaginal and genital skin, urinary problems, and gastrointestinal symptoms, may be long-term. Research has shown that estrogen protects women from cardiovascular disease, including heart attacks and strokes, by depressing blood cholesterol levels. Estrogen also protects women's bones from becoming brittle, as in osteoporosis, and when the levels of estrogen fall sharply, as they do in menopause, we no longer have such protection against these health risks. According to Dr. Miriam Stoppard, "approximately three-quarters of all women will have some symptoms related to the suddenness of estrogen withdrawal, all of which can be treated."[43]

Treatment for the symptoms of menopause has focused on hormone replacement therapy (usually referred to as HRT). Yet the decision to use estrogen replacement causes a dilemma for many women, for although there are a great many benefits, they are not without some risk. For example, estrogen replacement therapy has been shown to reduce hot flashes, night sweats, memory deterioration, aging skin, and a number of other menopausal symptoms. But on the other side of the controversy, estrogen replacement has been associated with an increased incidence of cancer of the uterine lining, fluid retention, an increase of benign fibroid tumors of the uterus, and a higher rate of breast cancer, particularly in women with a family history of the disease. Hormone replacement has only been around for a few decades and its long-term and far-reaching effects may not be fully known. And, as the number one prescription drug in America, some doctors are "handing out these hormones like M&Ms."[44] A full investigation of alternatives to HRT will very likely change the options for women in the future. Herbal therapies, change in diet, exercise, yoga, vitamins, relaxation techniques, homeopathy, energetic therapies, and various other healing practices hold tremendous promise for making menopause less symptomatic, and might be used in place of or in combination with HRT in the future. On the other hand, many women swear that HRT has dramatically changed their life by reducing symptoms of menopause, increasing libido and sexual appetite, and speeding them on their way to what Margaret Mead referred to as "post menopausal zest." Clearly the decision to use HRT should be made individually by each woman, in consultation with an understanding and knowledgeable health care provider who is aware of her personal and family health history.

Although some see menopause as *the* critical midlife issue for women, I do not agree. Instead, it is one of many integrated bodymind changes—physiological, psychological, and spiritual—that are a part of the midlife process. Unlike the onset of menstruation (menarche) or pregnancy, menopause is not a clearly defined event or condition, and there are no standards against which to measure one's particular experience of it. "Menopause," Terri Apter writes, *"accompanies* women's midlife, but, in my sample of women—35 of whom had experienced or were experiencing menopause—it did not cause the crises and growth I observed. Menopause played no single, specific role in midlife development. Menopause is simply the cessation of menstruation. It has no universal meaning other than that."[45]

For example, in recent years some women have begun welcoming and celebrating their movement toward the "wisdom of the crone," the leaving of their fertile, childbearing years behind as they travel toward "holding the wise blood inside," as shamans have described this time of life for women. From this perspective, menopause is not viewed as a disease of estrogen deficiency but rather as part of a process of transition and opportunity. Other women, particularly those who have built a great deal of their self-identity in the role of mother to the exclusion of other aspects of the Self, or who overly value youthfulness, may have a more difficult journey. I am not saying, however, that women who see menopause as an opportunity for transformation and empowerment will not experience any of its physical or psychological symptoms. Instead, these symptoms can be seen and understood as part of the process of change that is happening both internally and externally at midlife.

Some writers speak of a "male menopause" that occurs at midlife. It is clear that the word itself is a misnomer. Men's reproductive systems do not stop functioning at a certain age, as do women's ovaries. Similarly, men's fertility does not cease at midlife. Most healthy men continue to have sufficient sperm to father children well into old age. Nevertheless, some men at midlife will experience a change in virility and sexual libido; some will experience impotence (defined here as an inability to achieve or sustain an erection). If menopause for women is the "Silent Passage," as Gail Sheehy has called it, then this change in some men's sexual vitality is surely the "Unspeakable Passage."[46] But in spite of not having clear language to discuss this aspect of men's (both heterosexual and homosexual) midlife passage, it is important that it be understood. Research has shown that about half of American men over the age of forty have experienced midlife impotence to varying extents.[47]

Impotence in men at midlife can sometimes be accounted for by a number of physiological variables such as pelvic injury, cardiac disease, atherosclerosis (fatty deposits in the blood vessels which cause circulatory abnormalities), spinal cord injuries, neurological problems, Peyronie's disease, diabetes, or cancer. Some impotence may be due to the side effects of medication as well as a response to heavy consumption of alcohol. Low levels of testosterone have been implicated in the etiology of both impotence and lack of sexual appetite, although various studies suggest that only five to thirty-five percent of men experience impotence due to hormonal problems.[48] Other researchers, however, report that declines in male hormones, called androgens, and especially in testosterone are the major factor in midlife impotence. Some studies have suggested that there may be an underlying decline in both total testosterone and free testosterone with advancing age,[49] and that there is an established correlation between impotence and age.[50] However, other studies have found that the relationship between impotence and age is far stronger when the samples looked at were men sixty-five and older, well past the age of midlife.[51]

It is clear that more research must be directed toward understanding the complex factors underlying impotence. But sexual appetite and behavior in all people, both men and women, depends on a complicated and exquisitely integrated relationship between physical, social, emotional, and psychological variables. Dr. Herbert Benson of Harvard Medical School, a pioneer in the understanding of bodymind, observes, "In reality, while patients with erectile dysfunction are thought to demonstrate an organic component, psychological aspects of self-confidence, anxiety, and partner communication and conflict are often important contributing factors."[52]

In addition to the potential influence of testosterone and other physical or endocrinological factors, it is clear that psychological and cognitive elements contribute to midlife impotence. Men in our culture are given a double-edged sword. On the one hand, our cultural values have a clear split between spirit and matter: many men and women are detached from the body and from Eros and sexuality in general. Men, though, are conditioned to put great faith in the importance of virility and sexual performance. Male role models and heroes throughout time have been noted for their potency and sexual prowess. Just as sacred images of the Goddess were found scratched into cave walls, so too was the image of the *phallus* with its life-giving energy. But patriarchy and the dichotomy of matter and spirit have wounded men just as they have women. They have reduced sexuality to a physical act devoid of any spiritual meaning or connection to larger reality. James Hollis writes: "Men, as well as women, labor always under the heavy shadow of ideologies, some conscious, some inherited from family and ethnic group, some part of the fabric of a nation's history and its mythic soil. This shadow is an oppressive weight on the soul. Men labor under it, oppressed and blighted in spirit. The experience of this weighty shadow is saturnine. The definitions of what it means to be a man—male roles and expectations, competition and animosity, the shaming and devaluing of many of men's better qualities and capacities—all lead to the crushing weight."[53] It is no wonder that at a time like midlife—when so much appears to be in flux, when so much of youth and vigor must be relinquished in the service of full maturity—sexual expression, which relies on such an exquisite balancing of physical, psychological, and spiritual energies, would reflect the ennui and confusion of this passage. The man himself may not consciously understand the depth of the transformation that is sweeping what he knew of himself away, but his penis does.

Sexuality is a form of empowerment and expression of the Self. Jung understood the relationship between the life energy of the libido and phallic, masculine energy: "a phallic symbol does not denote the sexual organ, but the libido, and however clearly it appears as such, it does not mean *itself* but is always a symbol of the libido."[54] Jungian analyst Eugene Monick notes that Jung's understanding of psychic energy, of libido, "includes such elemental human requirements as creativity, connection with the 'other,' and ecstasy, the spiritual movement from ego to Self."[55] Allowing for freely flowing psychic energy and uncovering the authentic Self are central to the tasks of midlife. It is no surprise that the bodymind would symbolically express this confusion in impotence.

By midlife, the splitting of spirit and matter has taken its toll on all human beings, regardless of gender, throughout our lives. But midway on our journey through life we are being given opportunities to reintegrate these powerful bodymind energies. The liberation of the contents of our repressed shadow, our inner integration of masculine and feminine, and our movement toward the Self always releases libido. And our midlife journey will, necessarily, take us on a pilgrimage to reclaim our own lost reverence for the sacredness and mystery of our body, its relationship to spirit, and its most joyful sexual expression. We can sense the flow of energy and life in the manner that Rumi describes: "There's no blocking the speechflow-river-running-all-carrying momentum that true intimacy is."[56]

At midlife, we need a release from the old prescriptions and beliefs about our bodies, about sexuality, about spirit and matter. Men have been taught to tightly control themselves and their world. Women are given more latitude for emotional expression in general, but not in the realm of Eros. The full extent of the repression of female sexuality is described by writer David Steinberg: "Women who allow themselves the range of sexual expression taken for granted by men are likely to be seen, metaphorically, as witches, whores and sex-demons, and may well (again, metaphorically) be burned at the stake."[57] We need a new paradigm, one in which all of us, men and women alike, feel free to express the sacred erotic energy that is a part of our humanity. Aldo Carotenuto, Jungian analyst and professor at the University of Rome, observes: "Because sexuality has long been subject to prohibitory limits, it is in this area that our approach to another person becomes particularly dramatic. We may believe ourselves to be unconstrained, but this shows itself to be a delusion whenever we are seriously presented with an opportunity to freely express our sensuality. Therefore we could say that the art of loving, of eroticism, coincides with transgression. By way of the erotic, human beings are enabled to break the internal prohibitions—to veto the veto."[58] By breaking these internal prohibitions and welcoming the energy of the Self, Eros, sexuality, and the sensual will always have a place in our lives, regardless of our age or position in the life cycle. We begin the journey by honoring the sacredness of light in matter, of loving and living in our body. We must come to understand, at the very core of our being, what William Blake meant when he said: "That call'd Body is a portion of soul discern'd by the five senses."[59]

Paule Marshall's character, Avey Johnson, who was described in some detail in Chapter Five, comes eventually to the end of her journey, having left behind who she was and discovered who she is becoming. Her full awareness of the transformation that has been taking place is through her body. Avey Johnson, like many of us by midlife, has lost her Self in the course of her unconscious life. Her great-aunt Cuney had named her Avatara after Cuney's grandmother, who had been brought to America on a slave ship and had taught her about how the Ibos just picked up their chains and walked back to Africa, right across the water. But by midlife, Avey had long ago left Avatara behind ("Great-aunt Cuney had saddled her with the name of someone people had sworn was crazy . . ."). From a bureaucrat at the Department of Motor Vehicles to a widow on a cruise ship vacation, Avey Johnson finds herself at the conclusion of Marshall's exquisite novel on the edge of pure awakening. She has been brought by an old man she has met,

Lebert Joseph, to the little island of Carriacou in the Caribbean, where she attends a ceremony honoring the ancestors. Without her conscious participation, her sacred body enters into the realm of both mystery and connection and she finds her true name, her authentic Self:

> And for the first time since she was a girl, she felt the threads, that myriad of shiny, silken, brightly colored threads (like the kind used in embroidery) which were thin to the point of invisibility yet as strong as the ropes at Coney Island. Looking on outside the church in Tatem, standing waiting for the *Robert Fulton* on the crowded pier at 125th Street, she used to feel them streaming out of everyone there to enter her, making her part of what seemed a far-reaching, wide-ranging confraternity.
>
> Now suddenly, as if she were that girl again, with her entire life yet to live, she felt the threads streaming out from the old people around her in Lebert Joseph's yard. From their seared eyes. From their navels and their cast-iron hearts. And their brightness as they entered her spoke of possibilities and becoming even in the face of the bare bones and the burnt-out ends.
>
> She began to dance then. Just as her feet of their own accord had discovered the old steps, her hips under the linen shirtdress slowly began to weave from side to side on their own, stiffly at first and then in a smooth wide arc as her body responded more deeply to the music. And the movement in her hips flowed upward, so that her entire torso was soon swaying. Arms bent, she began working her shoulders in the way the Shouters long ago used to do, thrusting them forward and then back in a strong casting-off motion. Her weaving head was arched high. All of her moving suddenly with a vigor and passion she hadn't felt in years, and with something of the stylishness and sass she had once been known for. . . . Avey Johnson could not have said how long she kept her arms raised or how many turns she made in the company of these strangers who had become one and the same with people in Tatem. Until suddenly Lebert Joseph did something which caused her arms to drop and her mind to swing back to the yard and the present moment. He had remained at her side all along, watching her dance with the smile that was at once triumphant and fatherly, and dancing himself, the slow measured tramp. But as her arms went up and her body seemed about

to soar off into the night, his smile faded, and was replaced by the gaze that called to mind a jeweler's loupe or a laser beam in its ability to penetrate to her depth. His eyes probing deep, he went to stand facing her in front. His oversized hands went out, bringing to a halt for a moment the slow moving tide around them. And then he bowed, a profound, solemn bow that was like a genuflection. . . .

To her utter bewilderment others in the crowd of aged dancers, taking their cue from him also, began doing the same. One after another of the men and women trudging past, who were her senior by years, would pause as they reached her and, turning briefly in her direction, tender her the deep almost reverential bow. Then singing, they would continue on their way.

One elderly woman not only bowed but stepped close and took her hand. Cataracts dimmed her gaze. The face she raised to Avey Johnson was a ravaged landscape of dark hollows and caves where her wrinkled flesh had collapsed in on the bone. Her chin displayed the beginning of a beard: a few wispy white hairs that curled in on themselves. An old woman who was at once an old man. . . .

"Bercita Edwards of Smooth Water Bay, Carriacou," she said, and holding on to Avey Johnson's hand she peered close, searching for whatever it was she possessed that required her to defer despite her greater age. "And who you is?" she asked.

And as a mystified Avey Johnson gave her name, she suddenly remembered her great-aunt Cuney's admonition long ago. The old woman used to insist, on pain of a switching, that whenever anyone in Tatem, even another child, asked her her name she was not to say simply "Avey," or even "Avey Williams," but always, "Avey, short for Avatara."[60]

Some Thoughts and Suggestions

1. Take some time to reflect on the ways you treat your body. Make a list and write it down. Use two headings: "Ways I honor my body" and "Ways I dishonor my body." Be particularly aware of issues such as diet, exercise, stress reducers, toxic habits, and so on. On your list of "dishonoring," honestly think about how these habits, behaviors, and attitudes give you plea-

sure. Then consider both their short-term and long-term effects. Take each item separately and write down the ways you could change these in healthier directions. Then one by one set goals for these changes. Begin to incorporate the changes into your life. Program in frequent rewards for accomplishing both short-term and long-term goals. If you need to, get help to make these changes. For example, you might try psychotherapy, Alcoholics Anonymous, Narcotics Anonymous, Overeaters Anonymous, or other twelve-step programs; nicotine patches; joining Jazzercise, an aerobics class, or a health club; or taking t'ai chi classes. Consult with your doctor before beginning an exercise program, particularly if you are out of shape and haven't been physically active. Find healthy alternatives to giving your body what it wants.

2. Enter into an Active Imagination—a conversation with your body. What is your body trying to tell you? Do you have chronic or consistent physical symptoms or health problems? What might those symptoms be trying to express? What is the symbolic meaning of the symptoms?

3. Look carefully for ways in which the body is portrayed in dreams. Both the symbolic symptoms of the body and images of the body in dreams are important paths to healing and to learning about the Self.

4. Explore the notion of the energetic body. There are many types of body work and therapies that work directly with this phenomenon. From learning t'ai chi to various forms of meditation to working with an energetic healer, there are many opportunities for self-knowledge and healing. At the very least, read some of the excellent books on the subject listed in the notes to this chapter.

5. Discover what your body needs from you and give it in healthy, life-affirming ways. Would a weekly massage be a way for you to ward off the negative effects of stress and illness? If you have a sweet tooth, can you be satisfied with a juicy orange or low-fat yogurt instead of high-fat ice cream? Can sweetness be reinterpreted so that your body will get what it needs by listening to some beautiful music?

6. Look at the ways in which you express your sexuality. Are you free and comfortable, or unexpressive in this aspect of your life? What were you

taught about sexuality? What myth are you living that doesn't reflect who you really are inside? How do you want the second half of your life to be different?

7. Explore some of the wonderful books and resources on bodymind. You will be amazed.

CHAPTER 11

Understanding and Helping

For at bottom, and just in the deepest and most important things, we are unutterably alone, and for one person to be able to advise or even help another, a lot must happen, a lot must go well, a whole constellation of things must come right in order once to succeed.
RAINER MARIA RILKE, *LETTERS TO A YOUNG POET*, 1934

THIS CHAPTER is specifically for people whose loved one is in the midst of the midlife transition. It is impossible to describe any hard and fast rules about what you should do to be supportive and helpful, since everyone will experience a unique journey at midlife; yet just as a gardener cannot make a plant sprout or mature, good gardeners can help a plant to flourish by weeding, watering, tending, and caring for the fragile new growth. Here are some gardening tips:

Understand that the midlife passage needs room and space to proceed.

In Chapter Five, I described the process of growth and change at midlife as like being in a chrysalis, the cocoonlike structure in which a caterpillar dissolves and emerges as a butterfly. Like this metamorphosis, the midlife transition is a process of gestation and slow changes. For what we can know and see about a person during this period is not necessarily what we will get when the transformation is complete. In other words, the confusion and distress characteristic of the beginning and middle of the journey is part of an evolution toward greater self-understanding. At midlife, we recognize that we have left behind important parts of our Self and have the strong psychological and spiritual motivation to reclaim them. Yet although this is the underlying energy behind the process, many people do not immediately recognize what is happening, or understand that the confusion and the pain they are feeling are part of normal adult development. As we have already seen, at midlife people may feel dissatisfied with their marriage or relationship, with their job, or with life in general, or they may experience anxiety, depression, or sadness which seems to have no external cause. Some may say that they feel "empty," and may find themselves asking questions like "Who am I?" and "What is my life really about?" To you they may appear distressed, bewildered, and "not like their old self." But these symptoms and changes are all part of a process that is moving toward releasing parts of the personality that have concealed the real person inside.

This is not to say that some Frankensteinian process is occurring and your loved one will emerge from the chrysalis unrecognizable to you. In fact, some of the most important changes may not be readily observable to anyone but the person experiencing them. Although the process and changes of midlife are described as a relinquishing of the "false self," we have to remember that underneath that false self lies an ego that organizes and integrates new information and self-understanding into consciousness. Psychologist Charles Tart writes, "It is not as if you kill false personality but rather that (1) you get enough sense of who your deeper, inner self is and (2) you develop enough mindfulness and focus to put the energy back into your essential self."[1]

If you have raised or been around children, then you understand that they go through stages of development. For example, a two-year-old will cry and scream if her parents want to leave her with a babysitter, but by the time she is a few years older, she has outgrown that developmental stage and may be quite happy to see her favorite babysitter come to take care of her for the evening. Most adolescents go through a period of time in which they are rebellious and difficult to deal with, when it seems that no matter what parents suggest, they want to do things in just the opposite way. But by the time an adolescent grows into a young adult, the rebelliousness passes. The same adolescent that couldn't stand his parents and their rules may grow up, in just a few short years, to be good friends with them. Like these stages of development, the midlife journey is a time of a great many changes in attitude and viewpoint. Just as we cannot see the growth that is taking place in the caterpillar enclosed in the chrysalis, we cannot always see the growth that is occurring in an individual at midlife, for the journey is a deeply interior one that is often unconscious and may be difficult to describe. Yet these conflicts and changes are likely to express themselves in outer behavior.

Helping someone through the midlife transition requires patience and a willingness to trust in the person and the process itself. As much as we may love someone, as honestly as we would like to see their suffering end, we cannot go through the process for them. Deeply personal, midlife is a journey that is, essentially, undertaken alone.

Melanie began to experience many symptoms of the midlife crisis after she suffered two significant losses in her life. Her brother Dave who had always been in excellent health, had been diagnosed with cancer and died six months later in spite of chemotherapy and radiation treatments. During Dave's illness their mother suffered a stroke and was unable to communicate or care for herself. Melanie's training as a nurse, her family role of caretaker, and the fact that she lived in the same city as her mother and brother all but dictated that she would be the one to provide most of the support and help to her family members. Her sister, Angie, lived in the same town and helped as she could by placing her three very young children in day care for part of each morning. Their other two brothers lived across the country, and although they were emotionally and financially supportive, they could not meet the day-to-day needs of their brother and mother. Melanie's husband, Matt, was supportive and loving. Often he would prepare special meals and try to get her to take some time for herself. He'd suggest going to a movie or renting a video so that she could take a brief respite from the hard work and sorrow she was experiencing. Given the tragedy of the situation in which she found herself, Melanie couldn't have asked for greater love and support.

Melanie hardly had a chance to grieve after her brother's death. Although they were the closest in age of all the children, had been great friends when they were young, and remained so as adults, all of Melanie's time and energy were being taken up by caring for her mother, whose condition continued to worsen. Ten weeks after Dave's death her mother died. Although she still had the loving support of her husband, remaining brothers, and sister, Melanie suddenly felt alone and despondent. Her grief became a catalyst for a deep descent into the underworld, where she began to distrust all of the beliefs she had held throughout her life. At forty-three, Melanie began to question all of the values by which she had lived. Her deep faith in God was shaken and she felt angry and helpless. "I don't understand life at all," she said as she choked back tears. "I don't know who I am anymore. I don't know what I want for my life."

At first, Melanie's family was extremely supportive of her. But her process of grieving did not conform to theirs, and they were unaware that grieving may take a very long time for some. They further did not understand that her losses had sparked the psychological and spiritual crises of midlife for her. In spite of his great love for her, Matt became increasingly frustrated with Melanie's "depression," as he called it, when she had not returned to "normal" more than a year after her mother's death. He pointed out that before all the losses in her family, Melanie had been the "life of the party," outgoing, and a real "people person." "I'm not depressed, exactly," she would counter. "Something is changing inside of me and I just don't feel like being as social as I used to be." For the first time in her life, Melanie seemed to need and want more time to herself, a fact that Matt, her siblings, and her friends had difficulty understanding or accepting.

Melanie's midlife changes frustrated and confused Matt. He wanted to make things better for her, couldn't stand to see her suffering, and kept insisting that she "get over it." He didn't understand that Melanie needed time to comprehend and adjust emotionally to the internal changes that life had delivered to her. "Talk to me," he would say, begging for some explanation. But Melanie *couldn't explain to him what was really happening inside of her because she didn't really understand it herself.* It was beyond words. Melanie needs the time and space to understand for herself what is going on and changing inside of her.

Be ready to listen, but don't try to solve problems that are not yours to solve.

When a loved one is going through the midlife passage, the role that you play is best described as that of *companion.* The word "companion" means "a person who accompanies or associates with another, one who lives with, assists, or travels with another." The word is from the Late Latin *companio,* "one who eats bread with another." This is a wonderful description of how you can help your loved one at midlife, or at any other time of life for that matter. Your job and role is *not* to solve their problems but rather to accompany and be there as a loving, supportive presence. It is best to communicate feelings such as, "I know that you are going through a challenging, difficult time. I love you. I'm here for you and am happy to listen when and if you want to talk," or, "I don't know what I can do to help you through this, but I want you to know that I'm here and will wait for you to tell me if there is anything I can do." It is not useful and may even be harmful, though well-intentioned, to say, as Matt did to Melanie, "When are you going to get over this?" Specific suggestions about how to resolve the problems or reduce the symptoms will fall on deaf ears and will only add to the distress. Avoid communicating ideas like, "Why don't you just quit your job if you're that unhappy?" "Why don't you just get a divorce if you hate your life?" or "If you would only stop thinking about yourself so much, you'd be a lot happier."

Your role in supporting and helping a loved one at midlife is one of containment. Like a pot that holds a plant or a bucket that holds water, the container is and is not a part of the inner process that is occurring to someone in the midlife passage. Good containers maintain proper *boundaries* for the essence they contain. Imagine a houseplant which is seeded in a pot that is too small. At some point it will wither and die because it doesn't have room to grow. On the other hand, if a houseplant is uncontained and has nothing firm in which the soil can rest, the dirt will be all over the floor and there will be nowhere for the plant to set its roots.

It is considerably easier to determine how large a pot is necessary to grow a houseplant than to know how much space and room are necessary for the growth of human beings. And understanding and accepting the importance of healthy interpersonal boundaries is easier than living them out. Many people, especially women, have been taught to take on a great deal of responsibility for other people's emotions and direction in life. But while there is much to be valued in feeling a loving connection and compassion for others, we must resist the kind of codependency (a much overused word and concept, but one with some relevance here) that allows us to take on responsibility for people and things over which we have no control. Trust your instincts, and communicate clearly and with good healthy boundaries that require your loved one to take full responsibility for his or her decisions. We have to learn to follow the advice of Albert Camus: "Don't stand behind, I might not lead; Please don't lead, I might not follow; Just walk beside me and be my friend."[2]

Look within yourself to understand your reactions.

During the most difficult stage of a midlife crisis, Cindy found herself questioning her whole life. She had married Mark when they were both quite young, and together they raised a large family of six children. All but one were grown and living on their own. Their sixteen-year-old son, Alan, in the midst of high school, was popular and active in several sports. He was only at home to grab a quick bite and to sleep. By six-thirty in the morning he was off to school and didn't return until well after dark. Alan had a great relationship with his parents but was very involved with his own life, as is usual for a healthy teenager. At midlife, Cindy began to feel a sense of emptiness and lack of meaning. She had done a fine job as a mother; her kids were all healthy, good people. "Now what?" Cindy asked herself. Having defined herself for all of her adulthood in the role of mother, she was now at loose ends and didn't know what to do with the rest of her life.

At forty-five Cindy decided to enter nursing school, and Mark was completely supportive. He understood that now with the children grown and Alan well on his way to adulthood, Cindy wanted to explore other avenues, other aspects of her life. Initially, Mark had great respect for Cindy's courageous decision. He knew that she was concerned that she was too old to start school again and wouldn't remember how to study. In fact, she did extremely well during her first semester and made the dean's list. Mark was, understandably, very proud of her and threw a dinner party to celebrate her success.

During the second semester, Mark's attitude began to change. He felt lonely and left out of Cindy's life. She was very busy with her studies and never seemed to have time to spend with him anymore. Cindy was working hard to keep a balance between her schoolwork and her marriage and family, but it was true that she wasn't as available as she had been to accompany Mark on his errands, work in the yard with him, or engage in the kind of social life they had in the past. In spite of Cindy's efforts not to put all of her time and energy into school, Mark became increasingly irritable and began to make sniping comments like, "I'm going to work in the yard this afternoon but I'm sure you're too busy to help out," or, "Brian and Karen asked us for dinner this weekend but I told them we couldn't because you'd be too busy."

Cindy was constantly asking Mark what was wrong, but he denied that anything was bothering him. He only said that he was "tired and stressed out from work," or "had a bad headache, that's all." Mark couldn't admit, even to himself, that he was feeling abandoned, unloved, and jealous because Cindy wasn't giving him the same kind of attention that she always had. He could hardly understand these feelings himself. After all, he was truly proud of her and did understand her need to find new interests and challenges now that the kids were grown.

The changes that a loved one will go through at midlife *will* affect the lives of other people. Sometimes these changes will feel strange and uncomfortable. Often we may feel that we are "losing" someone. In this case, Mark needed to look within himself to understand why he was having problems with Cindy's return to school. His own feelings of abandonment, his unloved-child complex, were being intensified by the changes in Cindy's life. At stressful times of change, marriages and relationships may be at great risk. Mark could have continued to blame Cindy for his lonely and frightened feelings and the marriage most likely would have deteriorated. Instead, Mark did a very wise thing. He began to ask himself why he was having such strong feelings of abandonment and anger. Cindy was the woman he loved, and when he could free himself of the terrified feelings even for a moment, he understood that she still loved him and was doing everything in her power to let him know it. By looking inside himself, Mark began to understand that he had always felt unlovable. His own parents had been cold and unable to express any kind of feelings for their children. By becoming conscious of his feelings, Mark could begin to take responsibility for them instead of projecting them onto Cindy. This recognition alone began to change Mark. As time went on, he was able to tell Cindy that he needed to set aside special times for the two of them to be together. She agreed and they began to make a "date" for dinner, a movie, or a special event every weekend. Mark also rekindled his interest in fly-fishing, something he had put aside with the responsibilities of fatherhood and work. He began to spend some time with his friends at a nearby river and became quite an expert at fly casting. He fished while Cindy studied. Cindy and Mark began to communicate at a deeper, more intimate level than they ever had before. They knew that life was going to be different than it had been in the past. But they also understood that their life together could be even better, immensely richer, as each of them pursued the challenges and interests that gave meaning and importance to their lives.

Your reaction to the changes experienced by a loved one at midlife can tell you a great deal about yourself if you look honestly and clearly at what you are feeling and experiencing. It is easy to blame your loved one for what you are feeling—but this is both unconscious and dangerous. Relationships can be easily destroyed when we project and blame others instead of understanding ourselves and our reactions. It takes far more courage and insight to be willing to look inside. It is critical to ask ourselves questions like, "Why is this upsetting to me?" "What am I contributing to this situation that is making it feel so bad to me?"

Midlife is a time of taking on the full responsibilities of maturity and adulthood. But being tolerant and patient does not mean that you must endure morally reprehensible or abusive behavior. I am not suggesting here that you tolerate behavior that is unacceptable to the deepest part of you. You do not have to go along with a spouse who says, for example, "I'm so confused about my life that I'm going to have a few affairs to find out what it is I really want." You do not have to take on an extra job to support a partner who has left his or her job in order to have time to conduct an inner search for the meaning of life. You do not have to sell your house to finance your partner's sailing trip around the world to "find herself." You do not have to stand idly by while a friend or family member engages in alcohol or substance abuse as a way of combating or denying the turmoil that lies underneath their awareness. Just as you must take responsibility for your own feelings and develop insights and awareness as to their origins, so must everyone else.

At midlife, we are dealing with a new, unfamiliar terrain: we are meeting the unconscious in our inner lives, but at the same time we must live in the outer world. And we must be responsible for our behavior, for the outer world, in which we continue to live, is filled with moral imperatives and commitments. Carl Jung, describing his own "confrontation with the unconscious" at midlife, writes of the importance of maintaining one's responsibilities and relationships even in the wake of great inner chaos: "It was most essential for me to have a normal life in the real world. My family and my profession remained the base to which I could always return, assuring me that I was an actually existing, ordinary person. The unconscious contents could have driven me out of my wits. But my family, and the knowledge: I have a medical diploma from a Swiss university, I must help my patients, I have a wife and five children, I live at 228 Seestrasse in Küsnacht—these were actualities which made demands upon me and proved to me again and again that I really existed, that I was not a blank page whirling about in the winds of the spirit. . . . No matter how deeply absorbed or how blown about I was, I always knew that everything I was experiencing was ultimately directed at this real life of mine. I meant to meet its obligations and fulfill its meanings."[3]

James Hollis echoes these thoughts, offering wise counsel to those immersed in the underworld of midlife, when he writes: "To find and follow one's passion is not necessarily to take off, as Gauguin did to Tahiti, for there are commitments to honor, people whose lives are affected by our decisions and something to say for staying a course to which we have a moral responsibility. Yet we are still obliged to live our passion lest our lives remain trivial and provisional, as if some day all would become clear and choices easy. Life is seldom clear and easy; yet choice is what defines and validates a life."[4]

Be supportive of positive changes.

Growth at midlife can be very frightening, making us feel very fragile. It is important to find a healthy balance of encouragement and containment. The changes that your friend or loved one is making at midlife deserve to be nurtured and respected even though you might not understand them or choose them for yourself.

Danny had spent his life working as a master carpenter for a home-building company. His family and friends always relied on him because he was solid and responsible and always did what he said he would do. Because of his honesty and straightforwardness his friends said, "With Danny, what you see is what you get." But Danny had always had a secret that he never shared with anyone else, even his wife. He had always wanted to be an actor. At thirty-nine he could no longer contain this lifelong desire, and he called a local community theater group to see if he could become involved in some of their productions. Because of his skills in carpentry he started out by working on set construction. He began to make some new friends and felt excited to be a part of the efforts to mount shows for the community. At first his old friends didn't even seem to notice this new passion, but when it began to interfere with his spending time with them they began to tease him. "Why do you want to go pound nails after pounding them all day?" they joked.

The more time Danny spent around the theater, the more interested he became in the plays they were producing that season. One of the directors gave him a copy of a script and asked if he was interested in auditioning for a small part that he "looked right for." The part only had a few lines, but Danny was both terrified and excited about the prospect of realizing his dream, even if it was only in his local community. He auditioned and got the part. While his wife and family were very proud of him, he was hesitant to tell his old friends because they had already razzed him about getting involved with the theater group in the first place—and that was just for being a glorified carpenter. But the rehearsals conflicted with the nights that he usually went with his friends to play pool; he would have to tell them that he wouldn't be on the team for the next few months, and of course they would want to know why. When he finally told his friends, they teased him mercilessly: "Good idea, Danny, maybe Spielberg will be in the audience and you'll be the next Harrison Ford." "Aren't you too old to be dressing up in costumes?" "It's stupid. You're too old to go to Hollywood now." Danny felt like calling the director and telling him he wasn't available to do the part; he would just say, "There's too much rehearsal time, I'm too busy."

In the end, Danny kept the part and did very well with it. But the attitudes of his friends had almost crushed the vulnerable growth he achieved by accepting new challenges and new dreams. Notice that Danny was not threatening to quit his job or leave his family homeless in order to pursue a career in acting. In fact, his exploration of community theater was an excellent move, since he could realize some of his dreams while continuing to be the responsible adult that he is. His friends could have honored his courage in trying something that was so close to his heart, rather than ridiculing him for it.

As we provide support and encouragement for a friend or loved one at midlife, we must be careful not to project our critical, judgmental views onto the delicate being who cautiously emerges from the chrysalis. Accepting even what we do not understand is central to the act of loving. As we age and change in life, knowing that we will continue to be loved by those people who are important to us offers a powerful sense of containment and foundation. As the poet May Sarton noted, "Sunlight pours into my study from four windows. Year by year the turquoise silk has faded to a gentle watery blue, the brilliant embroidery has softened, and it is lovelier than ever. 'We love the things we love for what they are,' Robert Frost reminds us. And he means, I think, that we love them as they change . . . as well as for what they once were."[5]

Being a good container and helper during the midlife passage can include *praying and sending loving energy* to the person we love. Although our minds may not always understand the ways in which prayer works, there is much evidence that it can hold enormous power. At a time in our life when we may be feeling helpless to stop the suffering of a loved one experiencing a crushing midlife passage, prayer offers hope and opportunity.

Learning more about the midlife passage can give great insight to understanding what your loved one is going through. *Continue to read about midlife.* Be willing and open, though not insistent, to talk about it.

There are no right or wrong ways to be a companion on a midlife journey. The most important thing of all is, of course, to provide love. Love fully and unconditionally and trust that for every raging squall at sea there will be a time of calm and peace. Poet Anne Sexton provides a view of helping that goes straight to the soul. Poetry, unlike most prose, has the capacity to reach the part of our heart that is not tempered by logic and reason. As you read this poem, listen carefully to the words that inspire wisdom. Sexton understands that the inner journey of a loved one touches your life too, and not without creating its own brand of pain and heartache. But in the end, the only thing that matters is love, and with love as your guide you will be a companion of special and sacred grace.

Big Heart
wide as a watermelon,
but wise as birth,
there is so much abundance
in the people I have:
Max, Lois, Joe, Louise,
Joan, Marie, Dawn,
Arlene, Father Dunne,
and all in their short lives
give to me repeatedly,
in the way the sea
places its many fingers on the shore,
again and again

and they know me,
they help me unravel,
they listen with ears made of conch shells,
they speak back with the wine of the best region.
They are my staff.
They comfort me.
They hear how
the artery of my soul has been severed
and soul is spurting out upon them,
bleeding on them,
messing up their clothes,
dirtying their shoes.
And God is filling me,
though there are times of doubt
as hollow as the Grand Canyon,
still God is filling me.
He is giving me the thoughts of dogs,
the spider in its intricate web,
the sun
in all its amazement,
and a slain ram
that is the glory,
the mystery of great cost,
and my heart,
which is very big,
I promise it is very large,
a monster of sorts,
takes it all in—
all in comes the fury of love.[6]

CHAPTER 12

Concluding Thoughts

All true things must change and only that which changes remains true.
CARL JUNG, "THE NATURE AND ACTIVITY OF THE PSYCHE"

AT MIDLIFE we are beset by changes of enormous magnitude. Consciously or unconsciously we will have to acknowledge that life as we have known it is no more. The values, ideals, and beliefs that served us well on the first half of our journey are simply not up to the task of meeting the challenges of life's afternoon. We are changing, life around us is changing. We are being swept into our destinies of aging, death, and eternity. The Greek philosopher Heraclitus rightly understood that life is a moving flow that persists without our permission and certainly without our control. "You cannot step into the same river twice,"[1] he wrote, recognizing that rivers, like human lives, are continually changing as new water rushes down their banks. Whether we enter this flow unconsciously and "squealing like a pig," or with surrender, grace, and courage in pursuit of transformation, is a decision that each of us is charged with making at midlife.

Ram Dass tells a wonderful story that illustrates our relationship to the great flow of time and existence. With his typical good humor and insight he tells of an old Chinese man sitting on the porch, too old to work in the garden. His son, who is tilling the garden with the rest of the family, looks up at the old man and thinks, "He's so old. All he does is eat food. What good is he? It's time for him to be done." So the son makes a box and puts it on a wheelbarrow. He rolls the box up to the porch and says, "Father, get in." When the father gets into the box, the son puts the cover on it and heads toward the cliff. As he reaches the edge of the cliff, the son hears a knocking from inside the box. "Yes, Father?" he says. The father replies, "Son, I understand what you're doing and why you're doing this, but might I suggest that you just throw me over and save the box. Because there is a good chance your children will need it."[2]

At midlife we are acutely aware of the endings yet to come. We may already have experienced major losses, such as the death of parent or loved one, the termination of a marriage or important relationship, the loss of a job or a life role that has defined us for many years, a physical illness or change in our health or vitality. Some of the losses and changes may be more subtle: a bulge around our middle, thinning hair, wrinkles, the awareness that we may have reached the apex of our career, the knowledge that we will never be a kicker for the Redskins or a rock 'n' roll singer. That there are losses yet to come should be clear to those of us in the middle years. But sometimes the changes and disappointments arrive at such a fast and furious pace we may feel like Sisyphus pushing his boulder up the mountain only to have it roll back down.

At midlife we know that the "times they are a-changing," and we must change with them or suffer the consequences. Jung observed that any person who pretends that the second half of life is no different from the first must "pay with damage to his soul."[3] Abraham Maslow describes the fear of growth and change, the avoidance of our transpersonal potential, as the "Jonah Complex," after the biblical figure who tried to avoid his divine mission.[4] William Blake admonishes us to understand that change is inherent in our lives, and that we must follow that change with our perception and awareness though human beings may insist on seeing things "thro' narrow chinks of his cavern." "The man who never alters his opinions is like standing water, and breeds reptiles of the mind," he writes.[5]

When we feel lost in the woods at midlife, it is seductive to let our opinions, like standing water, remain calcified and inert. We may try to convince ourselves that nothing has really changed, that the symptoms we've been experiencing are just a bump in the road. At such a time it is not always easy to remember that the trials of our most difficult experiences can provide us with enormous opportunity for transformation. Jung understood this transformation as an initiation during which a new, more conscious relationship between the personal ego and the Self could be established. The liberation of our shadow, our darkest, most unconscious energies, is part of a quest, not for perfection, but for completion.

It is my hope that this book has emphasized the opportunity that midlife offers for authentic change and a meaningful and rich second half of life. I have not attempted to dodge the dark side by painting a picture of midlife as filled only with wondrous experiences. It is only in "holding a tension of the opposites," in seeking a *balance* between the realities of our human experience and its possibilities, that we can move toward a greater consciousness, our authentic personality, and unconditional self-love. Jung argued for this process of individuation if only to avoid living what he called the "provisional life," by which he meant a life of unconsciousness, routine, and emptiness, in which one is unable to make decisions and change with the flow of one's own reality. Like a leaf on the wind, the man or woman living this stagnant existence will see life slip away in fantasies and "could have, should have beens," until time runs out and there is no longer any opportunity to live with meaning, celebration, and grace.

At midlife we are being asked to decide how we will live. We can continue to go about our business as if nothing has changed or will change, or we can grab hold and truly live as we have never lived before. Isabel Allende, the celebrated author of *House of the Spirits,* suffered through the death of her twenty-seven-year-old daughter. Describing both her grief and her awakening at age fifty-two, she offers a breathtaking insight about life, which becomes all the more relevant at midlife. "I finally understood what life is about; it is about losing everything. Losing the baby who becomes a child, the child who becomes an adult, like the trees lose their leaves. So every morning we must celebrate what we have."[6]

The metamorphosis which will allow us to live fully and celebrate each morning is available to each and every one of us as part of our human endowment. We need not have any special abilities or knowledge to begin the journey, just a willingness to look inside and to open ourselves to our potential. And it is not just Carl Jung who echoes this optimism; writers and thinkers from all traditions have understood that the life of every human being is a journey filled with suffering and pain, but from which a wiser, more awakened being may emerge. Camus wrote, "In the depth of winter,

I finally learned that within me there lay an invincible summer."[7] In a particularly alchemical moment, Rumi writes: "Copper doesn't know it's copper, until it's changed to gold."[8]

The initial task before us is to begin. And our beginning will require a descent into the inner world. Jung begins the first line of his autobiography with this understanding: "My life is a story of the self-realization of the unconscious."[9] A story told in India illuminates why this inner journey is of such significance and power. It concerns an argument among the gods as to where to hide the secret of life so that men and women cannot find it:

> Bury it under a mountain, one god suggested, they'll never find it there.
>
> No, the others countered, one day they will find a way to dig up the mountain and uncover the secret of life.
>
> Put it in the depths of the deepest ocean, another god suggested, it will be safe there.
>
> No, said the others, some day humankind will find a way to travel to the depths of the ocean and will find it.
>
> Put it inside them, another god said, men and women will never think of looking for it there.
>
> All the gods agreed, and so it is said the gods hid the secret of life within us.[10]

The psychological and spiritual transformation that is possible through the rigors and pain of the midlife journey do not occur on the surface. *As in all good myths and stories, true metamorphosis occurs in the depths of the underworld.* This underworld of suffering, loss, fear, and confusion, this confrontation with the unconscious, creates a refiner's fire from which we can emerge transformed. While we are ordinary people who live ordinary lives, at midlife we can more fully appreciate the mythic qualities of our existence. At midlife we struggle with the same human issues of birth, death, resurrection, suffering, striving, and meaning as have all the great heroes and heroines throughout time. Joseph Campbell says of our common struggle, "I think that what we're seeking is an experience of being alive, so that our life experiences on the purely physical plane will have resonances within our own innermost being and reality, so that we actually feel the rapture of being alive."[11]

At midlife we are being drawn to the mythical reality of the underworld for the miracle of healing and the rebirth of the soul. While there are many, many myths and stories that describe what happens in the underworld, I particularly like one told by Joan Halifax in her book on shamanism and related by Allan Chinen in *Once Upon a Midlife.* This story, told by the Native American Chumash tribe of California, tells of a powerful wizard named Axiwalic, who becomes very ill but is not able to heal himself. He leaves his village to go off into the woods alone to die, but on the way he meets a spirit who offers him a cure. The spirit takes him down into the underworld, where he must sit in a great hut and wait. After a long while, every kind of animal in the world, from bears to mice to bison, appears to him. They all defecate on Axiwalic, until he is buried under a pile of feces. Then the animals bathe him, cure him of his illness, and return him to his people.[12] Many on the journey of midlife can appreciate the accuracy of the image of Axiwalic buried in excrement as they reflect on the beginnings of their own initiation into the second half of life.

At midlife we can recognize that we are living in the polarities of opposing forces, between Yin and Yang, light and dark, known and unknown, visible and invisible. Neither old nor young, we have no control over our ultimate destiny and yet we have the power to transform within it. We may attempt to avoid the ravages of the middle passage by allowing our unconscious to lead us as we meander, half asleep, toward the rest of our life. But if we do so, we will experience a royal battle of psychological, physical, and spiritual symptoms as the relentless, uncompromising Self pushes for expression against our unwillingness to change and grow. W. H. Auden expresses this inner conflict with a keen observation:

We would rather be ruined than changed;
We would rather die in our dread
Than climb the cross of the moment
And let our illusions die.[13]

Instead of forestalling our appointment with life, we may instead choose to awaken and become who we are meant to be, though this will require an extended visit to the underworld. "Knowing others is wisdom; Knowing the self is enlightenment," writes Lao-Tzu.[14] The words "Know thyself" are inscribed in ancient Greek on the outer walls of the temple to

Apollo at Delphi from which the wisdom of the Oracle was delivered. "The unexamined life is not worth living," said Plato.[15]

By midlife we have left so much of ourselves as a sacrifice on the altar of conformity that most of us are encased in a deep coating of defensiveness and grief. In mournings both deep and subtle we long for our Self, for our instincts, our passion, our joy at the simple reality of being alive. We are, many of us, living our lives like the character played by Jack Nicholson in Mike Nichols's film *Wolf,* a middle-aged man who has lived and is living a very conventional life. A subdued, unassuming, "civilized," intellectual editor in chief at a New York publishing house, he has allowed life to move him toward a great inner emptiness. His gentleness comes not from any deep-seated serenity but simply from a lack of passion for his life: he is a "nice guy" who rarely experiences sexual passion with his wife and is unable to defend his territory against the maraudings of an insincere, manipulative, and dangerous younger adversary who feigns friendship and loyalty while coveting not only his job but his wife as well. While driving home from a meeting in Vermont, through snow and on an icy road, the editor accidentally hits a wolf with his car. Thinking he has killed the animal, he attempts to pull it to the side of the road, when it suddenly leaps to life and bites him on the arm. He is apparently unharmed, but within a few days he begins to experience a strange array of unusual symptoms, which announce themselves through a heightened acuity of sensation. He can hear, see, and smell not like a man but like a wolf. Under the spell of nightfall and the energy of the moon, he begins to transform into a wolf with all of its primitiveness, passion, and instinctive energy.

This reintegration of our original instincts, passionate nature, and authentic Self is an archetypal theme at midlife. Clarissa Pinkola Estes, writing on the myths and stories of the wild-woman archetype, reflects on this need to restore the instincts to their natural function in our lives: "So what is the point of this reclamation and focus, this calling back of the hawk, this running with the wolves? It is to go for the jugular, to get right down to the seed and to the bones of everything and anything in your life, because that's where your pleasure is, that's where your joy is, that's where a woman's Eden lies, that place where there is time and freedom to be, wander, wonder, write, sing, create and not be afraid . . . the ability to see what is before us through focusing, through stopping and looking and smelling and listening and feeling and tasting. Focusing is the use of all of our senses, including intuition."[16]

A story from India, told by Joseph Campbell, mirrors the central themes of *Wolf* and of Dr. Estes's work, as it describes the loss and delight in recovery of our true selves:

A female tiger was just about ready to give birth to a cub when she spotted a herd of goats grazing in a field. She had been unsuccessful in the hunt and was exhausted and starving, but she pulled together all of her energy and leaped at them. She was so tired that she died in midair, but the tiger cub was born healthy and alert. The maternal goats nursed him and brought him up to think of himself as a goat. He was in every way like the goats: he ate grass and bleated like a goat. He never questioned that he was anything other than a goat. After a long time the herd was attacked by a powerful old tiger. All of the goats scattered and ran, except for the tiger-goat. The old tiger looked at the tiger-goat and roared: "What are you doing here?" The tiger-goat only bleated and pawed at the ground, continuing to nibble at the grass. The old tiger grabbed the tiger-goat by the scruff of the neck and dragged him over to a small pool of water. Forcing him to look at his own reflection, he bellowed, "Look, you have the pot-face of a tiger, just like mine." The tiger-goat continued to bleat. The old tiger then dragged the tiger-goat over to a place where he had hidden freshly killed meat. Ripping off a piece of meat, the old tiger forced it into the mouth of the tiger-goat. At first the tiger-goat was sickened. "Then he experienced the warmth of the blood—no grass ever tasted like this—as it trickled down his gullet and into his belly. He began to feel elated, intoxicated. His lips smacked; he licked his jowls. He arose and opened his mouth with a mighty yawn, just as though he were waking from a night of sleep—a night that had held him long under its spell for years and years. Stretching his form, he arched his back, extending and spreading his paws. His tail lashed the ground, and suddenly from his throat there burst the terrifying, triumphant roar of a tiger. When the roar was finished, the old tiger demanded gruffly, 'Now do you know what you really are?' "[17]

The need at midlife to recapture our animal instincts for living life with gusto and independence is critical. But it is important to remember that our passionate instincts contain a gentle and interconnected side of human nature as well. Human beings long for intimacy, recognition, trust, community, civility, and the deep sense of being part of a tribe. Just as our more independent animal nature is repressed in a society as complex as our own, so too are these softer sides of our nature. Robert Wright reminds us, "The problem with modern life, increasingly, is less that we're 'oversocialized' than that we're undersocialized—or that too little of our 'social' contact is social in the natural, intimate sense of the word."[18]

Coming to an understanding of our own authentic nature can be a complex endeavor. First, because we are always changing, so that no self-definition can ever be wholly static. Like the river, we are flowing, in a process of change, for all of our lives. But more important, by midlife we may no longer know the person from the mask. Our authentic instincts and personality have been so covered over that we bleat like tiger-goats and forget what it is like to be fully alive and yet also a part of the tribe. The new revelation of self-knowledge is not an instantaneous affair. J. Krishnamurti, a spiritual teacher who adhered to no strict tradition but urged people to look into themselves and the nature of their experience, writes: "So to be what you are is an extremely arduous affair; if you are at all awake, you know all these things and the sorrow of it all. So you drown yourself in your work, in your belief, in your fantastic ideals and meditations. By then you have become old and ready for the grave, if you are not already dead inwardly."[19]

But midlife offers another chance to know the truth about ourselves. Recognizing "consciousness as a precondition to being," Jung understood the importance of self-knowledge, not only for the process of individuation and the pursuit of wholeness in the individual but for the future of humankind and the fate of our planet. In order to know what we are contributing to the whole, each of us must "know relentlessly how much good he can do, and what crimes he is capable of, and must beware of regarding the one as real and the other as illusion. Both are elements within his nature, and both are bound to come to light in him, should he wish—as he ought—to live without self-deception or self-delusion."[20]

It is in this larger, cosmic sense that we may discover our full meaning at midlife. For the midlife journey is not simply about aging or making changes in our outer life. It is about the discovery of personal meaning in one's inner life. It is about the recognition of the sacred in everyday experience. It is about understanding that while we are just a grain of sand in the great flow of time, we are, each of us, unique and necessary to the fulfillment of some cosmic plan. "Evolution," writes Teilhard de Chardin, "is an ascent towards consciousness."[21]

The relationship between our individual consciousness and that of the universe is told in an old Chinese proverb that describes the layers surrounding a single human being. We change the world when we change ourselves, and the light of consciousness, like the energy of all light, continues into the eternity.

If there is light in the soul,
There will be beauty in the person.
If there is beauty in the person,
There will be harmony in the house.
If there is harmony in the house,
There will be order in the nation.
If there is order in the nation,
There will be peace in the world.[22]

I truly hope that this book has provided food for thought and some comfort as you traverse the sometimes frightening, sometimes exhilarating terrain of the midlife journey. There are no coherent maps that can give explicit directions, nor any gurus who can lead you by the hand. It has to be enough to know that while the journey may feel immensely and terrifyingly lonely, you are held in the heart of a universe that embraces you with enduring love and compassion and wishes you Godspeed on your journey. Perhaps the proper path from here is best explained by a story about Rumi and his passionate friendship with a wandering ecstatic called Shams of Tabriz. Shams is said to have taken Rumi's books and thrown them into a fishpond. "Now," he told him, "you must live what you know."[23]

Notes

CHAPTER 1

1. Gail Sheehy, *Passages,* New York: Bantam Books, 1974, pg. 14.
2. Anthony Stevens, *On Jung,* New York: Penguin Books, 1990, pgs. 183–84.
3. James Hollis, *The Middle Passage,* Toronto: Inner City Books, 1993, pg. 17.
4. *People* magazine, "Mr. Bridge," November 8, 1993, pgs. 50–53.
5. Carl Jung, "Marriage as a psychological relationship," *CW,* 17, par. 331.*
6. Carl Jung (Recorded and Edited by Aniela Jaffé), *Memories, Dreams, Reflections,* New York: Vintage Books, 1965, pg. 179.
7. Ibid., pg. 177.
8. Anthony Stevens, *On Jung,* New York: Penguin Books, 1990, pg. 166.
9. Carl Jung, "The Stages of Life," *CW,* 8, par. 399.
10. Sheldon Kopp, *An End to Innocence,* New York: Macmillan, 1978, pg. 48.

CHAPTER 2

1. M. Esther Harding, *The i and the Not i,* Princeton, NJ: Princeton University Press (Bollingen Series), 1965.

**CW* refers to the *Collected Works* of Carl Jung, published by the Princeton University Press (Bollingen Series). Citations include the volume number and the paragraph number for easy reference. Reprinted by Permission of Princeton University Press.

2. Abraham Maslow, *Toward a Psychology of Being,* Princeton, NJ: Van Nostrand, 1962.
3. Carl Jung, "Definitions," *CW,* 6, par. 757.
4. Abraham Maslow, "Deficiency Motivation and Growth Motivation." In M. R. Jones (Ed.), *Nebraska Symposium on Motivation,* Lincoln: University of Nebraska Press, 1955. See also S. R. Maddi, *Personality Theories: A Comparative Analysis,* Homewood, IL: Dorsey Press, 1972, for a discussion of actualization theorists.
5. Daryl Sharp, *C. G. Jung Lexicon: A Primer of Terms and Concepts,* Toronto: Inner City Books, 1991, pg. 68.
6. Carl Jung, "The Psychology of the Transference," *CW,* 16, par. 400.
7. Joseph Campbell with Bill Moyers, *The Power of Myth,* New York: Doubleday, 1988, pg. 123. Also see James Hollis, *Tracking the Gods: The Place of Myth in Modern Life,* Toronto: Inner City Books, 1995.
8. Joseph Campbell, *The Hero With a Thousand Faces,* Princeton, NJ: Princeton University Press (Bollingen Series), 1949 (second ed., 1968), pg. 30.
9. Joseph Campbell, op. cit., pg. 30.
10. George Lucas, who wrote, produced, and directed the *Star Wars* trilogy, was an avid student of Campbell's work on the hero myth. The deeply resonating themes of this film series are solidly based on strong archetypal patterns and images that are found in the hero myths of all cultures. Campbell admired Lucas's work immensely, and in fact, the interviews conducted with Campbell by Bill Moyers for the PBS series *The Power of Myth* were conducted at Lucas's Skywalker Ranch in California.
11. Sheldon Kopp, *Guru: Metaphors from a Psychotherapist,* New York: Bantam Books, 1976, pg. 128. This is a fascinating collection of metaphors for the process of psychotherapy.
12. James Hollis, *The Middle Passage: From Misery to Meaning in Midlife,* Toronto: Inner City Books, 1993, pg. 41.
13. A. Schopenhauer, *Parerga and Paralipomena: Short Philosophical Essays* (E. F. J. Payne, translator), Oxford: Clarendon, 1974, pg. 102.
14. Marion Woodman, *Holding the Tension of the Opposites* (audiotape), Boulder, CO: Sounds True Recordings, 1991.
15. Mary Oliver, "The Journey." In *Dream Work,* New York: Atlantic Monthly Press, 1986, pgs. 38–39. Many thanks to poet David Whyte for introducing me to this wonderful piece at the Common Boundary conference in 1993.
16. S. Kierkegaard, *Fear and Trembling, the Sickness Unto Death,* Garden City, NY: Doubleday Anchor, 1954, pg. 159.
17. Lenore Thomson Bentz, "Seasoned Reflections on Midlife Transition" (an interview with Aryeh Maidenbaum and Daniel Levinson), *Quadrant,* 1992, Vol. 25, No. 1, pg. 9.
18. Carl Jung, *Memories, Dreams, Reflections,* New York: Vintage Books, 1965, pg. 326.
19. Calvin S. Hall and Vernon J. Nordby, *A Primer of Jungian Psychology,* New York: New American Library, 1973, pg. 32.
20. Adapted from Anthony Stevens, *On Jung,* New York: Penguin Books, 1990, pg. 29.
21. Carl Gustav Jung (1875–1961). While Jung's work offers great insight and understanding to the process of transformation and change at midlife as well as throughout life in general, it is important to note that Jung himself would have resisted any kind of "guru" status. He strongly felt that his ideas were flowing rather than static set-in-stone theories and that they should be added to and changed by future

generations of thinkers who struggled to understand the same kind of human and metaphysical problems as he had. He, in fact, was concerned about allegiance to a particular individual rather than a body of thought that Freud had insisted on and, thus, was not too keen on people referring to themselves as "Jungians." Upon hearing of this usage he commented: "I'm glad I'm Jung and not a Jungian." Carl Jung, *Letters,* Vol. 1 (1946), G. Adler (Ed.), Princeton, NJ: Princeton University Press, 1975, pg. 405. Also cited by Aryeh Maidenbaum, Executive Director of the C. G. Jung Foundation for Analytical Psychology, in the Foreword to Robert Hopcke, *A Guided Tour of the Collected Works of C. G. Jung,* Boston: Shambhala, 1992, pg. ix, and Harry A. Wilmer, *Understandable Jung,* Wilmette, IL: Chiron, 1994, pg. 4.

22. A number of writers have addressed the issue of consciousness. In addition to the many Jungian writers, they include scientists, philosophers, and religious teachers throughout the ages. The following texts may be of interest: Erich Neumann, *The Origins and History of Consciousness,* Princeton, NJ: Princeton University Press, 1954; Julian Jaynes, *The Origin of Consciousness in the Breakdown of the Bicameral Mind,* Boston: Houghton Mifflin, 1976; Jeffrey Mishlove, *The Roots of Consciousness (revised ed.),* Tulsa, OK: Council Oak Books, 1993; Daniel C. Dennett, *Consciousness Explained,* Boston: Little Brown, 1991; Robert Ornstein, *The Psychology of Consciousness,* New York: Harcourt Brace Jovanovich, 1977 (second ed.); Robert Ornstein, *The Evolution of Consciousness,* New York: Simon and Schuster, 1991; Robert Ornstein (Ed.), *The Nature of Human Consciousness: A Book of Readings,* San Francisco: W. H. Freeman, 1976; Itzhak Bentov, *Stalking the Wild Pendulum: On the Mechanics of Consciousness,* New York: Bantam Books, 1977; John Rowan Wilson, *The Mind,* New York: Time-Life Books, 1969.
23. Jack Kornfield (Ed.), *Teachings of the Buddha,* Boston: Shambhala, 1993.
24. Interestingly, the coming of consciousness and creation itself appears in the cultures and religions of all people as the creation of light. Ernst Cassirer, *The Philosophy of Symbolic Forms, Vol. 2* (Ralph Manheim, translator), New Haven: Yale University Press, 1953–57, pg. 94 ff. (3 volumes). Cited in Erich Neumann, *The Origins and History of Consciousness,* Princeton, NJ: Princeton University Press, 1954.
25. Carl Jung, *CW,* 11, par. 935.
26. Jean Shinoda Bolen, *Crossing to Avalon,* San Francisco: Harper, 1994, pg. 194.
27. Carl Jung, "Psychology and Alchemy," *CW,* 12, pg. 28.
28. Carl Jung, *CW,* 8, par. 382.
29. Carl Jung, *CW,* 9 i, par. 99.
30. For example, the archetype of the Mother (what we instinctively expect "Mother" to be: nurturant, protective, loving) lays the groundwork for our own relationship with our real, personal mother. The characteristics and behaviors of our own real mother may or may not coincide with our unconscious expectations. Our own mother may not be able to provide even the basic aspects of mothering. Our personal experience will form into a complex (e.g., a "negative mother complex") through the law of similarity and the law of contiguity. That is to say, an archetype becomes active when a person comes into proximity (contiguity) with a situation or person who is similar to the archetype in question. "When an archetype is successfully activated, it accrues to itself ideas, precepts, and emotional experiences associated with the situation or person responsible for its activation, and these are built into a complex which then becomes functional in the personal unconscious." The extent to which the complex is unconscious will determine its effect on other re-

lationships. A man may marry and the outer relationship with his wife is one of partner/lover/spouse, but his real unconscious expectations are for "mother" and he operates as if expecting his wife/partner to respond to him in the ways of the negative mother. See Anthony Stevens, op. cit., pgs. 32–35. Also see Anthony Stevens, *Archetypes,* New York: Quill, 1983.

31. Calvin S. Hall and Vernon J. Nordby, op. cit., pg. 51.
32. Carl Jung, *Memories, Dreams, Reflections,* pg. 325.
33. Rainer Maria Rilke, "A Book for the Hours of Prayer." In Robert Bly (translator), *Selected Poems of Rainer Maria Rilke,* New York: Harper and Row, 1981, pg. 13.
36. Interestingly, most "primitive" cultures believe that the source of consciousness is more likely to reside in the center of the body.
35. Carl Jung, *Memories, Dreams, Reflections,* pg. 304.
36. Ibid., pg. 302.
37. Jean Shinoda Bolen, *The Tao of Psychology: Synchronicity and the Self,* San Francisco: Harper and Row, 1979, pg. 7.
38. Aldous Huxley, *The Perennial Philosophy,* New York: Harper Colophon Books, 1945, pg. 2 (discussed in Larry Dossey, *Recovering the Soul: A Scientific and Spiritual Search,* New York: Bantam Books, 1989, pgs. 48–49).
39. Aldous Huxley, Ibid. pg. 7.
40. The Gospel of Thomas, discovered in 1945 as part of the Coptic texts of the Nag Hammadi library. *The Gospel of Thomas: The Hidden Sayings of Jesus* (Marvin Meyer, translator), New York: HarperCollins, 1992, pg. 55.
41. *A First Zen Reader,* compiled and translated by Trevor Leggett, Tokyo: Charles E. Tuttle, 1960, pg. 46.
42. Scripture quotations are from the New Revised Standard Version of the Bible, copyright 1989 by the Division of Christian Education of the National Council of the Churches of Christ in the U.S.A. Used by permission. All rights reserved. *Holy Bible—The New Revised Standard Version.* Nashville: Thomas Nelson, 1989, pg. 188.
43. Daniel Matt, *The Essential Kabbalah: The Heart of Jewish Mysticism,* San Francisco: Harper, 1995, pg. 25.
44. Seng Ts'an, "Believing in Mind." In Eknath Easwaran, *God Makes the Rivers to Flow: Selections from the Sacred Literature of the World* (second ed.), Tomales, CA: Nilgiri Press, 1991, pg. 96.
45. "The Upanishads," *The Sacred Books of the East,* Vol. 1 (F. Max Muller, translator), London: Oxford University Press, 1926, pg. 136.
46. A. C. Ross, *Mitaukuye Oyasin,* Fort Yates, ND: Bear, 1989.
47. Teilhard de Chardin, *The Phenomenon of Man,* New York: Harper and Row, 1955.
48. Carl Jung, *Psychology and the East* (R. F. C. Hull, translator), Princeton NJ: Princeton University Press, 1978, pg. 69.
49. Edward Edinger, *Ego and Archetype,* Boston: Shambhala, 1992, pg. 103.
50. Carl Jung, "Psychology and Religion: West and East," *CW,* 11, par. 509. The full quotation is: "Among all my patients in the second half of life—that is to say, over thirty-five—there has not been one whose problem in the last resort was not that of finding a religious outlook on life. It is safe to say that every one of them fell ill because he had lost what the living religions of every age have given to their followers, and none of them has been really healed who did not regain his religious outlook. This of course has nothing whatever to do with a particular creed or membership of a church."

51. The Gospel of Saint Thomas, pg. 53.
52. Carl Jung, "Psychology and Alchemy," *CW,* 12, par. 126.

CHAPTER 3

1. For an excellent and full discussion see Anthony Stevens, *On Jung,* New York: Penguin Books, 1990, chapter 5.
2. Robert Hopcke, *Persona: Where Sacred Meets Profane,* Boston: Shambhala, 1995, pg. 3.
3. Karen Horney, *Neurosis and Human Growth,* New York: W. W. Norton, 1950, pg. 65.
4. Carl Jung, "The persona as a segment of the collective psyche," *CW,* 7, par. 245 ff.
5. Robert Bly, *A Little Book on the Human Shadow,* New York: Harper and Row, 1988, pg. 17.
6. Carl Jung, *Aion, CW,* 9ii, par. 423.
7. Rainer Maria Rilke, *Letters to a Young Poet* (M. D. Herter Norton, translator), New York: W. W. Norton, 1963, pg. 69.
8. Carl Jung, *Memories, Dreams and Reflections,* New York: Vintage Books, 1965, pg. 181.
9. Carl Jung, "The psychology of the child archetype," *CW,* 9i, par. 285.
10. Carl Jung, "Psychological aspects of the mother archetype," *CW,* 9i, par. 179.
11. Carl Jung, *CW,* 6, par. 708.
12. Cited in Betty Edwards, *Drawing on the Right Side of the Brain* (revised ed.), Los Angeles: Jeremy Tarcher, 1989, pg. 34.
13. Barbara G. Walker, *The Woman's Dictionary of Symbols and Sacred Objects,* New York: Harper and Row, 1988, p. 18.
14. Carl Jung, "A psychological theory of types," *CW,* 7, appendix, par. 923.
15. Anthony Stevens, op. cit., pg. 146.
16. See John Sanford, *The Invisible Partners,* New York: Paulist Press, 1980.
17. James Hollis, *The Middle Passage: From Misery to Meaning in Midlife,* Toronto: Inner City Books, 1993, pg. 47.
18. Jelaluddin Rumi, in Coleman Barks with John Moyne, *The Essential Rumi,* San Francisco: Harper, 1995, pg. 106.
19. Thomas Moore, *Soulmates,* New York: HarperCollins, 1994, pg. 23.
20. K. Bradway, "Jung's Psychological Types," *Journal of Analytical Psychology,* 1964, Vol. 9, pgs. 129–35.
21. In addition to introversion and extroversion, Jung described *four function types.* These function types refer to the way (or ways) in which we take in the world. Two he categorized as rational and two as irrational.

    The rational functions include both *thinking* and *feeling.* The word "rational" is used because both of these functions use certain criteria to organize and decide about the nature of their experience. The thinking function is rational and able to make logical judgments about things. Thought, logical inference, and cognition are the tools for making sense of the world. The feeling function has to do with values. It decides whether something is acceptable or not, right or wrong, good or bad.

    The two "irrational" functions are called *intuition* and *sensation.* The term "irrational" was selected because these function types do not decide so much as experience the world. Intuition tells us about future possibilities. Having a "hunch" or a "sixth sense" are examples of intuition. It can be described as an unconscious perception. An intuitive person sometimes finds "complex ideas coming to him as a complete whole, unable to explain how he knew. These visions, intuitions or hunches may show up in any realm—technology, sciences, mathematics, philosophy, the arts, or one's social life." Sensation is "sensible," and this function is based on the observation of facts. Personal experience through the physical senses provides the foundation for these facts. Sensation types perceive the world through what they see, hear, touch, and feel. They would rather work with known facts than look for possibilities or relationships between things. See, for example, Carl Jung, "A psychological theory of types," *CW*, 7. Combining these two attitude types (extroversion and introversion) and the four functional types (thinking versus feeling and sensation versus intuition) allows for eight *psychological types*. In the 1950s Isabel Myers, in collaboration with her mother, Katharine Briggs, devised the Myers-Briggs Type Indicator (MBTI©). This tool for identifying personality types became very popular and brought Jung's ideas to the attention of the general public. These authors added an additional category: judging versus perceiving. *Judging* refers to the preference for closure, the need to establish clear deadlines, and in short, liking things to be decided upon and settled. *Perceiving,* on the other hand, is a preference to keep things open and fluid, wanting options open, and being willing to let things emerge or unfold.

Using the Myers-Briggs scheme, with their additional category of judging/perceiving, it is possible to identify sixteen different psychological types. Myers and Briggs assigned each of the attitudes and functions a letter: Extroversion (E), Introversion (I), Thinking (T), Feeling (F), Intuition (N—the "I" is already used by introversion), Sensation (S), Judging (J) and Perceiving (P). Allowing for all the possible combinations of these characteristics produces the sixteen types. Each type is designated with a four-letter code such as ISTP or ESTJ. For example, on the Myers-Briggs, I am an ENFP (Extroverted-Intuitive-Feeling-Perceiving). See Eleanor Corlett and Nancy Millner, *Navigating Midlife: Using Typology as a Guide,* Palo Alto, CA: CPP Books, 1991, for an interesting view of midlife as experienced by the different psychological types. Also see David Keirsey and Marilyn Bates, *Please Understand Me: Character and Temperament Types,* Del Mar, CA: Prometheus Nemesis, 1984.

22. Carl Jung, "The phenomenology of the spirit in fairytales," *CW,* 9i, par. 431.

CHAPTER 4

1. Sogyal Rinpoche, *The Tibetan Book of Living and Dying,* San Francisco: Harper, 1992, pg. 25.
2. Ibid.
3. Deepak Chopra, *Ageless Body, Timeless Mind,* New York: Harmony Books, 1993. Also see Deepak Chopra, *Unconditional Life,* New York: Bantam Books, 1991.
4. George P. Church, "Jobs in an Age of Insecurity," *Time* magazine, November 22, 1993, pgs. 32–39.
5. Lisa Genasci, "Sick at Work," *Virginian-Pilot and Ledger-Star,* March 23, 1995, pg. D1.
6. *Time* magazine, op. cit.

7. Linda McGonigal, Benicia, California, unpublished poem, 1994.
8. Marion Woodman, *The Pregnant Virgin,* Toronto: Inner City Books, 1985, pg. 16.
9. Howell Raines, *Fly Fishing Through the Midlife Crisis,* New York: William Morrow, 1993, pg. 200.
10. Clarissa Pinkola Estes, *Women Who Run With the Wolves,* New York: Ballantine Books, 1992.
11. Ibid., pgs. 134–35.
12. Carl Jung, *Memories, Dreams, Reflections,* New York: Vintage Books, 1965, pg. 314.
13. Ibid.
14. Stephen Levine, *Who Dies? An Investigation of Conscious Living and Conscious Dying,* New York: Doubleday, 1982, pgs. 5–6.
15. Ibid., pg. 5.
16. See a wonderful article about AIDS and spirituality by Mark Matousek, "Savage Grace," *Common Boundary,* May/June 1995, pgs. 22–31.
17. "Godfather Death," in *The Complete Grimm's Fairy Tales,* New York: Pantheon Books, 1944, pgs. 209–12. Clarissa Pinkola Estes offers a beautiful telling of this tale, in addition to other myths and stories about the passing from life to death, on her audiotape titled *The Radiant Coat,* Boulder, CO: Sounds True Recordings, 1990.
18 William Butler Yeats, *The Collected Poems of W. B. Yeats,* New York: Macmillan, 1963.
19. Peter O'Connor, *Understanding the Midlife Crisis,* New York: Paulist Press, 1981, pgs. 48–49, notes that in all the interviews he conducted with men at midlife, there was not a single one in which a man had not come to the recognition that "time was running out."
20. J. P. Ellman, "A Treatment Approach for Patients in Midlife," *Canadian Journal of Psychiatry,* October 1992, 37 (8), pgs. 564–66.
21. June Singer, *Boundaries of the Soul,* New York: Doubleday, 1972, pgs. 9–10. Also see Richard Bode, *First You Have to Row a Little Boat,* New York: Warner Books, 1993.
22. *Holy Bible: The New Revised Standard Version,* Nashville: Thomas Nelson, 1989, pgs. 153–88
23. Carl Jung, "Answer to Job," *CW,* 11. See also Edward F. Edinger, *Transformation of the God-Image: An Elucidation of Jung's Answer to Job,* Toronto: Inner City Books, 1992, for a thorough discussion of Jung's ideas on this subject.
24. C. S. Lewis, *The Problem of Pain,* New York: Macmillan, 1962, pg. 97.
25. Theodore Roethke, *The Collected Poems of Theodore Roethke,* New York: Anchor Books, 1975, pg. 231.
26. Sogyal Rinpoche, op. cit., pgs. 28–29.
27. Merle Shain, *Hearts That We Broke Long Ago,* New York: Bantam Books, 1983, pg. 21.
28. Carl Jung, *Memories, Dreams, Reflections,* pgs. 358–59.
29. Viktor E. Frankl, *Man's Search for Meaning,* New York: Washington Square Press, 1984, pg. 135 (originally published in Austria in 1946; English translation by Beacon Press, 1959).
30. Ibid. Introduction by Gordon Allport, pg. 12.
31. Stephen Levine, *Healing Into Life and Death,* New York: Anchor Books, 1987, pgs. 12–13.
32. Sogyal Rinpoche, op. cit., pg. 193.

33. Sogyal Rinpoche, *Tibetan Wisdom of Living and Dying* (series of audiotapes), Boulder, CO: Sounds True Recordings, 1993.
34. Caryle Hirshberg and Marc Ian Barasch, *Remarkable Recovery,* New York: Riverhead Books, 1995; Andrew Weil, *Spontaneous Healing,* New York: Alfred A. Knopf, 1995.
35. Rainer Maria Rilke, *Letters to a Young Poet,* New York: W. W. Norton, 1963, pg. 35.

CHAPTER 5

1. Rainer Maria Rilke, *Selected Poems of Rainer Maria Rilke,* translated from the German and with commentary by Robert Bly, New York: Perennial Library, 1981, pg. 21. The full poem reads:

> *You darkness, that I come from*
> *I love you more than all the fires*
> *that fence in the world,*
> *for the fire makes*
> *a circle of light for everyone,*
> *and then no one outside learns of you.*
>
> *But the darkness pulls in everything:*
> *shapes and fires, animals and myself,*
> *how easily it gathers them!—*
> *powers and people—*
>
> *and it is possible a great energy*
> *is moving near me.*
>
> *I have faith in nights.*

2. Mary Kay Blakely, *Wake Me When It's Over: A Journey to the Edge and Back,* New York: Times Books, 1989.
3. Robert Michael Pyle, *The Audubon Society Field Guide to North American Butterflies,* New York: Alfred A. Knopf, 1981, pgs. 20–22.

   Note: A fascinating convergence of technology and knowledge about life is afoot among a group of people, including many schoolchildren, who track the migration of the beautiful monarch butterfly and communicate their findings via the Internet. More information is available on the World-Wide Web at http://informns.k12.mn.us. Also see Sue Halpern, "Winged Victories," *NetGuide,* February 1995, pgs. 52–56, and Sue Halpern, *Migrations to Solitude,* New York: Vintage Books, 1993.
4. Marion Woodman, *The Pregnant Virgin,* Toronto: Inner City Books, 1985, pg. 7.
5. Murray Stein, *In Midlife,* Dallas: Spring Publications, 1983, pgs. 24–25.
6. Paule Marshall, *Praisesong for the Widow,* New York: Dutton, 1984.
7. Ibid., pgs. 31–32.
8. Ibid., pg. 37.
9. Ibid., pgs. 82–83.
10. Marion Woodman, op. cit., pg. 175.

11. Ibid., pg. 179.
12. Ibid., pg. 178.
13. Paule Marshall, op. cit., pgs. 204–5.
14. Erik Erikson, *Childhood and Society,* New York: W. W. Norton, 1963. Also see Erik Erikson, *Identity, Youth and Crisis,* New York, W. W. Norton, 1968.
15. David Whyte, "Tilicho Lake," *Where Many Rivers Meet,* Langley, WA: Many Rivers Press, 1990, pg. 23.
16. Peter Kramer, *Listening to Prozac,* New York: Viking, 1993.
17. Anthony Storr, *Solitude: A Return to the Self,* New York: Ballantine Books, 1988, pg. 18. Also see Sue Halpern, *Migrations to Solitude,* New York: Vintage Books, 1992; David A. Cooper, *Silence, Simplicity and Solitude,* New York: Bell Tower, 1992.
18. Thomas Moore, *Care of the Soul,* New York: HarperCollins, 1992, pg. 137.
19. Sogyal Rinpoche, *The Tibetan Book of Living and Dying,* San Francisco: Harper, 1992, pg. 11.
20. Ibid.
21. May Sarton, *Journal of a Solitude,* New York: W. W. Norton, 1973, pg. 11. Also see, by this author: *Plant Dreaming Deep,* New York: W. W. Norton, 1968; *The House By the Sea,* New York: W. W. Norton, 1981; *At Seventy: A Journal,* New York: W. W. Norton, 1984.
22. Thomas Moore, op. cit., pg. 286.
23. Nancy Wood, "Solitude," in *Spirit Walker* (with paintings by Frank Howell), New York: Doubleday, 1993, pg. 51.
24. Barbara Walker, *The Woman's Encyclopedia of Myths and Secrets,* New York: Harper and Row, 1983. This is a fascinating and exhaustive collection of scholarship into history, legend, and myth.
25. Marsilio Ficino, *The Book of Life* (Charles Boer, translator), Dallas, TX: Spring Publications, 1980, pg. 96, 116. Cited in Thomas Moore, op. cit., pg. 172.
26. Howell Raines, *Fly Fishing Through the Midlife Crisis,* New York: William Morrow, 1993, pg. 79.
27. Nicholas Cummings, "Behavioral Health After Managed Care: Opportunity for Professional Psychology," *Register Report,* January 1995, Vol. 20 (3) and 21 (1), pg. 1.
28. Gregory Dennis, "Therapy Under Siege," *New Age Journal,* May/June 1994, pg. 93.
29. Carl Jung, "The Structure and Dynamics of the Psyche," *CW,* 8, par. 417–531.
30. Carl Jung, *Memories, Dreams, Reflections,* New York: Vintage Books, 1965, pg. 197.
31. Carl Jung, *CW,* 8, par. 982.
32. Jean Shinoda Bolen, *The Tao of Psychology: Synchronicity and the Self,* New York: Harper and Row, 1979, pgs. 16–17.
33. *The Gospel of Thomas: The Hidden Sayings of Jesus,* Interpretation by Harold Bloom, San Francisco: Harper, 1992, Saying 24.
34. Ibid., Saying 113.
35. Jean Shinoda Bolen, op. cit., pg. 4.
36. Lao-Tzu, *Tao te Ching: A New English Translation* (Stephen Mitchell, translator), San Francisco: Harper, 1988, pg. 56.
37. Robert Michael Pyle, *The Audubon Society Handbook for Butterfly Watchers,* New York: Charles Scribner's Sons, 1984, pg. 157.
38. Carl Jung, *CW,* 9ii, par. 125.

39. Satinover and Bentz, Ibid., pg. 25.
40. Allan B. Chinen, *Once Upon A Midlife,* Los Angeles: Jeremy Tarcher, 1992, pg. 168.
41. Ibid., pg. 204. Also see Robert Bosnak, *A Little Course in Dreams,* Boston: Shambhala, 1988, chapter 6.
42. Carl Jung, *CW,* 8, par. 787.
43. Carl Jung, "The Development of Personality," *CW,* 17, par. 335.
44. Erik Erikson, *Identity, Youth and Crisis,* pg. 138.
45. Viktor Frankl, *Man's Search for Meaning,* New York: Washington Square Press, 1984, pg. 131.
46. Ibid., pg. 132.
47. Paule Marshall, op. cit., pg. 256.
48. Viktor Frankl, op. cit., pg. 132.
49. Emily Dickinson, poem #598, *The Complete Poems of Emily Dickinson,* Boston: Little Brown, 1960 (first published in 1929, conjectured to have been written in 1862). Note: Emily Dickinson did not title any of her poems.
50. Thomas Moore, op. cit., pg. i.
51. Carlos Castaneda, *The Teachings of Don Juan,* New York: Washington Square Press, 1968, pg. 107. Cited in Jack Kornfield, *A Path with Heart,* New York: Bantam Books, 1993, pg. 12.

INTRODUCTION TO SECTION TWO

1. Jack Kornfield, *A Path with Heart,* New York: Bantam Books, 1993, pg. 8.
2. Thomas Kuhn, *The Structure of Scientific Revolutions,* Chicago: University of Chicago Press, 1962. Kuhn used the word "paradigm" to describe conceptual systems that dominate scientific and societal thinking during a particular period of scientific evolution. Every new paradigm initiates a new way of looking at things and, as such, is both positive and progressive. However, since no scientific theory can be expected to explain the enormous complexity of the universe, at a certain point data will emerge that are incompatible with a prevailing paradigm. Because people have embraced the prevailing paradigm, they assume that it is both true and complete. Many people will resist information that does not conform to the prevailing way of seeing things. For example, until the beginning of the twentieth century, Western science and philosophy was based squarely on the foundations of Newtonian theories in physics and Descartes's philosophical ideas about the nature of matter and spirit. The findings and evidence provided by physicists such as Albert Einstein, Niels Bohr, Wolfgang Pauli, and others demonstrated that Newtonian physics, while applicable to some parts of reality, could not accommodate what happened at the subatomic level of analysis. See Stanislav Grof, *Ancient Wisdom and Modern Science,* Albany: State University of New York Press, 1984; John Hitchcock, *The Web of the Universe: Jung, the "New" Physics, and Human Spirituality,* New York: Paulist Press, 1991; Michael Talbot, *The Holographic Universe,* New York: HarperCollins, 1991; Fritjof Capra, *The Tao of Physics,* New York: Bantam Books, 1983; Gary Zukav, *The Dancing Wu Li Masters,* New York: Bantam Books, 1979.
3. Carl Jung, *CW,* 11, par. 144. Jung eventually concluded that this process of individuation was at work in inorganic material as well as living matter (e.g., the formation of crystals). But individuation finds its highest expression in human beings. See: Anthony Stevens, *On Jung,* New York: Penguin Books, 1990, pg. 187.

4. Hazrat Inayat Khan, *The Art of Being and Becoming,* New Lebanon, NY: Omega, 1982, p. xiii.

CHAPTER 6

1. Pierre Teilhard de Chardin, *The Evolution of Chastity* (René Hague, translator), London: William Collins, 1972. Reprinted in Pierre Teilhard de Chardin, *On Love and Happiness,* San Francisco: Harper, 1984, pg. 16.
2. Ysaye Barnwell, "The Power of a Vocal Community," *Nourishing the Soul: Discovering the Sacred in Everyday Life, Common Boundary's 13th Annual Conference,* November 12–14, 1993, Crystal City, Virginia. Audiotape—Boulder Co: Sounds True Recordings, 1993.
3. Eleanor Bertine, *Close Relationships: Family, Friendship, Marriage,* Toronto: Inner City Books, 1992, pg. 13. This volume is an edited reprint of *Human Relationships: In the Family, In Friendship, In Love,* by Eleanor Bertine, 1958.
4. Abraham Maslow, "A Dynamic Theory of Human Motivation," *Psychological Review,* 1943, Vol. 50, pgs. 370–96. Also see Abraham Maslow, *Motivation and Personality* (second ed.), New York: Harper and Row, 1970.
5. Rollo May, *Man's Search for Himself,* New York: New American Library, 1967, pg. 25 (first published in 1953 by W. W. Norton).
6. Carl Jung, "The Psychology of the Transference," *CW,* 16, par. 454.
7. Pierre Teilhard de Chardin, *Human Energy* (J. M. Cohen, translator), London: William Collins, 1969, pg. 32.
8. Thomas Moore, *Soulmates,* New York: HarperCollins, 1994, pg. 71.
9. Robert Wright, "Our Cheating Hearts," *Time* magazine, August 15, 1994, pg. 46. This article was adapted from Robert Wright, *The Moral Animal: Evolutionary Psychology and Everyday Life,* New York: Pantheon Books, 1994.
10. Ibid.
11. Michael Liebowitz, *The Chemistry of Love,* Boston: Little, Brown, 1983.
12. See Diane Ackerman, *A Natural History of Love,* New York: Vintage Books, 1995.
13. Robert Johnson, *We: Understanding the Psychology of Romantic Love,* San Francisco, Harper, 1983, pg. xiii. Note: The image of courtly romantic love was described recently in the popular media when the courtship of actors Nicolas Cage and Patricia Arquette was discussed on television, and in newspapers and magazines. According to these reports, Nicolas Cage first met Patricia Arquette in a Los Angeles coffee shop in 1987 and announced to her that he had fallen in love with her, even though they had just met, and wished her to send him on a "quest" so that he might prove it. Arquette told Cage to bring her a black orchid and a signature from reclusive author J. D. Salinger. Since black orchids do not exist, Cage spray-painted a purple one and then paid two thousand dollars for a letter signed by Salinger. In spite of the completion of the quest, eight years passed and the couple saw each other only about four times during that period. In 1995 Arquette called Cage and proposed, and they were married. Cage was quoted as saying Patricia was his "true soul mate" and "the person I would want to be if I were a woman." Here's hoping that these two lovers are entering into a conscious relationship or will withdraw projections and live a long and happy life together. *National Enquirer,* May 9, 1995, Vol. 69, No. 42, pg. 8.
14. *The New Yorker,* December 12, 1994, pg. 101.

15. Robert Johnson, op. cit., pg. 69. Also see Linda Schierse Leonard, *On the Way to the Wedding,* Boston: Shambhala, 1986.
16. Carson McCullers, *Ballad of the Sad Café,* New York: Bantam Books, 1971, pg. 26 (originally published by Houghton Mifflin, 1951). My appreciation to Ruth Frazier for the reminder of this wonderful book in her article "The Lover and the Beloved," *Skip Two Periods,* Vol. 7, No. 2, Spring 1990. Also see Jean Houston, *The Search for the Beloved,* Los Angeles: Jeremy Tarcher, 1987. The projection of unconscious psychic material operates in all forms of relationships. While the characteristics of anima/animus that Jung wrote about are clearest in very traditional relationships between men and women in heterosexual marriages, they also exist in less traditional relationships between men and women as well as in gay and lesbian relationships. See Emma Jung, *Animus and Anima,* Dallas: Spring Publications, 1957; Robert Hopcke, *Jung, Jungians and Homosexuality,* Boston: Shambhala, 1989; Betty Berzon, *Permanent Partners: Building Gay and Lesbian Relationships That Last,* New York: Plume, 1988.
17. Marie-Louise von Franz, *Projection and Re-collection in Jungian Psychology,* LaSalle, IN: Open Court, 1980, pg. 11.
18. Carl Jung, *CW,* 8, par. 507.
19. Daryl Sharp, *The Survival Papers: Anatomy of a Midlife Crisis,* Toronto: Inner City Books, 1988, pgs. 74–75. Also see Daryl Sharp, *Dear Gladys: The Survival Papers Book 2,* Toronto: Inner City Books, 1989.
20. James Hollis, *The Middle Passage,* Toronto: Inner City Books, 1993, pg. 32.
21. Rainer Maria Rilke, *Letters to a Young Poet,* New York: W. W. Norton, 1963 (revised ed.), pg. 59.
22. Carson McCullers, op. cit., pg. 29.
23. Erich Neumann, *The Great Mother: An Analysis of the Archetype,* Princeton, NJ: Princeton University Press (Bollingen Series), 1972 (originally published in 1955), pg. 3.
24. Kathie Carlson, *In Her Image,* pgs. 3–4.
25. Riane Eisler, *The Chalice and the Blade,* San Francisco: Harper, pg. 24.
26. Adrienne Rich, "Re-forming the Crystal," in *Poems Selected and New 1950–1974,* New York: W. W. Norton, 1975, pg. 228. Also see Susan Griffin, *Woman and Nature,* New York: Harper Colophon Books, 1978; Shirley Nicholson (Ed.), *The Goddess Reawakening: The Feminine Principle Today,* Wheaton, IL: Quest Books, 1989; M. Esther Harding, *Woman's Mysteries,* New York: Harper and Row, 1971; Marion Woodman, *The Pregnant Virgin,* Toronto: Inner City Books, 1985; Robert Johnson, *Femininity Lost and Regained,* New York: Harper and Row, 1990; Fred Gustafson, *The Black Madonna,* Boston: Sigo Press, 1990; Christine Downing, *The Goddess: Mythological Images of the Feminine,* New York: Crossroad, 1989; Edward Whitmont, *Return of the Goddess,* New York: Crossroad, 1989; Sylvia Brinton Perera, *Descent to the Goddess: A Way of Initiation for Women,* Toronto: Inner City Books, 1981. For an excellent anthology about the conscious feminine, see Connie Zweig (Ed.), *To Be A Woman: The Birth of the Conscious Feminine,* Los Angeles: Jeremy Tarcher, 1990.
27. Robert Bly, "The Hunger for the King in a Time with No Father." In Patricia Berry (Ed.), *Mothers, Fathers,* Dallas: Spring Publications, 1990, pg. 2.
28. *Washington Post,* "Nearly a quarter of kids grow up without fathers," *Virginian-Pilot and Ledger-Star,* April 24, 1995, pg. A2.

29. Robert Bly, op. cit., pg. 3.
30. Ibid., pg. 5.
31. Ellen Gray, "Group urges us to go without TV this week," *Virginian-Pilot and Ledger-Star,* April 23, 1995, pg. E7. Data based upon Nielsen surveys and TV-Free America.
32. Alvin Toffler, *The Third Wave,* New York: William Morrow, 1980, pg. 44.
33. Peter Laslett, "The Comparative History of Household and Family." In John F. Crosby, *Reply to Myth: Perspectives on Intimacy,* New York: John Wiley, 1985, pg. 366.
34. Lillian Rubin, *Just Friends,* New York: Harper and Row, 1985, pg. 17.
35. James Hollis, *The Middle Passage,* Toronto: Inner City Books, 1993, pg. 94.
36. Thomas Moore, op. cit., pg. 72.
37. Ralph Waldo Emerson, "Friendship," *The Writings of Ralph Waldo Emerson, Vol. 1* (Essays, first and second series), New York: Brentanos, 1910, pg. 131. For a more contemporary and readily available citation, see William J. Bennett, *The Book of Virtues,* New York: Simon and Schuster, 1993, pgs. 336–37.
38. Judith Viorst, *Necessary Losses,* New York: Fawcett, 1986, pg. xi.
39. Cited in Lillian Rubin, *Just Friends,* New York: Harper and Row, 1985, pg. 17.
40. Steve Duck, *Friends, For Life: The Psychology of Close Relationships,* New York: St. Martin's, 1983, pgs. 141–42.
41. Lillian Rubin, op. cit., pg. 10.
42. Ralph Waldo Emerson, op. cit., pg. 132.
43. Lillian Rubin, op. cit., pg. 13.
44. Aristotle, quoted in Diogenes Laertius, *Lives of Philosophers,* New York: Putnam, 1925, Book 5, section 20.
45. Carmen L. Caltagirone, *Friendship as Sacrament,* New York: Alba House, 1988, pg. xvi.
46. Mary Wollstonecraft. Cited in Janice G. Raymond, *A Passion for Friends,* Boston: Beacon Press, 1986.
47. Thomas Moore, op. cit., pg. 93.
48. Jelaluddin Rumi, "The Friend," in *Night and Sleep,* Cambridge, MA: Yellow Moon Press, 1981.
49. Janie Sams and David Carson, *Medicine Cards: The Discovery of Power Through the Ways of Animals,* Santa Fe, NM: Bear, 1988.
50. Samuel A. Corson and Elizabeth O'Leary Corson, "Companion Animals as Bonding Catalysts in Geriatric Institutions." In Bruce Fogel (Ed.), *Interrelations Between People and Pets,* Springfield, IL: Charles C. Thomas, 1981, pgs. 146–74.
51. E. Friedmann, S.A. Thomas, A.H. Katcher, and M. Noctor, "Pet Ownership and Coronary Heart Disease Patient Survival," *Circulation,* 58:II-168 (Abstr), 1978. Also cited in Bruce Fogel, *Pets and Their People,* New York: Penguin Books, 1983, pg. 28.
52. Marie-Louise von Franz, cited in Eleanora M. Woloy, *The Symbol of the Dog in the Human Psyche,* Wilmette, IL: Chiron, 1990, pg. 23. Of related interest: Elizabeth Marshall Thomas, *The Hidden Life of Dogs,* Boston: Houghton Mifflin, 1993.
53. Walt Whitman, "Song of Myself" (originally published in 1855), in Richard Gray (Ed.), *American Verse of the Nineteenth Century,* London: J. M. Dent, 1973, pg. 117. Also cited in Samuel A. Corson and Elizabeth O'Leary Corson, op. cit.
54. Eugene Kennedy, *On Being a Friend,* New York: Continuum, 1982, pg. 45.

55. Ralph Waldo Emerson, op. cit., pg. 134.
56. Alvin Toffler, op. cit., pg. 25.
57. Thomas Moore, op. cit., pg. 100.
58. Carl Jung, *Psychological Reflections: A New Anthology of His Writings 1905–1961,* Jolande Jaffe and R. F. C. Hull (Eds.), Princeton, NJ: Princeton University Press, 1970.
59. ABC Television, *20/20* program, March 25, 1994.
60. Al Gore, *Earth in the Balance: Ecology and the Human Spirit,* New York: Plume, 1992, pg. 29.
61. Chief Seattle, letter to President Franklin Pierce, 1855, cited in Joseph Campbell with Bill Moyers, *The Power of Myth,* New York: Doubleday, 1988, pgs. 34–35. Also see Hyemeyohsts Storm, *Seven Arrows,* New York: Ballantine Books, 1972.
62. Mark Gerzon, *Coming Into Our Own.* New York: Delacorte Press, 1992, pg. 187.
63. W. H. Auden, "As I walked out one evening" (November 1937), in *W. H. Auden: Selected Poems,* Edward Mendelson (Ed.), New York: Vintage Books, 1979, pg. 62. Also see Edward Mendelson, *Early Auden,* New York: Viking, 1981, pg. 237. Also cited in Marion Woodman, *Holding the Tension of the Opposites* (audiotape), Boulder, CO: Sounds True Recordings, 1991.
64. Dastoor Minocher Homji, "The Cows Are Many Colors, but the Milk Is the Same," in Stanislav Grof (Ed.), *Ancient Wisdom and Modern Science,* Albany: State University of New York Press, 1984, pg. 49.
65. James Hollis, op. cit., pg. 16.
66. Marion Woodman, *The Pregnant Virgin,* pg. 166. (Poet and essayist E. B. White wrote about the importance of Thoreau's *Walden* as the "only book I own, although there are others unclaimed on my shelves. Every man, I think, reads one book in his life, and this one is mine. It is not the best book I ever encountered, perhaps, but it is for me the handiest, and I keep it about me in much the same way one carries a handkerchief—for relief in moments of defluxion or despair." (*The New Yorker,* May 23, 1953). Marion Woodman's *The Pregnant Virgin* has been that handkerchief for me during my passage of midlife.
67. John Bradshaw, *Homecoming: Reclaiming and Championing Your Inner Child,* New York: Bantam Books, 1990, pg. 7.
68. Jane Howard, *Families,* New York: Berkley Books, 1980 (originally published by Simon and Schuster, 1978).
69. Thomas Moore, op. cit., pg. 94.
70. Karl Menninger
71. The Earthworks Group, *50 Simple Things You Can Do to Save the Earth,* Berkeley, CA: Earthworks Press, 1989.

CHAPTER 7

1. W. B. Yeats, "The Second Coming," in G. D. Sanders, J. H. Nelson, M. L. Rosenthal (Eds.), *Chief Modern Poets of Britain and America,* New York: Macmillan, 1970, pg. I-121.
2. Strephon Kaplan-Williams, *The Jungian-Senoi Dreamwork Manual,* Novato, CA: Journey Press, 1980, pg. 36. Also see Strephon Kaplan-Williams, *Dreamworking: A Comprehensive Guide to Working with Dreams,* San Francisco: Journey Press, 1991.
3. T. C. McCluhan, *Touch the Earth,* New York: Promontory, 1971, pg. 56. Also cited

in John A. Sanford, *Dreams and Healing,* New York: Paulist Press, 1978, pg. 6. Also see Mircea Eliade, *Shamanism: Archaic Techniques of Ecstasy,* Princeton, NJ: Princeton University Press, 1964; Benjamin Kilborne, "Ancient and Native People's Dreams," in Stanley Krippner (Ed.), *Dreamtime and Dreamwork,* Los Angeles: Jeremy Tarcher, 1990, pgs. 194–203.

4. Morton Kelsey, *Dreams: A Way to Listen to God,* New York: Paulist Press, 1978, pg. 74. Also see Morton Kelsey, *God, Dreams and Revelation,* Minneapolis: Augsburg, 1974; John Sanford, *Dreams: God's Forgotten Language,* Philadelphia; Lippincott, 1968; Morton Kelsey, *Encounter with God,* Minneapolis: Bethany Fellowship, 1972; Morton Kelsey, *Healing and Christianity,* New York: Harper and Row, 1974; Morton Kelsey, *The Christian and the Supernatural,* Minneapolis: Augsburg, 1976; Louis M. Savary, Patricia H. Berne, and Strephon Kaplan-Williams, *Dreams and Spiritual Growth,* New York: Paulist Press, 1984.
5. Talmud, in A. Cohen, *Everyman's Talmud,* New York: Schocken, 1978, pg. 287. Cited in Jeremy Taylor, *Dreamwork,* New York: Paulist Press, 1983, pg. 5. Also see Jeremy Taylor, *Where People Fly and Water Runs Uphill,* New York: Warner Books, 1992, and Robert Van de Castle, *Our Dreaming Mind,* New York: Ballantine Books, 1994, for an excellent review of the role of dreams in politics, art, religion, and psychology from ancient civilizations to present-day scientific research.
6. Scripture quotations are from the New Revised Standard Version of the Bible, copyright 1989 by the Division of Christian Education of the National Council of the Churches of Christ in the U.S.A. Used by permission. All rights reserved. *Holy Bible: The New Revised Standard Version,* Nashville: Thomas Nelson, 1989, pgs. 479–80 (Job 33: 15–16). Cited in James A. Hall, *Patterns of Dreaming,* Boston: Shambhala, 1991, pgs. 8–9.
7. *Holy Bible,* op. cit., Matthew 1:20–22, 24; 2:12–13, 19–22. For other biblical references to dreaming, see Numbers 20:11, Daniel 4:10–18, Deuteronomy 18:10, Genesis 16:7; 20:3; 21:17; 28:12; 31:24; 32:24–29; 40:5–19; 41:1–32.
8. James A. Hall, op. cit., pg. 15.
9. Sigmund Freud (1909), *The Interpretation of Dreams* (A. A. Brill, translator), New York: Modern Library, Random House, 1950. Freud modified his original ideas about dreams during the course of his life and work. But the idea that a dream is a disguised fulfillment of a repressed wish continues to be a major tenet of classical psychoanalytic theory. See James A. Hall, op. cit., pgs. 15–43; Ernest Jones, *The Life and Work of Sigmund Freud,* New York: Basic Books, 1961; Sigmund Freud, *A General Introduction to Psychoanalysis,* New York: Washington Square Press, 1968 (originally published by Boni and Liveright, 1924).
10. Carl Jung, *Memories, Dreams, Reflections,* New York: Vintage Books, 1965, pg. 147.
11. The relationship between Freud and Jung is both intellectually and emotionally stimulating. See Linda Donn, *Freud and Jung: Years of Friendship, Years of Loss,* New York: Collier Books, 1988.
12. Carl Jung, *Memories, Dreams, Reflections,* pg. 161.
13. Carl Jung, "The Practical Use of Dream Analysis," *CW,* 16, par. 319. Also see Fraser Boa, *The Way of the Dream: Conversations on Jungian Dream Interpretation with Marie-Louise von Franz,* Boston: Shambhala, 1994. This is an excellent introduction to Jung's ideas about dreams by one of his most brilliant and illustrious students and colleagues. There is also a film series with von Franz that is wonderful. The series is produced by Fraser Boa and is called *The Way of the Dream,* by Windrose Films, 1988. Also

see Stephen Segaller and Merrill Berger, *The Wisdom of the Dream: The World of C. G. Jung,* Boston: Shambhala, 1991.

14. N. Kleitman and E. Aserinsky, "Two Types of Ocular Motility During Sleep," *Journal of Applied Physiology,* 1955, Vol. 8, pgs. 1–10. Note: Later studies have shown that dreaming may not be strictly restricted to REM sleep only. Some dreams may occur during non-REM (NREM) sleep. Additionally, more recent studies have demonstrated correlations between dream content and the direction of eye movements, between small muscle or limb movements and middle-ear activity. See Ramon Greenberg, "Dreams and REM Sleep—An Integrative Approach," in William Fishbein (Ed.), *Sleep, Dreams and Memory,* Jamaica, NY: Spectrum, 1981, pgs. 125–33.
15. William Fishbein, Introduction in William Fishbein (Ed.), op. cit.
16. W. Dement, "The Effect of Dream Deprivation," *Science,* 1960, Vol. 131, pgs. 1705–7. Cited in James A. Hall, *Patterns of Dreaming,* Ibid, pg. 90.
17. "There is a growing body of research with other animals and plants demonstrating rhythmic patterns of metabolic activity during sleep (and analogous cyclic dormant periods) which are strikingly similiar to the patterns of REM sleep in more complex organisms. There is substantial reason to believe that *all* living things may participate in the dream state. It is interesting to note that shamans and mystical thinkers of all persuasions have said for centuries that this is the case, and now contemporary science has begun to verify it experimentally." Jeremy Taylor, *Dreamwork,* Ibid, pg. 6.
18. James A. Hall, op. cit., chapter 3.
19. James A. Hall, op. cit., pgs. 102–3.
20. Carl Jung, *CW,* 8, par. 505.
21. This metaphor is elaborated very nicely by James A. Hall, *Jung: Interpreting Your Dreams* (audiotape), Los Angeles: Audio Renaissance Tapes.
22. Carl Jung, *CW,* 16, par. 304.
23. Dreams may also include images, allegories, and rebuses (representations of a phrase by a picture). For the purposes of this discussion, the use of the term "symbol" will include these variations. See Edward C. Whitmont and Sylvia Brinton Perera, *Dreams, a Portal to the Source,* London: Routledge, 1989.
24. Carl Jung, *CW,* 15, par. 105.
25. Carl Jung, *Man and His Symbols,* New York: Doubleday, 1969, pg. 4.
26. Roy Dreistadt, "An Analysis of How Dreams are Used in Creative Behavior," *Psychology,* February 1971, Vol. 8, No. 1, pgs. 24–50. Also cited in Phyllis R. Koch-Sheras, E. Ann Hollier, and Brooke Jones, *Dream On: A Dream Interpretation and Exploration Guide for Women,* Englewood Cliffs, NJ: Prentice-Hall, 1983, pg. 132.
27. Robert Louis Stevenson, "A Chapter on Dreams," *Memories and Portraits, Random Memories, Memories of Himself,* New York: Charles Scribner's Sons, 1925. Also cited in Carl Jung, *Man and His Symbols,* pg. 25, and in Phyllis R. Koch-Sheras et al., op. cit., pg. 132.
28. Roy Dreistadt, op. cit., pgs. 24–50. Also cited in Carl Jung, *Man and His Symbols,* pgs. 25–26.
29. W. Kaempffert (Ed.), *A Popular History of American Invention,* New York: Charles Scribner's Sons, 1924, Vol. 2, pg. 385. Also cited in Jeremy Taylor, op. cit., pgs. 6–7, and Phyllis R. Koch-Sheras et al., op. cit., pgs. 132–33.

30. Interestingly, this is the same term, "big dream," used by the Elgoni people, who live in the jungles of Elgon in East Africa, to describe dreams that appear to come from something other than a personal source. See E. A. Bennett, *What Jung Really Said,* New York: Schocken, 1983, pg. 99.
31. Edward C. Whitmont and Sylvia Brinton Perera, op. cit., pg. 56.
32. Mary Ann Mattoon, *Understanding Dreams,* Dallas: Spring Publications, 1984, pg. 140.
33. Carl Jung, *CW,* 18, par. 473. Also cited in Mary Ann Mattoon, op. cit., pg. 140.
34. Cited in Edward C. Whitmont and Sylvia Brinton Perera, op. cit., pg. 8.
35. Clarissa Pinkola Estes, *In The House of the Riddle Mother* (audiotape), Boulder, CO: Sounds True Recordings, 1991.
36. James A. Hall, *Jungian Dream Interpretation: A Handbook of Theory and Practice,* Toronto: Inner City Books, 1983, pg. 34.
37. Carl Jung, *CW,* 12, par. 403.
38. James A. Hall, *Jungian Dream Interpretation,* pg. 34.
39. Carl Jung, *CW,* 16, par. 320. Also see James Hillman, *Archetypal Psychology: A Brief Account,* Dallas: Spring Publications, 1983.
40. Carl Jung, *CW,* 10, par. 320.
41. Carl Jung, *CW,* 8, par. 509.
42. Marion Woodman, *Dreams: Language of the Soul* (audiotape), Boulder, CO: Sounds True Recordings, 1991.
43. *The Interpretation of Dreams: Oneirocritica of Artemidorus* (R. J. White, translator), Park Ridge, NJ: Noyes Press, 1975. Also cited in James A. Hall, *Patterns of Dreaming,* pg. 265.
44. Carl Jung, *CW,* 8, par. 556.
45. Edward C. Whitmont and Sylvia Brinton Perera, op. cit., pgs. 79–80.
46. Joseph Campbell with Bill Moyers, *The Power of Myth,* New York: Doubleday, 1988, pg. 40.
47. *The Complete Grimm's Fairy Tales,* New York: Pantheon Books, 1972, pgs. 160–66. For an analysis of this fairy tale and an enumeration of its themes, also see Gertrud Mueller Nelson, *Here All Dwell Free,* New York: Doubleday, 1991; Marie-Louise von Franz, *The Feminine in Fairy Tales,* Dallas: Spring Publications, 1972; Marion Woodman, *Leaving My Father's House,* Boston: Shambhala, 1992; Clarissa Pinkola Estes, *Women Who Run With the Wolves,* New York: Ballantine Books, 1992.
48. The whole realm of the humanities, science, archaeology, religion, literature, art, poetry, mythology, fairy tales, and folklore from all cultures can contribute to understanding the archetypal images in dreams. Thus the realm from which the psyche may draw its symbols is limitless. And there can be no definitive list of the sources of information that can help us in understanding the broad range of archetypal symbols. But here are some references that I have personally found very helpful and that may be of interest: Good general dictionaries (e.g., if you are only to have one or two books on the subject): *The Herder Symbol Dictionary,* Wilmette, IL: Chiron, 1986; J. C. Cooper, *An Illustrated Encyclopaedia of Traditional Symbols,* New York: Thames and Hudson, 1988. Other books that I have found to be very helpful and that are available at many bookstores and in libraries: Beverly Moon (Ed.), *An Encyclopedia of Archetypal Symbolism,* Boston: Shambhala, 1991; Herbert Spencer Robinson and Knox Wilson, *Myths and Legends of All Nations,* Savage, MD: Littlefield Adams, 1990; Bergen Evans, *Dictionary of Mythology,* New York: Laurel, 1970; J. C. Cooper, *Sym-*

bolic and Mythological Animals, New York: Aquarian/Thorsons, 1992 (also in this series: J. C. Cooper, *The Aquarian Dictionary of Festivals;* Jan Knappert, *The Aquarian Guide to African Mythology, Indian Mythology, Pacific Mythology;* Page Bryant, *The Aquarian Guide to Native American Mythology;* John and Caitlin Matthews, *British and Irish Mythology;* Derek Walters, *Chinese Mythology*); Patricia Monaghan, *The Book of Goddesses and Heroines,* St. Paul: Llewellyn, 1990; Barbara G. Walker, *The Woman's Dictionary of Symbols and Sacred Objects,* San Francisco: CA: Harper, 1988; Barbara G. Walker, *The Woman's Encyclopedia of Myths and Secrets,* San Francisco: Harper, 1983; Joseph Campbell with Bill Moyers, *The Power of Myth;* Joseph Campbell, *The Hero with a Thousand Faces.* Princeton, NJ: Princeton University Press, 1968; Joseph Campbell, *The Inner Reaches of Outer Space: Metaphor as Myth and as Religion,* New York: Harper and Row, 1988; Joseph Campbell, *Transformations of Myth Through Time,* New York: Harper and Row, 1990; Joseph Campbell, *Myths to Live By,* New York: Bantam Books 1972; Joseph Campbell, *The Masks of God,* New York: Penguin Books, 1962 (4 volumes: *Primitive Mythology, Oriental Mythology, Occidental Mythology, Creative Mythology*); Merlin Stone, *When God Was a Woman,* New York: Harcourt Brace Jovanovich, 1976; Merlin Stone, *Ancient Mirrors of Womanhood* (2 volumes), New York: New Sibylline Books, 1979; Charlene Spretnak, *Lost Goddesses of Early Greece,* Boston: Beacon Press, 1978; *The Complete Grimm's Fairy Tales;* Marie-Louise von Franz, *Alchemy,* Toronto: Inner City Books, 1980; Marie-Louise von Franz, *Creation Myths,* Dallas: Spring Publications, 1972; Donald Sandner, *Navaho Symbols of Healing,* Rochester, VT: Healing Arts, 1991; H. W. Janson, *History of Art,* New York: Harry N. Abrams, 1963; Karen Armstrong, *A History of God,* New York: Ballantine Books, 1993. Additionally, see all forms of religious writing: the Bible, the Talmud, the Koran, and Taoist, Buddhist, and Hindu texts as well as sacred poetry.

49. Marion Woodman, *Dreams: Language of the Soul* (audiotape).
50. For an excellent discussion of the persona, see Robert Hopcke, *Persona: Where Sacred Meets Profane,* Boston: Shambhala, 1995.
51. Carl Jung, *Memories, Dreams, Reflections,* pgs. 182–83.
52. Ibid., pg. 183.
53. Ibid., pg. 183.
54. Edward Edinger, *Ego and Archetype,* Boston: Shambhala, 1992, pg. 182.
55. Carl Jung, *Memories, Dreams, Reflections,* pg. 196–97. Also see Carl Jung, "Concerning Mandala Symbolism," *CW,* 9i. Also see Heita Copony, *Mystery of Mandalas,* Wheaton, IL: Quest Books, 1989; José and Miriam Argüelles, *Mandala,* Boston: Shambhala, 1985.
56. John Sanford, *Dreams and Healing,* New York: Paulist Press, 1978, pgs. 33–34.
57. James A. Hall, *Patterns of Dreaming,* pg. 130.
58. Carl Jung, *CW,* 14, par. 706.
59. Robert Johnson, *Inner Work,* San Francisco: Harper, 1986, pg. 138. Also see Barbara Hannah, *Encounters with the Soul: Active Imagination as Developed by C. G. Jung,* Santa Monica, CA: Sigo Press, 1981; James A. Hall, *Clinical Uses of Dreams: Jungian Interpretation and Enactments,* New York: Grune and Stratton, 1977 (Hall refers to the process of vitalizing dream images as *dream enactment*).
60. Jamie Sams and David Carson, *Medicine Cards: The Discovery of Power Through the Ways of Animals,* Santa Fe, NM: Bear, 1988, pg. 109.
61. June Singer, *Boundaries of the Soul,* New York: Doubleday, 1989, pg. 343.

62. Carl Jung, *Memories, Dreams, Reflections,* pg. 302.
63. Robert Bly (translator), *Selected Poems of Rainer Maria Rilke,* New York: Harper and Row, 1981, pg. 53.
64. Mary Ann Mattoon, *Understanding Dreams,* Ibid., pgs. 178–183.
65. Jeremy Taylor, op. cit., pgs. 76–98.
66. Carl Jung, *CW,* 10, par. 325.

CHAPTER 8

1. Dylan Thomas, "The force that through the green fuse drives the flower," in G. D. Sanders, J. H. Nelson, M. L. Rosenthal (Eds.), *Chief Modern Poets of Britain and America,* New York: Macmillan, 1970, pg. I-395.
2. Howard Gardner, *Art, Mind and Brain,* New York: Basic Books, 1982, pg. 86.
3. Some researchers suggest that the origins of art and interest in symbolic expression may be seen in man-apes known as australopithecines who lived more than 3 million years ago. The most ancient art object in the world, the Makapansgat Pebble, was not crafted by human hands but was forged by nature. Nevertheless, its striking resemblance to a human face and the fact that it was found in a cave that could not have been its source have led to the idea that it was claimed as a treasured possession by our prehuman ancestors. See Desmond Morris, *The Human Animal,* New York: Crown, 1994, pgs. 186–88. Also see Desmond Morris, *The Biology of Art,* London: Methuen, 1962.
4. Michael D. Lemonick, "Ancient Odysseys," *Time* magazine, February 13, 1995, pgs. 64–67. Note: The cave near Avignon, France, is often refered to as the Chauvet Cave, after the name of a local park ranger, Jean-Marie Chauvet, who first discovered it. Also see Robert Hughes, "Behold the Stone Age," *Time* magazine, February 13, 1995, pgs. 52–62. Also see H. W. Janson, *History of Art,* New York: Harry N. Abrams, 1963.
5. In P. E. Vernon, *Creativity, Selected Readings,* New York: Penguin Books, 1970, pg. 109. Cited in Mike Samuels and Nancy Samuels, *Seeing with the Mind's Eye,* New York: Random House, 1975, pg. 240.
6. Abraham Maslow, *Toward a Psychology of Being* (second ed.), New York: Van Nostrand, 1968.
7. Rollo May, *The Courage to Create,* New York: W. W. Norton, 1975, pgs. 32–33.
8. Deena Metzger, *Writing for Your Life,* San Francisco: Harper, 1992, pg. 3.
9. Ibid.
10. Bruce Ballenger and Barry Lane, *Discovering the Writer Within,* Cincinnati: Writer's Digest Books, 1989, pg. 4.
11. Betty Edwards, *Drawing on the Right Side of the Brain* (revised ed.), Los Angeles: Jeremy Tarcher, 1989, pg. 65.
12. Pablo Picasso, cited in Julia Cameron, *The Artist's Way,* New York: Tarcher/Perigee, 1992, pg. 20.
13. Thomas Moore, *Care of the Soul,* New York: HarperCollins, 1992, pg. 198.
14. Plato, *The Ion,* in L. Cooper (translator), E. Hamilton, and H. Cairns (Eds.), *Plato: The Collected Dialogues,* New York: Pantheon Books (Bollingen), 1961, pgs. 218–21. Also see Plato, *Phaedrus, Ion, Gorgias,* and *Symposium* and passages from *The Republic* and *Laws,* translated by Lane Cooper, 1938 (Cornell University Press). Cited in

Albert Rothenberg and Carl Hausman, *The Creativity Question,* Durham, NC: Duke University Press, 1976, pgs. 31–33.

15. Samuel Taylor Coleridge, *Biographia Literaria: or Biographical Sketches of My Literary Life and Opinions,* Vol. 1, pgs. 144, 150–51, London: Rest Fenner, 1817—edition by John Shawcross, Oxford: Oxford University Press, 1907. Cited in Albert Rothenberg and Carl Hausman, op. cit., pgs. 61–63.
16. Desmond Morris, *The Human Animal,* pg. 188.
17. Translated in Makoto Ueda, *Literary and Art Theories in Japan,* Cleveland: Press of Western Reserve University, 1967, pg. 159. Cited in Richard P. Pilgrim, "Foundations for a Religio-Aesthetic Tradition in Japan." In Diane Apostolos-Cappadona (Ed.), op. cit.
18. Cited in Cecilia Davis Cunningham, "Craft: Making and Being." In Diane Apostolos-Cappadona (Ed.), *Art, Creativity and the Sacred,* New York: Crossroad, 1986, pg. 8.
19. Carl Jung, *CW,* 15, par. 110. In addition to Vol. 15 of the *Collected Works,* also see Vol. 5, "Symbols of Transformation," and Carl Jung, *Modern Man in Search of a Soul,* New York: Harcourt Brace Jovanovich, 1933.
20. Maya Angelou, "Shades and Slashes of Light." In Mari Evans (Ed.), *Black Women Writers 1950–1980: A Critical Evaluation,* New York: Anchor Books, 1984, pgs. 3–5. For interesting anecdotes about the process of writing by other well-known writers and creative thinkers, see Bill Strickland, *On Being a Writer,* Cincinnati: Writer's Digest Books, 1989; Milenko Matanovic (Ed.), *Lightworks: Explorations in Art, Culture, and Creativity,* Issaquah, WA: Lorian Press, 1985.
21. Mary Wigman, "The New German Dance." In Virginia Stewart (Ed.), *Modern Dance,* 1935.
22. Natalie Goldberg, *Writing Down the Bones,* Boston: Shambhala, 1986, pg. 37. Also see Natalie Goldberg, *Freeing the Writer Within* (audiotape), Austin, TX: Davenport Productions, 1988; Natalie Goldberg, *Wild Mind,* New York: Bantam Books, 1990; Natalie Goldberg, *Long Quiet Highway,* New York: Bantam Books, 1993.
23. Julia Cameron, op. cit. Also see Julia Cameron, *The Artist's Way* (audiotapes), Boulder, CO: Sounds True Recordings, 1993. Also see Joanna Field (Marion Milner), *On Not Being Able to Paint,* Los Angeles: Jeremy Tarcher, 1987.
24. See, for example, Sally Springer and Georg Deutsch, *Left Brain, Right Brain* (revised edition), New York: W. H. Freeman, 1985.
25. Betty Edwards, op. cit., pg. 40. Also see Tony Buzan, *Using Both Sides of Your Brain,* New York: Dutton, 1983; Barbara Meister Vitale, *Unicorns are Real: A Right-Brained Approach to Learning,* Rolling Hills Estates, CA: Jalmar, 1982; Henriette Klauser, *Writing on Both Sides of the Brain,* San Francisco: Harper, 1987; Gabriele Rico, *Writing the Natural Way,* Los Angeles: Jeremy Tarcher, 1983.
26. Roger W. Sperry, "Lateral Specialization of Cerebral Function in the Surgically Separated Hemispheres." In F. J. McGuigan and R. A. Schoonover (Eds.), *The Psychophysiology of Thinking,* New York: Academic Press, 1973, pgs. 109–229.
27. Arthur Koestler, *The Act of Creation,* London: Arkana, 1989, pg. 177 (first published by Penguin Books in 1964).
28. Thomas Moore, op. cit., pg. 199.
29. Paul Tillich, *The Courage to Be,* New Haven: Yale University Press, 1980, pg. 46. (originally published in 1952).
30. Abraham Maslow, op. cit., pg. 135.

31. Ibid., pg. 136.
32. Walt Whitman, cited in Allen Ginsberg, "Meditation and Poetics." In John Welwood, *Ordinary Magic: Everyday Life As Spiritual Path,* Boston: Shambhala, 1992, pg. 101. Excerpted from Allen Ginsberg, "Meditation and Poetics." In William Zinsser (Ed.), *Spiritual Quests: The Art and Craft of Religious Writing,* Boston: Houghton Mifflin, 1988.
33. Laura Byrne Paquet, "Risking it All," *Home Office Computing,* June 1995, pgs. 54–58. Also see Michael Warshaw (Ed.), "Great Comebacks," *Success,* August 1995, pgs. 33–46.
34. For example, see Janean Chun, Chythia E. Griffin, Erika Kotite, Heather Page, and Debra Phillips, "Entrepreneurs Across America," *Entrepreneur,* June 1995, pgs. 95–112. Also see Robert J. Weber, *Forks, Phonographs and Hot Air Balloons: A Field Guide to Inventive Thinking,* Oxford: Oxford University Press, 1992.
35. Peter O'Connor, *Understanding the Mid-Life Crisis,* New York: Paulist Press, 1981. See especially chapter 5. Also see Daniel J. Levinson et al., *The Seasons of a Man's Life,* New York: Alfred A. Knopf, 1978.
36. Gail Sheehy, *New Passages: Mapping Your Life Across Time,* New York: Random House, 1995, pg. 190.
37. Betty Friedan, *The Fountain of Age,* New York: Simon and Schuster, 1993, pg. 222.
38. John Naisbitt and Patricia Aburdene, *Re-Inventing the Corporation,* New York: Warner Books, 1985. Also see John Naisbitt, *Megatrends,* New York: Warner Books, 1983
39. Thomas Peters and Nancy Austin, *A Passion for Excellence,* New York: Random House, 1985. Also see Thomas Peters and Robert H. Waterman, Jr., *In Search of Excellence,* New York: Warner Books, 1982; Michael LeBoeuf, *Imagineering,* New York: Berkley Books, 1980.
40. Roger von Oech, *A Whack on the Side of the Head: How to Unlock Your Mind for Innovation,* New York: Warner Books, 1983. Also see Roger von Oech, *A Kick in the Seat of the Pants,* New York: Harper and Row, 1986.
41. Clarissa Pinkola Estes. *The Creative Fire* (audiotape), Boulder, CO: Sounds True Recordings, 1991.
42. Ibid.
43. Jelaluddin Rumi, "The Sheik Who Played with Children." In Coleman Barks with John Moyne (translators), *The Essential Rumi,* San Francisco: Harper, 1995, pg. 44.
44. Robert H. Hopcke, *A Guided Tour of the Collected Works of C. G. Jung,* Boston: Shambhala, 1992, pgs. 121–23.
45. Shunryu Suzuki, *Zen Mind, Beginner's Mind,* New York: Weatherhill, 1994 (first ed., 1970), pg. 14.
46. William G. Doty, "The Trickster." In Christine Downing (Ed.), *Mirrors of the Self: Archetypal Images That Shape Your Life,* Los Angeles: Jeremy Tarcher, 1991, pg. 237.
47. John E. Smelcer, "Raven Steals the Stars, Moon, and Sun," *A Cycle of Myths: Native Legends from Southeast Alaska,* Anchorage, Alaska: Salmon Run, 1993, pgs. 17–18.
48. Betty Edwards, op. cit. Interestingly, Eastern cultures have linguistic expression for intervals or gaps in time and space (*ma*), which describes the space between things or a musical rest as an interval in the temporal flow of music. The word *ku* is used as a term for "emptiness" or "nothingness." Western traditions do not include such concepts in language. See Richard Pilgrim, op. cit., pgs. 138–53. Also see Frederick Franck, *The Zen of Seeing,* New York: Vintage Books, 1973.

49. Natalie Goldberg, *Writing Down the Bones,* pg. 15.
50. Thomas Moore, op. cit., pg. 199.
51. Paracelsus, *Paracelsus: Selected Writings* (Jolande Jacobi Ed., Norbert Gurerman translator), Princeton, NJ: Princeton University Press, 1951, pg. 117.
52. Jelaluddin Rumi, "The Ground." In *Night and Sleep,* Cambridge, MA: Yellow Moon Press, 1981. Also see Coleman Barks with John Moyne (translators), op. cit.
53. See Kathleen Adams, *Journal to the Self,* New York: Warner Books, 1990; Ira Progoff, *At a Journal Workshop,* New York: Tarcher/Putnam, 1992; Sam Keen and Anne Valley-Fox, *Your Mythic Journey,* Los Angeles: Jeremy Tarcher, 1989.
54. Robert Bly, *A Little Book on the Human Shadow,* San Francisco: Harper, 1988, pg. 43.
55. Julia Cameron, *The Artist's Way.*
56. Gail Sheehy, op. cit., pg. 140.
57. George Eliot,
58. Natalie Goldberg, *Writing Down the Bones,* pg. 54.

CHAPTER 9

1. National Public Radio (NPR), *Morning Edition,* June 13, 1995. Many thanks to my good friend Alice Broome for alerting me to this wonderful story.
2. Kevin Fedarko and Mark Thompson, "All for One," *Time* magazine, June 19, 1995, pgs. 21–26.
3. Study commissioned by the Unity School of Christianity and cited in Rosemary Ellen Guiley, *The Miracle of Prayer,* New York: Pocket Books, 1995. The study was conducted in August 1993 by an independent organization, Fleishman-Hillard Research of St. Louis, Missouri, and consisted of a national mail survey of 1,500 households, with a response rate of forty percent. Another survey, commissioned by *Life* magazine and conducted by the Gallup Organization (December 17–19, 1993; telephone survey of 688 adults) found identical results to the Unity-sponsored study (sampling error ± 4.1 percent). "Why We Pray," *Life,* March 1994, pgs. 54–62.
4. Ibid., pg. 62.
5. Spindrift, Inc. "An Ancient Philosophy: A Modern Test," *The Spindrift Papers,* Vol. 1, 1975–1993 (P.O. Box 3995, Salem, OR 97302-0995). Cited in Larry Dossey, *Healing Words: The Power of Prayer and the Practice of Medicine,* San Francisco: Harper, 1993, pgs. 97–98. Also see Larry Dossey, *Recovering the Soul,* New York: Bantam Books, 1989. Also see Joan Borysenko, *Fire in the Soul: A New Psychology of Spiritual Optimism,* New York: Warner Books, 1993, and Jon Kabat-Zinn, *Full Catastrophe Living,* New York: Delacorte, 1990.
6. Randolph C. Byrd, "Positive Therapeutic Effects of Intercessory Prayer in a Coronary Care Unit Population," *Southern Medical Journal,* 81:7 (July 1988): 826–29. Also cited in Larry Dossey, *Healing Words,* pgs. 179–86, and Lois Duncan and William Roll, *Psychic Connections: A Journey into the Mysterious World of Psi,* New York: Delacorte, 1995, pgs. 209–10.
7. Larry Dossey, *Healing Words.*
8. June Singer, *Seeing Through the Visible World,* San Francisco: Harper, 1990, pg. xxi.
9. Carl Jung, *CW,* 11, par. 509. See footnote 54 in chapter 2 for the full quotation.
10. Carl Jung, *Memories, Dreams, Reflections,* New York: Vintage Books, 1965, pg. 325.
11. The word *spirit* is from the Latin *spiritus,* "to breathe, breath of God, inspiration."

The word *religion* is from the Latin *religio,* "bond between man and the Gods," perhaps from *religare,* "to bind back, to fasten."

12. Abraham Maslow, *Toward a Psychology of Being* (second ed.), New York: Van Nostrand, 1968, pg. 72.
13. Thomas Moore, *Care of the Soul,* New York: HarperCollins, 1992, pg. 219.
14. Chögyam Trungpa, "Earth and Space." In John Welwood (Ed.), *Ordinary Magic: Everyday Life as Spiritual Path,* Boston: Shambhala, 1992, pg. 29. Excerpted from Chögyam Trungpa, *The Myth of Freedom,* Boston: Shambhala, 1991.
15. Thich Nhat Hanh, in David Schiller, *The Little Zen Companion,* New York: Workman, 1994, pg. 371. Also see Thich Nhat Hanh, *Being Peace,* Berkeley, CA: Parallax, 1987; Thich Nhat Hanh, *The Present Moment* (audiotape series), Boulder, CO: Sounds True Recordings, 1994; Thich Nhat Hanh, *Living Buddha, Living Christ,* New York: Riverhead Books, 1995; Thich Nhat Hanh, *The Miracle of Mindfulness: A Manual on Meditation,* Boston: Beacon Press, 1975.
16. Jelaluddin Rumi, "The Waterwheel." In Coleman Barks with John Moyne (translators), *The Essential Rumi,* San Francisco: Harper, 1995, pg. 248.
17. Jack Kornfield, *A Path With Heart,* New York: Bantam Books, 1993, pg. 27.
18. Carlos Castaneda, *A Separate Reality: Further Conversations with Don Juan,* New York: Touchstone, 1971, pg. 50. Also see Carlos Castaneda, *The Teachings of Don Juan: A Yaqui Way of Knowledge,* New York: Touchstone, 1968; Carlos Castaneda, *Journey to Ixtlan: The Lessons of Don Juan,* New York: Touchstone, 1972.
19. Ram Dass, *The Only Dance There Is,* New York: Anchor Books, 1970, pg. 152.
20. John Welwood, Introduction, in John Welwood, *Ordinary Magic: Everyday Life as Spiritual Path.* Boston: Shambhala, 1992, pg. xxiii. This is an excellent book of excerpts from numerous writers and thinkers, a tremendous resource with which to begin. Also see Shunryu Suzuki, *Zen Mind, Beginner's Mind,* New York: Weatherhill, 1994 (first ed., 1970), and Trevor Leggett (translator), *A First Zen Reader,* Rutland, VT: Charles E. Tuttle, 1960.
21. Shunryu Suzuki, op. cit.
22. John Welwood, Introduction, op. cit., pgs. xxiii–xxiv.
23. Walpola Rahula, *What the Buddha Taught* (revised ed.), New York: Grove Press, 1974, p. 48 (originally published in 1959). Also see Tenzin Gyatso, the fourteenth Dalai Lama, *The Meaning of Life from a Buddhist Perspective,* translated and edited by Jeffrey Hopkins, Boston: Wisdom Publications, 1992; John Powers, *Introduction to Tibetan Buddhism,* Ithaca, NY: Snow Lion Publications, 1995.
24. Jon Kabat-Zinn, *Wherever You Go There You Are,* New York: Hyperion, 1994, pg. 8. This is an excellent book that provides specific mindfulness exercises, as is Jack Kornfield, op. cit., and Jack Kornfield, *The Inner Art of Meditation* (audiotape series), Boulder, CO: Sounds True Recordings, 1993. Also see Ram Dass, *Journey of Awakening: A Meditator's Guidebook,* New York: Bantam Books, 1990 (originally published in 1978); Charles T. Tart, *Living the Mindful Life: A Handbook for Living in the Present Moment,* Boston: Shambhala, 1994.
25. Natalie Goldberg, "Writing Fearlessly." In John Welwood (Ed.), op. cit., pgs. 90–98. Excerpted from Natalie Goldberg, *Writing Down the Bones,* Boston: Shambhala, 1986.
26. Mildred Chase, "Just Being at the Piano." In John Welwood (Ed.), op. cit., pgs. 108–114. Excerpted from Mildred Chase, *Just Being at the Piano,* Berkeley, CA: Creative Arts, 1985.

27. Eugen Herrigel, "Zen Archery." In John Welwood (Ed.), op. cit., pgs. 115–28. Excerpted from Eugen Herrigel, *Zen in the Art of Archery,* New York: Pantheon Books, 1953.
28. W. Timothy Gallwey, *The Inner Game of Tennis,* New York: Bantam Books, 1974. Also see Robert Pirsig, *Zen and the Art of Motorcycle Maintenance,* New York: William Morrow, 1974.
29. Annie Dillard, *Pilgrim at Tinker Creek,* New York: Harper and Row, 1974, pgs. 20–21 (this book won the Pulitzer Prize). Also see *Tickets for a Prayer Wheel* (1974), *Teaching a Stone to Talk* (1982), *An American Childhood* (1987), all by Annie Dillard and published by Harper and Row.
30. Terry Tempest Williams, *Refuge: An Unnatural History of Family and Place,* New York: Vintage Books, 1991, pg. 52. Also see Terry Tempest Williams, *An Unspoken Hunger,* New York: Pantheon Books, 1994.
31. William Carlos Williams, "Thursday." In A. Walton Litz and Christopher MacGowan (Eds.), *The Collected Poems of William Carlos Williams, Volume 1, 1909–1939,* New York: New Directions, 1986, pg. 157. Also cited in Allen Ginsberg, "Meditation and Poetics," in John Welwood (Ed.), op. cit., pg. 102.
32. Diane Ackerman, *A Natural History of the Senses,* New York: Random House, 1990.
33. Wallace Black Elk and Williams S. Lyon, *Black Elk: The Sacred Ways of a Lakota,* San Francisco: Harper, 1990, pg. 34.
34. Nancy Walker, "Mother's Words," in *Spirit Walker,* New York: Doubleday, 1993, pg. 18.
35. Cited in Jack Kornfield, *"The Seven Factors of Enlightenment."* In Roger Walsh and Frances Vaughan, *Paths Beyond Ego: The Transpersonal Vision,* Los Angeles: Jeremy Tarcher, 1993, pg. 58.
36. Cited in Elaine Pagels, *The Gnostic Gospels,* New York: Vintage Books, 1989, pg. xix.
37. John Sanford, *Dreams: God's Forgotten Language,* San Francisco: Harper, 1989, pg. 125.
38. Marion Woodman, *Rolling Away the Stone* (audiotape), Boulder, CO: Sounds True Recordings, 1989.
39. Lisa Beyer, "Crazy? Hey, You Never Know," *Time* magazine, April 17, 1995, pg. 22.
40. Carl Jung, *CW,* 7, par. 243.
41. Frank Hamilton Cushing, *Zuñi Folk Tales,* New York: Alfred A. Knopf, 1931, pgs. 34–53; Clarissa Pinkola Estes, *The Boy Who Married An Eagle: Myths and Stories about Male Individuation* (audiotape), Boulder, CO: Sounds True Recordings, 1991.
42. Ibid.
43. James Hollis, *The Middle Passage: From Misery to Meaning in Midlife,* Toronto: Inner City Books, 1993, pg. 22. Also see Randi Henderson, "The Gifts of Age," *Common Boundary,* September/October 1995, pgs. 24–31.

CHAPTER 10

1. Bill Moyers, *Healing and the Mind,* New York: Doubleday, 1993, pg. 253. The material in this book can also be seen in the PBS series (producer, David Grubin) of the same name.
2. Jeanne Achterberg, *Woman as Healer,* Boston: Shambhala, 1991, pg. 103.

3. Marion Woodman, *The Pregnant Virgin,* Toronto: Inner City Books, 1985, pg. 25.
4. Louise Farr, "How Stars Deal with Trauma of Growing Old in Tinseltown," Fairchild Publications. In the *Virginian-Pilot and Ledger-Star,* June 15, 1995, pg. E6.
5. Mark Seal, "Nell Newman's Organic Crusade," *New Age Journal,* March/April 1995, pg. 74.
6. Al Gore, *Earth in the Balance,* New York: Plume, 1992, pg. 28.
7. Carl Jung, Letter to Henry Murray, September 10, 1935, in *C. G. Jung Letters,* Vol. 2, pg. 160. Cited in John P. Conger, *Jung and Reich: The Body as Shadow,* Berkeley, CA: North Atlantic Books, 1988, pg. 109.
8. Carl Jung, *CW,* 8, par. 418. Also see Marie-Louise von Franz, *Psyche and Matter,* Boston: Shambhala, 1988; Edward C. Whitmont, *The Alchemy of Healing: Psyche and Soma,* Berkeley, CA: North Atlantic Books, 1993.
9. Pierre Teilhard de Chardin, *The Divine Milieu,* New York: Harper and Row, 1960, pg. 13.
10. Jack Kornfield, *A Path With Heart,* New York: Bantam Books, 1993, pgs. 7–8.
11. Jelaluddin Rumi, "Where Are We?" In Coleman Barks with John Moyne (translators), *The Essential Rumi,* San Francisco: Harper, 1995, pg. 15.
12. Deepak Chopra, *Quantum Healing: Exploring the Frontiers of Mind/Body Medicine,* New York: Bantam Books, 1990, pg. 48. Also see Deepak Chopra, *Unconditional Life,* New York: Bantam Books, 1991; Deepak Chopra, *Ageless Body, Timeless Mind,* New York: Harmony Books, 1993; Deepak Chopra, *Perfect Health,* New York: Harmony Books, 1990.
13. Stanislav Grof, *The Holotropic View,* San Francisco: Harper, 1990, pg. 7. Also see Stanislav Grof, *Ancient Wisdom and Modern Science,* Albany: State University of New York, 1984, pg. 10; James Jean, *The Mysterious Universe,* New York: Macmillan, 1930; Stanislav Grof, *East & West: Ancient Wisdom and Modern Science,* San Francisco: Robert Briggs Associates, 1983 (reprinted article from *Journal of Transpersonal Psychology*); Christina Grof and Stanislav Grof, *The Stormy Search for the Self,* New York: Tarcher/Perigee, 1990; Stanislav Grof and Christina Grof, *Spiritual Emergency,* New York: Tarcher/Perigee, 1989; Michael Talbot, *The Holographic Universe,* New York: HarperCollins, 1991; David Bohm, *Wholeness and the Implicate Order,* London: Routledge, 1987; Rupert Sheldrake, *A New Science of Life: The Hypothesis of Formative Creation,* Los Angeles: Jeremy Tarcher, 1981; Rupert Sheldrake, *The Presence of the Past: Morphic Resonance and the Habits of Nature,* New York: Random House, 1988; Gary Zukav, *The Dancing Wu Li Masters,* New York: William Morrow, 1979; Gary Zukav, *The Seat of the Soul,* New York: Fireside Books, 1989; Fritjof Capra, *The Tao of Physics,* New York: Bantam Books, 1988 (originally published in 1975); Fritjof Capra, *The Turning Point,* New York: Simon and Schuster, 1982; Fritjof Capra and David Steindl-Rast, *Belonging to the Universe: Explorations on the Frontiers of Science and Spirituality,* San Francisco: Harper, 1991; Stephen W. Hawking, *A Brief History of Time,* New York: Bantam Books, 1988.
14. See Bill Moyers, op. cit., chapter 4. Also see David Eisenberg with Thomas Lee Wright, *Encounters with Qi: Exploring Chinese Medicine,* New York: W. W. Norton, 1995 (first published in 1985); Paul Crompton, *The Elements of Tai Chi,* Corset, England: Element Books, 1990; Cheng Man-ch'ing and Robert W. Smith, *T'ai Chi,* Rutland, VT: Charles E. Tuttle, 1992 (first published in 1967); Herman Kauz, *Tai Chi Handbook,* New York: Doubleday, 1974; Yang Ming-shih, *T'ai-Chi Ch'aun,* Tokyo: Shufunotomo, 1992. Ta'i chi has been demonstrated to have significantly

positive effects on both physical and mental well-being. For example, a recent study published in the *Journal of the American Medical Association* (May 3, 1995) demonstrated that training in t'ai chi reduced falls and injuries in elderly people by significant margins. The study, conducted by Dr. Michael A. Province of Washington University School of Medicine in St. Louis, et al., included 2,328 elderly people who were trained in t'ai chi–type exercises. The results showed a reduced rate of falling of thirteen percent for those who practiced the exercises, and injuries were reduced by more than twenty-five percent compared to elderly people who did no exercise. According to federal data, six percent of all medical care dollars for the elderly were spent on care for injury from falls, and such falls are the sixth leading cause of death for the old. The medical costs associated with these kinds of injuries are more than $4 billion each year. Cited in the *Virginian-Pilot and Ledger-Star,* Wednesday, May 3, 1995.

15. See, for example, Judith H. Morrison, *The Book of Ayurveda: A Holistic Approach to Health and Longevity,* New York: Fireside Books, 1995. Also see books by Deepak Chopra listed above, note 13.
16. See, for example, Rosalyn Bruyere, *Wheels of Light: A Study of the Chakras,* Vol. 1, Sierre Madre, CA: Bon Productions, 1989; Shafica Karagulla and Dora van Gelder Kunz, *The Chakras and the Human Energy Fields,* Wheaton, IL: Quest Books, 1989; Barbara Ann Brennan, *Hands of Light,* New York: Bantam Books, 1988; Barbara Ann Brennan, *Light Emerging,* New York: Bantam Books, 1993; John Mann and Lar Short, *The Body of Light: History and Practical Techniques for Awakening Your Subtle Body,* Rutland, VT: Charles E. Tuttle, 1990; Geshe Kelsang Gyatso, *Clear Light of Bliss,* New York: Wisdom Publications, 1982; Jeffrey Mishlove, *The Roots of Consciousness* (revised ed.), Tulsa, OK: Council Oak Books, 1993. One writer, counselor, and astrologer, Barbara Hand Clow, writes that "during a midlife crisis, Eros, the life energy is rising and flowing upward in the physical body through all the subtle-energy systems—the chakras and the meridians—and opening the chakric centers of feeling so that it flows through the body more intensely. If we are counseled to honor and assist the opening of expanded energy channels at this time to not resist the powerful flow of erotic energy through the whole body, which I refer to as the "liquid light of sex," the cells in our bodies vibrate as if they are actually making love. . . . Experiencing elemental energy reawakens memory of the first creation of matter itself." See Barbara Hand Clow, *Liquid Light of Sex: Understanding Your Key Life Passages,* Santa Fe, NM: Bear, 1991, pg. 4.
17. Arnold Mindell, *Dreambody,* Boston: Sigo Press, 1982, pg. 29. Also see A. E. Powell, *The Etheric Double,* Wheaton, IL: Quest Books, 1987 (first published in 1925).
18. John White and Stanley Krippner, *Future Science,* New York: Anchor Books, 1977. Cited in Barbara Ann Brennan, *Hands of Light,* pg. 29.
19. See, for example, Barbara B. Brown, *New Mind, New Body, Biofeedback: New Directions for the Mind,* New York: Harper and Row, 1974. Also see W. Doyle Gentry (Ed.), *Handbook of Behavioral Medicine,* New York: Guilford Press, 1984; George Mandler, *Mind and Body: Psychology of Emotion and Stress,* New York: W. W. Norton, 1984; Hans Selye, *The Stress of Life* (second ed.), New York: McGraw-Hill, 1978.
20. Candace B. Pert, "The Wisdom of the Receptors: Neuropeptides, the Emotions and Bodymind," *Advances,* 3:3 (1986), pgs. 8–16. Also see Candace Pert, "The Chemical Communicators." In Bill Moyers, op. cit., pgs. 177–93.

21. Joseph Chilton Pearce, *The Crack in the Cosmic Egg: Challenging Constructs of Mind and Reality,* New York: Julian Press, 1988 (originally published in 1971).
22. Deepak Chopra, *Quantum Healing,* pg. 68.
23. Mark Gerzon, *Coming into Our Own,* New York: Delacorte, 1992, pg. 59. Also see Richard Carlson and Benjamin Shield (Eds.), *Healers on Healing,* New York: Tarcher/Putnam, 1989.
24. Bernie S. Siegel, *Peace, Love & Healing: Bodymind Communication and the Path to Self-Healing: An Exploration,* New York: Harper and Row, 1989, chapter 2. Also see Bernie S. Siegel, *Love, Medicine & Miracles: Lessons Learned About Self-Healing from a Surgeon's Experience with Exceptional Patients,* New York: Harper Perennial, 1986; Larry Dossey, *Meaning and Medicine,* New York: Bantam Books, 1991; Marc Ian Barasch, *The Healing Path: A Soul Approach to Illness,* New York: Tarcher/Putnam, 1993: Susan Sontag, *Illness as Metaphor,* New York: Vintage Books, 1978.
25. Carl Jung, *CW,* 8, par. 502.
26. Marion Woodman, op. cit., pg. 178.
27. O. Carl Simonton, Stephanie Matthews-Simonton, and James L. Creighton, *Getting Well Again,* New York: Bantam Books, 1988 (originally published by Jeremy Tarcher, 1978), pg. 3. Also see Norman Cousins, *Anatomy of an Illness as Perceived by the Patient,* New York: W. W. Norton, 1979; Roy Laurens, *Fully Alive: Healing the Body with the Hidden Mind,* Dallas; Saybrook, 1985; Andrew Weil, *Spontaneous Healing,* New York: Alfred A. Knopf, 1995; Caryle Hirshberg and Marc Ian Barasch, *Remarkable Recovery,* New York: Riverhead Books, 1995; Lawrence LeShan, *The Medium, the Mystic and the Physicist,* New York: Viking, 1974; Lawrence LeShan, *You Can Fight for Your Life: Emotional Factors in the Treatment of Cancer,* New York: M. Evans, 1977; Joan Borysenko, *Minding the Body, Mending the Mind,* New York: Bantam Books, 1987; Jeanne Achterberg, op. cit.; Jeanne Achterberg, *Imagery in Healing: Shamanism and Modern Medicine,* Boston: Shambhala, 1985; Jeanne Achterberg, *Bridges of the Bodymind,* Champaign, IL: Institute of Personality and Ability Testing, 1980.
28. Stanley Krippner and Alberto Villoldo, *The Realms of Healing,* Berkeley, CA: Celestial Arts, 1994, pg. 12. Also see Doug Boyd, *Rolling Thunder,* New York: Delta Books, 1974; Donald Sandner, *Navajo Symbols of Healing,* Rochester, VT: Healing Arts, 1991; Hyemeyohsts Storm, *Seven Arrows,* New York: Ballantine Books, 1972; Michael Harner, *The Way of the Shaman: A Guide to Power and Healing,* San Francisco: Harper, 1980; Joan Halifax, *Shamanic Voices: A Survey of Visionary Narratives,* New York: Dutton, 1979; Mircea Eliade, *Shamanism: Archaic Techniques of Ecstasy,* Princeton, NJ: Princeton University Press, 1964.
29. Carlos Castaneda, *Journey to Ixtlan: The Lessons of Don Juan,* New York: Simon and Schuster, 1972. Also see by Carlos Castaneda: *The Teachings of Don Juan: A Yaqui Way of Knowledge* and *A Separate Reality: Further Conversations with Don Juan.* Also see *Tales of Power* (1974), *The Eagle's Gift* (1981), and *The Art of Dreaming* (1993). Taisha Abelar, *The Sorcerer's Crossing,* New York: Penguin Arkana, 1992; Dan Millman, *The Way of the Peaceful Warrior,* Tiburon, CA: H. J. Kramer, 1980.
30. Cited in Betty Friedan, *The Fountain of Age,* New York: Simon and Schuster, 1993, chapter 2.
31. Michael Waldholtz, "Fountain of Youth May Not Be Fairy Tale, Study Finds," *Wall Street Journal,* October 16, 1992. Cited in Gail Sheehy, *New Passages: Mapping Your Life Across Time,* New York: Random House, 1995, pg. 8.

32. Deepak Chopra, *Ageless Body, Timeless Mind,* pg. 10.
33. Betty Friedan, op. cit.
34. From a documentary by *National Geographic Explorer,* aired on July 30, 1995. Also see a wonderful book about vigorous aging: Sarah L. Delany and A. Elizabeth Delany with Amy Hill Hearth, *Having Our Say: The Delany Sisters' First 100 Years,* New York: Dell, 1993; and Caroline Bird, *Lives of Our Own: Secrets of Salty Old Women,* New York: Houghton Mifflin, 1995; Cathleen Rountree, *On Women Turning Fifty,* San Francisco: Harper, 1993; Cathleen Rountree, *Coming into Our Fullness: On Women Turning Forty,* Freedom, CA: Crossing Press, 1991.
35. Terri Apter, *Secret Paths: Women in the New Midlife,* New York: W. W. Norton, 1995, pg. 202.
36. Robert Arnot, *Dr. Bob Arnot's Guide to Turning Back the Clock,* Boston: Little Brown, 1995, pgs. 4–5.
37. Carl Jung, *Memories, Dreams, Reflections,* New York: Random House, 1965 (originally published in 1961), pg. 297.
38. Catherine Maclay, "John T. Lescroart: No Day Job, Just Time to Write," *Publishers Weekly,* August 14, 1995, pgs. 60–61.
39. *Holy Bible,* John 9:1–3. Scripture quotations are from the New Revised Standard Version of the Bible, copyright 1989 by the Division of Christian Education of the National Council of the Churches of Christ in the U.S.A. Used by permission. All rights reserved. *Holy Bible: The New Revised Standard Version,* Nashville; Thomas Nelson, 1989, pg. 102.
41. Larry Dossey, *Healing Words: The Power of Prayer and the Practice of Medicine,* San Francisco: Harper, 1993, pgs. 13–15.
41. Bernie Siegel, *Love, Medicine & Miracles,* pg. ix.
42. Gail Sheehy, *The Silent Passage,* New York: Pocket Books, 1991.
43. Miriam Stoppard, *Menopause,* London: Dorling Kindersley, 1994, pg. 6.
44. Claudia Wallis, "The Estrogen Dilemma," *Time* magazine, June 26, 1995, pgs. 46–53.
45. Margaret Morganroth Gullette, "What Menopause Again?" *Ms.* July/August 1993, pgs. 34–37. Cited in Terri Apter, op. cit., pg. 202. In addition to the Gail Sheehy, Miriam Stoppard, and Claudia Wallis references listed above, see Margaret Morganroth Gullette, *Safe at Last in the Middle Years,* Berkeley, CA: University of California Press, 1988; Germain Greer, *The Change: Women, Aging and the Menopause,* New York: Alfred A. Knopf, 1992; Gayle Sand, *Is It Hot In Here or Is It Me?* New York: HarperCollins, 1993; Ann Mankowitz, *Change of Life: A Psychological Study of Dreams and the Menopause,* Toronto: Inner City Books, 1984; Susan S. Weed, *Menopausal Years: The Wise Woman Way,* Woodstock, NY: Ash Tree Publishing, 1992.
46. Gail Sheehy, *New Passages,* pg. 294.
47. Lawrence Altman, "Study Suggests High Rate of Impotence," *New York Times,* December 12, 1993. Cited in Gail Sheehy, *New Passages,* pg. 296. Also see the results of the Massachusetts Male Aging Study, *Journal of Urology,* January 1994; "Impotence," *NIH Consensus Statement,* National Institutes of Health Consensus Development Conference, Bethesda, Maryland, December 7–9, 1992.
48. Irwin Goldstein and Larry Rothstein, *The Potent Male: Facts, Fiction, Future,* Los Angeles: Body Press/Price Stern Sloan, 1990.
49. R. Mitchell, S. Hollis, C. Rothwell, W. R. Robertson, "Age-related Changes in

the Pituitary-Testicular Axis in Normal Men; Lower Serum Testosterone Results from Decreased Bioactive LH Drive," *Clinical Endocrinology*, May 42 (5), 1995, pgs. 501–7.

50. M. Jonler, T. Moon, W. Brannan, N. N. Stone et al., "Impotence and the Quality of Life," *British Journal of Urology*, May 1995, 75 (5), pgs. 651–55.
51. M. Perring and J. Moran, "Holistic Approach to the Management of Erectile Dysfunction," *British Journal of Clinical Practice*, May/June 1995, 49 (3), pgs. 140–44.
52. Herbert Benson et al., *NIH Consensus Statement*, National Institutes of Health Consensus Development Conference, Bethesda, Maryland, December 7–9, 1992. Cited in Gail Sheehy, *New Passages*, pg. 304.
53. James Hollis, *Under Saturn's Shadow: The Wounding and Healing of Men*, Toronto: Inner City Books, 1994, pgs. 9–10. Also see Robert Bly, *Iron John: A Book About Men*, New York: Vintage Books, 1992 (first published in 1990 by Addison-Wesley); Robert Moore, *Rediscovering Masculine Potentials* (audiotapes), Wilmette, IL: Chiron, 1988; Robert Moore and Douglas Gillette, *King, Warrior, Magician, Lover: Rediscovering the Archetypes of the Mature Masculine*, New York: Harper and Row, 1990; Robert Bly, James Hillman, and Michael Meade (Eds.), *The Rag and Bone Shop of the Heart*, New York: HarperCollins, 1992; Guy Corneau, *Absent Fathers, Lost Sons: The Search for Masculine Identity*, Boston: Shambhala, 1991; Robert Hopcke, *Men's Dreams, Men's Healing*, Boston: Shambhala, 1989; Robert Johnson, *He: Understanding Male Psychology*, New York: Harper and Row, 1977; Eugene Monick, *Castration and Male Rage: The Phallic Wound*, Toronto: Inner City Books, 1991; Eugene Monick, *Phallos: Sacred Image of the Masculine*, Toronto: Inner City Books, 1987; James Wyly, *The Phallic Quest: Priapus and Masculine Inflation*, Toronto: Inner City Books, 1989; Robert Bly and Bill Moyers, *A Gathering of Men* (videotape), Public Affairs Television, 1990; Jean Shinoda Bolen, *Gods In Everyman*, New York: Harper and Row, 1989.
54. Carl Jung, *CW*, 5, par. 329.
55. Eugene Monick, *Castration and Male Rage*, pg. 18.
56. Jelaluddin Rumi, "A Mouse and A Frog." In Coleman Barks with John Moyne (translators), op. cit., pg. 79.
57. David Steinberg, Introduction, in David Steinberg, *The Erotic Impulse: Honoring the Sensual Self*, New York: Tarcher/Putnam, 1992, pg. xvii.
58. Aldo Carotenuto, *Eros and Pathos: Shades of Love and Suffering*, Toronto: Inner City Books, 1989, pg. 66.
59. William Blake, "The Marriage of Heaven and Hell" (1793). In Alfred Kazin (Ed.), *The Portable Blake*, New York: Viking, 1974 (originally published in 1946), pg. 250.
60. Paule Marshall, *Praisesong for the Widow*, New York: Dutton, 1984, pgs. 249–51.

CHAPTER 11

1. Charles T. Tart, *Living the Mindful Life*, Boston: Shambhala, 1994, pg. 65.
2. Albert Camus,
3. Carl Jung, *Memories, Dreams, Reflections*, New York: Vintage Books, 1965 pg. 189.
4. James Hollis, *The Middle Passage: From Misery to Meaning in Midlife*, Toronto: Inner City Books, 1993, pg. 106.
5. May Sarton, *Plant Dreaming Deep*, New York: W. W. Norton, 1968, pg. 47.

6. Anne Sexton, "The Big Heart," in *Awful Rowing Toward God,* New York: Houghton Mifflin, 1975. Also cited in Marilyn Sewell, *Cries of the Spirit,* Boston: Beacon Press, 1991, pgs. 57–58.

CHAPTER 12

1. Heraclitus, in Charles H. Kahn, *The Art and Thought of Heraclitus,* Cambridge: Cambridge University Press, 1979, pg. 168.
2. Ram Dass, *Conscious Aging I and II: On the Nature of Change and Facing Death* (audiotapes), Boulder, CO: Sounds True Recordings, 1992.
3. Carl Jung,
4. Abraham Maslow, *Toward a Psychology of Being* (second ed.), Princeton, NJ: Van Nostrand, 1968. Cited in Roger Walsh and Frances Vaughan, *Paths Beyond Ego: The Transpersonal Vision,* Los Angeles: Tarcher/Perigee, 1993, pg. 110.
5. William Blake, "The Marriage of Heaven and Hell." In Alfred Kazin (Ed.), *The Portable Blake,* New York: Viking Penguin, 1994, pg. 261 (originally published in 1946).
6. Isabel Allende, *Paula,* New York: HarperCollins, 1994. Also see Margot Hornblower, "Grief and Rebirth," *Time* magazine, July 10, 1995.
7. Albert Camus, "Summer," *Return to Tipasa.* In Albert Camus, *Lyrical and Critical Essays,* New York: Alfred A. Knopf, 1969, pg. 169 (originally published in French in 1954).
8. Jelaluddin Rumi, "The Mouse and the Camel." In Coleman Barks with John Moyne (translators), *The Essential Rumi,* San Francisco: Harper, 1995, pg. 143.
9. Carl Jung, *Memories, Dreams, Reflections,* New York: Vintage Books, 1965, pg. 3.
10. Cited in James W. Jones, *In the Middle of This Road We Call Our Life,* San Francisco: Harper, 1995, pgs. 24–25, and Larry Dossey, Foreword, Caryle Hirshberg and Marc Ian Barasch, *Remarkable Recovery,* New York: Riverhead Books, 1995, pg. xvii.
11. Joseph Campbell with Bill Moyers, *The Power of Myth,* New York: Doubleday, 1988, pg. 5.
12. Joan Halifax, *Shaman: Wounded Healer.* London: Thames and Hudson, 1981. Cited in Allan B. Chinen, *Once Upon a Midlife: Classic Stories and Mythic Tales to Illuminate the Middle Years,* Los Angeles: Jeremy Tarcher, 1992, pg. 173.
13. W. H. Auden, from "The Age of Anxiety," in *Collected Poems,* ed. by Edward Mendelson, New York: Random House, 1976, pg. 407.
14. Lao Tzu, *Tao te Ching* (Gia-Fu Feng and Jane English, translators), New York: Alfred A. Knopf, 1972, #33.
15. Plato, "Apology," *The Dialogues of Plato.* In Robert Maynard Hutchins (Ed.), *Great Books of the Western World,* Vol. 7, Chicago: Encyclopaedia Britannica, 1952, pg. 210.
16. Clarissa Pinkola Estes, *Women Who Run With the Wolves,* New York: Ballantine Books, 1992, pg. 332.
17. Heinrich Zimmer, *Philosophies of India,* New York: World Publishing, 1956, pgs. 4–8 (first published in 1951 under the auspices of the Bollingen Foundation). Cited in Joseph Campbell, *Myths, Dreams and Religion,* Dallas: Spring Publications, 1970, pgs. 252–53.
18. Robert Wright, "The Evolution of Despair," *Time* magazine, August 28, 1995, pg. 56.

19. J. Krishnamurti, "Seeing Without the Observer." In John Welwood (Ed.), *Ordinary Magic: Everyday Life as Spiritual Path,* Boston: Shambhala Publications, 1992, pg. 52. Excerpted from J. Krishnamurti, *Krishnamurti's Notebook,* New York: Harper and Row, 1976.
20. Carl Jung, *Memories, Dreams, Reflections,* pg. 330.
21. Teilhard de Chardin, *The Phenomenon of Man,* New York: Harper and Row, 1959 pg. 258.
22. Cited in Jack Canfield and Mark Victor Hansen, *Chicken Soup for the Soul,* Deerfield Beach, FL: Health Communications, 1993, pg. vii.
23. Jelaluddin Rumi, *Night and Sleep.* Versions by Coleman Barks and Robert Bly. Cambridge, MA: Yellow Moon Press, 1981.

Acknowledgments

This book was made possible through the loving support and containment of my family: Nancy, Jim, Deanne, J. P., Deborah, Matthew, Katelyn, Judi, Ed, Brianna, Alyssa, Colby, Kay, Lu, Gilda, Kevin, Kirsta, Karen, Shelley, Dick, Chuck, Susan, Anna Marie, Chuck, Mabel, Buck, Nancy, Todd, Hilda, Paul, Tracy, Bob, Sam, Tracy, Christi, Keith, Elisabeth, Stewart, Karen, Steve, Brittany, Matt, Robin, Lanny, Paul Robert, and Jerry, who individually and collectively have taught me that love transcends all the changes, sometimes heartbreaking ones, that life presents to us. The memories and spirits of my mother, Mary, Fran, Sarah, Nana, Pop, my Grandmother and Grandfather Brehony, Mary and Peter, Aunt Kitty, Great-Uncle Jim, and my most beloved Uncle Jimmy surround me with loving energy now just as they did in life. My most deeply felt thanks and blessings to my father's special angel, his family and the transplant team at the University of Virginia Medical Center, who gave my father the gift of life and the rest of us more time to enjoy his humor, heart, and love. I have come to learn that family is defined not by static and unchanging relationships created by blood and snippets of DNA, but by that which is in your heart.

The caring and connection of my remarkable extended family is a container of great love and celebration: Teresa, George, Jean, Art, Mary, Bud, Leah, Patty, Paul, Eric, Kelly, Mike, Laura, Mary Ann, Bruce, Alex, Jackie, Artie, Janet, Timmy, Scott, Caitlyn, Colleen, Danny, Antoinette, Kristin, Danny, Michael, Ricky, Patty, Nicole, Ricky, Ryan, Michael, Jamie, Donna Beth, Matthew, Maura, Kevin, Robin, Dana, Shannon, Jude, "the boys," Patrick, Francis, Eric, Michael. I am blessed by this family, by those brought into my life by connections of blood and history as well as those discovered in the great wisdom of a universe that understands that there are no accidents and that we meet souls along our way that we will know, love, and learn from. My family has always given me a lifelong sense that Thomas Wolfe was wrong. You *can* go home again.

My life is blessed with many devoted friendships that are truly attached at the heart: Esther, Alice, Nancy, Kathryn L., Judy, Martha, Mary, Renée, Brenda, Debbie, Vivian, Margaret, Kim, Kathy, Peggy, Leslie, Linda, Pat, Jo, Elsie, Marni, Bogey, Parker, Shelly, Allison, Beth, Loren, Erik, Alex, Malcolm, Jahnna, Dashiell, Skye, Petie, Lyntoni, Barbara, Linda, Allison, Annette, Linda, J.T., Ann, Sandra, Kathy, Beth, Sherrye, Ann, Virginia, Ginger, Ruth, B.J., Pam, Marshall, Laura, Paul, Goodlet, Teresa, Tricia, Michael, Kelly, Sarah, Jamie, Carol, Jill, Kyle, Troy, Andrew, Nina, Jeff, Lawren, Sarah, Cullen, Deborah, Zelda, Roger, Steve, "Miss Billy," Jim, Debbie, Julie, Alice, Audrey, Susan, Debbie, Sandra, Diana, Chez, Pam, Lee, Linda, Kathy, Suebee, Catherine, Li'l Nancy, Maggie, Cathy, Tina, SusaDee, Colleen, Pam, Jo, Leslie, Charlotte, Wendy, Allison, Jakey, Tommy, Millicent, Teresa, Mike, Emma, Dolly, Vance, Gunner, Dylan, Carole, Terry, Judy B., the Sam & Omie's crew, Johanna, Dan, the Kline family, Ray, Dot, Charlene, Robert, Ryan, Brett, my friends at Dolphin Tales, Cahoon's and FatBoyz, the guys at Moe's Music, the Bird Brains, Sandy, Nancy, Joni, Trish, Dorry, Sarah, Hilary, Alan, Lois, Fran, Bob, Madeline, Bill, Sam, Barbara, Ron, Sandy, Max, Sally, Dayton, Helen, Chuck, Jazz, Madeline, Rachel, Alan, Robert, Julie, Sally, David, Carly, Jordan, Jerry, Justin, Kent, Hilary, Ray, Tony, Miss Peggy, all of Bill Pfeiffer's family and friends. A special thanks to my beloved friends, who also happen to be colleagues, and gave me their time, attention, and important honest contributions to early drafts of this manuscript: Caren, Jan, Kathy B-W, and Gayle. The four-leggeds: Dorothy and Miss Maude and all their tail-wagging pals and winged friends.

To all of my tribe, my longbody, I send undying love and heartfelt appreciation for your never-ending support and love. In each and every moment you testify to what Rumi meant when he wrote: "Friend, our closeness is this: that wherever you put your foot, feel me in the firmness under you." I feel each of you, every step of my way, in the firmness under me.

Throughout the years, my clients have given me the honor of accompanying them down part of their paths. With tears, laughter, and honest relationship they have taught me about courage, heart, and the ineffable human experience. I thank them.

A special note of thanks to Tom Bird, my mentor and friend, keeping me on track and providing the containment of courage when the weenie in me surfaced more often than I would like to admit. And to Barbara not only for her computer help, but more important, for her friendship and honesty. My thanks to the remarkable authors and copyright holders for permission to reprint from their work. To Lisa Ross, of the Spieler Agency, an agent with heart and an early, fervent belief that this book has something to say that can help people. To Susan Petersen, whose vision for Riverhead Books consistently raises the standards of publishing to the benefit of all who read to expand their horizons. To Dolores McMullan, who has made the technical and administrative process of publishing this book a pleasure. And especially to Cindy Spiegel, at Riverhead Books, an editor with soul, whose sharp imagination and skills made this book into something far better than I ever could have alone.

My gratitude to Marion Woodman, a precious resource to understanding the pain and the blessings of the passage. Her book, *The Pregnant Virgin,* saved my life. I'm thankful that I had the opportunity to tell her that. And to Nora, like Hecate at the crossroads, a lighthouse and a blessed guide when you're completely lost. To La.

To the Great Spirit and the Divine Light in all of us.

Kathleen A. Brehony
1996

Permissions

Figure 1, from *On Jung* by Anthony Stevens. Copyright © 1990 by Anthony Stevens. Used by permission of Penguin Books. Scripture quotations are from the *New Revised Standard Version of the Bible,* Copyright © 1989 by the Division of Christian Educators of the National Council of Churches of Christ in the USA. Used by permission. All rights reserved. W. H. Auden, excerpt from *Collected Poems by W. H. Auden.* Copyright © 1976 by Edward Mendelsohn, William Meredith, and Monroe K. Spears, executors of the estate of W. H Auden. Reprinted by permission of Random House, Inc. Barbara Bird, excerpts from personal letter. Used by author's permission. Joseph Campbell, excerpts from *Myth, Dreams, and Religion,* by Joseph Campbell. Copyright © 1970 by the Society for the Arts, Religion, and Contemporary Culture. Used by permission of Dutton Signet, a division of Penguin Books USA, Inc. T. S. Eliot, excerpt from "Little Gidding," in *Four Quartets,* copyright © 1943 by T. S. Eliot and renewed 1971 by Esme Valerie Eliot, reprinted by permission of Harcourt Brace & Company. Mark Gerzon, excerpts from *Listening to Midlife: Turning Your Crisis Into a Quest.* Copyright © 1992, 1996, by Mark Gerzon. Reprinted by arrangement with Shambhala Publications, Inc., 300 Massachusetts Avenue, Boston, MA 02115. Jakob and Wilhelm Grimm, excerpts from "Godfather Death" from *The Complete Grimm's Fairy Tales,* revised translations by James Stern. Copyright © 1944 by Pantheon Books, Inc., and renewed 1972 by Random House, Inc. Reprinted by permission of Pantheon Books, a division of Random House, Inc. C. G. Jung, excerpts from *Collected Works, Volume 8.* Copyright © renewed 1969 by Princeton University Press.

Reprinted by permission of Princeton University Press. C. G. Jung, excerpts from *Memories, Dreams Reflections,* translated by Richard and Clara Winston. Translation copyright © 1961, 1962, 1963, renewed 1989, 1990, 1991 by Random House, Inc. Reprinted by permission of Pantheon Books, a division of Random House, Inc. Stephen Levine, excerpt from *Healing Into Life and Death.* Copyright © 1987 by Stephen Levine. Reprinted by permission of Doubleday, a division of Bantam Doubleday Dell Publishing Group, Inc. Paule Marshall, excerpts from "Praisesong for the Widow." Copyright © 1983 by Paule Marshall. Reprinted by permission of the Putnam Publishing Group. All rights reserved. Linda McGonigal, Unpublished poem. Used by permission of the author. Deena Metzger, Excerpt from poem, page 3 from *Writing for Your Life,* by Deena Metzger. Copyright © 1992 by Deena Metzger. Reprinted by permission of HarperCollins Publishers, Inc. Stephen Mitchell, Excerpt from poem 56 from *Tao Te Ching* by Stephen Mitchell. Translation copyright © 1988 by Stephen Mitchell. Reprinted by permission of HarperCollins Publishers, Inc. Thomas Moore, Excerpts from *Care of the Soul,* by Thomas Moore. Copyright © 1992 by Thomas Moore. Reprinted by permission of HarperCollins Publishers, Inc. Thomas Moore, Excerpts from *Soul Mates,* by Thomas Moore. Copyright © 1994 by Thomas Moore. Reprinted by permission of HarperCollins Publishers, Inc. Mary Oliver, "The Journey," from *Dream Work.* Copyright © 1986, by Mary Oliver. Used by permission of Grove/Atlantic, Inc. All rights reserved. Rainer Maria Rilke, excerpts from pages 13, 21 (Entire poem in footnote), 53 from *Selected Poems of Rainer Maria Rilke, edited and translated by Robert Bly.* Copyright © 1981 by Robert Bly. Reprinted by permission of HarperCollins Publishers, Inc. Rumi, excerpts from *The Essential Rumi.* Translation © 1995 by Coleman Barks. Used by permission of Threshold Books, RD4, Putney, VT, 05346. Sent Ts'An, excerpt from "Believing in Mind," translated by Stephen Ruppenthal. From *God Makes the Rivers to Flow,* by Eknath Easwaran. Copyright © 1991 by Eknath Easwaran. Used by permission of Nilgiri Press. Anne Sexton, "The Big Heart," from *The Awful Rowing Toward God* by Anne Sexton. Copyright © 1975 by Loring Conant, Jr., Executor of the Estate of Anne Sexton. Reprinted by permission of Houghton Mifflin Co. All rights reserved. Daryl Sharp, excerpt from *The Survival Papers: Anatomy of a Midlife Crisis.* Copyright © 1988, by Daryl Sharp. Used by permission of Inner City Books. All rights reserved. Sogyal Rinpoche, excerpt from poem, page 25 from *The Tibetan Book of Living and Dying.* Copyright © 1993 by Rigpa Fellowship. Reprinted by permission of HarperCollins Publishers, Inc. Nancy Wood, "Solitude," "Mother's Words," from *Spirit Walker* by Nancy Wood, illustrations by Frank Howell. Copyright © 1993 by Nancy Wood. Used by permission of Doubleday, a division of Bantam Doubleday Dell Publishing Group, Inc. David Whyte, "Tilicho Lake." Copyright © 1990 by David Whyte. Used by permission of Many Rivers Company. All rights reserved. William Carlos Williams, "Thursday," from *Collected Poems: 1909–1939, Volume I.* Copyright © 1938 by New Directions Publishing Corp. Reprinted by permission of New Directions Publishing Corp. All rights reserved. Marion Woodman, excerpts from *The Pregnant Virgin: A Process of Psychological Transformation.* Copyright © 1985, by Marion Woodman. Used by permission of Inner City Books. All rights reserved.